THE OPTIONS EDGE + FREE TRIAL

The Wiley Trading series features books by traders who have survived the market's ever changing temperament and have prospered—some by reinventing systems, others by getting back to basics. Whether a novice trader, professional, or somewhere in-between, these books will provide the advice and strategies needed to prosper today and well into the future. For more on this series, visit our website at www.WileyTrading.com.

Founded in 1807, John Wiley & Sons is the oldest independent publishing company in the United States. With offices in North America, Europe, Australia, and Asia, Wiley is globally committed to developing and marketing print and electronic products and services for our customers' professional and personal knowledge and understanding.

THE OPTIONS EDGE
+ FREE TRIAL

An Intuitive Approach to Generating Consistent Profits
for the Novice to the Experienced Practitioner

Michael C. Khouw
Mark W. Guthner, CFA

WILEY

Published by John Wiley & Sons, Inc., Hoboken, New Jersey.
Published simultaneously in Canada.

For general information on our other products and services or for technical support, please contact our Customer Care Department within the United States at (800) 762-2974, outside the United States at (317) 572-3993 or fax (317) 572-4002.

Wiley publishes in a variety of print and electronic formats and by print-on-demand. Some material included with standard print versions of this book may not be included in e-books or in print-on-demand. If this book refers to media such as a CD or DVD that is not included in the version you purchased, you may download this material at http://booksupport.wiley.com. For more information about Wiley products, visit www.wiley.com.

Library of Congress Cataloging-in-Publication Data:

Names: Guthner, Mark, author. | Khouw, Michael, 1968– author.
Title: Options play : an intuitive approach to generating consistent profits for the novice to the experienced practitioner / Mark W. Guthner, Michael Khouw.
Description: Hoboken, New Jersey : John Wiley & Sons, Inc., [2016] | Series: Wiley trading | Includes

bibliographic references and index.
Identifiers: LCCN 2015043835 (print) | LCCN 2015049131 (ebook) | ISBN 9781119212416 (paperback) |

ISBN 9781119212447 (pdf) | ISBN 9781119212423 (epub)
Subjects: LCSH: Options (Finance)
Classification: LCC HG6024.A3 G88 2016 (print) | LCC HG6024.A3 (ebook) | DDC 332.63/2283—dc23
LC record available at http://lccn.loc.gov/2015043835

Cover image: Wiley
Cover design: © Timashov Sergiy/Shutterstock

10 9 8 7 6 5 4 3 2 1

CONTENTS

Introduction   1

CHAPTER 1   What Is an Option, and How Do
Options Work?   11

CHAPTER 2   Valuing Options with the Black–Scholes–
Merton Option-Pricing Model   29

CHAPTER 3   Trading Volatility   65

CHAPTER 4   Are Options Fairly Priced?   97

CHAPTER 5   Fundamental Option Strategies   125

CHAPTER 6   Portfolio Hedging Producing Enhanced
Returns   155

CHAPTER 7   Option Strategies for Special Situations   193

CHAPTER 8   Extracting Information from Options Prices   213

CHAPTER 9   Synthetics   235

CHAPTER 10   Home Runs   253

CHAPTER 11   Strike-Outs   277

Notes   305

Glossary   311

References   319

About Online Education and Option Trading Tools   323

About the Free Trial   329

Index   331

CONTENTS

We would like to thank EZTrade.Com for providing us with historical time series data concerning asset, index and option prices along with the associated implied volatility data used to generate the charts and analysis provided in this book. In addition, economic and interest rate data used came from the Federal Reserve Economic Database (FRED, Research.StLouisFed.Org) provided by the Federal Reserve Bank of St. Louis. Finally, data concerning the energy markets came from The International Energy Agency (IEA, IEA.Org) and the US Department of Energy (DOE, Energy.Gov)

CONTENTS

Options on stocks, indices, and futures often get a bad rap. Journalists, pundits, and casual market observers criticize these derivative financial instruments as too complicated, subject to abuse, and difficult to understand, value, and trade profitably. They go on to claim that they are a structural cause of financial calamities and something should be done to limit their use. Many seasoned investment professionals are unnecessarily intimidated by derivative instruments in general, and options in particular. After all, there are a host of options available to trade on individual stocks, market indeces, bonds, commodities, and other financial assets. With so many choices in standardized exchange-listed options, and an infinite number of bespoke products available over the counter,[i] selecting the best option to satisfy one's investment objectives can be daunting. Complicating the task is their flexibility. Options are customizable and often constructed into unusual-sounding structures. Finally, the mathematics sophisticated practitioners' use to price and hedge options are intimidating to some as well.

If those concerns have prevented you from trading options, you might be surprised to learn that even if you are new to the investment world, even if you have never bought or sold a stock, you have probably bought options without realizing it. If you have purchased airline tickets, property insurance, or life insurance, you have unwittingly bought an option. If you have applied to a number of colleges and received an acceptance letter, you have bought a free option. Options are a part of everyday life, and they are everywhere. Since options are a part of your everyday life, you can improve your standard of living by an awareness of options available all around you when arranging your financial affairs.

---

[i]Over-the-counter (OTC) or off-exchange trading of derivatives are executed directly between two parties without the supervision of an exchange.

Consider the conventional college acceptance. Once a college applicant is accepted, the person has the option, but not the obligation, to attend. He or she can choose to attend that college, attend another college, or not attend any college at all. The important point is that the college acceptance letter represents a right but not an obligation to attend an institution of higher learning. This is a fundamental characteristic of an option. The terms of the college acceptance letter give the would-be student optionality. There are exceptions to every rule of course. If the acceptance letter is presented in response to a request for "early decision" or "early action" and the college agrees, the applicant is obliged to attend that university. The acceptance letter is no longer an option, but a binding obligation.

How about an airline ticket? When one holds an airline ticket, one has the right, but not the obligation, to travel on a specific flight. When the traveler presents the ticket at the gate, the airline has the obligation to provide a seat. On the other hand, if a ticketholder chooses not to get on the plane or is unable to, the airline cannot compel the person to get onboard or ask for additional money. Most ticket purchasers exercise their option. They do so by actually taking the flight. In short, the ticketholder owns an option to fly or not fly.

Airlines know that some passengers will not exercise their right to take the contracted flight. To maximize profits, they want to be sure there is a passenger in every seat. To fill as many seats a possible, the airline will sell more options (i.e., airline tickets) than there are seats (i.e., naked options) on the designated flight. This places the airline at risk. If more passengers exercise their right to fly than available seats, they must provide additional compensation to the affected traveler. Some airline seat agrements offer full or partial refunds to travelers who do not fly. This option to get one's money back has value and airlines charge a premium for it. Travelers who are uncertain about their travel schedule are willing to pay this cancelation premium by paying a higher ticket price.

There are more than 25,000 flights per day in the United States, giving the traveling public a great deal of choices. Yet if you have ever flown, chances are you were able to sift through all those possibilities to choose the best ticket or at least one that suits your needs. Knowing where you wanted to go and when you wanted to get there, you could select the flight that was right for you. Moreover, you were able to determine whether the price of the ticket was one you were willing to pay without knowing all the costs that the airline incurs to provide that seat. While confronted with a multitude of travel options, you can develop a logical method for optimizing results. This is no different from the world of financial options. While there are a multitude of options to choose from, this book will help you develop a logical method for selecting options that meet your financial goals.

Perhaps the most common option for American consumers involving a major financial transaction is the closed-end auto lease with a buyout provision. When a consumer enters into a closed-end lease, that person gets to use the leased property for a fixed term, and has the right to buy the property for the agreed residual value when the contract expires. This person is not at risk if the market value of the vehicle turns out to be lower than the residual value stated on the initial lease contract. He can simply return the car and the lessor bears the loss in value if any. If the market value of the car turns out to be higher than the residual value (i.e., strike price) the consumer can purchase the car at the contractually stated residual value and keep it or sell it. Any gain enjoyed by purchasing the car at the residual value and selling it at market value accrues to the lessee. In short, it represents a purchase option (call) on the car leased.

These examples show that options in the real world have benefits to both the buyer and seller. Buyers get the flexibility they need and sellers get to capture the business revenue they desire. Both market actors are made better off showing that options are not necessarily a zero sum game. Properly employed, one participant does not have to gain at the other's expense. The same holds true for options in the financial markets. Both hedgers and speculators are made better off by trading options.

These examples show that people buy and sell options and are unaware that they are doing so. This is often the case in finance as well. While some might trade listed options explicitly, many investors trade options without ever intending to get involved with derivatives. If we take a deeper look into finance theory, we will recognize that there are options in financial instruments where none are advertised.

Finance is concerned with the dynamics of how money and financial assets are managed, and how corporations and governments raise debt and equity capital to finance their operations. While many might believe that finance is a hard science, it is in fact a social science peppered with a fundamental truth. At its core, finance is based on the concept of the time value of money. Time value of money suggests that money today is worth more than the same amount of money tomorrow. This intuitively makes sense, not only because of the potentially dilutive effects of inflation, but because someone can invest her money in a bank certificate of deposit, earn interest, and have more money in the future. The factor that equates currency today with currency tomorrow is the interest rate earned. Reflexively, to determine the value of money today, we discount the value of currency owed sometime in the future by some rate of interest. Based on this foundation, investment finance aims to price assets today.

What makes finance a social science is choice and how people go about making a selection among the choices presented to them. Another way of thinking about choice is that choices represent options. When investing in capital, you have the option of investing in a low-risk asset like a CD, which pays a low rate of interest, or investing in a more risky asset such as a corporate bond, which pays a higher rate of interest. The corporate bond is more risky because there is the possibility of losing money if the lender defaults. The investment challenge is filled with a multitude of options. If you want to take even more risk with the hope of making an even higher rate of return, you could allocate capital to common stocks or emerging market government bonds. At the end of the day, investment finance is primarily a social science, as it is concerned with how people make decisions under uncertainty characterized by risky outcomes.

The choices do not stop there. In the investment world, there are host of financial and real assets from which to choose as a means of growing capital. You could invest in any of the assets mentioned above, or in foreign currencies, commodities, private companies, or real estate, for example. Within each of these asset classes there are subcategories to consider. You could invest in growth stocks or value stocks. Alternatively, you could invest in commercial real estate, apartment buildings, or single-family homes, for example. The next step requires drilling down even further. What particular stock should you buy—or should you just invest in a mutual fund? Although you might be confronted with an unlimited amount of choices, what is attractive about these options is that they are free. You do not have to pay a premium to get these choices, and they generally do not expire. Free options have value, and one should seek them out and exercise them if and when it is advantageous to do so.

Options provide a way of assessing and managing risk. As you select from the universe of investment choices, the outcome of the investment is indeterminate in advance. What makes investment finance a particularly challenging endeavor is that people have to make decisions (exercise options) under uncertainty. This is what ultimately makes investment a social science. Option pricing theory helps investors understand how to value uncertainty and the volatility of potential outcomes. This is true because the level of risk and uncertainty of potential outcomes is a major component of the value of an option.

While the choices we make are simply a manifestation of the process for exercising an option, every investment vehicle has some element of an option imbedded in it. When one lends money to another entity, the borrower has the option to "pay as agreed" and perform on the loan or default on it. By electing to default, a borrower exercises the right to put the collateral pledged against the loan to the lender and walk away from the obligation. In this case, the loan has a put option imbedded in it. A put option gives the holder of that option the right but not the obligation to sell an asset to the seller of the option. The seller of a put option has the obligation to perform a promised task if the owner of the option chooses to exercise it. In the case of a loan, if the value of the underlying asset (i.e., collateral of the loan) falls below the face value of the loan, the borrower is better off defaulting on the loan and putting the collateral to the lender. If the value of the collateral remains above the value of the loan, the borrower is better off servicing the loan.

Another way of looking at this relationship is to view it from the standpoint of the borrower. The borrower is someone who owns the underlying asset and holds equity. If someone chooses to buy stock in a company, that investor owns a call option on the value of the company's assets. In the financial world, the owner of a call option has the right but not the obligation to buy an asset. The seller of the option has the obligation to perform should the owner of the option exercise this right. We can think of common stock as a call option on the company's assets. If the value of the company's assets rises, the shareholder can exercise the call option by selling the asset and repaying the loan. The amount of the loan represents the strike price of the call option. The common stockholder enjoys all the gains represented by the difference between the asset value and the loan's amount. If, on the other hand, the value of the company's assets falls below the value of the loan, the shareholder can let the call option expire worthless, and the stockholder walks away empty-handed. The lender takes over the asset and the relationship between the lender and the shareholder terminates.

In this book, we will take you through the educational process necessary to develop expertise in trading listed options and exposing options where you would never expect to find them. We will start with a crawl by covering the basics by defining and discussing the characteristics of options from a qualitative point of view. This will be followed with a discussion of options math approached from a practitioner's point of view.

To keep the concepts accessible, we will introduce the math and work through examples for clarity. This way, you can repeat these calculations on your own so you can later make them a part of your decision-making process. Options analytics is perfectly suited for the application of financial technology. For those who want to delve deeper, we provide access to decision support systems delivered over the web. With that foundation, we will discuss how investors can take advantage of shifts in volatility as part of their risk-management process. With the theoretical aspects of option trading under our belt, we move into the real world and examine the historical returns provided by options on the S&P 500. Success in option trading depends, in part, on using the right strategy at the right time. We cover basic option strategies that are commonly used by individuals and institutions alike. From there, we blend option strategies with historical performance to present alternatives to the traditional strategies that will put the odds on the side of the hedger and speculator. Finally, we take a close look at some investment professionals that have done well and others who failed miserably. We discuss how successful traders used options in unique and insightful ways to produce outsized gains over time. This is followed by examples of how very intelligent and sophisticated investors misused options or traded securities with option characteristics without knowing it. Our ultimate objective is to educate the reader. We want everyone who trades options to successfully meet their investment objectives. To that end, those who read and understand this book should become better traders and investors by understanding how options are priced and how they perform with changing market conditions as a foundation for risk management. It is also important to recognize hidden options wherever they may exist, particularly if they are free. The following is one such example.

Options are about choice.

Choice is good, and everybody in this world wants choice. Wealthy people have the most choice of all. They have the financial wherewithal to buy the things they want, like expensive houses, cars, boats, and so on, and the super wealthy can travel in luxury with the purchase of a private jet. They have the funds to do the things they want, such as traveling to exotic destinations and dining at the finest restaurants. With a big enough wallet, people can buy almost anything.

But what if you want the finer things in life and do not have the resources to pay for them? How do you get choice? The simple answer is . . . buy or create an option. Options are about choice. Pay a fee today, and have choices tomorrow. To minimize that fee, buy an out-of-the-money option and hope for the best. But how do you find an option that has the potential to deliver the lifestyle you want? You could try your luck at the lottery. The lottery ticket is the ultimate deep-out-of-the-money option. But let's get real; the chance of winning the "Mega Millions" lottery is 258.9 million to one. Not to worry, the chance of winning the "Powerball" lottery is much better at 175.2 million to one. But let's face it; these options are so far out of the money that they are virtually assured to expire worthless. Outside of a lottery ticket, we cannot simply buy an option on living the good life. Or can we?

Lenny Dykstra is an interesting character, and he found a way of buying an option on living the life of the rich and famous. Lenny Dykstra was born in 1963 and grew up in Southern California. His professional baseball career started in 1981 when the New York Mets drafted him in the thirteenth round. Lenny quickly became a star in the minor leagues. In 1983, for example, he led the Carolina League in at-bats, runs, hits, triples, batting average, and stolen bases. With a batting average of .358, 8 home runs, 105 stolen bases, and 105 walks, Lenny could get on base and score runs. Lenny played ball with Billy Beane, who later became general manager of the Oakland Athletics and was made famous outside the world of baseball when his story was told in a book and movie called *Money Ball*. Billy once said that Dykstra was "perfectly designed emotionally" to play baseball and had "no concept of failure." Lenny was destined to have a great career in baseball, and he debuted in the "Bigs" in 1985 at the age of 22. Lenny played in 1,278 games and achieved a lifetime batting average of .285 with 404 RBIs. His post-season batting average was even better, at .321. As a three-time all-star and MVP, Lenny commanded big bucks and earned a salary that exceeded $24 million over his career.

Lenny was famous for living the big life, and by the time he retired in 1996, it is said that he had saved just $5 million. With his lifestyle, this cash would not last forever. After retirement, he entered the business world, where he purchased a string of car washes. In addition, he had a partnership with Castrol called "Team Dykstra" Quick-Lube Centers in the Los Angeles area. He also had ownership interests in a ConocoPhillips fueling center, a real-estate development company, and finally, a venture to develop several "I Sold It on eBay" stores. His younger brother Kevin ran his business enterprise for him. Business was good, and Lenny's take from payroll was $1 million a year. Lenny spent his free time playing golf, signing autographs, and making media appearances. Last but not least, he managed his personal portfolio of stocks and he wrote a column for TheStreet.Com.

While this income and lifestyle is attractive to most of us, it was not good enough for Lenny. Mr. Dykstra had a bigger-than-life persona and enjoyed the nickname "Nails" during his Major League days. Mets fans gave him this nickname because of his hardnosed personality and fearless play. With greater ambitions in mind, Lenny sold his business interests in 2006 for over $50 million. After repaying $20+ million in debts and capital gains taxes, Lenny's net worth had increased nicely.

While Lenny was wealthy, he was not "super-wealthy." So how could he live far beyond his means by giving the appearance that he was living within his means? The short answer is, buy an option on the lifestyle. Options come in many different flavors. The options that investors are most familiar with are those traded on exchanges. One can buy an option on a stock and have the option to take ownership of that stock by exercising the option and paying the seller the strike price. Hard to see how this will help him live the big life. This only works if one picks the right options on the right stocks and makes a boatload of money. There is a second variety of option called the *synthetic option,* and these can be configured in ways only limited by one's imagination. A synthetic option can be constructed in such a way as to give the owner of the option all the rights, responsibilities, and privileges of owning an asset, without actually paying for it. You can live in the house, upgrade it to your liking, and sell it, if you so choose. As you are about to see, it is very important for the asset to hold its value, to keep the option alive. So you are required to spend some money along the way and perform regular maintenance to keep your assets in good shape.

Most of us buy synthetic options without really realizing it. When you buy a house and borrow money to do so, you are buying an option to use and keep the house. All you have to do is pay your option premium called a mortgage payment. The following should make this concept a bit clearer. Let's say you want to buy a house for $1 million. People traditionally put 20 percent down to buy a house. So you go to the bank, get a mortgage for $800,000, and show up to the closing with $200,000 and take ownership of the house, or at least you think you did. What actually took place economically is that you bought an option on a $1 million house and paid an up-front premium to get it. That option has a strike price equal to the face value of the mortgage, or $800,000. The time value of that option is paid over time. So long as the value of the house stays above $800,000, you are economically incented to make your mortgage payment and keep the ownership rights. With the ownership rights, you can keep it, or sell it, repay the mortgage, and keep the difference.

You can achieve the same lifestyle at a lower cash cost by making a smaller down payment. If you can find a lender that will let you buy the house with nothing down, you do not have to pay any premium up front. All you have to do is pay a higher ongoing option premium represented by a higher mortgage payment. This, of course, changes the strike price of your option. It is now an at-the-money option with a strike price of $1 million. So long as the price of the house does not fall below $1 million, you have the economic incentive to continue paying the option premium (i.e., the mortgage) to maintain the ownership rights. If the market price of the house falls to $900,000, for example, you have an incentive to stop paying the mortgage, let the option expire worthless, and allow the bank to repossess the house. Thought of another way, the owner of the house owns a put option. In exercising their option, the homeowner puts the house to the lender who must buy the house at the strike price of the option, which is equal to the face value of the mortgage.

Lenny Dykstra was very clever, or at least he thought so, by using this technique to buy an option on an extremely privileged lifestyle. In his pursuit for something bigger, he sold his $4 million house and purchased one in Thousand Oaks, California, for $18.5 million. Giving this piece of real estate even more cache, he bought the house from Wayne Gretzky, arguably the best professional hockey player to ever take the ice. *Money* magazine reported that his monthly payment was $120,000. The average interest rate on a 30-year fixed-rate mortgage in 2007 was 6.34 percent. This implies that Lenny put virtually nothing down. Said another way, he bought an at-the-money call option to use and own the house.

Run-of-the-mill rich people fly first class. The mega rich have their own private jet. In 2007, Lenny bought a Gulfstream jet for $2 million and spent an additional $500,000 to upgrade the interior. Anyone who has ever looked into owning a private jet or taking a fractional ownership in a jet knows that the FAA has very strict maintenance rules. The electronics and structure must be regularly examined and maintained and the engines have to be periodically rebuilt or replaced. Since he chose to buy an older model, it was a fuel hog making it expensive to fly. Jet aircraft are hard assets and one can borrow against hard assets. Anyone can create a synthetic option to use and own a jet aircraft by pledging it as collateral against the loan.

In 2008, Lenny started a magazine called *Players Club*. *Players Club* was a luxury magazine aimed at professional athletes. Articles were written to show players how to spend their vast incomes while holding onto their wealth. He wanted to help his colleagues make smart financial decisions and avoid the pitfalls of so many athletes who came before him. Professional athletics is riddled with players who made millions and ended up bankrupt in retirement. The concept had possibilities because the magazine would have a core readership of high-profile individuals, but it takes millions of readers to make a magazine financially successful. Option traders recognize equity in a business as an option on company assets. If the company does well, the option goes wildly in the money and the equity investors win big. If the company fails, the option expires worthless and the lenders eat the losses. With an uncertain value, Lenny unwittingly bought an out-of-the-money option on the success of a magazine. But that did not matter. The magazine gave Lenny the perfect excuse to live the lifestyle. What better way to appeal to the mega wealthy than to show them how to do it?

When you try to keep up with the mega rich, any car will not do. Lenny drove a Maybach, which sell for a minimum of $360,000, and with the appropriate configuration can cost far more. Furthermore, Maybachs are expensive cars to drive, maintain, and insure. "Keeping Living the Dream" was the *Players Club* tag line, but living that dream is an expensive endeavor. The magazine was destined to fail because expense control was not part of Lenny's business plan. He published *Players Club* from midtown Manhattan where rent ran $17,000 a month and each issue began with an Ode to Lenny. It was status that mattered, and well it should. If you want to buy out-of-the-money call options and you want the lenders to think they are selling out-of-the-money put options, image and perception matter. To sell those options, you have to have assets to borrow against, and Lenny borrowed wherever he could. When he could not leverage those assets any further, he borrowed from his credit cards, friends, employees, and relatives.

While all this was going on, Lenny fancied himself an investment and options guru. He used his notoriety to start an investment advisors service called "Nails Investments," where he claimed to have superior stock-picking skills that would help individuals substantially outperform the market. After he found a stock to endorse, he would recommend that they buy deep-in-the-money call options to take a position. This is one thing Lenny essentially got right. We show in Chapter 4, that deep-in-the-money options statistically outperform at-the-money or out-of-the-money options on a risk-adjusted basis. His idea was not based on statistical analysis, however. His assertion was that deep-in-the-money options is a "stock replacement" strategy. The price action of deep-in-the-money options is very similar to the price action of the underlying stock. But why make 10 percent when you can make 20 percent? The advantage of the stock replacement strategy is that you do not have to pay full price for the underlying stock. If you want to buy a $100 stock, buy a call with a $75 strike price. This way, one only has to put up $26 to $30, depending on time to expiration and implied volatility, instead of $100. This allows the investor to either take more positions or take bigger positions, or both. What was truly remarkable is his track record. To this day, his website says that he has had 389 wins and only one loss since he started making recommendations. True? False? You decide.

By late 2008, the jig was up. His magazine closed and the financial crisis decimated the value of everyone's assets, including Lenny's. Lenny had to start liquidating assets where his call options were in the money. Where liens exceeded the value of assets, he let the options expire worthless. At the end of the day, the house, car, jet, magazine, World Series ring, and more were gone. Poof! But Lenny owed more—tens of millions more. At this point, Lenny had no choice but to file Chapter 7 bankruptcy, which is a full liquidation to satisfy his remaining unsecured debts. It was not long before dozens of lawsuits were filed. The pressure of financial difficulties of this size was too much for Lenny to bear. As his empire and lifestyle were in full-blown collapse, Lenny went "all Charlie Sheen" and he returned to drinking and drugs. Because of the vast leverage involved, gambling with options will inevitably put the investor on the "E Ticket" ride of their lives. Many lose right out of the chute. The few that win big initially, more often than not lose it all due to excess risk taking, poor discipline, and general misunderstandings.

It does not have to be this way. People can use options to steadily build wealth with measured risks. Options do not bankrupt people. People's actions or should we say, misactions bankrupt people. We do not want to see anyone abuse or misuse options or see people have a few big wins or a few good years, only to crash and burn. To this end, this book is designed to help investors use options properly. Successful options traders use them to manage portfolio risks and to take educated positions with a predefined exposure to risk. To get there, investors must understand how options are priced, what drives their return performance, and what risk of loss they are taking. During this introduction, we introduced a number of terms and concepts that may be foreign to you. There is no reason to be intimidated by the terminology. We will explain these concepts later on to help you build greater comprehension of options as a derivative instrument. Included in this discussion is a presentation of the historical performance of index options and how you can use that information to construct option strategies that put the odds in your favor. We also provide a glossary of terms for quick reference. The first step in that process is to review the fundamentals of options. We urge the reader to focus on the issue of pricing dynamics and build an understanding of what happens when they age, and how they change as market conditions change.

■ Additional Resources

We feel support is critical to your success. To that end, we have teamed up with **OptionsPlay**, which is a financial technology firm that delivers stock selection and options analytics service over the web. Go to **OptionsPlay.com** for a free trial and subscription discounts.

We have also created a website called **TheOptionsEdge.com**. Go there to find interesting articles about investing, additional insights about options trading and our commentary on market action. We will also post places and dates where we will be speaking so you can come see.

## CHAPTER 1

What Is an Option, and How Do Options Work?

An option is a contract to buy or sell any specific item, which is referred to as the **underlying instrument,** asset, or interest. As with all contracts, there are two parties involved. An option contract is an agreement that gives the buyer or owner of the contract the opportunity, but not an obligation, to buy or sell the underlying instrument at their discretion. The seller, on the other hand, has the obligation to perform the seller's end of the bargain should the buyer choose to exercise their right to transact under the terms of the agreement.

The underlying instrument is commonly a financial instrument like a stock, an index of financial instruments, a basket of stocks such as an ETF, a bond or a currency. The underlying instrument does not have to be a financial instrument, however. An option may reference a physical good such as a commodity (oil, gas, gold, silver or copper) or an economic good such as electricity, water, or real estate, and so on. Since investors are interested in options as a means of pursuing certain financial and/or risk management objectives in their investment portfolios, this book will focus on options referencing financial assets, such as stocks and stock indexes. Rest assured that the principles underlying an option contract are universal. It is easy to take the concepts presented and apply them to other aspects of your economic life, be it the purchase or sale of real estate or the management of a business.

The terms and conditions of an option contract must be very precise. The contract defines when, how, and at what price the contract will be executed. For options on financial assets, there are a number of standard terms the buyer and seller must agree upon. Fortunately, options listed on exchanges have standardized terms. This makes financial options liquid and easy to trade. Once you know the basic standardized terms of an option contract, you are good to go. Firstly, an option contract will establish the price of a trade, if a transaction were to occur. A transaction only occurs, if and only if, the owner of the option choses to **exercise** their right to transact. When an owner of an option exercises their right to transact, they make the demand that the seller of the option perform to the terms and conditions of the option contract. When a contract is exercised, the obligation is fulfilled and the contract is terminated. The price at which a trade occurs is known as the **strike price**. The **contract multiplier** defines the amount of stock or commodity transacted under the option agreement. For options on equities, the contract multiplier is typically 100. This means that a single option contract references 100 shares of stock. As a result, when the owner of a call option on a stock exercises their right, the option seller must deliver 100 shares of stock. Options do not last forever. The contract will define the length of time an option will remain effective. Should the buyer choose to exercise their right under the option agreement and transact, the buyer must do so within this window of time. The date upon which an option expires is known as the **expiration date**. If the buyer of an option chooses not to exercise this right during the life of an option, it simply ceases to exist, and both parties go their merry way.

There are two basic types of options, puts and calls. The type of option the investors select to use is dependent on their investment goals and risk management objectives. Since there are millions of investors employing different strategies trading options, both types are actively traded in the financial markets every day. A **call** option is a bullish instrument. It gives the buyer the right, but not the obligation, to purchase the underlying instrument at a predetermined price. Investors buy call options with the expectation that the price of the underlying security will rise. The seller of a call does so with the expectation that the price of the underlying instrument will stagnate or fall. Investors might buy a call to manage risk as well. Investors who hold a short position on the underlying instrument, with the expectation the price of that asset will fall, are at risk the price will spike higher. Buying a call allows short sellers to limit their risk by allowing them to buy back their short position at a predefined price. A **put** option is a bearish instrument. It gives the buyer the right, but not the obligation, to sell the underlying instrument at a predefined price. Investors buy put options with the expectation that the price of the underlying instrument will fall. Like calls, puts can be used for hedging as well. If you are long the underlying stock, you might purchase a put option to limit losses should the price of that stock fall.

How Options Are Created, Extinguished, and Settled

Companies issue a fixed amount of stock, and those shares typically trade on an exchange. While options trade on exchanges much the same way stocks do, there is not a fixed amount of options outstanding. Options differ from stock in that they are created and destroyed as investors take positions during the normal course of trading. If Investor A wants to buy a call option on company XYZ, he instructs his broker to go to the exchange and find someone who wants to sell the same option. If he finds another investor or market maker, call her Investor B, who wants to sell that call with the same terms, and the two parties agree on a price, then a transaction takes place. Since Investor A does not own an option, he will **"buy to open"** a new position. If Investor B already owns the option she wants to sell, she will **sell to close** her current holding. In this process, an option is created and one is destroyed, and the total number of options outstanding does not change. If, on the other hand, there are no options outstanding or existing owners of the options do not want to sell, all is not lost. The broker finds a third party or market maker—call him Investor C, who wants to sell a call option he does not already own. Investor C **writes** a call option that does not currently exist and sells it to Investor A. Since Investor C does not own the option and is creating a new one, he **sells to open** a new position. Since Investor C sold something he did not own, he is now short an option. The writer of the option now has an obligation to perform against the option written should the buyer of that newly created option wish to exercise. Whenever an investor initiates a new long position while the writer simultaneously sells to open a new position, an option is created and open interest expands.

Just as an option is created when a willing buyer and writer are willing to transact, they can also be destroyed. While there is just one way to create an option, there are two ways for an option to be extinguished. If an owner—say, Investor B—of a call sells the existing position, she "sells to close." This takes the option out of her portfolio. If Investor C on the other side of the trade wrote the option in question, he "buys to close." This takes the short position out of his portfolio. With both sides of the agreement now terminated, the option no longer exists. Alternatively, the buyer of the call option can exercise the right to transact. The owner of the call informs the writer of the intention to exercise, and the writer must fulfill the obligation. The writer does so by selling stock to the owner of the call at the previously agreed upon strike price. Once the transaction is consummated, the terms of the option contract are fulfilled and the contract is extinguished. In the case of a put, the put owner could decide to exercise the right to sell at the agreed-on strike price. Once the writer fulfills the obligation to buy the put owner's stock, the option is extinguished.

To get a feel for the market interest and liquidity of a particular option, it is useful to know how many options are outstanding. One can observe how many options exist on exchange-traded options by examining the **open interest**. The open interest represents the total number of option contracts that are outstanding at any point in time. Open interest increases when options are created, and it falls when options are closed or exercised. The exchanges publish the open interest data for every stock, stock index, ETF, or any other asset underlying those options, parsed by strike price and expiration date.

There is another very important aspect to the mechanics of trading options. When trading a derivative instrument, investors make an agreement to perform some action in the future. In the case of a call option, the writer agrees to sell stock to the call buyer at a predetermined price, if the call buyer wants it. Within this arrangement, there is a risk that the writer may not fulfill their obligation due to financial distress or some other reason. The industry has addressed this risk by forming a nonprofit entity called the **Options Clearing Corporation** (OCC). The OCC regulates the trading of exchange-traded options and guarantees the performance of those contracts by standing between the buyer and seller of options. In this way, the OCC is the counterparty to all option contracts outstanding. The OCC is well capitalized and has strict collateral requirements investors must adhere to, if they want to write options. These collateral requirements ensure that the option seller will perform as promised. With this discipline, Standard and Poor's and Moody's rate the OCC AAA/Aaa respectively. This is an indication that the chances of a counterparty failure are immeasurably small. Since the OCC is financially strong and maintains an AAA credit rating, investors are assured the terms of their contract will always be fulfilled. If there were not a high-quality counterparty to all option transactions, investors who buy options would have to worry about the financial stability and reputation of their counterparties. Under these conditions, the value of options would be subject to the credit quality of the counterparty and liquidity would be suppressed, as investors would have to find creditworthy counterparties. By having the OCC as the counterparty for all transactions, investors can focus on the investment issues at hand and not counterparty risk. As an aside, financial institutions trade over the counter (OTC) between themselves when they need certain types of customized options. When executing these transactions, counterparty risk is an issue, and option buyers must do in-depth credit analysis to determine if the option writer has the wherewithal to perform as they promise.

■ Exercising an Option

Investors who trade options do so with the intention of speculating on the price of the underlying security or hedging an existing position. After a trade has matured as intended, the owner of an option has two choices. They can either sell their position at a gain or loss, or they can exercise the option. When call buyers exercise, they do so because they want to take delivery of the underlying instrument to add the position to their portfolio or to cover a short position. Most option traders close out their investment by selling their position prior to expiration. While the owner has the right to exercise, the option contract specifies *when* they can do so.

The exercise clause of an option contract comes in three basic forms, and they are referred to as the American, the European, and the Bermudan styles. In a **European**-style option, the owner of a call (put) can only exercise their right to buy (sell) the underlying security on the expiration date of the option. Option writers usually prefer to sell European options as this eliminates the surprise of having to deliver or buy stock when they might not be ready to do so.

At the other end or the spectrum is the **American**-style option. In an American-style option, the owner of an option has the right to exercise at any time on or before the expiration date. At the extreme, the owner can exercise an American-style option a split second after they buy it. Buyers of options tend to prefer American-style options as it gives them greater flexibility. Options always have value, so it is generally suboptimal to exercise early. There are rare occasions, however, when it is advantageous to do so. For example, a company might issue a large special dividend. Since the owner of a call does not have rights to the dividend, the owner must exercise a call and take delivery of the stock to get it. Since there is more flexibility in an American-style option, its value will always be as high as, or higher than, an equivalent European-style option.

In between the European- and American-style options is the **Bermudan**. In a Bermudan-style option, owners may only exercise their right to transact on specific dates defined by the contract. Most individual investors are not aware that this type of option exists, as they are most commonly used in the interest rate option and swap markets, which are dominated by institutional investors.

■ Assignment

A very important aspect of exchange-traded options is that they are generic. If there are 100 different investors holding call options on company XYZ stock with the same strike price and expiration date, every one of those investors holds an identical option. All the sellers of those options have written identical contracts as well. When an investor exercises an option, the question of assignment comes into play.

This might seem like a trivial issue, but it is something to consider when trading American-style options. When one of the hundred owners of the call options decides to exercise early, who among the option writers will have to perform on the other end of the transaction? As mentioned earlier, the counterparty for all option contracts traded on the exchange is the Options Clearing Corp (OCC). From the perspective of the OCC, its counterparty is the broker/dealer or customer that owns the option. When an option is assigned, the OCC chooses a broker(s) *at random* who has a customer(s) who has written the call option being exercised. At this point, the OCC has made an assignment to a broker/dealer, but the broker/dealer is not the ultimate counterparty. The broker/dealer has to assign the option exercise to one of their customers. They do so by one of two methods. They can assign the option on a purely random basis, or they can rank order their customer positions by the time and date the option was written and then assign the options on a first-in, first-out (FIFO) basis. The broker has the leeway to choose the method at its discretion. There is a limitation, however. The broker/dealer is required to use the same method all the time. This way, the broker/dealer cannot cherry-pick assignments to less-favored customers, or assign to customers instead of the firm's own proprietary trading book.

There was a time when customers had to instruct their broker to exercise their options at expiration. If a customer forgot to instruct the broker to exercise an in-the-money option, it would expire and the customer would lose out. At the same time, there would be an option writer who was not assigned when he should have been. In this case, the writer would collect a windfall. This is not an issue today, as most all brokers automatically exercise options for their customers at expiration if they are in the money.

Over-the-counter (OTC) options are more straightforward. OTC options are bilateral contracts, usually between large financial institutions or between a large financial institution and a large institutional investor such as a hedge fund. All the owner of the option has to do is simply inform the seller of his or her desire to exercise and the transaction occurs.

Deliverables

The deliverable on an option contract is usually the underlying instrument, but not always. For options on stocks and ETFs, the deliverable is the underlying stock or ETF. So when an investor exercises an option to buy XYZ stock, the option writer must deliver shares of that stock to the owner of the option. Options on indexes are different. Instead of delivering the basket of stocks to the owner of an option who chooses to exercise, which would be cumbersome and expensive, the option writer delivers cash. The amount of cash delivered is equal to the option's intrinsic value. For a call, this is equal to the index's closing price minus the strike price or zero if the option is out of the money. For a put option, it is equal to the strike price minus the closing index value or zero if the option is out of the money. So if the S&P 500 index is trading at 1,600 and the strike price of the call option is 1,500, the option writer must deliver $10,000$ ($[1,600 - 1,500] \times 100$, where 100 is the contract multiplier) to the owner of the option.

Behavior of Option Prices

A stockowner enjoys a return if the price of that stock rises and suffers a loss if the price of the stock falls. In this case, the payoff is symmetrical, as price changes lead to an equal return or loss. If the stock goes up 10 percent, the investor earns that amount. If the stock falls by 10 percent, the investor loses the same amount. Options, on the other hand, give the buyer an asymmetric payoff. Take the case of an *at-the-money* call, where the strike price of the option is identical to the price of the underlying stock. If someone owns an at-the-money call option and the price of the underlying stock rises, the owner can exercise their right under the option contract to buy the stock. In doing so, the investor buys the stock at the strike price of the option and immediately sells the stock at the higher market price. The difference between these two prices less the option premium paid represents the profit the investor earns. If the price of the underlying falls, the owner can simply let the option expire and avoid a large loss. The loss is limited to the premium paid on the option. Likewise, if someone owns at-the-money put options, and the price of the underlying stock falls, the owner can exercise the right to sell the underlying stock. In doing so, the owner sells stock at the strike price of the option and covers that short position by purchasing stock in the market at a lower price. Once again, the difference between the price paid in the marketplace and sold by exercising the option less the option premium paid is the profit the investor earns. If the price of the underlying rises instead, the owner of the put can simply let the option expire and avoid a large loss. This loss is simply limited to the premium paid for the option.

This is a case of "heads I win big, tails I break even or lose a small amount." Every investor, arbitrageurs in particular, wants such an asymmetrical payoff pattern. Asymmetry gives an investor the opportunity to earn positive rates of return with limited downside risk. This unique feature of options is what attracts speculators and hedgers alike to these financial instruments. The beauty of options is their flexibility in terms of time to expiration and strike price. If investors want more time for a trade to work out, they buy a longer-dated option. If they want to change the nature of the asymmetry, or make a trade-off between leverage and price sensitivity, they can do so by adjusting the strike price they select. Exhibit 1.1 shows a stick diagram for the payoff pattern for both a put and call option with a strike price on the underlying security of $25. Stick diagrams are useful for understanding how the price of an option might behave given differing prices of the underlying security. Furthermore, it helps one clarify the payoff pattern for complex transactions that use multiple options to achieve a particular objective. Bear in mind that the analysis of stick diagrams is not just a theoretical exercise; it shows the **intrinsic value** of an option or multi-leg option strategy. For a call option, it is measured by subtracting the strike price of the option from the market price of the underlying security. For a put option, it is measured by subtracting the market price of the underlying

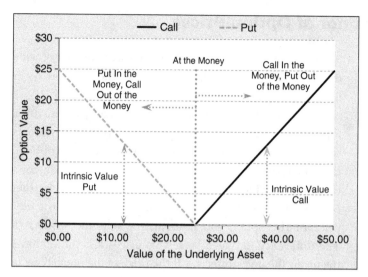

Exhibit 1.1   Payoff Pattern for a Put and Call with a Strike Price of $25

instrument from the strike price of the option. Only options that are in the money have intrinsic value. Furthermore, the intrinsic value of an option is equal to its market price at expiration.

The solid black line in Exhibit 1.1 represents the payoff pattern for a call option based on its intrinsic value (i.e., its value at expiration). Notice that as the price of the underlying instrument increases above the strike price, which is $25 in this case, the intrinsic value of the call option rises on a one-for-one basis. That is to say, if the stock rises by one dollar, so does the intrinsic value of the call. If however the price of the underlying falls below $25, the call does not have any intrinsic value and would expire worthless. The gray dotted line represents the payoff pattern of a put option. Notice that as the price of the underlying instrument falls below the strike price of $25, the intrinsic value of the put rises on a one-for-one basis. If, however, the price of the underlying rises above $25, the intrinsic value falls to zero and the put option would expire worthless.

This chart clearly shows the asymmetric nature of an option's payoff pattern. Assume for a moment that an investor wanted to own the stock of company XYZ, which is trading at $25 a share. One choice is to buy the shares and enjoy the gains if the price rises or suffer a loss if the price fell. An alternative is to buy a call option with a strike price of $25 at its intrinsic value. If the price of the shares rise, the investor enjoys a gain, if the share price falls, no loss is incurred. From the standpoint of a stick chart, this asymmetric pattern shows that owning a call option is always superior to owning the stock outright. As a result, we can conclude that an option has value above and beyond intrinsic value. The price one pays for an option above its intrinsic value is an option's **time value** (aka **time premium or volatility**

premium). The total value of an option, which is usually referred to as an **option premium,** is the sum of its intrinsic value and its time value. The purchaser of an option must pay this premium as a cost of capturing this asymmetric payoff. The premium is paid to the option writer, who takes the risk that the price of the stock will increase and they will have to sell stock to the call option buyer at a price below the stock's market price. This makes an option a **volatility instrument**. As volatility rises, so does the expected value of the option at expiration. Said another way, as volatility rises, the more likely the stock will trade substantially above the call option's strike price. As a result, the option premium is a function of an option's intrinsic value and a volatility premium is what the option writer demands for taking what is theoretically unlimited risk from selling a call. (The risk of selling a naked put is limited, as the asset price can only fall to zero.) This volatility premium will be discussed in greater detail below.

From an accounting standpoint, the premium paid by a purchaser of an option is known as a **net debt**. This is the amount the buyer places at risk when entering into a long option trade. If in the case of a call option, the price of the underlying stock rises, the premium will increase, resulting in a gain. Likewise, if the price of the underlying stock falls, the option premium will fall, resulting in a loss. In the case of a put option, if the price of the underlying stock falls, the premium will rise, resulting in a gain. Likewise, if the price of the underlying stock increases, the option premium will fall, resulting in a loss. In either case, if the price of the underlying security does not change as the option ages, the time premium of the option will fall, leaving the option buyer with a loss. When selling an option, the initial premium is subtracted from the proceeds of the sale to determine the profit earned, if any. On the flip side of the coin, the option writer collects the premium paid by the option buyer. This premium is compensation the option writer demands for providing an asymmetric return pattern enjoyed by the option buyer. Sellers of options take a significant risk that the price of the underlying security will move sharply against them and that under these circumstances, they would be required to fulfill their promise and perform on the contract.

From an accounting standpoint, the amount the option writer collects is known as a **net credit** as funds are deposited (credited) to the writer's account upon settlement of the trade. The option writer keeps these funds so long as the option sold remains outstanding. If the writer decides to cover the short position before the option expires, he must pay the current premium to buy back the option he previously sold. The writer's gain or loss is a function of the price that must be paid to buy back the option. If he can buy it back at a price lower than where it was originally sold, then he will capture a gain. If he has to pay a higher price, he suffers a loss. At the expiration date, one of two scenarios will occur. If the option is in the money, the owner of the option will exercise his right. The seller of a call option will have to deliver the underlying asset. Now that the seller is short that asset, she will have to buy it in the marketplace to make delivery. (Alternatively, she could maintain a short position. This would require the option seller to borrow the underlying asset and deliver it to the call buyer.) The amount of money it costs the writer to execute these transactions is equal to the intrinsic value of the option (plus commission). If the intrinsic value of the option is greater than the premium collected, the option writer suffers a loss. Naturally, if the option is out of the money at expiration, the option will expire worthless and the writer keeps the entire premium, which is equal to the profit on the trade.

■ Option Premium

Premium is another way to describe the price paid for an option. Like all financial instruments, the premium the buyer pays and the writer collects changes constantly over the life on an option. The direction and degree of change depends on a number of factors. As seen in the discussion above, when the price of the underlying changes, so will the intrinsic value of in-the-money put and call options referencing that underlying instrument. The price of the underlying security relative to an option's strike price is the primary determinant of the option premium. This is particularly true for options that are in the money. The expected volatility of returns on the underlying stock is a primary determinant of an option's value as well. The more volatile the returns on the underlying instrument are expected to be, the higher the value of both the associated puts and calls. As volatility rises, so does the potential for an extreme event. If the extreme event is a rise in price, the value of a call will enjoy a huge gain. Since options provide leveraged returns with respect to the price action of the underlying security, it is not uncommon for buyers of call options to capture returns that are hundreds of percent in magnitude. In such a scenario, the put will fall drastically in value and the owner can lose up to 100 percent of their investment should it expire worthless. If, on the other hand, the extreme event turns out to be a drop in price, the value of the put option will rise in value, possibly by multiples of the buyer's original premium. The value of the call option will go the other way and the owner can lose up to 100 percent of the premium paid.

With these dynamics in mind, it is easy to understand that as the uncertainty concerning the performance of the underlying instrument rises, we would prefer the asymmetric payoff pattern of an option vis-à-vis the underlying instrument. Volatility of returns on any asset continuously changes over time, as do investors' expectations concerning future volatility. To be effective at trading options, both buyers and sellers must develop a view on volatility over the life of the option they wish to trade. If market participants expect volatility to be high, option buyers bid up the price of options until they are indifferent between owning a call and owning the underlying stock, or owning a put versus taking a short position in the underlying stock. This applies to option writers as well. If option writers expect the volatility of asset price returns to be high, they will not sell any options until the premium rises to the point where they believe they are getting compensated for the risk they are taking. In short, volatility expectations drive option premiums. Only after these two parties agree on a premium will a transaction actually take place.

How we translate volatility estimates into option premiums across the strip of available strike prices and expiration dates is a matter of mathematics. Fortunately, academics have worked for decades on the question of option pricing. As a result, the theory of how to determine a fair price for an option is well developed and traders use models to price and value options. The most important of these models is the Black–Scholes–Merton option-pricing model, which was developed in the early 1970s. In Chapter 2, we delve into the mathematics of option pricing so anyone can become an expert in pricing options. Equally as important, the reader will gain an understanding of how the price of an option behaves as it ages and the investment environment changes from a mathematical perspective. Until then it is very important to develop some intuition about how market participants price options, and how those prices change as market conditions and investor expectations change. To build that intuition, we will focus on call options once again for a moment. Exhibit 1.2 shows an example of what the premium might look like for a three-month call option compared to a similar one at expiration. Notice that the buyer has to pay more than the intrinsic value of the option to the seller as payment for the asymmetric nature of an option's payoff pattern. For the most part, the market price of an option will be greater than the intrinsic value of an option. (There are rare circumstances when this is not the case for European options and we discuss those situations in later chapters.) The difference between the market price of an option and its intrinsic value is equal to the time value of an option. The time

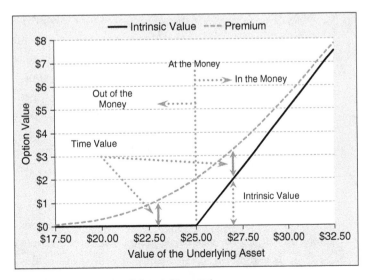

Exhibit 1.2   Premium = Intrinsic Value + Time Value

value of an option captures the investor's expectation of future volatility of returns on the underlying instrument. Naturally, time to expiration is a factor in time value as well. As the time to expiration increases, so does the time value of an option. This should be intuitively obvious because there is more time for the option to trade in the money sometime during its life.

An important concept in option valuation is the likelihood that an option will be exercised. This is determined, in part, by the relationship between the market price of the underlying instrument and the strike price. A call option is said to be **in the money** if the price of the underlying asset is greater than the strike price of the option. This is depicted by the area on the right-hand side of Exhibit 1.2. A put option is said to be in the money if the price of the underlying asset is less than the strike price. The value of an option increases as it moves further and further into the money simply because the intrinsic value of the option increases. If an option is far enough in the money, its price action will closely mimic the price action of the underlying asset. In other words, its price will move virtually dollar for dollar with the price of the underlying instrument. Now that the call option's price action closely follows that of the underlying instrument, it loses its asymmetric payoff pattern. The option no longer protects the owner from a large drop in the price of the underlying stock. As a result, the time value of the option falls as an option moves in the money. Exhibit 1.2 reveals this phenomenon, as the slope of the gray dotted line representing option premium is virtually the same as the slope of the intrinsic value line and the distance between these two lines narrows.

Similarly, a call option is said to be **out of the money** if the price of the underlying asset is less than the option's strike price. The area on the left-hand side of Exhibit 1.2 depicts this situation. A put option is said to be out of the money when the price of the underlying asset is greater than the strike price of the option. An option that is out of the money does not have any intrinsic value. Its value simply comes from the probability that it might trade in the money by the time it expires. As a result, as an option drifts out the money, it becomes less and less sensitive to the price of the underlying asset. Furthermore, it becomes less likely that the option will trade in the money by the time it expires. As a result, time value falls. This phenomenon is revealed in Exhibit 1.2 as well. If the option is far enough out of the money, the slope of the gray dotted line, representing the option price, approaches zero. This tells us that it has very little sensitivity to the price of the underlying asset. The price of the option approaches zero as well, as the probability the option will expire worthless becomes more certain.

When the price of the underlying asset is trading at the strike price of a put or call option, it is said to be **at the money**. Like out-of-the-money options, at-the-money options do not have any intrinsic value, either. It gets its value simply from the fact that there is roughly a 50:50 chance it will trade in the money at the expiration date. Since it falls in between in-the-money and out-of-the-money options, it shares characteristics of both. Its price action will move with the underlying security but will do so at a rate less than an in-the-money option and more than an out-of-the-money option. At-the-money options provide the greatest asymmetric payoff pattern. The option buyer risks little relative to the value of the underlying security, just 8 percent in this case. But there is the potential for the price of the underlying to rise far, far more. If the stock rises 20 percent, the option buyers will almost triple their money. If it falls by 20 percent, they will simply lose their premium. Since at-the-money options provide the greatest asymmetric return profile, they have the highest time premium.

◼ Moneyness

Option traders use shorthand terminology for the differential between the market price of the underlying security and an option's strike price. That word is **moneyness,** which is a numerical figure that is normalized to the price of the underlying security. An option that is at the money is said to have moneyness of 100, or 100 percent. If the strike price of the option is less than the market price of the underlying asset, it has moneyness less than 100. When moneyness is less than 100, a put option is out of the money and a call is in the money. The following is a numerical example for the computation of simple moneyness, which tells us how much an option is in or out of the money on a percentage basis.

Simple Moneyness

$$\text{Strike price } (K) = \$25.00$$
$$\text{Asset spot price } (S) = \$20.00$$
$$\text{Simple moneyness} = \frac{K}{S} \times 100$$
$$\text{Simple moneyness} = \$25.00/\$20.00 \times 100 = 125$$

Simple moneyness of 125 tells us that a call option is 25 percent out of the money relative to the price of the underlying asset. In the case of an equivalent put option, it tells us that it is 25 percent in the money. Moneyness is an important aspect of an option as it makes analyzing options between differing assets with differing prices more easily comparable. Just remember, when discussing options with moneyness less than 100, you are discussing options with a strike price less than the market price of the underlying asset. When discussing options with moneyness greater than 100, you are discussing options with a strike price more than the market price of the underlying asset.

While the concept of simple moneyness is relatively straightforward, there is a nuance to the analysis that sophisticated options traders take into consideration. In theory, investors should use the forward price of an asset, not the current spot price to determine an option's moneyness. The difference between the spot price and forward price of an asset is its cost of carry. The cost of carry is a function of the current rate of interest; the dividend yield of the underlying stock, index, or ETF pays a dividend; and the time to expiration of the option. This is an important component to the valuation of options. The following is an example of how to compute the forward price of an asset.

Forward Price

$$\text{Spot price } (S) = \$20.00$$
$$\text{Risk-free rate } (r) = 2\%$$
$$\text{Dividend yield } (d) = 1\%$$
$$\text{Time to expiration } (t) = 0.25 \text{ years}$$
$$\text{Forward price } = F = Se^{(r-d)t}$$
$$F = \$20.00 \times e^{(0.02-0.01)0.25} = \$20.05$$

In an environment of low interest rates or when we are estimating the forward price for a near-dated option, the forward price is not much different than the spot price. In this example, the difference is just $0.05. Under these circumstances, it is perfectly acceptable to use the spot price of the asset when computing moneyness. This is not the case for estimating moneyness in a high-interest-rate environment for a long-dated option. If the risk-free rate was 10 percent and the dividend yield was 1 percent, the forward price of a one-year option would be $21.88, which is $1.88 or 9.4 percent higher than the spot price. In this example of a $25.00 strike call, the correct estimate of the option's moneyness is 114 percent, not the moneyness of 125 estimated by simply referencing the current spot price of the asset. Given the current low-interest-rate environment, and the fact that most traders work with short-dated options, we do not have to pay too much attention to this distinction most of the time.

Simple moneyness is an absolute measure of how much an option is in or out of the money. This measure is a good shorthand method to understanding the behavior of a particular option under consideration. It is not the best measure of moneyness, however. Underlying this absolute measure of moneyness is the assumption that the volatility of returns on the underlying asset is constant over time. Anyone who trades the markets knows firsthand that markets go through periods of low and high volatility. Indeed professional volatility traders and market makers attempt to profit from fluctuations in volatility as a core element of their business model. When volatility is low, so is the time premium of an option. When volatility is high, option premiums are high as well. Volatility traders attempt to buy volatility when it is low and expected to rise, or sell it high when it is high and expected to fall, while managing other attributes such as sensitivity to the price of the underlying asset and time decay in the process.

An option that is out of the money is more likely to trade in the money when volatility is high versus in an environment when volatility is low. Therefore, measuring moneyness on an absolute basis is insufficient when comparing options on assets with distinctly different volatilities or options on the same asset during differing volatility regimes. To deal with this, sophisticated option traders use a standardized measure of moneyness. **Standardized moneyness** modifies absolute moneyness by dividing simple moneyness by the volatility of returns on the underlying instrument. With this measure, we are measuring moneyness in volatility terms. This measure is very similar to a *t*-stat, used in statistical analysis. The following is an example of the computation of standardized moneyness continued from the example started above.

Standardized Moneyness

$$\text{Standard deviation of returns} = 35\%$$

$$\text{Standardized moneyness} = \frac{\ln\left(K/F\right)}{\sigma\sqrt{t}}$$

$$\text{Standardized moneyness} = \frac{\ln\left(\$25.00/\$20.05\right)}{0.35\sqrt{0.25}} = 1.26$$

In this example, the standardized moneyness tells us that a call is 1.26 standard deviations out of the money. In other words, the underlying stock would have to produce a return greater than 1.26 standard deviations for a call to get in the money and a put with the same strike price to fall out of the money.

Consider for a moment that the stock is trading in a low-volatility environment. If volatility falls to 20 percent, the standardized moneyness estimate jumps to 2.19. This tells us that moneyness is 1.76 times as high as in the first case, making it far less likely the option will ever trade in the money. This is a very important way of thinking of moneyness in an environment where volatility is changing and testing various options strategies with historical data. Since options are complicated enough, we will explain concepts throughout this book using simple moneyness where possible. Bear in mind that you can sharpen your pencil and replace it with standardized moneyness in research and trading activities if you choose to do so.

■ The Relationship between Puts, Calls, and the Underlying Asset

While puts and calls on the same underlying instrument have different payoff patterns, they represent two sides of the same coin. Both contracts derive their value from the same underlying asset and the volatility of returns on that asset. When the price of the underlying rises, so does the price of a call, while the price of a put falls. When the price of the underlying asset falls, the price of a put increases while the price of a call declines. In short, calls move in the same direction as the price of the underlying instrument, while the price of a put moves in the opposite direction. Both puts and calls produce asymmetric payoff patterns. Both will increase in price when uncertainty rises and both will fall when volatility does the same. Since puts and calls are dependent, at least in part, on the value of the underlying security and the volatility of returns on the underlying instrument, their value must be related in some way. That relationship is known as **put–call parity**. Put–call parity defines an arbitrage condition between European put and call options with the same defining characteristic. More specifically, the two options must reference the same underlying security, have the same strike price, and expire on the same date. Those that trade and make markets in equity options are very familiar with the concept. The following is the mathematical relationship.

$$\text{Cash} + \text{Call option} = \text{Stock} + \text{Put option}$$

$$\text{Cash} = Ke^{-rt}$$

This equation is the standard formulation of put–call parity. It states that with cash and a call option, we can identically replicate the return performance of the underlying security (stock in this case) and a put option. The amount of cash required is equal to the present value of the strike price associated with the put and call options. Looking at the relationship more deeply, the intuition behind put–call parity becomes clear. An investor can buy a call option on a stock and hold cash equal to the strike price of the option. If the stock price is above the strike price, the investor exercises the option and gives up his or her cash and takes ownership of the company's stock. If the stock price is below the exercise price at expiration, the investor keeps their cash and the option expires worthless. The second half of the equation replicates that investment performance by purchasing shares in the company's stock and simultaneously purchasing a married put option. If the price of the stock is above the strike price at expiration, the investor keeps the shares and lets the option expire worthless. If the price of the stock falls below the strike price, the investor sells the shares to the seller of the put option, and now has cash equal to the strike price of the put option. The end result of following the strategy on the left-hand side of the equation is identical to the result of the right-hand side of the equation.

With this formulation, we can easily see why volatility moves the price of a puts and calls in the same direction. If implied volatility rises, pushing the price of a call higher, the price of a put must rise as well. If this were not the case, it would be cheaper to buy stock and sell a put than to hold cash and a call option. The individual investor will rarely see arbitrage opportunities like this as volatility traders, market makers, and computers run by high-frequency trading firms look for these opportunities. Once identified these sophisticated investors will sell calls and buy puts and stock until the discrepancy disappears. Small discrepancies exist all the time, but after paying a bid/offer spread to a market maker on the options and underlying stock plus commission to a broker, the advantage is eaten up by transaction costs.

Another way to look at put–call parity is to rearrange the equation and look at it from the perspective of holding stock outright.

$$\text{Stock} = \text{Call} - \text{Put} + Ke^{-rt}$$

By rearranging the general formula of put–call parity it becomes easy to see that we can replicate stock by purchasing a call, selling a put, and holding the present value of the option's strike price in cash. If at expiration, the call is in the money, the investor exercises the call, lets the put expire, and uses the cash on hand to purchase the underlying stock. If at expiration the put is in the money, the call will expire worthless and the stock will be put to the investor, who will pay for it with cash. Remember, put–call parity holds, if and only if the two options have the same strike price. If in the extraordinary circumstance the stock price is equal to the strike price of the put and call options, the investor can either exercise the call and take stock or let both options expire and hold cash with the same value. Alternatively, the investor can still buy stock by actively purchasing it in the marketplace. In all three scenarios, the investor ends up in the same place as simply buying the stock outright.

Put–call parity is a very important concept when formulating option strategies. There are situations when investors might want to synthetically create stock, puts, or calls, as it may be slightly cheaper than buying the securities outright. There are times when investors might want to create *cash* synthetically as well. Institutions do this all the time. In Chapter 9, the subject of synthetics based on put–call parity and other relationships is discussed in detail.

■ Leverage and Risk

Derivative products such as options, futures, and forwards, were developed as tools for risk transfer. Before the advent of derivatives, if someone had risk in their portfolio they did not want, their only choice was to sell the asset. Derivative products allow the investor to keep the investment and transfer some or all of the price risk to another market actor who is willing to take on that risk. A key attribute of derivatives products is leverage. It allows the investor to allocate just a fraction of the value of the investment they want to hedge to the hedging instrument.

Options, like most derivative financial products, provide a levered means of gaining exposure to a stock, market index, ETF, commodity, or other underlying asset. Option buyers pay a relatively small premium compared to the face value of the underlying instrument. In so doing, they experience a much larger gain or loss on the premium paid compared to the face value of the contract.

For example, assume an investor buys a three-month, at-the-money call when the underlying is trading at $25.00. Exhibit 1.2 shows the investor will pay $2.00 for this option contract. If the price of the underlying goes up $5.00 to $30.00, the rate of return on that asset is 20 percent ($5/$25). The option, on the other hand, will increase by $3.60 to $5.60, producing a return of 180 percent ($3.60/$2.00). This shows that the inherent leverage in an option gives the investor a big bang for the buck. While the investor sees a magnified return if price moves her way, she also suffers an outsized loss if price moves the wrong way. If the price of the underlying falls by $5.00 to $20.00, the loss is 20 percent. At the same time, the price of the option falls by $1.70 to $0.30, for an 85 percent loss. If the expected recovery in price does not materialize, the option will expire worthless resulting in a 100 percent loss.

One of the advantages of using options is that they limit risk relative to owning the underlying instrument outright. For example, instead of buying the underlying instrument at $25.00, assume the investor puts $23.00 in a money market account and spends $2.00 to buy a call option. If the underlying increases 20 percent to $30 a share, this strategy will produce a return of 14 percent ([$23 + $5.60]/$25.00), for a 14 percent gain. If, on the other hand, the price falls 20 percent to $20, this strategy suffers a 6.8 percent loss (1 − [$23.00 + $0.30]/$25.00). In the worst-case scenario, the price of the underlying stock would fall to zero if the company filed for bankruptcy, and stockholders would lose 100 percent of their investment. However, option holders would only lose the option premium of $2.00 or just 8 percent.

Leverage is a double-edged sword. If investors overleverage their portfolio by purchasing or selling options without holding the underlying security as a hedge or an adequate amount of cash, the results can be catastrophic. If they simply held the $2.00 call discussed above without cash, their returns would be either heroic (+180%) or disastrous (−85%), depending on what direction the underlying security went. It is very important when trading options to understand and quantify the risk before the trade is made. In the following chapter, we discuss option pricing, return dynamics, and risk metrics. This is the first step in effective risk management and strategy development for option traders. In later chapters, we build on this analysis and introduce various option strategies that maximize the potential for success by constructing strategies with moderate levels of leverage in some cases and/or self-hedging in others.

Effectively used, options can limit an investor's downside risk. The characteristic of limited risk comes with a cost, however. If the price of the underlying does not change over the life of an option, it will expire worthless. In the example of the $2.00 call option, the option buyer will lose 100 percent of the option premium and 8 percent on the combination of cash and call. If one bought the stock instead, they would have neither enjoyed a gained nor suffered a lost. Just like buying insurance, hedging and limiting risk often comes with a cost. One does not earn quite as much if price moves in the intended direction, but one can lose most or their entire option premium if price stagnates or moves in the wrong direction. The loss in value of an option as time passes is known as **time decay**. Managing time decay is a very important aspect of risk management in the context of both speculation and hedging. In our discussion of option strategies, we will uncover ways for investors to minimize loss due to time decay—and even profit by it, in some cases.

## CHAPTER 2

Valuing Options with the Black–Scholes–Merton Option-Pricing Model

If you want to trade options effectively for offensive or hedging purposes, it is critical to understand how options are priced and how they behave as market conditions change. The practice of using mathematics to price options came to the forefront in 1973 when Fischer Black and Myron Scholes published a paper titled "The Pricing of Options and Corporate Liabilities" in the *Journal of Political Economy*. This launched an avalanche of work in the area of option-pricing theory, starting with a paper written by Robert C. Merton called "Theory of Rational Option Pricing," which was published by the *Bell Journal of Economics and Management Sciences* in 1973. In this paper he derived and articulated a model, which is now known as the Black–Scholes–Merton option-pricing model. This model, or some modified version of it designed to take into account unique features of the underlying instrument, is the industry standard for pricing options on stocks, indexes, commodities, and other assets.

It is important to recognize that a model is simply a mathematical representation of a physical or economic system. The validity of that model rests on how the mathematical representation reflects how that system truly works. The way the model works is described by the assumptions made, which is the foundation upon which the model is built. Before delving straight into a model, it is imperative to hold a deep understanding of the assumptions made to develop an intuition into why it works, and to recognize under what situations it may not work. With an understanding beyond "plug and chug," you will greatly increase your chances of success when applying a mathematical representation to the investment markets. With that in mind, the following section describes the assumptions made to solve the option-pricing problem.

Assumptions of the Black–Scholes–Merton Option Pricing Model

Assumptions of the Black–Scholes–Merton option pricing model are:

- *The relationship between an option and its underlying instrument resides in an arbitrage-free environment.* Practically speaking, this means that we cannot trade an option against the underlying instrument in a risk-free manner and earn anything other than a risk-free rate of return. The B–S–M option-pricing formula is derived from a partial differential equation, which governs the price of an option over time. The implications of this equation suggest that if we continuously hedge an option with the underlying instruments *delta neutral*, we do not take any risk. Trading stock versus an option in this manner is a risk-free investment strategy and must therefore deliver a risk-free rate of return.

  This is a reasonable assumption for trading options in markets that never close, such as the currency market. Currencies continuously trade somewhere on the planet, allowing option traders to continuously hedge their currency options by taking the appropriate position in the underlying currency. This assumption is problematic for assets that trade for a limited time during the day. U.S. stock exchanges are only open a limited number of hours during the day. Companies often disclose news before or after market trading hours. This news might pertain to earnings, an acquisition, change in strategy, an accident, or legal entanglement, just to name a few. These news events impact the value of the affected company and its associated options. Since markets are not open, we cannot continuously hedge.

- *The price action of the underlying instrument follows geometric Brownian motion, with a constant drift and volatility.* Geometric Brownian motion is a continuous stochastic process where the logarithm of the price of the underlying asset follows a process of Brownian motion. Brownian motion describes the random movement of a particle suspended in a fluid or gas. That movement results from haphazard collisions with other atoms or molecules, making its path indeterminate ahead of time. The B–S–M model assumes that the price of financial assets behaves the same way. If the price of a financial asset is based on all available information as the efficient market hypothesis suggests, then price changes occur as new information comes out. Since consistent prediction of future events is extraordinarily difficult if not impossible, future asset prices are unpredictable. Since information continuously flows into the markets, prices continuously fluctuate. This behavior makes Brownian motion an applicable model for the returns on financial assets.

In a physical world, the movement of a particle moves continuously through the liquid in which it is found. It cannot disappear from its present location and magically appear somewhere else. This is where Brownian motion has the potential to break down as a descriptor of asset price returns. Asset prices move in very small increments most of the time. These increments are usually a penny or less. But there are times where random news events that flow into the market have a huge impact on the price of an asset. This can cause a huge instantaneous price jump. This is akin to a particle at the shallow end of a swimming pool magically showing up in the deep end. Price jumps occur around earnings announcements all the time. Companies usually report their earnings during nontrading hours. If those earnings come in much higher or lower than expectations, then the opening price following the news release might be substantially higher or lower than the closing price the previous day.

Another example is the drug approval process for a biotech company concerning a blockbuster drug that might cure a common disease. If the drug is approved, the share price might double or triple. If approval is denied by the FDA, the share price might fall by 50 percent or more. This is a binomial outcome in which price will either jump up or down. This does not resemble Brownian motion at all. So using a standard version of the B–S–M option model is not a useful method for pricing options around binomial events. Recognizing this, professionals use other option-pricing formulations under these circumstances.

It is important to recognize that Brownian motion assumes that the particle drifts at a constant rate like a leaf floating down a calm river. As it does so, it randomly moves from side to side at a consistent pace. Anyone who invests or trades securities in the financial market knows that volatility is anything but constant. There are very dull periods when volatility is very low. This is like the point of a river where the water almost stagnates. There are more normal times when the water in the river moves along at a measured pace and the turbulence in the water pushes the leaf randomly from side to side. Then there are those periods when the calm river turns into chaotic rapids. The leaf speeds up and then quickly slows down. Crosscurrents hurl the leaf from side to side. The behavior of a leaf floating down such a river is inconsistent with Brownian motion, but completely consistent with the behavior of asset prices. Anyone who actively manages their account knows that market dynamics put traders through periods of incredible boredom that can quickly change to periods of sheer terror. We might think that this could invalidate the B–S–M model, but it does not. It simply changes the way option and volatility traders use the model as a foundation for their decision-making process. This will become clear as you work your way through the book.

- *Both the underlying instrument and associated options trade in frictionless markets.* If we were to continuously hedge an option with the underlying instrument, as the model requires, we would continuously transact in the marketplace. For all practical purposes, a frictionless market is one where investors can buy or sell a security at the same price (i.e., no bid/offer spread). Furthermore, it assumes the markets are so large and deep that the act of trading does not have an impact on the price of the security traded. In addition, a frictionless market assumes that investors do not pay commissions to brokers who execute their trades.

Transactions costs are real, and they have a material impact on returns. The inclusion of transaction costs on the process of continuous hedging would drive down the value of an option for its owner and drive up the price for someone who sold an option. With these countervailing forces at play, assuming frictionless markets is a reasonable one but certainly not a perfect one. It also explains why the bid/offer spread demanded by market makers to trade an option is generally larger than the bid/offer spread demanded for the underlying security.

Furthermore, the assumption of frictionless markets is reasonable when trading options on equity market indexes such as the S&P 500, bond indexes, diversified baskets of commodities, and currency markets. These markets are huge and there are thousands if not millions of economic actors who transact in these markets throughout the trading day. These markets trade with very narrow bid/offer spreads, and only very large transactions have an impact on the price of these securities. This assumption becomes problematic for small, illiquid markets such as options on single stocks that have moderate market capitalizations (i.e., less than a few billion dollars). This is also the case for options on distressed assets, where liquidity is limited and uncertainty is high resulting in wide bid/offer spreads. Under these circumstances, transactions of nominal size can influence the market price of an option and its underlying security.

- *It is possible to buy or sell any amount of the underlying instrument, even fractional amounts.* Continuous hedging might require transacting very small amounts of the underlying instrument to offset small movements in the underlying security.

This is the least restrictive assumption made in the B–S–M model. We cannot trade a fraction of a share of stock, or a fraction of a commodity, currency, and so on as they trade in standardized amounts. As a result, this assumption is violated in real life. Practically speaking however, this has very little impact on the pricing and trading of options or their underlying instrument. Institutional investors typically trade options in large blocks. Since the option position is sufficiently large, the error introduced by transacting a full share of stock has an impact that is immeasurably small.

■ *Investors can borrow or lend at the risk-free rate.* To hedge a call option, the investor will sell short the underlying security. The B–S–M model assumes the cash generated by that short sale is invested in cash equivalents paying a risk-free rate of return. To hedge a put option, the investor will buy the underlying security and pay for the purchase by borrowing the necessary funds at the risk-free rate.

Financial institutions such as banks borrow from savers by taking deposits or by issuing securities in the capital markets. To generate revenue, they lend those funds to their customers at a higher rate. As a result, there is a structural difference between the cost of borrowing a person must pay, and the yield someone earns by lending money to the same institution. Brokerage firms do the same thing. When investors deposit funds in their brokerage account, they will earn some level of interest on the cash balance. If they borrow money, they pay the broker loan rate, which is far higher than the rate investors earn on their cash deposits. As a result, the assumption of borrowing and lending at the same rate is problematic for the individual investor. This is not the case for self-clearing broker/dealers. In the course of their market-making activities, they take on some long positions and short others. They use the proceeds from the short positions to pay for the securities purchased. They only need capital to cover the difference and post margin where necessary. Furthermore, the difference between the borrowing and lending rate is modest for large financial institutions such as commercial and investment banks. Since these are the market actors who price options at the margin, the assumption of borrowing and lending at the same rate is a sound one. Those who cannot borrow and lend at or close to the same rate must take this market imperfection into account when constructing an option strategy.

■ *There is no cost to borrow the underlying security.* The value of an option is determined by replicating the payoff pattern of an option by continuously trading the underlying security at the proper hedge ratio. Hedging an option entails running this strategy against an option to produce a risk-free rate of return. To hedge a call option, the investor will sell short the underlying instrument. The B–S–M option-pricing model assumes that the investor does not have to pay a fee of any kind to the owner of the underlying instrument for the privilege of borrowing that security to sell short as a hedge against the call. Likewise, when the investor hedges a put option, they buy stock as a hedge. The B–S–M assumes the owner of that stock cannot lend it out for a fee to earn additional income.

Assuming there is no cost to borrow or lend the underlying security is a reasonable assumption under most circumstances. Investors generally keep their securities with a broker/dealer for safekeeping. These securities are held in "street name," which means the broker/dealer is the owner of record even though their customers are the true owner of the securities. This allows the broker/dealer to lend securities to other customers or their proprietary trading desk at little or no cost. They do this because they earn a commission on the short sale transaction and will earn a second one when the short sale is covered. Furthermore, when an investor sells a security short, cash is generated. The broker/dealer holds on to that cash and invests it in short-term interest-bearing securities and keeps the interest earned. This is part of the broker/dealer business model for revenue generation to cover the cost of their securities lending program.

There are times however, when many investors want to sell a stock short because they expect its price to fall. Under this condition it becomes difficult for a broker/dealer to locate stock they can lend to their customers. Under these circumstances, the available stock is rationed using the pricing mechanism. Those willing to pay the most to borrow the stock will get it. Those unwilling to pay the price will not. The cost of borrowing distorts the price of an option. If a stock is expensive to borrow, the market maker who needs to sell stock short to hedge call options they have purchased must pay the cost of borrowing. This makes the call less valuable to them, so they will only buy a call if they can do so at a lower price to cover the cost of borrowing. High borrowing costs tend to drive the price of a put option up. If a market maker buys a put option, they must buy stock to hedge it. Now that they own stock, they can lend it out for a fee. This makes the put option more valuable to the market maker.

One might think that the no borrowing cost assumption is problematic. This is not the case, as the B–S–M model can be modified to capture the effect of borrowing costs. Furthermore, the distortion that borrowing costs introduce provides the sophisticated option trader with valuable information about the trading activity in the underlying security. This issue will be discussed in greater detail in Chapter 8.

Based on the assumptions above, Black, Scholes, and Merton showed that it is possible to create a risk-free investment composed of a long position in a stock and a short position in a call that will produce a risk-free rate of return. It is also possible to create a risk-free investment by purchasing stock and a put at the same time as well. Note also that there is no assumption concerning the expected rate of return on the underlying asset. Therefore, we can correctly conclude that the value of both puts and calls is independent of the expected price action of the underlying security.

While these assumptions may not describe the real world perfectly, they do so closely enough to make the B–S–M option-pricing model an invaluable tool in the management and pricing of options. To overcome the model's shortfalls, practitioners modify the model to take into account market structure, volatility dynamics, and special circumstances as they occur. How this is done is discussed throughout later chapters in this book. The remainder of this chapter will delve into the details of the B–S–M option-pricing model. In that discussion, we fully explain how professionals use it to price and manage individual options and portfolios of option positions. In later chapters, we will delve into methods of how investors might use the B–S–M option-pricing model to create and manage option strategies designed to capitalize on investment opportunities driven by unique market conditions. Furthermore we will show how professionals use violations of model assumptions to extract information from market prices, enhance portfolio returns, and manage risk.

▪ The Black–Scholes–Merton Option-Pricing Model[1,2]

The B–S–M option-pricing model is the most widely used option-pricing tool employed by professionals who trade options on equities and equity indexes. The beauty of the B–S–M is that it is a closed-form solution. This means that there is an equation or a finite group of equations that solve the mathematical problem. All we have to do is define the inputs and a unique solution will emerge.

The explicit form of the B–S–M option model for a particular financial asset will vary. For single-stock options that pay dividends on particular dates, the most accurate form of the model will incorporate specific dividends on precise dates. Stock indexes, on the other hand, are made up of a portfolio of stocks that pay dividends on different dates. When pricing options on indexes, it is useful to assume dividends are paid continuously. It is far simpler in practice to work with a dividend yield, which assumes dividends are paid continuously over the life of the option. The alternative requires an investor to determine the expected dividend payment every day of the year. This is time consuming, computationally expensive, and does not improve accuracy enough to make the work worthwhile. While it might be more accurate to price options on individual stocks by taking into account explicit dividend payments, most companies pay a moderate dividend of just a few percent of the share price per year. As a result, very little error is introduced by assuming continuous dividend payments. Dividends only become a significant issue when companies make special one-time payments that represent a substantial portion of the company's market capitalization. As a result, assuming continuous dividend payments for options on individual stocks is a reasonable one for companies paying moderate dividends.

The goal of the presentation below is to build the readers' intuition concerning the pricing and behavior of listed or OTC options. With this intuition, you should be able to make the computations necessary to manage a single option position, or a portfolio of options. With that in mind, we will discuss the most intuitive form of the B–S–M option-pricing model, which assumes continuous payment of dividends. That form of the model will be discussed below.

The following is the closed-form solution of the B–S–M option-pricing model we should use to value call and put options on an asset that pays a continuous dividend. It is worth noting that even though this form of B–S–M option-pricing model assumes continuous dividends, it will provide very accurate results in situations where the dividend yield on an individual stock is small.

Black–Scholes–Merton Option-Pricing Model for a Company or Index Paying a Continuous Dividend

$$C = Se^{-qt}N(d_1) - Ke^{-rt}N(d_2)$$

with the boundary condition that $C = \text{Max}(0,\ S - K)$ at expiration.

$$P = Ke^{-rt}N(-d_2) - Se^{-qt}N(-d_1)$$

with the boundary condition that $P = \text{Max}(0,\ K - S)$ at expiration.

$$d_1 = \frac{Ln\left(S/K\right) + \left(r - q + \sigma_S^2/2\right)t}{\sigma_S\sqrt{t}}$$

$$d_2 = d_1 - \sigma_S\sqrt{t}$$

where:

C = Price of a call option
P = Price of a put option
S = Current price of the stock or index
K = Strike price of the option
q = Dividend yield paid by the underlying stock or index
r = Risk-free rate
t = Time to option expiration
σ_S = Standard deviation of asset returns
$N(\ )$ = Cumulative standard normal distribution function

▪ Intuition behind the Option-Pricing Model

In the last chapter, we pointed out that there are two types of options. There is the American-style option, where the holder of the option can exercise at any time. These are the most common options the trade in the U.S. market. The other type is the European-style option, where option owners can only exercise their right on the expiration date. It is important to recognize that the B–S–M assumes the options are of the European variety. Even though the B–S–M model assumes an option can only be exercised at expiration, it can also be used to price American-style call options when the underlying instrument does not pay a dividend. This is true because it is never optimal to exercise an option before expiration. This assumption does break down for deep-in-the-money put options. A deep-in-the-money European put option will tend to have a lower price than an American-style put option at the margin due to cost of carry effects, whether or not the underlying pays a dividend.

To build an intuition about how an option is priced, it is useful to understand the various mathematical components of the model. Notice that the B–S–M call option-pricing model is broken up into two components, each containing a probability function. The following summarizes the meaning of these components.

- $N(d_1)$ is the expected, risk-adjusted value of receiving stock at expiration of the option, if and only if, the option finishes in the money. Said another way, it is a risk adjustment factor that quantifies how much the present value of the stock exceeds the current price of the stock *if* the option is exercised.

- $e^{-qt}N(d_1)$ represents the sensitivity of a call option's price to a change in the price of the underlying asset. This is referred to as an option's delta and will be discussed more below.

- Building on the above interpretation, $Se^{-qt}N(d_1)$ says that the value of a call option is determined in part by the price of the underlying asset, multiplied by the sensitivity of the options value to a change in the price in the underlying asset. Think of this as the expected benefit of purchasing the underlying asset outright.

- $N(d_2)$ represents the probability the option will expire in the money and be exercised.

- The second half of the B–S–M model $Ke^{-rt}N(d_2)$ represents the present value of the strike upon expiration times the probability the option will be exercised.

- The value of a call option is the difference between the present value of receiving stock at expiration less the present value of the option's strike price if the call option is exercised.

- The value of a put option is the difference between the present value of receiving cash at expiration less the present value of receiving stock if the put is exercised.

Example

With the B–S–M model clearly defined, it is useful to walk through an example to gain a deeper appreciation of an option's valuation and performance characteristics. To help in this endeavor, we will walk through a numerical example as we explain the theoretical foundation of option pricing and behavior. The inputs will be held constant throughout. For consistency and clarity, the numerical examples will examine both put and call options on a stock whose share price is the same as the strike price. Most practitioners think of these as at-the-money options, and for all practical purposes they are in a low interest rate environment. Theoretically speaking, the call option is ever so slightly in the money as the expected forward price of the stock at expiration is marginally higher than the current price owing to the drift in the price of the stock due to the cost of carry. The put option is ever so slightly out of the money for the same reason. Without further ado, the options we will examine have the following characteristics.

S = Stock price = $25.00 per share
K = Strike price = $25.00 per share
q = Dividend yield = 1.00%
r = Risk-free rate = 2.00%
t = Time to option expiration = 3 months or 0.25 of a year
σ_S = Standard deviation of stock returns = 35.00%

The first step is to determine d_1 and d_2.

$$d_1 = \frac{Ln\,(S/K) + \left(r - q + \sigma_S^2/2\right)t}{\sigma_S \sqrt{t}}$$

$$d_2 = d_1 - \sigma_S \sqrt{t}$$

$$d_1 = \frac{Ln\,(25/25) + (0.02 - 0.01 + 0.35^2/2)\,0.25}{0.35\sqrt{0.25}} = 0.1018$$

$$d_2 = 0.1018 - 0.35\sqrt{0.25} = -0.0732$$

An examination of the cumulate standard normal tables, we get the following values.

$$N(d_1) = N(0.1018) = 0.5405$$
$$N(d_2) = N(-0.0732) = 0.4708$$
$$N(-d_1) = N(-0.1018) = 0.4595$$
$$N(-d_2) = N(0.0732) = 0.5292$$

Plugging these inputs into the final formulation of the B–S–M option-pricing model, we get the following values.

$$C = Se^{-qt}N(d_1) - Ke^{-rt}N(d_2)$$
$$P = Ke^{-rt}N(-d_2) - Se^{-qt}N(d_1)$$
$$C = 25e^{-0.01\times0.25}0.5405 - 25e^{-0.02\times0.25}0.4708 = \$1.767$$
$$P = 25e^{-0.02\times0.25}0.5292 - 25e^{-0.01\times0.25}0.4595 = \$1.705$$

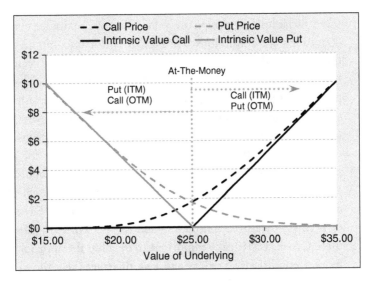

Exhibit 2.1 Price of an Option vs. Price of the Underlying

Since both of these options are structured with the same terms and reflect identical volatilities, they have very similar values. The call option, however, is slightly more valuable. This occurs because the call is ever so slightly in the money, while the put is ever so slightly out of the money. Recall that the cost of carry is a function of the risk-free rate and the dividend yield on the underlying security. Since the risk-free rate is greater than the dividend yield, the expected forward price ($25.06) is slightly higher than the current price of the stock ($25.00), placing a call ever so slightly in the money and a put ever so slightly out of the money.

The relationship between the price of the underlying security and the option's strike price is the biggest determinant of an options value. Exhibit 2.1 shows that as the price of the underlying security rises, the value of a call rises and the value of a put falls. Notice that as the options go extremely into the money, the option's price converges to intrinsic value. This occurs because deep-in-the-money options take on the performance characteristics of the underlying security. As they do so, they lose their time value.

▧ Understanding the Drivers of Option Prices

When trading options, it is very important to understand how investors' positions will behave for changes in market conditions. For a typical asset, there is only one variable to watch, and that is price itself. While this might also be true of an option, it is critically important from a risk-management perspective to understand why and by how much the price of an option changes. The B–S–M model indicates that there are six different factors that influence the price of an option. A change in any one of these variables will change the value of an option under consideration. Since market conditions are continuously in flux, it is not uncommon to experience changes in the price of the underlying security, volatility, and/or interest rates at the same time. To predict how the price of an option will behave for a change in any of an option's price drivers, mathematicians apply differential calculus to the B–S–M option-pricing formula to derive the equations necessary to explain the sensitivity to option prices for changes in individual market conditions. These partial differential equations quantify the sensitivity of an option's price for a small change in a single model input. Mathematicians routinely use Greek symbols and industry practice has embraced this academic convention and have given each of the sensitivities Greek names. The following is a discussion of the five main "Greeks" that practitioners use to predict, measure, and understand the behavior of option prices. Understanding these Greeks is critically important to develop the appropriate strategy given certain market conditions. Traders and risk managers use the Greeks as their foundation for hedging, managing, and reporting the risk of individual option positions and portfolio of options as well.

Delta (Δ)

Delta is a measure of the change in the value of an option given a change in the value of the underlying asset. It is the most important of the Greeks investors and market makers use to manage their option positions. Recall that a primary assumption in the derivation of the B–S–M option-pricing model is that a fair price of an option is determined by continuously hedging that option, delta-neutral for the life of the option, supposing a constant return volatility on the underlying instrument. Therefore, it is very important for traders to understand delta and how it behaves for changes in the underlying security. The delta for a call option will take a value that is greater than 0 but less than 1. The delta for a put will take a value that is less than 0 but greater than −1. Delta for both puts and calls is relatively intuitive, and the following provides some guidelines summarizing that intuition:

- If a call option is deep in the money, it is very likely to be exercised. Therefore, it will behave very much like the underlying instrument. If the underlying price rises by one dollar, the price of a deep-in-the-money call will rise by close to a dollar as well. In short, the delta for a deep-in-the-money call will approach the value of 1.0.

- The same can be said for put options except that puts move in the opposite direction of changes in the underlying security. If the underlying price falls by one dollar, the price of a deep-in-the-money put will rise by close to a dollar. Therefore, the delta for a deep-in-the-money put will approach the value of −1.0.

- If the option is deeply out of the money, it is very unlikely to be exercised. Therefore, it will have very little sensitivity to price changes of the underlying instrument and will barely move with the price of the underlying. Therefore, the delta for a deep-out-of-the-money option will approach the value of 0.0.

- If a put or a call option is at the money, it is just as likely to be exercised as not. Therefore, it will behave in between the two extremes of in- and out-of-the-money options. Consequently, the delta of at-the-money call options will approach a value of 0.5, and since a put moves in the opposite direction, its value will approach −0.5.

- The value of a call option rises with the price of the underlying asset and is therefore always positive. On the other hand, the value of a put option falls as the price of the underlying rises. Therefore, the delta of a put option is always negative.

- For non–dividend-paying stocks, the delta of a call minus the delta for a put with the same strike price and time to expiration will be equal to 1.0. For a stock or index that pays a dividend, the delta of a call minus the delta for an equivalent put will be somewhat less reflecting the present value of the fixed dividend.

The delta of an option is driven by the degree to which an option is in, at, or out of the money. Exhibit 2.2 shows the relationship between delta for the put and call under review as a function of the price of the underlying asset. Notice as the call goes deeper in the money, the delta moves toward 1.0 but does not quite get there. This shows that a deep-in-the-money option has an ever so slight bit of optionality to it. At the same time, the delta of the put option asymptotically goes to 0.0. Exhibit 2.2 points out a few other important facts about option-pricing behavior. First, notice that the curves are steepest for at-the-money options, which means the

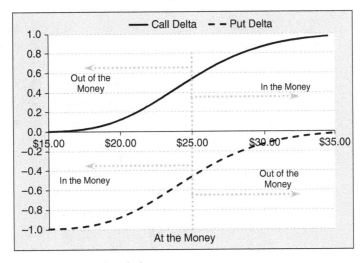

Exhibit 2.2 Delta vs. Price of Underlying Asset

delta changes most rapidly at this point. Second, deltas of puts and calls move in parallel. As the delta of a call moves toward 1.0, the delta of a put moves toward 0.0. As the value of a put's delta moves toward −1.0, the delta of a call moves toward 0.0. This is only true for a put and call pair referencing the same underlying security that have the same strike price and time to expiration.

The following are equations that professionals use to compute the delta for put and call options. In addition, we continue with our example and compute the deltas of the put and call options priced.

$$\Delta_{call} = \frac{\partial c}{\partial S} = e^{-qt}N(d_1) > 0$$

$$\Delta_{put} = \frac{\partial p}{\partial S} = e^{-qt}[N(d_1) - 1] < 0$$

$$\Delta_{call} = \frac{\partial c}{\partial S} = e^{-0.01 \times 0.25}0.5405 = 0.539$$

$$\Delta_{put} = \frac{\partial p}{\partial S} = e^{-0.01 \times 0.25}[0.5405 - 1] = -0.458$$

Assume for a moment that the price of the underlying asset rises by $2.00, from $25.00 to $27.00. To compute the predicted value of the options, we multiply the price change by the appropriate delta and add it to the initial asset value as indicated in the equation below. The following is a computation that predicts the new option values.

$$C_{New} = C_{Old} + \Delta_{Call} \times \Delta S$$
$$P_{New} = P_{Old} + \Delta_{Put} \times \Delta S$$
$$C_{New} = 1.767 + 0.539 \times 2.00 = \$2.848$$
$$P_{New} = 1.705 - 0.458 \times 2.00 = \$0.789$$

This method suggests the new value of the call is $2.848, while the new value of the put is $0.789. Contrast this to the values we obtain if we compute the price of the options directly from the B–S–M option-pricing model. To make the latter computation, we change the price of the underlying to $27.00. The model produces the correct price estimate for the call, which is $3.017, which is $0.169 more than using delta alone predicts. Using the B–S–M model to compute the correct price of the put reveals a value of 0.960, which is $0.171 higher than the linear estimate provided by delta. The question that comes to mind is, "Why is there a difference?" Furthermore, "Why does delta predict a lower price in both cases?" The answer is quite simple. The relationship between the price of the underlying asset and the option is nonlinear. This is reflected in the fact that the deltas are not constant as the price of the underlying asset changes as shown in Exhibit 2.2. Using delta alone assumes the relationship between an option's price and the price of the underlying asset is linear. Nonetheless, using delta gives a very good first-order approximation

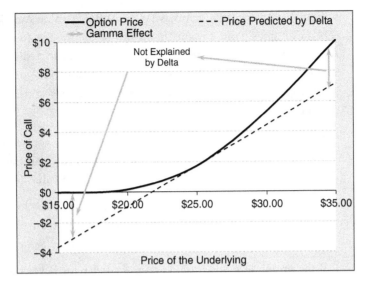

Exhibit 2.3 Call Option Price vs. Price of Underlying Instrument

of the value of options after a shift in the price of the underlying asset takes place. The nonlinearity of the relationship becomes clear by viewing Exhibit 2.3.

Notice that for small changes in the price of the underlying, the difference between the straight line represented by delta is virtually indistinguishable for the values obtained for the B–S–M option-pricing model. It is only for large moves in the price of the underlying asset that delta fails to explain the full movement in the price action of an option. That curvature in the option price relative to that of the price of the underlying asset is measured by a sensitivity factor called gamma.

Gamma (Γ)

We previously showed that delta is a measure of the change in the value of an option given a small change in the value of the underlying asset. In mathematical terms, delta is the first partial derivative of an option's price with respect to the price of the underlying asset. Further, we showed that delta has its own dynamic. The absolute value of delta rises as an option moves in the money and falls as it moves out of the money. This explains why there is a curvature in the relationship between the price of the underlying asset and the price of an option. **Gamma** is a measure of this curvature and indicates how fast delta changes for a change in the price of the underlying asset. In mathematical terms, **gamma** is the first partial derivative of delta with respect to the price of the underlying asset. This is the same as saying it is the second partial derivative of an option's price with respect to the price of the underlying asset. The gamma for a call option will take the value that is greater than 0 and theoretically has no upper bound. Very short term, slightly out-of-the-money options have very high gammas, as an option's value can skyrocket in percentage terms as it goes from a point that is out of the money to one that is in the money. A one-day, slightly out-of-the-money option can increase from pennies to dollars as it moves into the money just before expiration. Like delta, gamma for an option is relatively intuitive, and the following provides some guidelines summarizing that intuition.

- If the option is deep in the money, it behaves very much like the underlying instrument, which by definition does not have any gamma. Therefore, the gamma for a deep-in-the-money option will approach a value of 0.0.

- If the option is deeply out the money, delta will be close to zero and will barely move with a price change of the underlying instrument. Therefore, gamma for deep-out-of-the-money options will approach the value of 0.0, as well.

- If the option is at the money, its price behavior is very dependent on which way the price of the underlying goes. If the option goes in the money, its delta rises rapidly from 0.5 to 1.0 for a call, and −0.5 to 0.0 for a put. Likewise if a call option goes out of the money, its delta falls rapidly from 0.5 to 0.0, while the delta of the put moves from −0.5 to −1.0.

- From the analysis above, we see the use of delta alone underestimates the price rise of a call when the price of the underlying rises and overestimates the drop in an option's value when price falls. Just the opposite is true for a put option. In short, gamma improves the return characteristics of an option vis-à-vis the price of the underlying instrument. Gamma is a positive attribute, and taken alone, the more gamma an option has the better.

- A put and call with the same time to expiration and strike price will have the same gamma. This occurs because the rate of change of both option's deltas is the same as these options move in or out of the money. The chart in Exhibit 2.2 shows the delta for puts and calls with the same terms moving in parallel as both curves bend at the same rate and in the same direction.

Exhibit 2.4 shows the value of gamma for the put and call options highlighted in the ongoing example. Notice that as the options go deeper in or out the money, gamma falls toward zero. Further, Exhibit 2.4 points out a few important aspects regarding the behavior of gamma. First, gamma is highest for calls that are somewhat in the money and puts that are somewhat out of the money. This is the point where delta moves most rapidly. Second, as the price of the underlying moves away from this point, gamma drops quite rapidly.

Since the delta curves of puts and calls with the same terms move in parallel, the equation that governs gamma is the same for both instruments. To help build intuition about the computation of gamma, the following equation determines

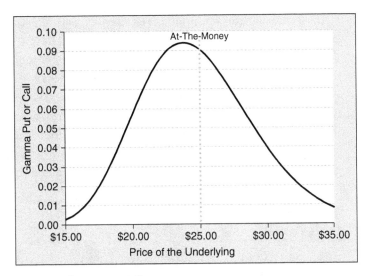

Exhibit 2.4   Gamma for a Put or Call

gamma for a put and call option. In addition, we continue with the example started above, and compute the gamma for the put and call options priced.

$$\Gamma_{\text{call, put}} = \frac{\partial^2 c}{\partial S^2} = \frac{\partial^2 p}{\partial S^2} = \frac{n(d_1)e^{-qT}}{S\sigma\sqrt{T}} > 0$$

Examining the standard normal density tables, we get the following value for $n(d_1)$.

$$n(d_1) = n(0.1018) = 0.3969$$

$$\Gamma_{\text{call, put}} = \frac{0.3969e^{-0.02\times0.25}}{25 \times 0.35\sqrt{0.25}} = 0.090$$

Now that we have computed gamma, we can repeat the price prediction analysis above and combine the effects of both delta and gamma to estimate the value of the options after the price of the underlying rises by $2.00. To compute the predicted value of the options we use a two-term Taylor series. (A Taylor series is a linearized representation of a function. It is the sum of any number of terms that are calculated from the value of the function's derivatives. In this case, delta is the first derivative and gamma is the second derivative.) The following is a computation of the new predicted value of these options.

$$C_{New} = C_{Old} + \Delta_{\text{Call}} \times \Delta S + (1/2) \times \Gamma \times \Delta S^2$$
$$P_{New} = P_{Old} + \Delta_{\text{Put}} \times \Delta P + (1/2) \times \Gamma \times \Delta S^2$$
$$C_{New} = 1.767 + 0.539 \times 2.00 + (1/2) \times 0.090 \times 2.00^2 = 3.025$$
$$P_{New} = 1.705 - 0.458 \times 2.00 + (1/2) \times 0.090 \times 2.00^2 = 0.968$$

By combining the sensitivities reflected by both delta and gamma, this method predicts the new value of the call at $3.025, while the new value of the put is $0.968. Contrast this to the values we obtain if we compute the price of the options directly from the B–S–M option-pricing model. Recall, the B–S–M tells us the fair value of the call after a $2.00 upward shift in the price of the underlying security is $3.017. Using the B–S–M model to compute the price of the put reveals a value of 0.960. Combining the effects of both of these metrics produces results that are spot on. By combining the effects of gamma with delta, we can now accurately predict the price of an option after a relatively large change in the price of the underlying security.

Vega (ν)

What makes an option different from other financial assets is that its value is derived in part by the return volatility of the underlying asset. The relationship between volatility and an option's price is a positive one, as an option becomes more valuable as the volatility of the underlying asset's returns increases. **Vega** is a measure of how sensitive an option's price is to a change in the volatility of the underlying asset. Because of this characteristic, options became one of the most important vehicles for managing volatility risk in an investor's portfolio. Options make volatility a tradable attribute, and many treat it as a unique asset class in its own right. Those that trade options in combination with the underlying asset or other options engage in an investment strategy known as **volatility arbitrage**.

Volatility trading allows an investor to profit from changes in implied volatility or the expected differential between implied volatility and realized volatility. **Implied volatility** is the uncertainty factor used to price an option at a point in time, as it represents investor's expectation of volatility over the life of the option. **Realized volatility** is the actual fluctuation in returns experienced over the life of the option or some other defined period of time. Volatility trading allows investors to take a view on uncertainty without an expectation of which way the price of the underlying asset will go. To implement a typical long-volatility trade, an investor buys a call option and sells short the underlying asset on a delta-neutral basis. Alternatively, the investor can buy a put and buy the underlying asset on a delta-neutral basis. When the price of the underlying asset moves, the option will outperform the return on the underlying asset no matter which way the price of the underlying asset moves. We showed how this phenomenon works in the previous discussion of delta. In the absence of time decay, the option outperforms the underlying asset due to the gamma effect, which was also described.

This idea of trading volatility is very important for both risk management and creating an offensive return profile. Volatility is a complex subject and investors must understand its nuances to implement a successful volatility-trading program.

To provide the necessary insight, Chapter 3 will discuss the ins and outs of volatility and reveal various strategies designed to maximize an investor's gain based on how the market prices uncertainty. Until then, it is important to take a closer look at how vega impacts the price of an option. While the intuition behind vega is relatively straightforward, there are aspects that one needs to keep in mind when constructing volatility strategies. The following is a discussion that provides a few guidelines concerning the amount of vega inherent in an option, which helps explain why an option behaves as it does. This intuition should prove useful as investors monitor their volatility positions:

- Volatility is one of the two primary determinants of an option's price. As the implied volatility of an option rises, so does the value of both a put and a call. Many practitioners believe that an option has a greater chance of finishing in the money as its implied volatility rises. As you will see toward the end of this chapter, this is only the case for out-of-the-money options. The real value comes from the fact that in a high-volatility environment, the price of the underlying asset is likely to go *further* in the money relative to a low-volatility environment.

- If the option is deep in the money, it behaves very much like the underlying instrument, which, by definition, does not have any sensitivity to volatility. Therefore, as a put or call moves deeper in the money, its sensitivity to volatility falls and vega moves toward a value of 0.0. This is reflected in the value of an option as its time value diminishes as it moves further into the money.

- If the option is deeply out of the money, it will have very little price sensitivity to the underlying instrument. These options have a very small probability of moving in the money by the expiration date. While the time value of the option changes at the margin, it is not greatly affected by a change in implied volatility. Therefore, vega for deep-out-of-the-money options will approach the value of 0.0, as well.

- At-the-money options lie between the in- and out-of-the-money options. These options only have time value and sit at an inflection point where they can capture intrinsic value if the price of the underlying moves in the appropriate direction. Therefore, all other things held constant, vega is highest for at-the-money options.

- Puts and calls with the same time to expiration and strike are equally impacted by changes in implied volatility. The time value of both instruments moves in the same direction, so they both have the same vega. This occurs because these instruments are two sides of the same volatility coin—namely, the volatility of the underlying asset.

- Vega is driven by time to expiration of an option as well. The buyer of an option locks in a certain level of volatility for the life of the option. The longer the time to expiration, the more volatility drives the value of an option. As you will see in the equation for vega, vega increases with the square root of time to expiration.

It is important to recognize that vega increases with time to expiration, but does so at a slower rate as the life of the option extends further into the future. Therefore, longer-term options have more vega than shorter-term ones, but it does not increase linearly.

■ Unbeknownst to most novice traders, a change in implied volatility will change the delta for options that are out of or in the money, while the delta for an at-the-money option is left relatively unchanged. This occurs because relative to volatility itself, the options have moved closer to their strike, so their deltas move toward the delta of an at-the-money option. Consequently, the delta of an in-the-money option will fall and an out-of-the-money option will rise if implied volatility increases.

Exhibit 2.5 shows the value of vega for our numerical example as a function of the price of the underlying security. Vega peaks for options when the price of the underlying asset is slightly above the strike price (i.e., equal to the forward price of the underlying asset) and tapers off as the price of the underlying instrument moves away from the option's strike price. Vega falls faster as the price of the underlying falls relative to how fast it falls when the price of the underlying rises. This occurs because the price of the underlying is unbounded on the upside, and is bounded by zero on the downside.

Exhibit 2.6 is a chart of vega as a function of the time to expiration on our $25.00 strike option, with the price of the underlying asset at $25.00 as well. Notice that the slope of the curve flattens as the time to expiration increases, and steepens rapidly as the time to expiration falls. This is an important attribute to consider if you are buying a delta-hedged option to capture a valuation change due to a

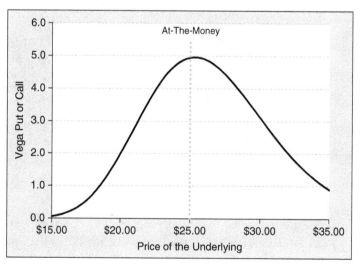

Exhibit 2.5   Vega (Put or Call) vs. Price of the Underlying Security

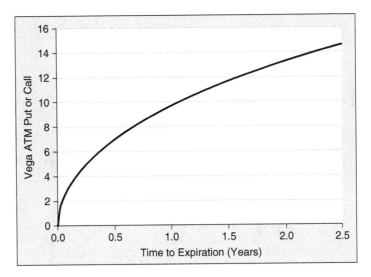

Exhibit 2.6   Vega vs. Time to Expiration

change in implied volatility. You must buy an option with a long enough time to expiration to "buy" enough vega to have a meaningful impact on the value of the trade. Furthermore, the option needs to maintain that sensitivity long enough for the trade to work out.

To help build intuition about the computation of vega and the effect of a change in implied volatility on the value of an option, the following equation is used to determinate its numerical value for both a put and call option. For consistency, we continue with the example started above, and compute the vega of the put and call options priced.

$$V_{call,put} = \frac{\partial c}{\partial \sigma} = \frac{\partial p}{\partial \sigma} = Se^{-qT}n(d_1)\sqrt{t} > 0$$

$$V_{call,put} = 25e^{-0.01 \times 0.25}0.3969\sqrt{0.25} = 4.949$$

Now that we have computed vega, we can predict the new price of an option for a shift in the implied volatility while all other factors are held constant. Assume for this exercise that implied volatility rises 25 vol points from 35 percent to 60 percent. The following is a computation of the new predicted value of these options.

$$C_{New} = C_{Old} + v \times \Delta\sigma$$
$$P_{New} = P_{Old} + v \times \Delta\sigma$$
$$C_{New} = 1.767 + 4.949 \times 0.25 = 3.004$$
$$P_{New} = 1.705 + 4.949 \times 0.25 = 2.942$$

These estimates are just 0.004 different from the price obtained by using the B–S–M option-pricing formula directly, making it a very accurate prediction tool for managing implied volatility in a single position or portfolio of options.

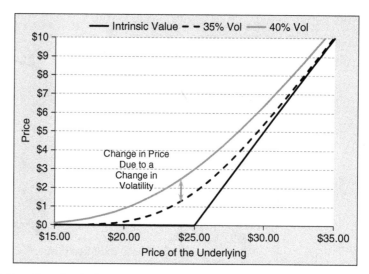

Exhibit 2.7   Effect of Volatility on the Option Performance Curve

It is important for options investors to be aware of the impact that volatility has on the performance characteristics of an option itself. In Exhibit 2.7, we see that the value of a call option rises across the curve. Notice that at-the-money options increase more than options that are either in or out of the money. This dynamic causes the option's performance curve to flatten. The net effect of this flattening is that the absolute value of delta rises for both in- and out-of-the-money options. With a flattening of the performance curve, gamma falls as well. This is an important characteristic when it comes to constructing portfolio hedges, which is discussed in Chapter 7. We will address this dynamic in more detail during that discussion.

Theta (Θ)

The price of an option is related to the life of that option. The longer it exists, the probability the option will trade in the money sometime over its life increases and the potential to trade far in the money increases as well. Most investors think of an option's price as its cost. We think that interpretation is a bit misguided. The true cost of an option is measured by its **theta**, which indicates how fast an option loses value as it ages. Option decay is the dynamic that option buyer hates, but it is the price they pay to capture the asymmetric return profile measured by gamma. Time decay causes many investors to lose money, as the price movement does not occur to the degree anticipated in the time period desired. Option writers, on the other hand, embrace time decay, as it is the source of their income and profits. Therefore, we need to gain a deep understanding of how an option ages to manage this risk. Option buyers need to construct strategies that minimize this source of performance drag, while option writers should employ strategies that maximize this effect. The first step in that process is to build some intuition around this factor. The following are some key points to keep in mind.

Theta is related to an option's time to expiration. Specifically, the rate of option decay falls as time to expiration increases. This is a bit counterintuitive because longer-term options have a higher price than short-term options. The reason this occurs is because volatility over a defined period of time does not increase linearly. It increases by the square root of time ($\sigma_T = \sigma_{Annual}\sqrt{T}$). For example, assuming an annualized volatility of 35 percent, the standard deviation of potential outcomes over a two-year horizon is 49.5 percent, while volatility over a month horizon is 10.1 percent. In short, the standard deviation of outcomes of a two-year option is 5 times higher than a one-month option, while its investment horizon is 24 times longer. While the price on a long-term option is higher than a short-term one, that price decay is spread out over a longer time period overwhelming the higher price. Exhibit 2.8 shows this explicitly.

Theta is also a function of moneyness. The premium for an at-the-money option is entirely composed of time value. Naturally, one would expect that it will decay fastest in dollar terms, and indeed, it does. The dotted black line in Exhibit 2.9 shows this phenomenon. As an option moves out of the money, time premium decreases and decay in price terms decreases along with it. When measuring an option's rate of time decay as a percentage of an option's price, this is not the case. Time decay as a percent of the option premium is highest for out-of-the-money options and lowest for in-the-money options. There is a simple reason for this, while an option that is either 5 percent in or out of the money has similar time premiums, the in-the-money option has a much higher premium owing to its intrinsic value. Intrinsic value does

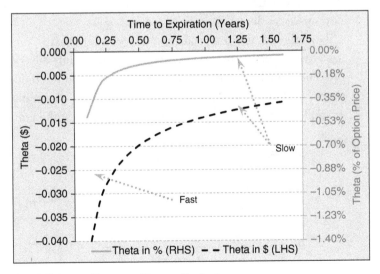

Exhibit 2.8   Call Option Decay vs. Time to Expiration

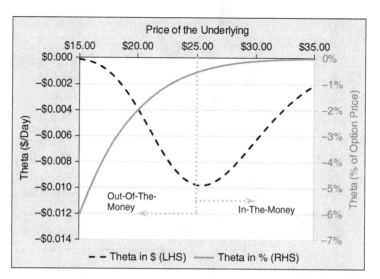

Exhibit 2.9 Three-Month Call Option Decay vs. Share Price

not fall with time, only time premium does. An out-of-the-money option does not have any intrinsic value. So even though the time decay is low in dollar terms, compared to a small base it can be quite large.

The formula used to compute theta is extraordinarily complicated, making it difficult to build intuition by interpreting its elements. This is not an impediment to successfully trading options, and the dynamics in the two charts above provide all the intuition we need to know concerning the management of time premium. Where possible, we just need to remember that—all other things held equal—in-the-money options decay slower than out-of-the-money options, and longer-dated options decay slower than shorter-dated ones.

Nonetheless, it is important to understand the math. The following equations are used to compute theta for call and put options. While the equations are quite similar, the difference lies in the fact that when a call is in the money, the put is out of the money and vice versa, so the signs are reversed. Naturally, we continue with the example already started, and compute the thetas of the put and call options priced.

$$\theta_{call} = -\frac{\partial c}{\partial T} = -\frac{Se^{-qT}n(d_1)\sigma}{2\sqrt{T}} + qSe^{-qT}N(d_1) - rXe^{-rT}N(d_2) \lessgtr 0$$

$$\theta_{put} = -\frac{\partial p}{\partial T} = \frac{Se^{-qT}n(d_1)\sigma}{2\sqrt{T}} - qSe^{-qT}N(-d_1) + rXe^{-rT}N(-d_2) \lessgtr 0$$

$$\theta_{call} = -\frac{25e^{-.010\times.25T}0.3969 \times 0.35}{2\sqrt{0.25}} + 0.01 \times 25e^{-0.010\times.25}0.5405$$
$$- 0.02 \times 25e^{-0.02\times.25}0.4708 = -3.564$$

$$\theta_{put} = -\frac{25e^{-.010\times.25T}0.3969 \times 0.35}{2\sqrt{0.25}} - 0.01 \times 25e^{-0.010\times.25}0.4595$$
$$+ 0.02 \times 25e^{-0.02\times.25}0.5292 = -3.316$$

Now that we have computed theta, we can predict the new price of both of these put and call options for the passing of time. Assume for this exercise that the options aged by 14 days, and nothing else has changed. The following is a computation of the new predicted value of these options.

$$C_{New} = C_{Old} + \theta_{Call} \times \Delta t$$
$$P_{New} = P_{Old} + \theta_{Put} \times \Delta t$$
$$C_{New} = 1.767 - 3.564 \times 14/365 = 1.630$$
$$P_{New} = 1.705 - 3.316 \times 14/365 = 1.578$$

The price of the call option using the B–S–M option-pricing model is 1.627, which is just 0.003 less than the estimate. The price of the put option using the B–S–M pricing model is 1.574, which is just 0.004 less than the estimate. This confirms that theta is indeed a good measure of the price decay a buyer suffers and an option writer enjoys as an option ages.

Rho (ρ)

When buying call options, investors hold options and cash to replicate the return performance of the underlying security. The investors can invest that cash in an interest-bearing instrument to augment their returns. As a result, an option's price is sensitive to a change in interest rates. From a risk-management perspective, this Greek is not as heavily weighted in the process as the other ones, because it takes significant moves in the risk-free rate to have a meaningful impact on the price of an option. Notwithstanding the fact that rho takes a back seat to the other Greeks, it is a relevant factor in option pricing, and we need to understand this metric. The intuition about how interest rates affect the price of puts and calls is relatively clear:

- Investors have the choice of buying call options instead of buying the underlying outright. Since the price of a call is small compared to the underlying instrument, investors hold a great deal of cash when replicating a stock with options. The investor places that cash into money market securities and earns interest. If interest rates rise, the investor earns a higher rate of return, making options a superior choice. In response to higher interest rates, investors bid up the price of calls until the financial advantage of doing so is arbitraged away.

- Just the opposite happens for puts. If investors want to short a stock, they can buy puts as an alternative. When self-clearing institutional investors like a bank or broker/dealer shorts stocks, they can invest the proceeds in money market

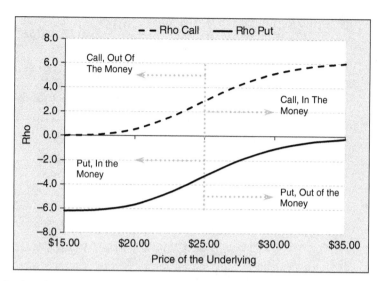

Exhibit 2.10 Rho for Call and Put Options vs. the Price of the Underlying

securities. As interest rates rise, the return on the cash proceeds increases, making a short sale superior to buying puts. As a result, the value of puts will fall until the financial advantage disappears.

■ The more a call option is in the money, the higher its price. Furthermore, its price behavior becomes more and more like that of the underlying instrument. The same is true for a put, but its price moves in the opposite direction. As a result, the cost of carry of an option becomes a growing determinant of its value. Exhibit 2.10 shows how rho changes for the options in our numerical example as a function of the price of the underlying security. One can quickly see that in-the-money options are far more sensitive to interest rates than out-of-the-money options. Furthermore, put options have just the opposite relationship to interest rates vis-à-vis calls.

To help build intuition about the computation of rho, the following equations are employed to determine an option's sensitivity to a change in the risk-free rate. As always, we continue with the example started above, and compute the rhos of the put and call options priced.

$$\rho_{call} = \frac{\partial c}{\partial r} = TXe^{-rT}N(d_2) > 0$$

$$\rho_{put} = \frac{\partial p}{\partial r} = -TXe^{-rT}N(-d_2) < 0$$

$$\rho_{call} = 0.25 \times 25e^{-0.02 \times 0.25}0.4708 = 2.928$$

$$\rho_{put} = -0.25 \times 25e^{-0.02 \times 0.25}0.5292 = -3.291$$

Now that we have computed rho, we can predict the new price of both put and call options when interest rates change. Assume for this exercise that the risk-free rate increases from 2 to 4 percent. The following is a computation of the new predicted value of these options.

$$C_{New} = C_{Old} + \rho_{Call} \times \Delta r$$
$$P_{New} = P_{Old} + \rho_{Put} \times \Delta r$$
$$C_{New} = 1.767 + 2.928 \times 0.02 = 1.826$$
$$P_{New} = 1.705 - 3.291 \times 0.02 = 1.639$$

The new price of the call option using the B–S–M option-pricing model is 1.828, which is just 0.002 more than the estimate. The price of the put option using the B–S–M pricing model is 1.642, which is just 0.003 more than the estimate. Rho predicted these changes within a few tenths of a penny. This confirms that rho is indeed a good measure of an option's sensitivity to interest rates. Notice how insensitive these short-term options are to a change in the risk-free rate. A doubling of the risk-free rate causes the call to rise and the put to fall by about 6 cents. Rho becomes an issue with longer-dated options. As a rule of thumb, rho should become part of the analysis if you are trading options longer than one year. If instead of pricing three-month options you were pricing one-year options, these at-the-money instruments would be almost four times more sensitive to rates.

Phi (Φ)

Last but not least is an option's sensitivity to a change in the underlying asset's dividend yield, and the cost of borrowing the underlying security. Like rho, this Greek is not heavily weighted in the risk-management process under normal circumstances because it takes a significant move in the dividend yield to have a meaningful impact on the price of an option. In fact, we might argue that a change in a company's dividend policy will have a greater impact on the value of the underlying security than on the associated options. When a company increases its dividend, it signals to the market that the financial prospects of the firm are improving and that the improvement is expected to continue long into the future. This will tend to drive the price of a company's stock up. Likewise, when a company cuts its dividend, it usually does so because of falling profits or it is suffering financial distress and management needs to preserve cash to navigate the hard times ahead. This tends to push the price of the company's stock down. As a result, the delta effect will overwhelm the cost of carry effect of a change in dividend payments.

We find phi most useful for managing options with high or growing short interest in the underlying security. When hedge funds identify a company struggling financially, they often sell short its stock in the hopes of capitalizing on a fall in the price of the company's shares. To do this, they borrow stock from their broker or other entity and sell it in the marketplace. The new owner of the stock is entitled to the dividend the company might pay, and the short seller is required to pay that dividend on the stock sold short. When investors borrow stock in order to sell it short, they might have to pay a fee for doing so. This fee has the same effect on the cost of carry for the short seller as paying the dividend. When a stock becomes hard to borrow, it also becomes expensive to do so. The cost of borrowing a stock can go from virtually nothing to 10 percent or more in a matter of days if there is high demand for the company's shares by short sellers. Phi provides a good approximation for the impact on the price of an option for fluctuations in the cost of borrowing the underlying security. The intuition concerning the stock borrowing rate and dividend yield effect on the price of puts and calls is relatively straightforward:

- Investors have the choice of buying call options instead of buying the underlying stock outright. While the owner of a call has the right to buy the underlying stock, the owner does not have rights to the dividend paid by the company to shareholders. All other things being equal, this makes a call less valuable relative to the underlying asset. As the dividend rises, the value of the call falls relative to the underlying security.

- The same logic applies to borrowing costs. Assume an investor sells a call to a market maker. That market maker is now at risk. They will lose money if the value of the stock falls. To eliminate the risk that the price of the underlying might fall, she must sell the appropriate amount of stock short. If borrowing costs are nil, she does not have to consider this in her analysis. If, on the other hand, she has to pay a rate of 5 or 10 percent of the market price of the stock per year to borrow the stock, it is more expensive for her to hedge her long call position. As a result, the value of the call is less valuable as it becomes more expensive to hedge.

- The exact opposite is true when making a market in a put option. A market maker who buys a put is now at risk that the price of the underlying asset could increase. To cover that risk, she buys stock on a delta-neutral basis. If that stock is expensive to borrow, she can now lend out that stock and collect a fee. This allows her to pay a higher price for the put.

Exhibit 2.11 shows how phi changes for the options discussed in our numerical example as a function of the price of the underlying security. We can quickly see that these two lines are not parallel, as in the case of rho. Rho for a put and a call move in parallel for changes in the underlying security because they are measures of sensitivity and are a function of the option's strike price, which is fixed, and the probability they will expire in the money, which rises and falls in equal amounts but in the opposite direction. Phi, on the other hand, is a function of the price of the underlying security, which drives the option's price and the option's delta.

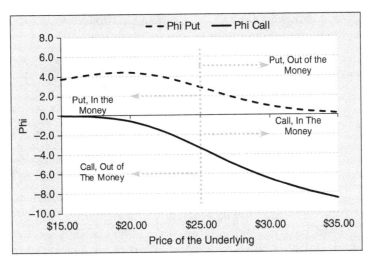

Exhibit 2.11 Phi for a Call and Put Option vs. Price of the Underlying Asset

The cross product of an option's price and its delta is not linear, resulting in a nonlinear relationship between phi for a put and call. Furthermore, since the dividend yield is held fixed, the dollar amount of the dividend falls as the price of the underlying security falls, causing the spread between the two curves to narrow at the margin as well. Nonetheless, the important takeaway of this analysis is that in-the-money options have a greater sensitivity to a change in the dividend yield than out-of-the-money options. Furthermore, an increase in dividends will result in a rise in the price of a put and a fall in the price of a call. This relationship should be intuitive. An increase in the dividend yield will lower the forward price of the underlying security, making a call less valuable and a put more valuable.

To help build intuition about the computation of phi, the following equations are appropriate for the determination of an option's sensitivity to a change in the dividend or borrowing rate of the underlying security. As always, we continue with the example started above, and compute the phis of the put and call options priced.

$$\phi_{call} = \frac{\partial c}{\partial q} = -TSe^{-qT}N(d_1) > 0$$

$$\phi_{put} = \frac{\partial p}{\partial q} = TSe^{-qT}N(-d_1) < 0$$

$$\phi_{call} = -0.25 \times 25e^{-0.01 \times 0.25}0.5405 = -3.370$$

$$\phi_{put} = 0.25 \times 25e^{-0.01 \times 0.25}0.4595 = 2.865$$

Now that we have computed phi, we can predict the new price of both put and call options when dividend or borrowing rates change. Assume for this exercise that the dividend yield (or borrowing rate) increases from 1 to 3 percent (or 0 to 2 percent in the case of the borrowing rate). The value of these two options will change by the following amounts. The following is a computation of the new predicted value of these options.

$$C_{New} = C_{Old} + \phi_{call} \times \Delta q$$
$$P_{New} = P_{Old} + \phi_{put} \times \Delta q$$
$$\Delta_{call} = 1.767 - 3.370 \times 0.02 = 1.700$$
$$\Delta_{put} = 1.762 + 2.865 \times 0.02 = 1.762$$

The new price of the call option using the B–S–M option-pricing model is 1.701, which is just 0.001 more than the estimate. The price of the put option using the B–S–M pricing model is 1.763, which is also just 0.001 more than the estimate. In other words, a tripling of the dividend yield (or an increase in the stock borrowing rate from 0 to 2 percent) causes the calls to fall and puts to rise by about 6 cents. Phi predicted these changes within a tenth of a penny. This confirms that phi is indeed a good measure of the price decay a buyer suffers as an option ages. Assume for a moment that the stock became expensive to borrow and the borrowing rate jumped to 10 percent per annum. Phi predicts the value of the call would fall by $0.34 and the put would rise by $0.29. These are very large moves, considering the price of the underlying security did not change. One must be sure to include the cost of borrowing the underlying security, if any, to accurately price an option.

◼ Putting It All Together: The Total Differential and Return Attribution

The power of using the Greeks to get a sense of the risk of holding an option or portfolio of options is that it allows one to put aside a complicated formula and focus on just a few metrics. Using the Greeks to measure sensitivities allows one to quickly and accurately figure out where the risks are before a trade is made. This is quite handy, as we can quickly review a number of option strategies and pick the one that best fits our expectations and risk tolerances. Furthermore, it allows us to compare portfolio and performance expectations ex-ante (i.e., at the beginning for the investment horizon) with what actually took place. Knowing where the returns came from ex-post (i.e., at the end of the investment horizon) enables the investor to learn from past trades, both good and bad. Everyone makes mistakes, and building a feedback loop into investment activity is necessary to constantly improve overtime. This is particularly important in a volatile environment where all the factors that drive option prices are fluctuating. We might not fully appreciate where returns come from without a full return attribution.

One of the strengths of examining the partial differentials (i.e., the Greeks) discussed in this chapter is that their effects are additive without significant loss of accuracy. This allows the investor to parse returns by their source. Total return is simply the sum of the pieces. In the case of a call option, the total differential is defined by the following equation:

$$\Delta C = \left(\frac{\partial C}{\partial S}\right) dS + \frac{1}{2}\left(\frac{\partial^2 C}{\partial S^2}\right) dS^2 + \left(\frac{\partial C}{\partial \sigma}\right) d\sigma + \left(\frac{\partial C}{\partial t}\right) dt$$
$$+ \left(\frac{\partial C}{\partial r}\right) dr + \left(\frac{\partial C}{\partial q}\right) dq$$

or, more generically,

$$\Delta C = Delta \times \Delta S + 0.5 Gamma \times \Delta S^2 + Vega \times \Delta\sigma + Theta \times \Delta t + Rho \times \Delta r$$
$$+ Phi \times \Delta q$$

While rather long, the interpretation and implementation of this equation is quite simple. The previous examples are simply each of the components of this total differential. The only step left is to sum the pieces and lay out the results in a logical and insightful way. Exhibit 2.12 brings all the pieces together. Each column represents an option valuation assuming just one factor changed. The column at the far right-hand side is the total scenario that incorporates all the changes at once. By comparing the total with its component parts, we can identify the exact sources of gain and loss.

Notice that the return attribution analysis of each input variable change results in a small error, while the cumulative error is larger than the sum of the pieces. This

	Beginning	Scenario Components					End
Stock Price	25	27	25	25	25	25	27
Strike Price	25	25	25	25	25	25	25
RFR	2%	2%	2%	2%	4%	2%	4%
Dividend Yield	1%	1%	1%	1%	1%	3%	1%
Time to Maturity	0.25	0.25	0.25	0.212	0.25	0.25	0.212
Volatility	35%	35%	60%	35%	35%	35%	60%
Greeks	Values	Predicted Changes					
Delta	0.539	1.078					
Gamma	0.090	0.180					
		1.258					1.258
Vega	4.949		1.237				1.237
Theta	−3.564			−0.137			−0.137
Rho	2.928				0.059		0.059
Phi	−3.370					−0.067	−0.067
Predicted Price		3.025	3.004	1.630	1.826	1.700	4.117
B–S–M Model Price	1.767	3.017	3.001	1.626	1.827	1.701	3.968
Error		0.008	0.003	0.004	−0.001	−0.001	0.149
Error in Percent		0.25%	0.10%	0.26%	−0.07%	−0.09%	3.76%

Exhibit 2.12   Return Attributions

occurs because linearizing what are obviously curvilinear relationships introduces some error. It is important to recognize that the above analysis takes into account the big, first-order, sensitivity factors. The second-order effects are not captured in this analysis. When any of the market-based inputs change, be it price of the underlying security, volatility, time, or interest rates, it has an effect on all the values of the Greeks. For example, a change in volatility has an effect on delta, gamma, and the other Greeks. To capture all the secondary effects, one would have to build a 5 × 5 matrix to incorporate how a change in volatility changes the other Greeks, and how a change in time does the same. Doing so would address the $0.150 tracking error shown above, but the effort would be both impractical and unnecessary for anybody but market makers and big hedge funds. For the average investor, the uncertainty of all the market factors far outweighs any benefit that might come from digging deeper.

This analysis shows how market factors affect the price of an option. But there is another Greek many option traders consider before putting in a trade. They want to know the probability that an option will expire in the money. They also might want to know the probability that an option will trade in the money sometime during its life. This is particularly important to option writers who want to capture a yield by selling an option they expect to expire worthless. The probability that an option will expire in the money is known as **zeta.**

Zeta (ζ) Probability of Expiring in the Money

Buyers purchase options or a combination of options with the expectation they will rise in price. Sellers write options or combination of options with the expectation they will fall in price and hopefully expire worthless. One of the ways of handicapping a trade beforehand is to assess the probability that the option will expire in the money. This is particularly useful for those who sell options. Their goal is to collect premium, witness the option expire worthless, and repeat the process all over again. These folks are implicitly making the wager that options will expire out of the money. More broadly, when writing an uncovered call, the investor is hoping the price of the underlying security stagnates or falls. When writing an uncovered put, the investor is hoping the price of the underlying stagnates or rises. Investors who write covered calls usually want to hold on to the underlying asset, but are hoping to capture some additional income by writing options that expire worthless. Covered call writers maximize their return when the price of the underlying security rises to the strike price of the option at expiration. At this level, the underlying asset reaches its highest price possible with the option simultaneously expiring worthless.

Just as with the Greeks that describe price behavior, there is a Greek for determining the probability that an option will expire in the money. This Greek is called zeta. The intuition concerning it is really quite simple. The more an option is

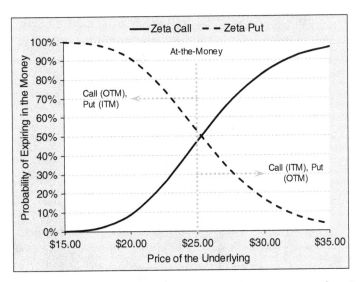

Exhibit 2.13   Probability of Call and Put Options Expiring in the Money vs. Share Price

in the money, the more likely it is that it will be in the money at expiration. The further out of the money it is, the less likely it will expire in the money. Exhibit 2.13 shows the probability the put and call in the ongoing example will finish in the money at expiration as a function of the price of the underlying security.

Since the probability of finishing in the money is an important determinant concerning the value of an option, it is a component of the B–S–M option-pricing formula. The formulas for making this important computation are presented below. The following is a computation of the probability an option will expire in the money.

$$\zeta_{call} = N(d_2)$$
$$\zeta_{put} = N(-d_2)$$
$$\zeta_{call} = N(-0.0723) = 0.4708 \ \text{ or } \ 47.1\%$$
$$\zeta_{put} = N(0.0723) = 0.5292 \ \text{ or } \ 52.9\%$$

When analyzing a put and call with the same strike price and expiration date, as we are in this case, only one or the other will be exercised. Therefore, the probability that the call will be exercised, plus the probability that the put will be exercised, is equal to 100 percent. (There is the possibility that the underlying will be at the strike price at expiration. Statistical theory tells us that the probability of any single event occurring is infinitesimally small and therefore zero.)

Zeta$_{Ever}$ (ζ) Probability of Trading in the Money

Investors who trade options are also concerned with the probability that an option will trade in the money at some point in its life. For the lack of a better term, we call this Zeta$_{Ever}$. Since there is an infinite number of paths the price of the underlying security can follow, the formula for Zeta$_{Ever}$ is far more complex. The set of formulas required to compute Zeta$_{Ever}$ is presented below.

$$Zeta_{Ever,Call} = Min\left[\left(\frac{K}{S}\right)^{\mu+\lambda} N(-z) + \left(\frac{K}{S}\right)^{\mu-\lambda} N\left(-z + 2\lambda\sigma\sqrt{t}\right), 1\right]$$

$$Zeta_{Ever,Put} = Min\left[\left(\frac{K}{S}\right)^{\mu+\lambda} N(z) + \left(\frac{K}{S}\right)^{\mu-\lambda} N\left(z - 2\lambda\sigma\sqrt{t}\right), 1\right]$$

$$z = \frac{\ln\left(\frac{K}{S}\right)}{\sigma\sqrt{t}} + \lambda\sigma\sqrt{t} \quad \mu = \frac{(r - q) - \frac{\sigma^2}{2}}{\sigma^2} \quad \lambda = \sqrt{\mu^2 + \frac{2r}{\sigma^2}}$$

To show how the probability of expiring in the money differs from the probability that an option will ever trade in the money, we will examine the example options assuming the price of the underlying security is $22.50. We make this assumption because the probability the option will trade at or in the money when the stock price equals the strike price is 100 percent by definition.

$$\mu = \frac{(0.02 - 0.01) - \frac{0.35^2}{2}}{0.35^2} = -0.4184$$

$$\lambda = \sqrt{-0.4184^2 + \frac{2 \times 0.02}{0.35^2}} = 0.7082$$

$$z = \frac{\ln\left(\frac{25}{22.5}\right)}{0.35\sqrt{0.25}} + (0.7082)(0.35)\sqrt{0.25} = 0.7260$$

$$Zeta_{Ever,Call} = \left(\frac{25}{22.5}\right)^{-0.4184+0.7082} \times 0.2339 + \left(\frac{25}{22.5}\right)^{-0.4184-0.7082} \times 0.3163$$
$$= 52.2\%$$

$Zeta_{Ever,Put} = 100.0\%$, *because it is already in the money*

The probability the three-month, $22.50 strike call will trade in the money at some point in its life is 52.2 percent. The probability it will be in the money on the expiration date is just 25.0 percent. How many people who write naked calls 10 percent out of the money realize there is a greater than 50 percent chance it will trade in the money sometime over the option's life? We suspect few people do. Investors who sell naked out-of-the-money options to collect premium with the hope of the option expiring worthless should keep a sharp eye on Zeta$_{Ever}$. Margin requirements increase very rapidly as an option moves from out of the money to in the money. Those who pursue a strategy of selling naked options must be sure to have excess capital available to address the potential requirement to post additional margin. This excess capital will give the investor the flexibility to ride out the fluctuations in price. Without excess capital available, the investor will suffer a

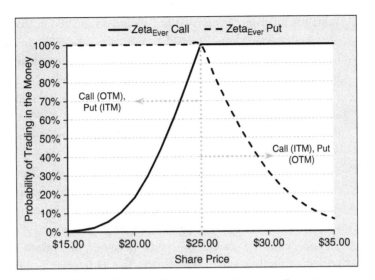

Exhibit 2.14 Probability of Call Option Trading in the Money vs. Share Price

margin call, which will take him out of the position, forcing a loss and eliminating the potential profits available from option decay. Investors who overwrite calls on long positions or puts on short positions need to understand the probability an option will expire in the money. When selling calls against an asset held in one's portfolio, the investor is giving away some potential upside in return for the yield generated from the premium collected. One should balance the potential for capital gains with the need for income.

Exhibit 2.14 shows the probability a put or a call with a $25.00 strike price will trade in the money. Notice how quickly both of these lines go to 100 percent as the price of the underlying security approaches the strike price. This is a very important risk-management issue for investors who like to write naked options. Those who write options at or just out of the money should plan on making delivery, as the odds suggest they will have to do so most of the time.

Final Thought

This chapter was designed to build an understanding of option pricing and dynamics for the novice and expert alike. With this groundwork in place, we now have the foundation necessary to take the next steps and use these derivative instruments to speculate on market action or to hedge individual positions or entire portfolios. A major determinant of an option's price is the implied volatility of the underlying asset. This is a measure of investor expectations for the uncertainty of the underlying's price over the course of an option's life.

For most assets, we look directly at price to determine the market's opinion of value. This is not the case for options. While we can observe an option's price, value is a function of the volatility assumed reflected in that market price. From this perspective, one should consider an option a *volatility instrument*. With the proper hedge, investors can use options to trade volatility. Take the following example. If you believe a stock will be more volatile in the future than what option prices suggest, you could buy the option, and hedge it delta neutral. This will produce an above-risk-adjusted rate of return if your view turns out to be correct. Grabbing the gamma effect when the price of the underlying security moves more than the option price suggests is one way a volatility trader captures this value. If you believe a stock will be less volatile in the future than what an option's price suggests, you could sell an option and hedge it delta neutral with the underlying instrument and capture a return in excess of the risk-free rate by capturing the option's price decay as the price of the underlying instrument stagnates.

Since volatility makes the price behavior of options far different from other securities, understanding the nature and characteristics of volatility is paramount to success. Unfortunately, volatility is not a very well understood concept for many individual investors. Some institutional investors understand every last nuance of volatility and option-pricing behavior. Some do not. With that in mind, the following chapter is devoted to a discussion of volatility, starting with the basics and moving to the complex. With that as a foundation, you will be better equipped to use options in a more prudent and profitable fashion.

## CHAPTER 3

Trading Volatility

Options are different from most financial instruments in that their value is derived, at least in part, by the uncertainty of future returns on the underlying asset. This makes options very important financial instruments as they provides a way for investors to take a view on this uncertainty or hedge it. Most every model, be it for a physical system or more esoteric ones such as those applied to economic or financial systems, depends on inputs that are observable. In the B–S–M model presented in Chapter 2, we see that there are a number of input variables that drive the price of an option. Specifically, the value of a put or call option is a function of the stock price (S), strike price (K), the dividend yield (q), the risk-free rate (r), the borrowing cost of the underlying security (b), the time to expiration of the option (t), and the volatility of the underlying asset (σ). The biggest drivers of an option's price, are the difference between the strike price and the price of the underlying security, the time to expiration, and the volatility of returns on the underlying asset.

With a mathematical equation of option prices in hand, we might think that valuing an option is a simple process. This, however, is not the case. We can directly observe all the model's inputs with the exception of one very important variable: the volatility of returns on the underlying asset. *Volatility* is a risk characteristic that describes the uncertainty in the price action of the underlying security. Among other things, it tells the investor something about the probable range of outcomes for an asset's price over a given period of time.

Both practitioners and academics define volatility as the annualized standard deviation of returns of the asset in question. Since there is a statistical formula for computing volatility of returns, we could compute volatility from historical price action and apply it to the B–S–M model to determine the appropriate price of an option. This, unfortunately, is an inappropriate way of using the B–S–M model for valuing an option. Investors are not concerned with what has taken place in the past. They buy or sell investments based on what they expect to happen in the future. The problem with using historical data to estimate volatility is that it looks backward in time. Historical data tell us something about how an option should have been priced in the past. Unfortunately, the value of an option today is dependent on what the price action of the underlying security will likely be in the future. Therefore, we must make a distinction in the option valuation exercise between volatility experienced in the past and expectations of volatility in the future. This distinction leads us to different measures of volatility.

The backward-looking measure of volatility is known as historical or **realized volatility,** which some call *statistical volatility*. The forward-looking measure used to price an option at a particular point in time is the investor's **expected volatility**. When applied to an option-pricing model, it produces a valuation, which is consistent with the investor's expectation of an asset's risk characteristic. The market price of an option is a compilation of investor expectation of price action concerning the behavior of the underlying asset over its life. Said another way, the quoted price of an option is a reflection of the "market's" opinion of volatility over the life of the contract. To estimate the market's expectation of volatility, we use the market price of an option as a model input and apply it to an option pricing formula. The pricing model is applied in reverse with the objective of finding the volatility measure that corresponds with that market price. The solution determined by this process is known as an option's **implied volatility**. Implied volatility is the measure of risk that is imbedded in the market price of an option that results from the price discovery process. This unique framework changes the way we should think about option valuation. Sophisticated investors think in terms of implied volatility as a surrogate for price.

Understanding the distinction and interrelationship between realized volatility and implied volatility is critical to understanding how the market prices options and how investors should construct the best option strategies. The following will discuss these two measures in greater detail.

◼ Realized Volatility

The price of all assets changes continuously. The price of some assets like technology and biotech stocks often change a great deal from day to day. Other assets like short- and intermediate-term government bonds remain relatively stable. Asset pricing models, the B–S–M option model included, generally assume that the volatility of an asset's returns remains constant over time. Every investor knows from observation that this is simply not the case. Prices of financial assets such as stocks, bonds, commodities and currencies, and real goods such as real estate and food, for example, go through periods of price stability, and at other times they go through periods of sheer chaos. Throughout the trading day, financial assets change hands continuously, and each successive trade generally takes place at a different price. The same holds true over any time period, be it day-by-day, week-by-week, month-by-month, or year-by-year. These changing prices represent an asset's realized volatility.

A proper measure of risk is independent of trend. The price of an asset might trend up, down, or sideways over time. Around that trend, however, are continuous price fluctuations. The price of an option at any point in time is independent of trend or its expected trend. A close examination of the B–S–M option-pricing model reveals that we do not need a return expectation for the underlying security to accurately price an option. It is only necessary to make an estimate of volatility. In short, the price of an option is only concerned with uncertainty and not trend. Realized volatility is an unbiased measure of past uncertainty as it is simply reflects past fluctuations in price over the time period studied. (In order to maintain a distinction between realized volatility and implied volatility going forward, we will use rVol as a shorthand notation for realized volatility, and iVol for a shorthand notation for implied volatility.)

Since volatility is not directly observable, it must be estimated. Volatility can be estimated on a historical basis by computing the standard deviation of returns the asset has displayed in the past. The formula for estimating standard deviation assumes that observations of the variable being studied are "independent and identically distributed." When applied to financial assets, it means that the return observed yesterday will have no impact on the returns observed today or any day in the future. Furthermore, it assumes that volatility of returns is fixed over time. While these assumptions might hold true some or most of the time, market observers know that returns on financial assets violate both of these assumptions at the margin.

There are times when prices *autocorrelate*. Autocorrelation is a measure of how much yesterday's price action affects today's price action and we witness autocorrelation when the price of an asset trends in one direction or another. We see autocorrelation all the time, particularly in market indexes. There are times when the stock, commodity, real estate, currency markets, etc. go up day after day, or down day after day, for weeks or months on end.

We witness the violation of the fixed-volatility assumption as well. Statistical measures of volatility based on historical data will differ if measured over different lengths of time or examined over different time periods. Estimates of volatility over a one-month period will differ from one determined over a three-month period, which will differ from an estimate over a one-year period. Every market observer noticed that the volatility of returns on equities was much higher in 2008 than it was in 2007 or 2011. As a result, we know from an examination of historical realized volatility that uncertainty is anything but fixed over time.

The standard disclaimer of investment managers is that "past performance is no guarantee of future results," and so it is with realized volatility. If we use a historical measure of volatility to price an option today, we are explicitly making the assumption that volatility in the future will be the same as it was in the past. We know from experience, however, that realized volatility is not stable, but it is a reasonably unbiased first guess at what it might be in the future. Option traders do not price options based entirely on past performance. Traders might consider historical volatility when they develop an expectation of future uncertainty, but in the end they must anticipate future volatility correctly to be successful in their trading activities. One thing we can be sure of is that future volatility will differ from volatility experienced in the past most if not all of the time.

Implied Volatility

Investing is about future opportunities and risk of loss. When buying a stock, fundamental investors are less concerned about where the stock price traded in the past and more interested in its value today and in the future. Just because its market price is less than its historical trading range does not mean the stock price cannot fall further. The same holds true for volatility. Since volatility is a prime determinant of an option's price, investors should be concerned with their expectations of volatility of the underlying asset going forward. This makes pricing options challenging to say the least. You should recognize that volatility, like price, is ultimately subjective.

Investors observe the price of an option quoted in the marketplace but not the volatility assumption that contributes to that price. To find the volatility assumed by the marketplace, we need to apply the quoted price to an option-pricing model to determine a level of volatility that coincides with the quoted price. The measure of uncertainty revealed is the option's implied volatility. Determining an option's implied volatility is a bit tricky. Since we cannot solve for volatility implicitly by algebraically rearranging the B–S–M option-pricing formula, we need to use a process of trial and error. The process starts with a guess at an option's iVol. That figure is applied to the B–S–M option-pricing model to compute the option's price. If the resulting price is too high, a lower guess is applied and a new option price is determined. If the resulting option price is too low, we make a higher guess at volatility and the option price is determined. This process continues until a level of volatility is found that produces the price quoted in the marketplace. The volatility that causes the option-pricing model to produce the quoted market price is the option's implied volatility (iVol).

Since iVol is the risk parameter that produces the stated market price of the option, practitioners use iVol as a way of thinking about price and value. There are a number of advantages of using iVol as a valuation and pricing indicator. First, it is standardized and indicates uncertainty on an annualized basis. This way, iVol is applicable to any option expiration. It does not matter if the option under review is a one-month, three-month, one-year, or longer dated option. Second, it is normalized to the price of the underlying asset. This way, we can compare the price of an option on a $25.00 asset with one on a $45.00 asset. Assume, for a moment, that we are comparing three-month, at-the-money options on a $25.00 asset and a $45.00 asset. For simplicity, assume they trade at the same iVol. The premium on the option referencing the higher-priced asset will be higher than the premium on the lower-priced asset. At first blush, we might conclude that the higher-priced option is more expensive. But by using iVol as a valuation measure, we would rightly conclude that both assets are trading at the same risk level and valuation.

Since iVol is the valuation metric to focus on, the challenge of valuing an option rests with estimating the appropriate implied volatility. Once a trader has a view on the appropriate level of iVol, a trading strategy will emerge. Options where the iVol is higher than an investor's expectation of future rVol are candidates for sale. Options where the iVol is lower than the investor's expectation of future rVol are candidates for purchase. This insight does not make trading options any easier than trading any other asset. Just as no one knows what the price of an asset will be in the future, no one knows with certainty what volatility an asset will display over the life of the option. Nor do we know if the iVol on an option will change over its life or simply remain the same.

Many traders use rVol as a basis for building an estimate of iVol. The efficient market hypothesis tells us that past volatility is a reasonably unbiased estimator for future volatility. While this might be true most of the time, it is certainly not true all of the time. Volatility traders go far beyond an analysis of rVol to estimate iVol. These investors look for fundamental reasons why an asset may become more or less volatile relative to past performance. Is the company subject to a takeover? Is it coming out with a new product? Is it expanding into new markets? Is there a change in management or corporate strategy coming down the pike? These and hundreds of other reasons influence the value and volatility a company's stock price might experience. In short, there are a number of drivers and factors to consider when assigning the appropriate volatility to an option.

To complicate matters further, options on the same asset may trade at different iVols for differing strike prices. Furthermore, options on the same asset may trade at different iVols for differing times to expiration. These differences are a reflection of investors' belief on when price-moving events might occur, and the expected size of those price movements. Alternatively, it may simply reflect that there is more investor uncertainty in the short term versus the long term, or vice versa. Since options on the same asset trade at different iVols depending on their strike price and time to expiration, institutional option traders chart iVol against these terms. In doing so, they create two-dimensional charts to reveal the relationship. A graph showing the relationship between iVol and moneyness is known as a *skew chart*. "Moneyness" describes the relative position of an option's strike to the forward price of the underlying instrument. For example if the forward price of the underlying instrument is $100, then the 95 strike put would have a moneyness of 95 percent. Puts and calls with a strike price of 100 would have a moneyness of 100 percent. Options with a strike price of 105 would have a moneyness of 105 percent and so on. A plot of iVol versus time to expiration is known as the *term structure of volatility*. This chart tells the investor what the market thinks about near-term versus longer-term uncertainty. Arbitrageurs and market makers often combine these charts into one picture forming a *volatility surface*. Since the volatility surface puts skew and term structure on one chart, it is handy at identifying a particular option that might be mispriced versus all the rest. To get a greater understanding of the characteristics of iVol across the family of options associated with a particular asset, the following section discusses the charts and graphs professional investors use to understand how the market is pricing options at any point in time.

■ Skew and the Volatility Smile

One of the assumptions of the B–S–M option-pricing model is that volatility is constant over time and known in advance. With knowledge of that volatility, the price of an option is determined. One could only wish that derivative valuation and trading were that simple. We know from an examination of historical volatility that an asset's volatility of returns is anything but constant. Since volatility is one of the primary determinants of an option's price, practitioners work around this flaw by using an expectation of future volatility as a pricing metric. They do this by combining current market conditions and expectations concerning the probability of future events along with historical experience to estimate the expected volatility of the underlying instrument over the life of an option. With this estimate, they determine what they believe to be a fair price for that option. In practice, however, traders know that both realized and implied volatility fluctuates depending on market conditions.

This fact is not lost on the market's ability to price options. An important method for viewing the market's opinion of option prices for a particular asset is revealed in a graph of iVol versus moneyness (or strike price). While option-pricing theory suggests that the implied volatility should be the same for all options on the underlying asset, practitioners know that implied volatility varies as a function of strike price. There are two shapes one typically encounters when examining implied volatility across the universe of available strikes:

- **Volatility skew:** Under most circumstances, iVol for equity options with moneyness less than 100 (i.e., out-of-the-money puts and in-the-money calls) is higher than those for options with moneyness greater than 100 (i.e., in-the-money puts and out-of-the-money calls). This is known as the volatility skew.

- **Volatility smile:** Sometimes options with moneyness less than and greater than 100 possess an iVol greater than that of at-the-money options. This creates a smile shape when iVol is charted against moneyness. This is known as the volatility smile or a lopsided smile often referred to as a smirk.

Whether the chart of iVol versus moneyness takes the shape of a skew or a smile, practitioners generally refer to this chart generically as a skew chart. Exhibit 3.1 shows a few examples of skew typically seen in the marketplace.

Options-pricing theory suggests that volatility is constant over time, so this begs the question "why does implied volatility vary by strike price?" The short answer is, this is the way the market modifies option-pricing models to incorporate market realities that violate model assumptions. The following looks at this phenomenon more closely.

- Every market observer knows that prices tend to climb a flight of stairs but take the elevator down. Said another way, prices tend to fall faster than they rise. Therefore, traders who sell downside put options know that realized volatility would probably be high if those options are going to be exercised. So they discount that potential when pricing put options. One explanation for this market dynamic is that fear is a more powerful emotion than greed. To avoid losses, investors tend to dump shares first and ask questions later when bad news hits the markets. Just as there is an excess of sellers, there tends to be a shortage of buyers during market panics. Under stressful market conditions, few investors try to "catch a falling knife" and bid for stocks as their price falls sharply. As liquidity dries up, sellers must discount their assets further to entice another investor to step in and

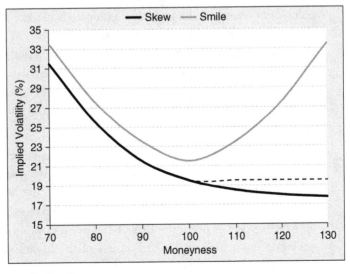

Exhibit 3.1 Volatility Skew

buy it from them. The price of downside options captures this phenomenon by pricing in higher volatility for the potential of the sharp downside scenario.

- Option-pricing models assume price movements are continuous but equity markets are not open 24 hours a day. Major news announcements often occur during nontrading hours. Companies typically announce earnings before or after the close of trading. This causes the share price to jump once the exchanges open for business. Skew is one way market participants capture "jump risk" into the price of an option.

- There is a technical reason for skew to exist, as well. Most investors are long assets. Some of those investors will want to protect the value of their assets by purchasing downside puts. As a result, there is a natural demand for out-of-the-money puts that pushes their market price and iVol up. On the flipside of the coin, the only natural seller of puts are those who are short the underlying instrument. Since there are far fewer people who are short relative to those who are long, more puts are demanded than supplied. To bring these two forces into balance, the price of out-of-the-money puts needs to rise to induce some market participant to provide the insurance that put buyers want.

- Since most investors are long assets, some will want to write covered calls to generate income. As a result, there tends to be natural suppliers of upside calls. By the same token, there are not as many natural buyers of out-of-the-money calls who simply want to speculate on higher prices. Therefore, there tends to be more sellers of upside calls than buyers, which tends to depress their price and therefore their implied volatility.

- There can also be a fundamental reason for skew with some underlying instruments. For example, if a particular company's balance sheet is levered (that is, it has net debt, rather than net cash), a fall in the price of a company's stock results in greater financial leverage on a market-value basis. More leverage translates into higher equity volatility. Because the implied volatility is a measure of the expectation in the percentage change in the value of equity, the amount of financial leverage held on a company's balance sheet should theoretically be reflected in option premiums.

- When markets get chaotic and market participants believe a large price shift is about to occur, investors bid up the price of deep in- and out-of-the-money options. This reflects the fact that traders discount a distribution of potential outcomes with "fat tails." That is, they expect extreme events. Out-of-the-money options have lower premium than at-the-money options. Option buyers are often willing to pay a little extra iVol on out-of-the-money options for the ability put up less capital up front when they believe a big move is at hand. This phenomenon reveals itself on the skew chart with high implied volatilities for options with both low and high moneyness. This phenomenon is common in the commodities markets, where prices can spike up just as fast as they might collapse.

To gauge whether downside puts are cheap or expensive on a historic basis, it is useful to chart skew over time. When skew is high on a historical basis, downside puts (those with moneyness less than 100 percent) are usually expensive relative to those with moneyness of 100 or higher. This phenomenon typically occurs when investors fear the potential for a large random unforeseen negative event. Since skew is associated with fear, it is a barometer for market sentiment. Market prices tend to find a bottom when fear is high and tend to peak when investors become complacent. As a result, not only is skew a good measure of relative value, it provides clues to future price action.

The discussion above describes skew as a function of an option's moneyness. Many investors look at skew this way, as it is relatively straightforward. But the exact definition of skew is important if we are to properly interpret the current state of option prices and how skew varies over time. We believe the best way to compute absolute skew is to compute the difference between iVol of options with 80 moneyness from that of options with 100 moneyness, as the following equation indicates.

$$\text{Absolute skew} = iVol_{80\ Mny} - iVol_{100\ Mny}$$

Some practitioners define absolute skew a little differently. They define absolute skew as the divergence in iVol for in- and out-of-the-money options. To compute absolute volatility on this basis, they take the difference between iVol of options with 80 percent moneyness and that of options with 120 percent moneyness. We caution investors to stay away from this measure as iVol on upside options distorts this measure. If the shape of the skew chart shifts from a skew to a smile, the latter measure will indicate that skew has fallen, when, in fact, this might not be the case. The only way to get a consistent measure of skew is to focus on downside options relative to those with an at-the-money strike.

While absolute skew is a common measure of the difference in iVol between downside puts and at-the-money options, it is important to recognize that there are other very important ways to measure skew. Many sophisticated practitioners, particularly volatility traders, normalize skew for the level of volatility expected on the underlying asset. They do this by dividing the absolute skew by the implied volatility of options with 100 percent moneyness. The equation for computing relative skew is shown in the following equation:

$$\text{Relative skew} = \frac{(iVol_{80\ Mny} - iVol_{100\ Mny})}{iVol_{100\ Mny}}$$

Traders observe that absolute skew tends to rise when volatility rises, and fall when volatility falls, which distorts a historical analysis making it more difficult to define what is "normal." Measuring skew relative to the level of volatility removes this effect, providing a more insightful measure of relative value among options with differing strikes. After all, a 5 percent skew for an asset that has a 25 percent at-the-money iVol has a different meaning from a 5 percent skew for an asset with a 50 percent iVol. By eliminating the effect of the level of volatility on skew, it tends to be a more stable and meaningful measure over time. In high-volatility environments, absolute skew might rise but relative skew often remains stable and might even fall a bit. This might occur when implied volatility of at-the-money options captures some of the risk that is being priced in out-of-the-money options.

Exhibit 3.2 plots the same data as that shown in Exhibit 3.1, but presents skew on a relative basis. Notice that the shapes of these curves are the same as those for absolute skew, but they are now measured in terms of volatility. The x-axis indicates moneyness in terms of the number of standard deviations the strike price is away from an at-the-money option. This makes it easier to see how the market is pricing extreme moves in the price of the underlying security. In this case, the option prices are suggesting that the seller of downside protection (i.e., puts) needs 12 additional "Vol clicks" to compensate for the risk that the price of the underlying security will fall by 1.5 standard deviations or more.

Volatility in standard deviation terms is not the only other alternative approach to measuring skew used by sophisticated practitioners. Some practitioners take the ratio of an iVol for 80 percent moneyness options and divide it by iVol for an at-the-money option. Still others use delta as a normalizing factor. These investors might track iVol for a 25 delta put versus iVol on a 50 delta put to track skew over time. This gives traders a measure of how much it costs to buy or sell delta across the available strike universe. At the end of the day, the appropriate measures

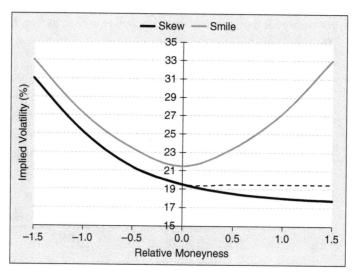

Exhibit 3.2   Skew in Volatility Terms

of skewness are subjective and different traders prefer different measures, and they might use different measures under different circumstances. To avoid jumping down a rabbit hole, we will stick with absolute skew throughout this book. We thought, however, the reader needs to be aware of these other methods of measuring skew and you should explore these methods more deeply as your curiosity warrants.

Term Structure of Volatility

The term structure of volatility is an explicit expression of the market's view on future implied volatility. In graphical terms, it is simply a chart of iVol for differing times to expiration typically for at the money options. It is analogous to the term structure of interest rates that bond investors use to judge the relative value of bonds across the maturity spectrum. The shape of the term structure curve takes varying shapes, depending on the markets expectation of uncertainty over time, and the potential for a unique event at a particular point in time. Given these variables, the term structure curve takes one of four basic shapes that signal how the market discounts future price action of the underlying security:

1. *Upward sloping*: Much of the time, the term structure of implied volatility is upward sloping. This is a reflection of the fact that investors tend to have a better handle on how the price of the underlying security is likely to behave in the near term relative to the long term. Since investors are more uncertain about what might happen in a year relative to what might happen in a month, sellers of those longer-term options will tend to demand a higher risk premium. Since sellers of options must perform if the buyer exercises their rights, and they are at risk for an amount far higher than the option premium, they need to be compensated for the risk taken. As a result, option writers tend to have more influence over the price of longer-dated options at the margin.

2. *Flat:* Sometimes the term structure of implied volatility is flat. Under these circumstances, the market is pricing near-term risks similarly to long-term risks. While a flat term structure is consistent with the assumptions made in formulating the B–S–M option-pricing model, this structure does not occur very often at the front end of the curve. It is very common to see flat term structures at the long end of the curve, particularly for market indexes. Realized volatility on market indexes is far more stable on indexes compared to those on individual stocks. From a technical standpoint, this shape indicates there is a balance between those willing to buy and sell options.

3. *Downward sloping:* Many times, the term structure of implied volatility is downward sloping. This usually occurs when market participants believe there is a price-moving event in the near future. Such an event might be the announcement

of earnings, or an industry specific report to be released by the government or an industry trade group on a specific date. A few examples are the number of cars sold by the auto industry, the book-to-bill ratio for the semiconductor industry, or overall consumer spending. A downward-sloping curve indicates that market participants believe that the release of that information will cause a sharp jump or fall in the price of the underlying asset, and sellers of options are demanding a premium for the risk of a short-term price jump, and buyers are willing to pay a premium to capitalize on that price action.

Financial distress can cause the term structure of volatility to invert for individual companies as well. Companies in financial distress are at risk of bankruptcy, which is a binomial event. These companies are under extreme pressure in the short to medium term, and implied volatilities will reflect this. Survival bias causes the implied volatility to fall as time to expiration increases. This happens because if the company can get over its short- to intermediate-term crisis, it is likely to survive in the long run. At the same time, when the probability of default/bankruptcy reaches an extreme, the time to expiration on the associated option comes into question. In a default scenario, the effective option expiration may accelerate, as the underlying stock may no longer trade, or simply go to zero. This has the effect of shortening the expected life of the option. Under these circumstances, investors will not pay for time value beyond the expected default date. This will be reflected in a depressed iVol on long-dated options, resulting in an inverted term structure.

Downward-sloping term structures are common on market indexes during bear markets. It is an indicator that investors en masse are scared of additional price declines over the near and intermediate term. To protect their existing portfolios from a loss in value, investors will buy near-dated puts, driving up implied volatility at the short end of the curve. Since bear markets eventually end, and investors tend to prefer options with smaller premiums, investors do not bid up the price of long-dated puts nearly as much. Since volatility is expected to be high for a defined period of time, implied volatility on longer-dated options will revert toward a longer-term mean.

4. *Hump shape:* The term structure might take a hump shape for the same reason that the term structure is downward sloping. The difference lies in when investors expect a sharp jump in price. Humpiness is something we see more often in individual stocks. If, for example, drug and biotech companies submit their drugs and medical products for approval from the FDA, oftentimes the approval date is either known or predictable. Since there are no information-driven price moves in the near term, implied volatility on short-dated options will be low. By the same token, options that expire long after the approval date will also be low. The real uncertainty lies around the approval date. Therefore, options that

expire shortly after the expected approval date will have the greatest price uncertainty. This uncertainty will be reflected by an elevated implied volatility zone on these options.

When selecting the term to maturity for options to use in your own investment strategy, it is important to be aware of the factors driving the term structure of an option's volatility. In doing so, you will be able to select the appropriate option or combination of options that meet your investment objectives. Exhibit 3.3 shows the various shapes in the term structure of iVol that drove the price of options on the S&P 500 index in the past. Strategies for capitalizing on certain shapes of the volatility curve will be discussed in Chapters 5 and 7.

Exhibit 3.3 shows the term structure of iVol on the S&P 500 for three specific dates. The dates were chosen as they reflect common, yet extreme, term structures. The gray line is an example of an inverted term structure, which occurred on October 15, 2008. The year 2008 was marked by one of the most fierce, global, financial crises in modern history. Financial institutions were going under and the stability of the financial system was in jeopardy. The price of risk assets had been falling for about a year and investors feared more losses lay ahead. Not only was realized volatility far above its historic norm, investors anticipated more of the same as the crisis continued to deepen. Investors were in a panic and purchased short-dated options to protect their portfolios against large losses. This investor preference for short-dated options relative to long-dated ones caused the term structure to invert.

The black dotted line is a more typical term structure, which occurred in early 2012. The Federal Reserve was in the midst of continued quantitative easing (i.e., easy monetary policy) and investors felt that the liquidity injection would support asset prices. As a result, investors believed assets prices would be well behaved

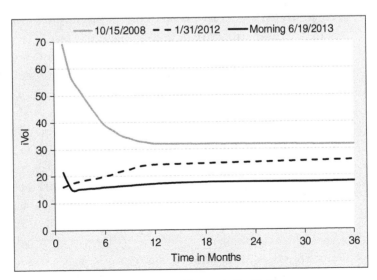

Exhibit 3.3   Term Structure of Implied Volatility on S&P 500 Options

in the near term, but there was uncertainty about when the easy money policy would end. As a result, option prices reflected greater long-term uncertainty and long-term options traded at a higher price relative to shorter-dated ones.

In the middle of June 2013, the term structure of volatility on the S&P 500 was relatively flat. This was a reflection that volatility of returns on stocks had been subdued for quite some time, hovering around 12 percent, which is about 7 Vol clicks below the S&P 500s realized volatility over the long term. Option prices suggested that the era of super-low volatility was coming to an end and longer-term volatility of 17 to 18 percent could be expected, with 15 percent volatility in the intermediate term. In addition, investors expected the Federal Reserve to announce that it would begin the process of reducing its purchases of U.S. Treasury and agency-sponsored mortgage-backed securities. If such an announcement were made, option traders speculated that it would create a one- or two-day volatility event. This is reflected by the volatility premiums demanded on very short-dated options.

Volatility Surface

Skew and term structure are two-dimensional pictures of iVol that traders use to summarize market pricing for options referencing a particular asset. While these are powerful ways of looking at option pricing, they do not show all the combinations of strikes and maturities. To capture this information in a two-dimensional chart, we would have to draw a skew graph for each of the available maturities traded, and a term structure for every strike as well. There is no reason to believe that skew on options with shorter expiration dates should be the same as options with a long time to expiration. Furthermore, it might be difficult to quickly identify the cheapest or most expensive options available. To assist in identifying inconsistencies in iVol, sophisticated volatility traders and market makers create a *volatility surface*. Combining the information contained in the skew and term structure charts produces a single picture creating the volatility surface. The volatility surface is a three-dimensional representation of implied volatility on the underlying instrument at a fixed point in time. It shows traders how options are priced as a function of both moneyness and term to expiration. Examining iVol in this way, we can quickly identify options that might be trading at premiums or discounts to their peers.

If a dislocation in the volatility surface appears, volatility traders must act fast as these dislocations generally do not last long. The iVol for an option with a particular strike and term to expiration usually deviates from that of similar options due to technical factors. Implied volatility might be high for a particular option due to the activity of a large buyer who is willing to pay up to get a trade done. Implied volatility might be depressed for a particular option due to a seller who is willing to pay for liquidity to get her trade done. An institutional investor might need a particular structure to hedge a particular risk and is willing to pay a liquidity premium to get it. This might distort different parts of the volatility surface. Arbitrageurs who trade volatility will jump on these opportunities by selling peaks on the volatility surface, while hedging that position by purchasing another option that might be trading on or below the surface, or by delta hedging with the underlying instrument. Exhibits 3.4 and 3.5 are examples of the volatility service for options on the S&P 500.

As a final thought, the existence of a volatility surface represents an interesting dilemma from a theoretical perspective. If we are able to model the value of an

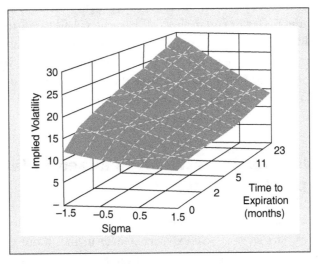

Exhibit 3.4   Volatility Surface January 13, 2013

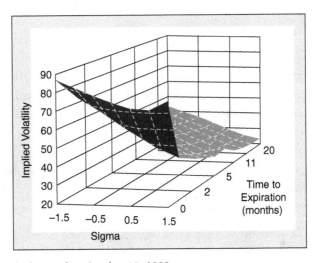

Exhibit 3.5   Volatility Surface October 15, 2008

option by making an assumption about the volatility of the underlying, how can it be consistent to have different volatility assumptions for options with the same expiration? It is important to remember that all these options reference the same underlying asset, which will ultimately realize one particular level of volatility. At some level, the volatility surface reflects practitioners' judgments addressing issues surrounding the uncertainty of realized volatility over time. It is their attempt to bend the B–S–M option-pricing model without breaking it. But this has practical implications about how traders manage their positions. Making different volatility assumptions for differing options means an option trader is hedging the Greeks of each option differently. Furthermore, it has implications for spread trading. If an investor can buy an option at 20 percent volatility and sell another one with the same time to expiration at 30 percent volatility, in theory the investor should be able to lock in an arbitrage profit. Furthermore, it should be possible to value that spread with one specific measure of volatility, which will differ from the iVol used to price the individual options in the spread. These are interesting implications, and we will discuss how to incorporate nuances in the volatility surface to optimize trade structures in later chapters.

The Relationship between Realized Volatility and Implied Volatility

One of the keys to successful option trading is to accurately predict the realized volatility an asset will experience over its life. If our estimate of future volatility is greater than the iVol extracted from market prices, we should get *long volatility* and buy an option and dynamically hedge it delta neutral to lock in the difference. If our estimate of future volatility is less than the iVol extracted from market prices, we should get *short volatility*.

If iVol contains the collective knowledge of all market participants, we should expect to find that iVol is a good unbiased estimator of future realized volatility. Furthermore, since it contains all available information, we should expect to find that iVol is a better estimator of future realized volatility than historical realized volatility. The academic work that examined this question with respect to options on the S&P 500 supports this hypothesis. As a result, we should expect to see rVol and iVol move up and down together.

Exhibit 3.6 compares iVol on three-month, at-the-money options to 90-day realized volatility from January 1, 2005, to June 30, 2013. A close look at this chart reveals a few interesting facts:

- IVol seems to lead rVol. Notice that iVol rises before rVol and it leads on the way down as well. This is what we would expect if iVol were a good predictor of future rVol.

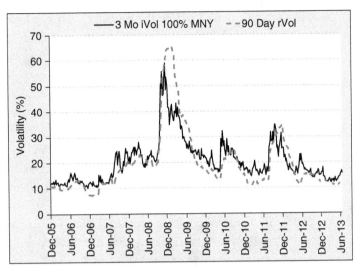

Exhibit 3.6   Three-Month iVol versus 90-Day rVol

- Over the time period studied, iVol overestimated rVol by 0.73 Vol points. This suggests that there is a small bias in iVol's predictive capability. Furthermore, it submits that at-the-money options on the S&P 500 are slightly overvalued, on average. However, this is not always the case. In the latter part of 2008 and early 2009, iVol underestimated forward rVol by a considerable amount. During this time, at-the-money options on the S&P 500 were considerably undervalued.

- IVol is about 1.8 times more volatile than rVol. This should not come as a surprise as iVol exists at a moment in time, while rVol is an estimated average over a period of time.

- Volatility in general rises faster than it falls. It seems the option traders react quickly to shocks and market stress, but are slower to give the all-clear signal after a shock has occurred.

- Volatility spikes occur most frequently when the market moves lower, rather than higher. This is consistent with the price path most investors have likely observed. Securities prices sometimes move sharply lower in short time frames and can drift higher over longer periods.

- Volatility is strongly mean reverting. The average iVol over this period was 19.5, while the average rVol was 18.4. When volatility was less than these averages, it tended to drift up. When it was above these averages, it drifted back down.

The fact that volatility follows a mean reversion process is very important for option traders. It tells us that when volatility moves to an extreme, it does not stay there long. Given this dynamic, option traders can maximize returns by purchasing volatility when it is well below the mean. This is not because the expected return is necessarily high, but rather because the payoff, or leverage afforded by options, becomes most asymmetric. Risking a small amount can provide huge levered returns. By contrast, when volatility greatly exceeds the mean, selling volatility is generally preferred as the probability of profit is greater. A shift in iVol can also provide important clues to changes in market sentiment as well. When iVol hits an extreme, it signals that the market's directional momentum may be about to change course. For example, in general, options time premiums fall as securities prices rise, reflecting complacency. When the prices of options start rising even as the market reaches new highs, it can signal that market participants who use options may be preparing for a decline. We saw examples of this in the summer of 2011 and 2013. Similarly when steep market declines are accompanied by falling time premiums, traders may be signaling that they believe a near-term bottom may be at hand, a dynamic witnessed in March 2009, which proved to be one of the best buying opportunities for equities in a century.

How to Trade Volatility

There are a number of ways to trade volatility. The most important is based on the ideal of continuously hedging, which is the arbitrage condition upon which options are priced. At its core, investors are trading an option against the underlying security. In this process, the option is traded against a synthetic option in a process known as gamma scalping. Some techniques use options exclusively. All volatility-trading techniques have different characteristics. Some perform best in choppy environments, while others perform better in trending markets. Some are more sensitive to changes in implied volatility, while others respond better to changes in realized volatility. At the end of the day, it is important to understand the behavioral differences in volatility-trading strategies in order to use them effectively. The following discussion takes a closer look at how both retail and professional investors can trade volatility.

Gamma Scalping

Options are priced based on a dynamic arbitrage condition between the option and the underlying security. If an investor buys a call and continuously hedges it delta neutral, he will earn a risk-free rate of return if the iVol on the option purchased matches the rVol experienced over the life of the option. To keep the trade delta neutral when hedging a call option, the underlying is purchased as the price of the underlying increases and the underlying is sold as its price declines. The purchaser of the call option will earn a return in excess of the risk-free rate if the iVol paid turns out to be less than rVol. Likewise, the purchaser will earn a return less than the risk-free rate if the iVol paid is more than the rVol experienced over the life of the option. The process of trading an option and hedging it with the underlying security is knows as **gamma scalping**.

Exhibit 3.7 shows why volatility trading using options versus its underlying security gets the name *gamma scalping*. This chart shows how an option trades relative to the underlying security. The black dotted line shows the performance of the underlying security, while the solid black line shows the performance on a three-month, $25.00 strike call. Notice that for any instantaneous movement in the price of the underlying, the option outperforms. As a result, value is created every time the price of the underlying security changes. This technique of volatility trading gets its name because the price appreciation of an option relative to the underlying security is quantified by gamma. This gain is not free, however. Investors pay a premium for an option, and that premium decays every day. The volatility trader earns a net gain when the gains from gamma exceed the losses from time decay, which is quantified by theta.

Gamma scalping is a common technique employed by volatility traders to capture excess returns by taking a view on iVol versus rVol. The previous paragraph described how a trader gets *long volatility*. Traders can also get long volatility by purchasing a put and stocks at the same time as well. To get *short volatility*, an investor sells a call and buys stock on a delta-neutral basis as a hedge. If the iVol sold on the call exceeds rVol over the life of the option, the trade will be successful and the investor will earn a return in excess of the risk-free rate. If the iVol sold on the

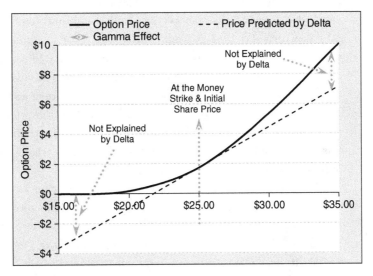

Exhibit 3.7 Gamma Scalping

call is less than the rVol experienced, the investor will earn a return that is less than the risk-free rate. Investors can also sell volatility by selling a put and stock delta neutral at the same time.

The process of gamma scalping is straightforward as it is a mechanical technique based on a formula. Transaction costs make volatility trading more complicated, however. If an investor continuously hedged throughout the trading day, bid/offer spreads and commissions would guarantee that the volatility trader would lose every time. To be successful, investors must manage transaction costs by trading only when the delta of the trade drifts far enough away from zero to the point where it introduces directional risk that exceeds one's risk tolerance. In practice, therefore, successful volatility traders must manage both their transaction costs and directional risk.

Since gamma scalping is the fundamental method for volatility trading, it is important to work through an example so we can build a practical intuition about what is taking place. Exhibit 3.8 is a simulation showing the math behind the gamma scalping trading technique. In this example, we simulate selling volatility. To do this, we sell a 90-day, $1,632 strike call on the S&P 500, while delta hedging by purchasing the appropriate amount of stock. The simulation starts with an index price of $1,600. The implied volatility incorporated into the option's price is 20 percent, and we assume realized volatility is 20 percent as well. The initial risk-free rate is 2 percent and we assume this stays constant. To make the math clean, we rebalance the option/underlying pair once everyday (including weekends, like currencies do) and the trade lasts for 30 days.

Over this 30-day simulation, the trade produced a return of $1.015 as the price of the option sold decayed, resulting in a gain of $12.637. The act of hedging entails buying high and selling low. This process resulted in a loss of $11.622. This return was produced on an average capital commitment of $616.19 producing a 30-day return of 0.1646 percent (1.015/616.7) or an annualized return of 2 percent (0.1646 × 365/30). This simulation confirms that if an option is sold and the realized volatility turns out to be equal to the implied volatility of the option sold, a process of continuous hedging will produce a return equal to the risk-free rate. The arbitrage condition that is the foundation of option pricing demands it. To get a sense of how traders can make or lose money volatility trading, Exhibit 3.9 builds on this analysis and summarizes the results of volatility trading when realized volatility differs from the iVol of the option sold.

The solid black line in Exhibit 3.9 shows the gain or loss we would earn by entering a short volatility trade though gamma scaling (short call, delta hedged with stock). If realized volatility manifests at 10 percent over a 30-day period, we earn $9.60, and if it comes in at 30 percent, we would lose $12.64. When entering into a volatility trade, it is useful to know what your risks are in advance without going through the exercise of such a simulation. You can perform a risk analysis ex-ante to

Day	Asset Price	Change	Return	Call Price	Change	Return	Call Delta	Net Return	Assets
90	1600.00			52.57			0.46		683.65
89	1584.90	−15.10	−0.94%	45.53	−7.04	−13%	0.42	$0.09	622.68
88	1590.29	5.39	0.34%	47.45	1.92	4%	0.43	$0.35	643.19
87	1588.90	−1.38	−0.09%	46.47	−0.98	−2%	0.43	$0.38	636.71
86	1574.48	−14.42	−0.91%	40.16	−6.31	−14%	0.39	$0.11	577.99
85	1542.12	−32.36	−2.06%	28.41	−11.74	−29%	0.31	−$0.96	452.59
84	1545.06	2.94	0.19%	29.00	0.59	2%	0.32	$0.33	461.59
83	1537.33	−7.72	−0.50%	26.29	−2.71	−9%	0.30	$0.26	431.29
82	1555.01	17.68	1.15%	31.57	5.28	20%	0.34	−$0.02	495.71
81	1582.54	27.53	1.77%	41.48	9.90	31%	0.41	−$0.57	604.38
80	1557.34	−25.20	−1.59%	31.65	−9.83	−24%	0.34	−$0.46	501.28
79	1559.19	1.85	0.12%	31.92	0.27	1%	0.35	$0.36	506.80
78	1563.40	4.21	0.27%	33.02	1.11	3%	0.35	$0.35	521.89
77	1566.13	2.73	0.17%	33.63	0.60	2%	0.36	$0.37	531.27
76	1591.01	24.88	1.59%	43.01	9.38	28%	0.43	−$0.41	634.22
75	1615.20	24.19	1.52%	53.67	10.66	25%	0.49	−$0.36	738.80
74	1615.60	0.40	0.02%	53.43	−0.23	0%	0.49	$0.43	740.12
73	1596.60	−19.00	−1.18%	44.17	−9.26	−17%	0.44	−$0.08	655.32
72	1617.54	20.94	1.31%	53.52	9.34	21%	0.50	−$0.17	747.93
71	1628.27	10.73	0.66%	58.55	5.03	9%	0.52	$0.29	796.01
70	1606.33	−21.93	−1.35%	47.27	−11.28	−19%	0.46	−$0.23	696.13
69	1606.50	0.17	0.01%	46.91	−0.36	−1%	0.46	$0.44	696.10
68	1612.35	5.85	0.36%	49.22	2.31	5%	0.48	$0.40	722.24
67	1630.96	18.61	1.15%	58.16	8.94	18%	0.53	−$0.04	808.18
66	1600.82	−30.14	−1.85%	43.01	−15.15	−26%	0.44	−$0.86	667.15
65	1585.02	−15.80	−0.99%	35.93	−7.08	−16%	0.40	$0.07	592.96
64	1595.47	10.46	0.66%	39.79	3.86	11%	0.43	$0.28	639.89
63	1583.57	−11.90	−0.75%	34.50	−5.29	−13%	0.39	$0.22	583.00
62	1580.29	−3.28	−0.21%	32.80	−1.69	−5%	0.38	$0.41	566.06
61	1576.24	−4.04	−0.26%	30.87	−1.93	−6%	0.37	$0.40	545.49
60	1600.00	23.75	1.51%	39.93	9.06	29%		−$0.37	
Mean			0.00%			−0.91%			616.7
Cumulative			0.00%			−24.04%		1.015	
Volatility			**20.0%**			**320%**			
Beta						15.9			

Exhibit 3.8   Volatility Trading Simulation iVol = rVol

estimate potential gains and losses you could experience by performing a parametric analysis by using vega. Recall from Chapter 2 that vega is the sensitivity of an option's value for a change in volatility. The black dotted line is an estimation of the gain or loss we might earn using this method. As with most parametric methods, it provides a first-order linear estimate of gains and losses.

Using vega to estimate potential gains and losses raises an interesting question: How should we compute both delta and vega when the expected realized volatility is different from the implied volatility that determines the option's transaction price? Most traders use the implied volatility of the option traded to compute delta and

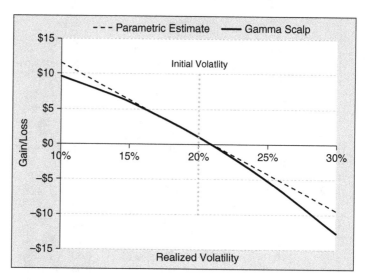

Exhibit 3.9   Volatility Trading Simulation Sensitivity Analysis

gamma, and most risk managers demand traders use this method. It is important to be aware that this can introduce some error in the hedge. The value of an option is, to some degree, path dependent. If we expect an rVol that is lower than iVol, then we expect price to follow a narrower path. This narrower path will have an effect on returns and the way we might want to manage a volatility trade. If iVol turns out to be lower than expected, the delta of the hedge will be too high at the margin if we use the iVol that determines the option's price. Remember, delta increases as implied volatility increases for out-of-the-money options. As a result, if we are looking for a drop in volatility, we should hedge the options somewhat "light." If the volatility forecast is correct, the realized returns and the estimated returns will line up more closely.

In Chapter 2, we touched on the subject of path dependency. Recall that the B–S–M option-pricing model assumes constant volatility. We know that volatility fluctuates, and this has an impact on the price of an option. An option derives its value from the underlying instruments. As discussed in that chapter, the primary determinants of an option's value are the price of the underlying asset, the volatility of returns on that asset, and the moneyness of the option. Since models for pricing options assume investors can replicate an option by continuously trading the underlying security, gamma scalping is the most common way investors trade volatility.

Since gamma scalping requires trading after every significant move in the price of the underlying asset, transaction costs in the form of commissions and bid/offer spreads can add up over time, particularly for the retail investor who trades in moderate size. For those who want to take a more buy-and-hold approach, there are other strategies to take advantage of large anticipated price moves. The following is a discussion of some of the common strategies investors use to capitalize on large moves in the price of an asset when they do not have an opinion about the direction of that move.

Straddles

Often, investors believe a news event will occur that will drive the price of a stock, commodity, or currency sharply higher or lower. This is a typical stance investors take when a biotech company is awaiting the decision from the FDA concerning the approval or denial of a new drug. Biotech companies tend to be small companies and live or die based on the performance of one or just a few therapies. To take advantage of situations of high uncertainty, investors often purchase a straddle. A straddle is a two-legged trade in which an investor buys a put and a call with the same strike price and the same time to maturity. In buying a straddle, most investors pick a strike price that is at or very near the price of the underlying security. The purchaser of a straddle earns a profit if the price of the underlying moves a long way from the strike price of the two options, as is typical of long volatility strategies. The risk of loss in a straddle is limited to the premium paid up front.

The beauty of a long straddle is that the investor can win no matter which way the price moves, so long as it moves far enough. If the price of the underlying rises or falls the investor enjoys a gain. On its face, this looks like a low-risk strategy, but there are significant risks. The challenge of employing this strategy is timing. Time decay is the enemy of option buyers. Since an investor is buying both a put and a call at the same time, the investor is taking on roughly twice the time decay, or, of a single leg option trade. It is important to understand that the value of a straddle will fall quite rapidly as the investor waits for the anticipated event. If the event does not manifest, the straddle will most likely lose value. There is a second risk one needs to be aware of when trading straddles. If the investor is investing for a catalyzing event, iVol on the two options is likely to be above normal levels. Even if the event manifests and the share price moves, implied volatility is likely to fall after the announcement and the price movement occurs. This vega effect will cause the time premium to fall and the value of the straddle will decline, all other things held equal. At the end of the day, one does not have to get directions right, but they must get magnitude right to earn a positive return. As a result, when placing a straddle trade, you must incorporate a fall in implied volatility when modeling the price movement needed to break even on the trade. The best time to use a straddle is when iVol is low and you expect it to rise over time coincident with a price shock.

Exhibit 3.10 shows the payoff pattern for a long straddle with different times to expiration. The gray dotted line is the payoff pattern for a 12-month straddle, the solid gray line is the payoff pattern for a 3-month straddle, and the solid black like shows the value of the straddle at expiration (also equal to its intrinsic value). Exhibit 3.10 also summarizes the Greeks for the three-month straddle.

A long straddle is not a leveraged play on small changes in the price of the underlying security. This becomes apparent when observing the initial delta for the trade. Calls have positive delta and puts have negative delta. Combined, the initial delta of a straddle is close to zero. It is just 0.08 in the case of a three-month straddle.

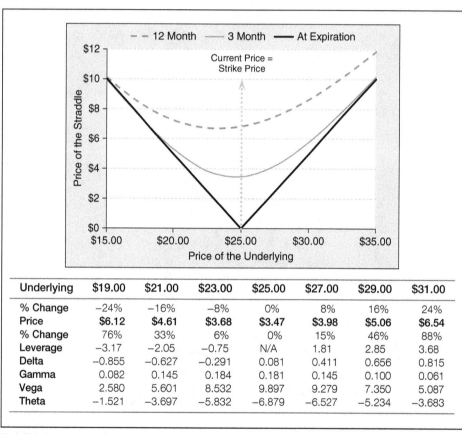

Underlying	$19.00	$21.00	$23.00	$25.00	$27.00	$29.00	$31.00
% Change	−24%	−16%	−8%	0%	8%	16%	24%
Price	$6.12	$4.61	$3.68	$3.47	$3.98	$5.06	$6.54
% Change	76%	33%	6%	0%	15%	46%	88%
Leverage	−3.17	−2.05	−0.75	N/A	1.81	2.85	3.68
Delta	−0.855	−0.627	−0.291	0.081	0.411	0.656	0.815
Gamma	0.082	0.145	0.184	0.181	0.145	0.100	0.061
Vega	2.580	5.601	8.532	9.897	9.279	7.350	5.087
Theta	−1.521	−3.697	−5.832	−6.879	−6.527	−5.234	−3.683

Exhibit 3.10 Payoff Pattern for a Long Straddle

Upside maximum gain = Unlimited

Downside maximum gain = Strike − Premium paid

Maximum loss = Option premium

Upper breakeven = Strike + Premium paid

Lower breakeven = Strike − Premium paid

Probability of expiring worthless ≅ 0

Notice that gamma is highest when the share price is equal to the strike price of the two options. So, as the price of the underlying moves away from $25, the delta of the trade moves in the investor's favor. The investor is getting "longer" as the share price rises and *shorter* as the share price falls. Since the premium paid on this straddle is $3.47, the break-even levels are $21.53 and $28.47. If the price of the underlying rises above or below these levels by expiration, the investors will earn a profit. Movement beyond these ranges adds to the investor's gain quite rapidly.

Notice how time works against the investor of a long straddle. The value of the 12-month at-the-money straddle is $6.85. After 9 months, that straddle would fall to $3.47 for a $3.38 loss if the price of the underlying security does not change. Since theta increases as the time to maturity falls, performance drag in the last three months of the one-year straddle is about as much as the first nine months. This provides an important clue to choosing an expiration date for a straddle. If we are investing based on the hypothesis that the price of the underlying security is going to trend in one direction, we should buy longer-dated straddles. This way, the effect of time decay is minimized and there is more time for the price of the underlying asset to move to an extreme. In the last chapter, we showed that long-dated options are more sensitive to changes in iVol than short-dated ones. If you are investing to capture a catalyzing event, it is best to use very short-dated options to minimize the effects of a potential collapse in implied volatility after the catalyzing event takes place.

Strangles

A strangle is similar to a straddle, the difference being that out-of-the-money options are purchased instead of at-the-money options. The structure gets it name because the strike prices of the two options "strangle" the current price of the underlying security. To construct a strangle, we purchase a put with a strike price below the price of the underlying and buy a call with a strike price above it. Like a straddle, the buyer of a long strangle will earn a profit as the price of the underlying security moves outside the strikes by an amount greater than the premium paid. The advantage of a strangle versus a straddle is that it requires less premium up front and suffers a slower time decay. This does not come without cost, however. To earn a profit, the price of the underlying has to move further up or down to generate a gain.

Exhibit 3.11 shows the payoff patterns of a long strangle with different times to expiration. The gray dotted line is the payoff pattern for a 12-month strangle. The solid gray line is the payoff pattern for a three-month strangle. The solid black line shows the payoff pattern for a strangle at expiration, which is also equal to its intrinsic value. Exhibit 3.11 summarizes the Greeks for the three-month straddle.

Like the straddle, the long strangle is not a levered play on small changes in the price of the underlying security. Strangles becomes levered to the price of the

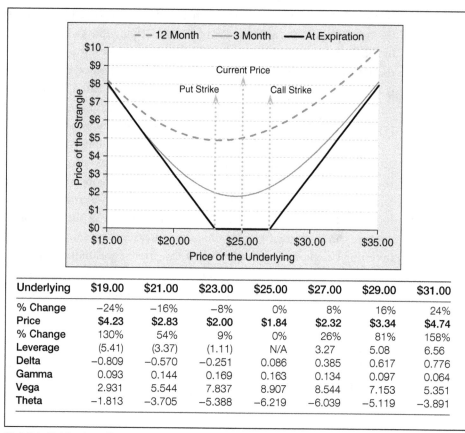

Underlying	$19.00	$21.00	$23.00	$25.00	$27.00	$29.00	$31.00
% Change	−24%	−16%	−8%	0%	8%	16%	24%
Price	**$4.23**	**$2.83**	**$2.00**	**$1.84**	**$2.32**	**$3.34**	**$4.74**
% Change	130%	54%	9%	0%	26%	81%	158%
Leverage	(5.41)	(3.37)	(1.11)	N/A	3.27	5.08	6.56
Delta	−0.809	−0.570	−0.251	0.086	0.385	0.617	0.776
Gamma	0.093	0.144	0.169	0.163	0.134	0.097	0.064
Vega	2.931	5.544	7.837	8.907	8.544	7.153	5.351
Theta	−1.813	−3.705	−5.388	−6.219	−6.039	−5.119	−3.891

Exhibit 3.11   Payoff Pattern for a Long Strangle

$$\text{Upside maximum gain} = \text{Unlimited}$$
$$\text{Downside maximum gain} = \text{Put strike} - \text{Premium paid}$$
$$\text{Maximum loss} = \text{Option premium}$$
$$\text{Upper breakeven} = \text{Call strike} + \text{Premium paid}$$
$$\text{Lower breakeven} = \text{Put Strike} - \text{Premium Paid}$$
$$\text{Probability of expiring worthless} = 1 - Zeta_{Put} - Zeta_{Call}$$

underlying as it moves above the call strike or below the put strike. In the example above, the strangle is structured with one put for every call, and each of the strikes are out of the money by $2. With this structure the three-month strangle initially has a small positive delta of 0.086. Many traders want an unbiased outcome, and will weight the trade delta neutral by buying slightly more puts. In this case, one would buy 1.3 (0.367/0.281 − 1) puts per call, as the calls possess 0.086 more deltas. Notice that gamma is highest when the share price is between the strike prices of the two options. So as the price of the underlying moves above the call strike or below the put strike, the delta of the trade moves in the investor's favor. Since the premium paid on the three-month straddle is $1.84, the break-even levels are $21.16 and $28.84. (Notice these bands are wider than the straddle described above.) If the price of the underlying rises above or below these levels by expiration, the investors will earn a profit. Like the straddle, movement beyond these ranges adds to the investor's gain quite rapidly.

Since a strangle, like a straddle, is *long gamma,* it will suffer time decay. The value of the 12-month at-the-money straddle is $5.061. After nine months, that strangle would fall to $1.84 for a $3.22 loss if the price of the underlying asset does not change. Notice, this is very similar to the time decay suffered in a straddle as well. Many investors prefer strangles to straddles, as there is a lower premium at risk. However, there is a significant chance a strangle will expire worthless (35.3 percent, in this case), whereas the probability of a straddle expiring worthless is nil. As a result, a straddle is likely to have intrinsic value at expiration. This trade-off is something to think about when deciding between a straddle and a strangle.

Calendar Spreads

A long *calendar spread,* also known as a *horizontal spread,* is an option structure where an investor buys a long-dated option and sells a shorter-dated one with the same strike price on the same underlying asset. The cost or net debit of a calendar spread is the difference between the premium paid on the longer-dated option and the premium collected on the shorter-dated option.

A calendar spread represents a different kind of volatility trade. If you are long volatility using gamma scalping, you will gain if the implied volatility rises or if realized volatility increases. If you are long volatility using a straddle or a strangle strategy, you will gain if the implied volatility rises or the price of the underlying security trends in one direction or the other. Like gamma scalping, you will also enjoy a gain if implied volatility rises using a calendar spread. This occurs because the vega of the long-dated option is greater than the vega for the short-dated option. As a result, if iVol rises, the value of the long-dated option will rise more than the short-dated option. This makes a calendar spread a great alternative if you are expecting a jump in iVol because the amount of capital one has to commit is moderate compared to a long call, short stock pair.

Since most investors do not trade calendar spreads and are therefore unaware of their unique characteristics, an example in in order. In this example, the investor purchases a 12-month $25.00 strike call and sells a three-month call with the same strike. For simplicity, a 35 percent iVol is assumed for both options. Exhibit 3.12 shows the relationship between the value of this calendar spread versus implied

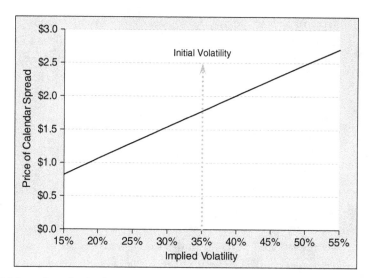

Exhibit 3.12   Value of Calendar Spread versus iVol, Price of Underlying Held Constant

volatility. This chart assumes that the change in iVol for both options changes by the same amount. From the perspective of the term structure of volatility, this represents a parallel shift in the curve either up or down. Notice that the relationship is linear so this is a very useful structure for taking a position in anticipation of a change in implied volatility. When considering a calendar spread as a volatility-trading vehicle, one should pay particular attention to long-dated volatility. Vega on the long-dated option is much higher than vega on a short-dated option. So the price action of iVol at the long end of the term structure will be the real driver of success or failure with this technique.

A calendar spread is a bit different from a traditional volatility trading strategy. What makes it different from straddles and strangles, for example, is that it does not benefit from a change in realized volatility. In fact, it is hurt by it if that volatility manifests as a large jump or a trend in the price of the underlying security.

Exhibit 3.13 shows the payoff pattern of the calendar spread given an instantaneous change in the price of the underlying security. The solid black line indicates the payoff pattern for the base case scenario, whereas the gray dotted line shows how the payoff patter shifts if iVol jumps higher. The difference between the two shows another way of displaying the calendar spread's sensitivity to iVol. Exhibit 3.13 shows that vega is 4.723 for this trade, so the value of the spread will increase by $0.04723 for every percentage point increase in iVol. Since the delta of both the long- and short-dated options are similar, the delta of the calendar spread is close to zero and just 0.036 in this case. Nonetheless, this gives the trade a small positive bias to a rise in the price of the underlying security. The slight upward slope in the curves above reveals this effect. Notice that as the price of the underlying security

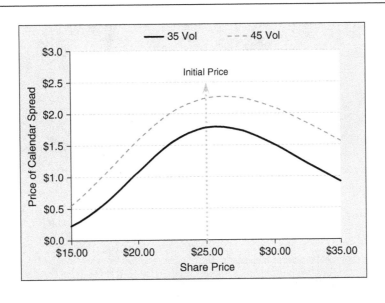

Underlying	$19.00	$21.00	$23.00	$25.00	$27.00	$29.00	$31.00
% Change	−24%	−16%	−8%	0%	8%	16%	24%
Price	$1.07	$1.97	$3.36	$5.31	$7.80	$10.72	$13.98
Change (%)	−80	−63	−37	0	47	102	163
Leverage	3.33	3.93	4.59	N/A	5.84	6.36	6.79
Delta	0.207	0.195	0.128	0.036	−0.047	−0.099	−0.121
Gamma	0.009	−0.021	−0.043	−0.046	−0.035	−0.018	−0.004
Vega	5.051	5.142	4.813	4.723	5.110	5.731	6.218
Theta	−0.229	0.555	1.400	1.798	1.589	0.987	0.313

Exhibit 3.13   Value of Calendar Spread versus Underlying Price

drifts away from the strike price of the two options, the value of the position falls. This occurs because the gamma of the shorter-dated option is somewhat higher than the longer-dated option, making the trade net gamma negative (i.e., −0.046). As a result, the delta of the trade becomes more negative when the price of the underlying security rises, and becomes more positive when the price of the underlying asset falls.

Since a calendar spread is gamma negative, we should expect it to be theta positive, and this is indeed the case. Exhibit 3.14 shows how the value of the calendar spread will change as times passes assuming the price of the underlying security does not change. In the previous chapter, the B–S–M model reveals that the time decay of an option falls as the time to expiration increases. Since a long calendar spread is a combination of a long-dated option and a short-dated one, theta is positive. This phenomenon works to the benefit of the trade. As time passes, and

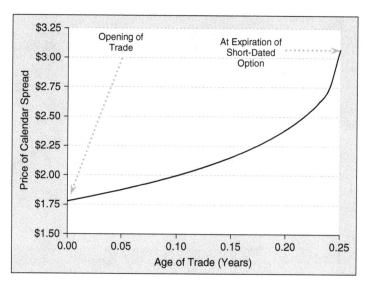

Exhibit 3.14   Value of Calendar Spread versus Time, ATM Strikes

the price of the underlying might drift away from the strike price, time decay offsets the capital loss and provides a return push.

Final Thought

In this chapter, we laid down the foundation every investor and option trader needs to know to understand how realized and implied volatility behaves. In addition, we discussed the volatility surface and how it affects the price of options. With this foundation, we presented a number of volatility-trading strategies we can use to take advantage of certain market conditions. One of the most important takeaways from this discussion is that options are valued based on the notion that volatility is not static. Implied volatility rises and falls as investors handicap the price risk in the underlying security. Realized volatility rises and falls depending on news flow and what actually is taking place in the market.

Options derive their value based on the assumption that investors can hedge an option by continuously trading with the underlying instrument. Most investors do not trade options in this fashion. Continuously hedging is a process followed by market makers as they attempt to run a matched book and by volatility traders who attempt to capitalize on fluctuations in iVol and/or rVol. Most investors trade options to hedge existing positions or to express a view on the underlying asset. In doing so, they construct strategies designed to meet those objectives. To achieve these goals, investors tend to buy and hold their positions for a period of time. As this chapter shows, there are a number of ways to trade volatility—either exclusively with options or by trading options and the underlying security in tandem. There are several ways to express a directional view of an asset. The question is, "What is the best strategy to employ?" Should you buy a call, sell a put, or trade options in combination? After all, there are a host of strike prices and expirations to choose from, and some strategies perform better than others depending on the situation, an investor's viewpoint, and market conditions.

In Chapter 2, we delved into how options are priced and presented some mathematics discussing their risk/performance characteristics. This is the theoretical background needed to understand how options behave. The question left unanswered is, "Are options fairly priced from the perspective of the buy-and-hold investor?' We know that if implied volatility turns out to be equal to realized volatility, the volatility trader should earn a risk-free rate of return. But how will the buy-and-hold investor make out? In the following chapter, we will delve into how options behave from the perspective of the buy-and-hold investor. To do this we will examine the historical performance of index options to uncover insights that go beyond the theoretical. With this combination of practical and theoretical knowledge, finding the best trades will become routine.

## CHAPTER 4

Are Options Fairly Priced?

It is often said that individual investors, and indeed many institutional investors, lose money when trading options. Statistics on this matter do not seem to exist, so we cannot point to any data to prove the validity of this assertion. We do know, however, that those that make markets in options run profitable enterprises. If this were not the case, they would go out of business. They earn revenue from commissions and capturing the bid/offer spread as they buy and sell to their customer base.

Ex-ante, investors buy and sell options to achieve a particular goal. That goal might be to anticipate a directional move in the price of the underlying security, make a bet on future volatility of returns, or hedge a risk and reduce volatility. Value from the investor's perspective is one of profit opportunity or risk management. It is important to remember that investors transact only if they see value in doing so. Looking at an option transaction in isolation without regard to the portfolio objectives as a whole, it is simply a bilateral agreement between two parties. From this perspective, trading in derivative instruments represents a zero sum game ex-post. The gain made by a long is reflected by a loss by the short and vice versa. Since market makers run a profitable enterprise, it is fair to say that investors might be losing out on risk-adjusted returns. When investors use options for both directional trades and hedging it seems that directional traders do not get the returns they are looking for on average, and hedgers do not get all the protection they desire if market makers capture extra value. This leads us to believe that market folklore is indeed correct, and that option investors tend to underperform on a risk-adjusted basis.

The efficient market hypothesis suggests that all securities, be they assets or derivative products, reflect all available information in the marketplace and are fairly priced. If this is the case, investors should earn a fair rate of return for the risk they take after adjusting for transactions costs. This should be the case no matter what strategy they follow over the long term. Said another way, a fairly priced asset should provide a fair risk-adjusted rate of return over the long hall. A portfolio of fairly priced assets should provide a fair risk-adjusted rate of return as well. Since investors seem to systematically come up short when applying options to their overall portfolio strategy, we need to ask the question, "Why do most investors who participate in the options market end up with the short end of the stick?" This is not a problem peculiar to investors who employ options. Most mutual funds that manage portfolios of stocks and bonds underperform their index benchmark they attempt to replicate or outperform, for example.

Systematic underperformance is a particularly perplexing question because options are priced in an arbitrage-free environment. That is to say, we cannot continuously trade an option against the underlying security and earned a superior risk-adjusted rate of return. This tells us that on average, options are fairly priced relative to the underlying instrument. Since options are instrument that allow investors to earn significant gains with a small capital commitment, most investors are intrigued by the opportunity presented by purchasing put and call options. In our experience, most investors tend to be a buyer of options. Since there has to be a seller for every buyer, market makers tend to be net short options. If investors tend to underperform and market makers tend to outperform on a risk-adjusted basis, this market structure suggests that options behave as if they are overpriced.

Herein lies the paradox. If options are priced in arbitrage-free environment, then both buyers and sellers of options should earn a fair risk-adjusted rate of return over time. To answer the question, "Are options fairly priced?" we need to delve more deeply into why sellers of options seem to get the upper hand over option buyers. To begin to answer that question, we need to start with an analysis of option pricing in the context of a generalized asset-pricing model. The primary hypothesis we make in choosing an asset-pricing model is the assumption of rational pricing. If option prices are fair, then there is a rational reason for the prices and returns we observe historically. We should expect to see that price and return behavior in the future should reflect what we see in the historical data. If we were to simply argue that option prices are irrational, then there would be no concrete reason for the returns we observe in the options market. This would suggest that market participants price options in a haphazard manner, which we believe is simply not the case. We believe that the market, in fact, prices assets fairly as postulated by the efficient market hypothesis. An outgrowth of that hypothesis is the capital asset pricing model (CAPM), which prices assets as a function of both the return on a risk-free asset and the market risk imbedded in the security itself. To analyze the return behavior of options, we will use CAPM as a mathematical construct to examine the historical return behavior of both put and call options. This model for pricing assets falls out of modern portfolio theory, which is based on the premise that investors will construct portfolios in a way that maximizes return and minimizes risk. These concepts are described in greater detail below.

Modern Portfolio Theory (MPT)

Modern portfolio theory (MPT) is a concept of investment finance that is concerned with how a rational investor constructs a portfolio. It rests on the proposition that investors want to maximize their financial well-being (i.e., desire high returns) but are risk averse (i.e., want to avoid or at least minimize losses) at the same time. In practice, MPT has evolved into a mathematical model that attempts to maximize a portfolio's expected rate of return given a particular level of risk. This is equivalent to minimizing risk for a given level of expected return. Within this framework, risk is defined and quantified as the standard deviation of returns. The objective of maximizing risk-adjusted rates of return is achieved through diversification. This is a process of selecting a group of investments that, as a package, produces a higher rate of return at a lower level of risk than any of the individual assets held in the portfolio. The benefits of diversification are achieved when the combination of assets held are not perfectly positively correlated. Under these circumstances, the value of the assets held in the portfolio do not necessarily rise or fall at the same time. When the value of some assets increases, the value of others assets might climb, fall, or stay the same. The best diversifying asset is one that is negatively correlated to the price action of other assets in the portfolio. A negatively correlated asset will increase in price when others fall, and vice versa. With such an asset, the portfolio will enjoy low volatility of returns. Through diversification, we should earn the expected rate of return on the individual assets in the long run, but endure a lower level of return volatility throughout the investment holding period. The following are the equations used to quantify return and risk. Put together, they allow the investor to construct an optimal portfolio.

$$Maximize \ E(R_p) = \sum_{i=1}^{N} w_i E(R_i)$$

$$Subject \ to: \ \sigma_p^2 = \sum_{i=1}^{N} \sum_{j=1}^{N} w_i w_j \sigma_i \sigma_j \rho_{i,j}$$

$$\sigma_p = \sqrt{\sigma_p^2}$$

where:

$E(R_i)$ = the expected rate of return on an individual asset in the portfolio

w_i = the weight of the individual assets in the portfolio

σ_i = standard deviation volatility of returns on the individual assets

$\rho_{i,j}$ = the correlation of returns among assets in the portfolio

$E(R_p)$ = the expected rate of return on the portfolio

σ_p = standard deviation (volatility) of returns on the portfolio

The first equation states that the expected rate of return of a portfolio is simply a weighted average of the expected returns of all the individual investments in a portfolio. The second equation states that the variance of a portfolio is a weighted average of the covariance of returns of all the investments that make up the portfolio. It is easy to see from this equation that as correlation ($\rho_{i,j}$) for any of the security pairs falls, so does the portfolio variance. Lastly, the standard deviation of returns on the portfolio is simply the square root of the portfolio's variance. Optimization routines are used to determine the best mix of risk assets to achieve the objective of maximizing return for a given level of risk. The first step in this process is to find the highest returning portfolios across the risk spectrum. Upon completion of this exercise, a curve of optimal portfolios is revealed. This curve is known as the *efficient frontier* of risky assets and is indicated by the curved black line in Exhibit 4.1.

In Exhibit 4.1, each of the black dots represents a different asset. Due to the benefits of diversification, optimization routine finds unique portfolios that will maximize its rate of return for any given level of risk. Those portfolios drawn across a spectrum of risks will produce the efficient frontier of portfolios, which provide better risk return characteristics than holding any one asset. As a result, the efficient

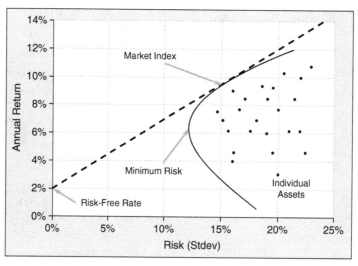

Exhibit 4.1   Efficient Frontier, Borrowing, and Lending Line

frontier of investible portfolios lies above and to the left of all the individual assets. It should be noted that while there is an optimal portfolio of risky assets for every level of risk, there is one portfolio that is better than all others no matter what level of risk a trader considers. Since the investment opportunity set contains all the investment opportunities in the marketplace, the portfolio that is superior to all others is the market portfolio. This is the case because this is the portfolio that the universe of all investors in aggregate holds. It is superior to all others because it only possesses market risk, as all the unique risks associated with individual investments are diversified away. Since market risk is the only characteristic the market pays for, it will pay the highest rate of return per unit of risk.

To find the characteristics of this *market portfolio,* a line is drawn from a point on the *y*-axis at a level equal to the risk-free rate to the highest point on the efficient frontier. This is a point where that line is just tangent to that curve. The resulting line is known as the *borrowing and lending line.* Notice that the borrowing and lending line, shown as the black dotted line in Exhibit 4.1, lies above the efficient frontier. The borrowing and lending line offers investors another investment opportunity. Investors who are willing to take more risk to get a higher expected rate of return should borrow money and invest the proceeds into the optimal market portfolio. This way, they will earn a higher rate of return for the risk they are willing to take relative to any other choice. Likewise, investors who are more risk averse should divide their capital between the risk-free asset and the market portfolio. This provides a higher returning portfolio at a defined level of risk than simply investing in a lower risk portfolio found on the efficient frontier. It can even provide investment opportunities that have far lower risk than the least risky portfolio of risk assets.

With the market portfolio and its risk/return characteristics defined, a trader can now determine the expected rate of return on any asset. As the market portfolio by definition only carries market risk, it provides the benchmark for pricing risky assets. The valuation model based on the characteristics of the market portfolio as a yardstick is known as the capital asset pricing model.

◼ Capital Asset Pricing Model (CAPM)

The capital asset pricing model is a mathematical construct used to determine the appropriate expected rate of return for any asset. Any asset evaluated in isolation will have return characteristics that are driven by the action of the overall market (i.e., market risk) and factors that are unique to the asset in question (i.e., asset specific risks). Since investors can diversify a portfolio and eliminate unique risks, CAPM does not consider an asset's unique risks when determining an appropriate rate of return. It only compensates for nondiversifiable risk, which is market risk. Therefore, an asset's sensitivity to market risk is the only driver of the asset's expected rate of return.

The sensitivity of an asset's unique returns to returns produced by the overall market is measured by a term called beta (β). Beta is unique for each asset and suggests that there is a linear relationship between as asset's return and its sensitivity to the market's returns. Simply stated, as beta increases, so does the asset's expected rate of return. An asset whose return is completely unrelated to systemic risk merely earns the risk-free rate of return. Therefore, the total expected rate of return for any asset is a combination of the risk-free rate plus the asset's sensitivity to market risk. This relationship is defined in the equations below.

$$E(R_i) = R_f + \beta_i[E(R_m) - R_f]$$
$$\beta_i = \frac{\sigma(R_i, R_m)}{\sigma_m^2} = \frac{\rho_{i,m}\sigma_i}{\sigma_m}$$

where:

$E(R_i)$ = the expected rate of return on an individual asset
$E(R_m)$ = the expected rate of return on the market portfolio
R_f = the risk-free rate of return
β_i = the measure of an assets sensitivity to the market risk premium
σ_m^2 = variance of market returns
$\rho_{i,m}$ = the correlation of an asset to the market
σ_i = standard deviation (volatility) of an asset's return

The intuition behind these equations is relatively straightforward. The expected return on assets i is the sum total of the risk-free rate of return plus an expected return premium as compensation for market risk taken. The return premium on the market portfolio is simply the difference between the expected return on the market portfolio and the risk-free rate $[E(R_m) - R_f]$. Beta defines the sensitivity between the market's return premium and the asset in question. It is equal to the covariance of the return on assets i and the return on the market portfolio, divided by the variance on the market portfolio. Stated another way, beta is equal to the correlation of return of assets i relative to the market portfolio, times the volatility of assets i divided by the volatility of the market portfolio. Theoretically, beta is unbounded. It can take a value of a large positive or negative number. Most assets, however, have a beta that is greater than zero and less than two. Since beta is a factor that is unique to a particular asset, it is the driver of expected returns relative to all other assets. Exhibit 4.2 provides additional intuition concerning beta.

The *security market line* is the manifestation of the capital asset pricing model formula presented above. It represents a visual representation between an asset's beta and its expected rate of return. Specifically, beta lies on the *x*-axis and expected return lies on the *y*-axis. By knowing an asset's beta, we can compute the asset's expected rate of return. Active investors are always looking for assets that are underappreciated by the market. If investors believe an asset is underpriced, they

Beta Value	Interpretation	Example
$\beta < 0$	Asset price generally moves in the opposite direction of the market.	Put options
$\beta = 0$	Asset price movement is unrelated with the movement of the market.	Short-term U.S. Treasury securities
$0 < \beta < 1$	Asset price moves in the same direction of the market but with less volatility.	Real estate, consumer product, and utility stocks
$\beta = 1$	Asset price moves in the same direction of the market with the same volatility.	Cyclical stocks, market index ETFs
$\beta > 1$	Asset price moves in the same direction of the market but with more volatility.	Natural resource, emerging market, and technology stocks, call options

Exhibit 4.2   Description of Beta and Examples

expect it to produce a rate of return that is higher than the CAPM would predict. Such an asset would fall above the capital market line. If investors believe an asset is overpriced, they expect it to produce a rate of return that is lower than CAPM would predict. Such an asset would fall below the capital market line. The act of buying cheap assets and selling expensive ones pushes asset returns to the capital market line over time.

The efficient market hypothesis argues that this process of value arbitrage ensures that all assets fall on or near the capital market line. Those assets that fall on this line are fairly priced, as investors are only being compensated for nondiversifiable risks. Exhibit 4.3 shows the security market line. The slope of that line indicates how much additional return we might expect to earn by taking on more market risk.

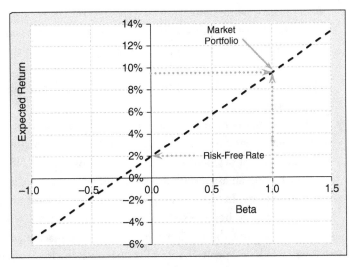

Exhibit 4.3   Relationship between Returns and Market Risk

This chart clearly shows that as an asset's beta increases, so does its expected rate of return. Assets with very high betas should possess high-expected rates of return. One of the criticisms of CAPM is that many high-risk assets such as penny stocks, mineral exploration stocks, and so forth do not produce high rates of return over time. It is important to remember that one of the underlying assumptions of CAPM is that assets are efficiently priced. Because of their small market capitalization, most penny stocks do not get widespread investor attention. With few people trading these issues, the share price of penny and mining stocks are subject to price manipulation. These issues are also very illiquid and suffer from large bid/offer spreads that consume any value an investor might uncover. In short, these stocks are anything but efficiently priced. Furthermore, unique risk far outweighs the market risk in these issues, and information about the issuing company is generally not well disseminated or understood by market participants at large. As a result, CAPM is a poor model to apply when estimating expected returns for these kinds of investments. The model performs best for large capitalization stocks.

Notice that the capital market line suggests that assets with small negative betas should have a small positive expected rate of return that is less than the risk-free rate. Should an asset have a large negative beta, CAPM tells us that such an asset should actually have a negative expected rate of return. At first blush, this might seem counterintuitive. After all, an asset with the negative beta will be risky when measured in terms of its standard deviation of returns. Since it is a risky asset, you might think that you should earn the risk premium on that asset.

Remember, however, that price discovery takes place in an arbitrage-free environment. If an asset with a negative beta had a positive risk premium, it could be combined with another asset possessing a positive beta that also has a positive risk premium. A clever investor could combine these two assets to form a portfolio with a beta of zero, while delivering an expected rate of return that is above the risk-free rate. Since an asset with a beta of zero should produce an expected rate of return equal to the risk-free rate, a portfolio of assets must do the same. Otherwise, there is an arbitrage opportunity. If such an opportunity existed, investors would buy the asset with a negative beta pushing its price up until it produced an expected negative rate of return.

The reason a person holds a risky asset is that they expect its value to rise over time. If an investor expected its price to fall, a rational person would sell the risky asset (or sell it short) and buy it back at a lower price. It is difficult to envision an investor buying an asset with a negative expected rate of return. But this is the case with put options. Investors buy put options, which have negative betas and expected rates of return, to hedge existing positions or to capitalize on a fall in the price of an asset they, but not the market, anticipates. The market prices risky assets at a level that will produce a positive rate of return over any investment horizon. If the market expects the price of risky assets to rise over time, then by necessity, the market also expects the price of a put option on that asset to fall over time. Does this make the purchase of put options a suboptimal investment choice? After all, investors buy put options all the time to protect the value of individual investments or their portfolio.

Evaluating Historical Returns on Put Options

The fact that assets possessing a negative beta should produce a negative rate of return over time has interesting implications for the expected returns on put options. Since put options have negative delta, this means they have the same return dynamic as an asset with negative beta. Therefore, put options should have an expected rate of return that is less than the risk-free rate under all circumstance. If the negative delta of a put option is large enough, it should produce a negative expected rate of return outright. Therefore, we should expect investors that buy put options on a regular basis to suffer negative rates of return and lose money.

The first step in verifying this proposition is to simply examine the historical returns on put options controlling for time to expiration and moneyness. To do this, we will evaluate the historical returns of put options on the SPDR S&P 500 ETF (SPY), which seeks to track the performance of the S&P 500 stock index. We chose the S&P 500 index because institutional investors use it as a proxy for the market index. This index represents the 500 largest companies in the United States and has a multitrillion-dollar market capitalization. SPY and its associated options, along with S&P 500 index futures and its options, are actively traded. Furthermore, options on this index are very liquid, and high-quality volatility and price data are available going back to January 2005. If any asset and associated options are efficiently priced, it certainly should be this one.

To compute the returns on the put options, we must first compute their price. To compute that price, we use the B–S–M option-pricing model. On each evaluation date, we input the risk-free rate, dividend yield, and implied volatility taken from the end-of-day volatility surface. The monthly return on the option is simply a reflection of its price change over that time. The monthly returns on the S&P 500 are derived from the price change on the index plus dividends paid over that same time. Beta of an option, like delta, is a function of an option's moneyness and its time to expiration. Consequently, we should expect the return dynamics for different options to behave differently. For completeness, one of the goals of this analysis is to determine if there is consistency in performance across the volatility surface. It is logical to assume that this may not be the case, because the volatility surface is not flat. We explained in the last chapter that the term structure of volatility is generally upward sloping but there are times when it inverts. Furthermore, there is a volatility skew that takes the shape of a smile from time to time. The S&P 500 will actually experience a single volatility over a given time period. At the same time, there is a matrix of implied volatilities across the surface. Given this artifact of option pricing, you might expect options with certain strikes and expiration to outperform others. If this is the case, this analysis will reveal which options are best to buy and which options are best to sell on average.

The result we get from this analysis is really quite remarkable. Exhibit 4.4 summarizes the historical *monthly* return characteristics for a one-month put option on the S&P 500.

The top row of Exhibit 4.4 indicates the moneyness of the option under review. Recall that 90 percent moneyness means the option's strike price is 10 percent below the asset's market price, while 110 percent moneyness means the option's strike price is 10 percent above the asset's current market price. 100 percent moneyness represents an option that is at the money. A close examination of Exhibit 4.4 reveals some interesting characteristics about put option return behavior. Puts that are 10 percent out of the money produce a 95.4 percent *monthly* loss on average. The median loss is 100 percent. Investors who buy a one-month put option on the S&P 500 that is 10 percent out of the money should expect a total loss, and that it is a rare event for investors who buy short-dated index puts to earn a profit. In fact, a close examination of the individual data points indicate a one-month, 90-moneyness put produced a profit just 0.8 percent of the time and suffered a loss 99.2 percent of the time.

At the other end of the spectrum, one-month puts that are 10 percent in the money produce an average monthly loss of 6.6 percent and the median loss is 11.1 percent. Investors who buy 10 percent in-the-money, one-month put options on the S&P 500 should expect a monthly loss about 62 percent of the time. Said another way, investors in these options have a better chance of earning a return, as they will do so 38 percent of the time. During the time period studied, investors in these options suffered a total loss just 0.8 percent of the time. Naturally, at-the-money options performed somewhere in between these two extremes. Exhibit 4.4 reveals one clear conclusion: The more out of the money a put option is, the more likely it is to lose value over time and will do so at an ever-increasing rate.

Moneyness	90	92	94	96	98	100	102	104	106	108	110
Median	−100	−100	−100	−100	−100	−100	−67.0	−33.5	−21.1	−14.6	−11.1
Average	−95.4	−89.8	−80.3	−71.3	−59.5	−38.6	−29.1	−19.0	−12.2	−8.7	−6.6
St. Dev.	47.2	58.7	90.7	103.1	105.9	105.9	89.6	72.3	58.0	47.6	39.9

Exhibit 4.4 Historical Monthly Returns in Percentage on One-Month S&P 500 Put Options

Options come in multiple expirations. Actively traded options on SPY extend out years if LEAPS (Long-Term Equity Anticipation Securities) are included, which are long-term options. We know from an analysis of the Greeks derived from the B–S–M model that longer-dated options have different characteristics than shorter-dated ones. Longer-dated options decay more slowly than shorter-dated ones and have less gamma, all other factors being equal. Furthermore, with longer-dated options there is more time for the investment to work out in favor of the option buyer. Therefore, one might expect longer-dated options to outperform shorter-dated ones. Exhibit 4.5 compares the returns on one-month put options with those that have 2, 3, 6, and 12 months to expiration. As with Exhibit 4.4, returns are displayed as a function of moneyness. For those who want to review the results numerically, they are presented in tabular form in the notes found at the end of the book.

Exhibit 4.5 shows the historical *monthly* total return for put options on the S&P 500 covering the period from January 2005 to July 2015 for options of various terms to expiration. Since put options by definition possess a negative delta, the price of the put option should rise when the value of the index falls, and fall when the price of the underlying rises. As explained above, the capital asset pricing model tells us that securities with negative betas should deliver returns that are less than the risk-free rate. Furthermore, if the absolute value of beta is large enough, such securities should deliver negative rates of return over time. This is what we observe for put options on the S&P 500 for all expirations. While most practitioners might expect to lose money when purchasing put options used to protect the value of their portfolios, few are aware of just how large the losses have been historically. The gray dotted line in Exhibit 4.5 shows the average monthly returns of one-month put options across a variety of strike prices. The gray dashed lines, solid gray line, and the solid black

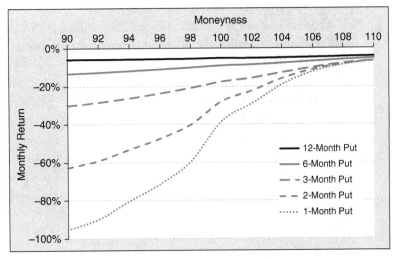

Exhibit 4.5   Historical Monthly Returns on S&P 500 Index Put Option Returns

line reveal the monthly returns for 2, 3, 6, and 12-month options, respectively. Comparing monthly returns for put options across the expirations spectrum confirms our expectations. As the time to expiration increases, the rate of loss declines. Said another way, returns improve as the time to expiration of index puts increases.

What is surprising, however, is the size of the monthly losses for options, which are just marginally out of the money or even at the money, even long-dated ones. In the case of a one-month at-the-money put option, we should expect to lose just over 38 percent of the option's value over a one-month holding period. For a similar three-month put option, we should expect it to lose just over 17 percent of the option's value over a one-month holding period. For a similar 12-month put option, expect it to lose over 5 percent of the option's value given a one-month holding period. The average loss on short-dated put options is a truly remarkable result. Remember, a one-month at-the-money put option should expire in the money about 50 percent of the time.

As a final point, note that as a put option moves into the money, its return improves markedly for short-dated options. The expected loss on a one-month or three-month option that is 10 percent in the money is just about 6 percent. There is a simple reason for this. As an option moves further in the money, it behaves more like the underlying security and less like an option on that asset. This occurs because the value of the option is increasingly derived by intrinsic value and less by time value, which falls as an option ages.

One can draw a clear conclusion from the data: When buying put options, expect to lose money. The only question is, how much? When purchasing put options, the preference should be for longer-dated ones that are in the money. When selling put options, the preference should be for shorter-dated out-of-the-money options. Finally, this analysis confirms the notion that assets with negative betas should produce negative rates of return over time.

While an analysis of the historic returns on put options is intriguing in its own right, it does not answer the question of whether put options are fairly priced. The question is, "Do the negative returns revealed in the analysis above represent a fair return on a risk-adjusted basis?" To answer this question, we must risk-adjust the returns. That is to say, we must remove the effects of beta from historical returns to see if puts provide excess, subpar, or fair returns after adjusting for the market risk embedded in these derivative instruments.

To measure the risk-adjusted performance of put options on the S&P 500, we look to the asset-pricing framework to determine if these derivative instruments provide a fair, albeit a negative, rate of return after adjusting for market risk. To do this, we revisit and reformulate the capital asset pricing model:

$$R_{put} = R_f + \beta_{put}[R_{SP500} - R_f] + \epsilon$$

Or

$$\alpha_{put} = R_{put} - \beta_{put}[R_{SP500} - R_f] - R_f$$

where:

$$\epsilon \cong E[N(0, \sigma_{error})] = \alpha_{put}$$

R_{put} represents the actual return on a put option with the S&P 500 as the underlying asset. R_{SP500} and R_f represent the return on the S&P 500 index and the return on a risk free asset over the same time period respectively. It is useful to think of β_{put} as a risk adjustment factor. Since the value of a put rises when the price of the underlying falls, we expect beta for a put to be negative. If puts closely track the returns in the S&P 500 but in the opposite direction, beta times the return on the S&P 500 should be a good predictor of returns on put options. It represents the sensitivity of a put option on the S&P 500 relative to the return on the S&P 500. There may be other factors at play that the model does not explain, which introduces noise in the analysis. If put options are fairly priced, ϵ should have a value of zero with some uncertainty around that estimate.

if ϵ is not equal to zero, α_{put} is the factor that will indicate if historical returns are fair on a risk-adjusted basis. It represents the portion of actual returns on put options that the return on the S&P 500 does not explain. When α_{put} is greater than zero, it indicates that the option outperformed the S&P 500 on a risk-adjusted basis. Under these circumstances, we would be better off buying a put as an alternative to shorting the S&P 500 index. If α_{put} turns out to be less than zero, it indicates that the option underperformed the S&P 500 on a risk-adjusted basis. In this case, we would be better off selling the S&P 500 index as an alternative to buying a put. When α_{put} is equal to zero, it indicates that the option outperformed in line with the S&P 500 on a risk-adjusted basis. Under these circumstances, we would be indifferent between buying a put and employing a strategy of shorting the S&P 500 index as a hedge.

To compute the coefficient β_{put}, we regress the monthly returns of puts against the returns on the S&P 500, holding moneyness and time to expiration constant. We repeat the regression analysis across various combinations of moneyness and expiration. By examining the returns across a strip of strikes and expirations, we can determine if the return characteristics across these descriptors are consistent.

Exhibit 4.6 summarizes the return characteristics for one-month put options on the S&P 500 parsed by moneyness. In addition, the coefficients alpha and beta are determined to quantify the risk-adjusted performance of these puts along with their sensitivity to the underlying index. To indicate how well the CAPM describes the relationship between the S&P 500 and its associated one-month put options, r-squared and correlation are summarized as well.

Money-ness	90	92	94	96	98	100	102	104	106	108	110
Median	−100.0	−100.0	−100.0	−100.0	−100.0	−100.0	−69.0	−33.5	−21.1	−14.5	−11.1
Average	−95.4	−89.8	−80.3	−71.3	−59.5	−38.6	−29.1	−19.0	−12.2	−8.7	−6.6
St. Dev.	47.2	58.7	90.7	103.1	105.9	105.9	89.6	72.3	58.0	47.6	39.9
Alpha	−92.6	−85.2	−72.5	−61.4	−47.9	−25.9	−17.5	−9.1	−4.1	−1.9	−0.9
Beta	−4.7	−7.9	−12.9	−16.5	−19.1	−20.9	−19.1	−16.3	−13.5	−11.3	−9.5
R-Sqrd	0.16	0.29	0.33	0.42	0.54	0.68	0.81	0.90	0.96	0.98	0.99
Correlation	0.40	0.54	0.57	0.65	0.74	0.83	0.90	0.95	0.98	0.99	1.00
% Gain	0.8	3.2	4.8	7.9	15.1	27.0	29.4	32.5	35.7	37.3	38.1
% Loss	99.2	96.8	95.2	92.1	84.9	73.0	70.6	67.5	64.3	62.7	61.9

Exhibit 4.6 Historical Performance Characteristics on One-Month S&P 500 Put Options

What is readily apparent from Exhibit 4.6 is that not only are returns negative for all levels of moneyness, but alpha is negative for all levels of moneyness as well. This is a clear indication that puts provide subpar rates of return. Digging a little deeper, it seems that alpha is related to the quality of fit and correlation to the underlying index. Notice that as a put option moves out of the money, r-squared and correlation fall, and alpha falls along with it. For puts that are further in the money, the quality of fit and correlation improve. This tells us that intrinsic and time value of an option play an important role in how an option performs. Options that are out of the money only have time value. That time value decreases rapidly as time passes. Therefore, for way-out-of-the-money options, theta is the primary driver of returns and price changes of the underlying security are secondary. Options that are deep in the money have far more intrinsic value than time value. As a result, the return on deep-in-the-money options is dominated by returns on the underlying instrument. Option decay has only a minor role to play.

This is an interesting result indeed. It suggests that anything but deep-in-the-money puts will substantially underperform on a risk-adjusted basis. Furthermore, the best one can hope for from buying a put option is to earn an almost fair risk-adjusted rate of return. The next question is, "How does time to expiration affect the performance of put options?"

Exhibit 4.7 shows a pattern of alpha, which is not dissimilar to the pattern of monthly returns we see in Exhibit 4.5. The gray dotted line indicates the performance on one-month put options across the moneyness spectrum. Those that are out of the money show huge negative alphas, while those that are deeply (i.e., 10 percent) in the money produce alphas that are very near zero. The gray dashed line shows the performance profile of three-month put options. It shows that out-of-the-money puts perform substantially better than one-month puts, but that is no consolation. Puts with three months to expiration still exhibit substantial underperformance on

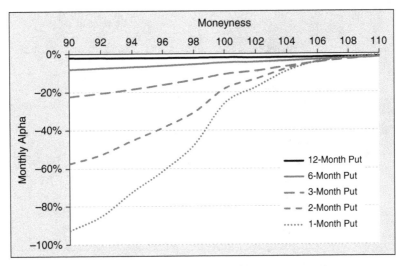

Exhibit 4.7 Historical Return Alphas on S&P 500 Index Put Options

a risk-adjusted basis. However, those that are in the money by 6 percent or more provide similar returns as their one-month cohorts. The solid black line shows the performance of 12-month puts. Interestingly, these longer-dated puts have an entirely different performance profile. They produce returns that are much more in line with their risk. Specifically, these options produced risk-adjusted returns that were negative by less than 1 percent, across the moneyness scale. The degree to which a 12-month put option is in, at, or out of the money does not seem to significantly influence its historical performance.

The above analysis once again confirms that in-the-money puts perform better than out-of-the-money options and long-dated options perform better than shorter-dated ones. While the relationship between moneyness and performance seems to be fairly linear, this is not the case with respect to expiration. Three-month puts behave more like twelve-month puts than one-month puts. This suggests that put option buyers would do well to extend expirations by just a few months. Equally as interesting, there does not seem to be a combination of strikes and expirations that put the odds in favor of the put buyer. The best result the put option buyer can expect is almost a fair rate of return.

In the final analysis, very-short-dated put options on the S&P 500 index seem to behave far differently than longer-dated options or even those that are just a few months longer. The question is why. Data in Exhibit 4.6 suggest r-squared and correlation are related to alpha. Exhibit 4.8 shows the relationship between the alpha of put options on the S&P 500 and the correlation of returns between those options and the returns on the S&P 500 itself. Recall that in a simple linear regression, correlation is simply the square root of r-squared.

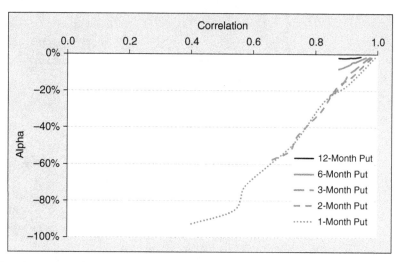

Exhibit 4.8 Historical Alpha versus Correlation

The gray dotted line in Exhibit 4.8 shows the relationship between alpha on one-month put options and the correlation of returns between those put options and the returns on the S&P 500. Notice that as correlation falls, so does alpha. Furthermore, that relationship seems to be robust and close to linear. The gray dashed line shows the relationship between r-squared and alpha for three-month options. As the reader can see, the same linear relationship between alpha and r-squared holds true for three-month put options. As correlation falls, so does alpha, and curves present very close to each other. It is not surprising to see three-month options perform better from this perspective as three-month options decay at a slower rate than one-month options. The solid black line represents the relationship between excess returns on twelve-month put options and r-squared. Interestingly, for these longer-dated put options, there does not seem to be a strong relationship between excess returns and r-squared. This is a fascinating result. Shorter-dated put options seem to have a return characteristic all their own, which is relatively unrelated to the returns generated by the underlying instrument.

To understand this phenomenon a little bit more, it is useful to examine beta as a function of moneyness. This holds the key as to why three-month options have return characteristics that look more like twelve-month puts, as opposed to one-month puts.

Exhibit 4.9 shows the relationship between the moneyness of a put option and its beta. The gray dotted line shows the relationship between beta on one-month put options and its moneyness. Notice that the beta on a one-month put is most negative for an at-the-money option, and it falls off as it moves in or out of the money. We might expect beta to fall as moneyness increases above 100 simply because the option price is driven by intrinsic value and less by time value. It therefore behaves

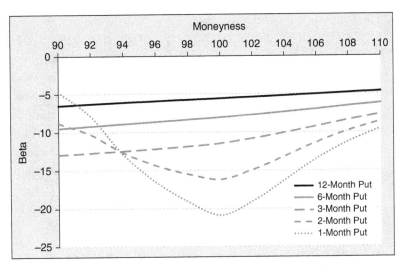

Exhibit 4.9 Put Betas versus Moneyness

more like the underlying asset. Furthermore, as the price of the option increases, its leverage to price changes of the underlying asset falls as well. Extending this line of thinking, we might expect the absolute value of beta to rise as a put option falls further out of the money, simply because it is becoming a more leveraged instrument. This is indeed the case for longer-dated options. The gray line and the solid black line display the relationship between a put option's moneyness and its beta for a six-month and twelve-month options, respectively. Notice that these are near linear relationships. As moneyness rises, the absolute value of beta falls, and it does so at the same rate whether these longer-dated options are in or out of the money.

One-month options behave differently. Beta for a one-month option falls as it moves out of the money. This phenomenon occurs because theta increases exponentially as the time to maturity falls. As a result, short-dated put options relentlessly fall in price rapidly due to time decay and this overwhelms the effects of price movement of the underlying security. In short, the price of the underlying security has to fall significantly and rapidly for it to overcome price decay on a short dated out-of-the-money put. It is predictable for the price of a short-dated put to fall, even if the price of the underlying instrument falls moderately. This is far different behavior compared to longer-dated options, which explains why one-month options do not behave like their longer-dated cohorts.

It is fair to say that most market observers and investors would not expect the results revealed by this close analysis of historical returns. With this insight uncovered, we now have the perspective necessary to improve trading and hedging performance. Given the negative alpha in put option returns, its relationship to moneyness, and time to expiration, we can make a few conclusions. All other things being equal, *one should favor longer-dated put options over shorter-dated ones.* In addition, *one should favor in-the-money put options versus those that are out of the money.* With this in mind, in the next few chapters, we will show how to incorporate this important insight when constructing option-trading strategies. Before getting into trading topics, there is more to learn about how option prices behave as they age. Put–call parity tells us that put options do not trade in a vacuum. Puts can be created synthetically by purchasing an asset and simultaneously selling calls on that asset. Since the returns on puts and calls are related, albeit in the opposite direction, we might expect call options to have similar return characteristics as put options, particularly as it pertains to alpha. The next section takes a closer look at the historical performance of call options on the S&P 500 index.

Evaluating Historical Returns on Call Options

A call option has a positive delta. Therefore, it should increase in price if the price of the S&P 500 increases, and produce a negative rate of return when the index falls. This is the definition of positive beta as well. Since the S&P 500 produced a 0.7 percent average monthly rate of return over the time period studied, we would expect a positive rate of return on its associated call options. We showed that the performance of put options is driven, at least in part, by the time to expiration and their moneyness, so we should expect that these factors influence the returns on call options as well.

Exhibit 4.10 shows the historical returns of call options on the S&P 500 from January 2005 to July 2015. Notice that call options produce a return pattern that

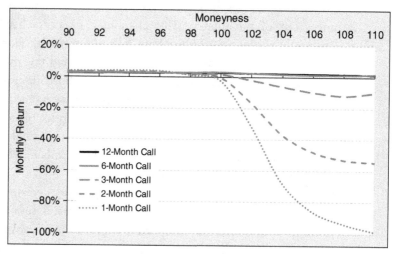

Exhibit 4.10   Historical Returns on S&P 500 Index Call Options

is very similar to those formed by put options, as revealed in Exhibit 4.5. Like those produced by one-month out-of-the-money put options, out-of-the-money call options produce very negative rates of return. Contrary to in-the-money puts, which produced negative returns, deep-in-the-money calls produced small but positive monthly rates of return of about 1-3 percent. At the other end of the expiration spectrum, 12-month call options produced positive rates of return, across all moneyness examined.

For a closer look at the numbers please see the tables in the notes at the end of the book. Interestingly, short-dated in-the-money calls produce a higher rate of return than longer-dated in-the-money calls. Not surprisingly, this relationship reverses for out-of-the-money calls. Just like put options, returns are highly negative for shorter-dated calls that are out of the money. Given these results, the CAPM would predict negative alphas for calls across the spectrum of moneyness and expiration.

Exhibit 4.11 shows the alpha produced by call options parsed by moneyness and time to expiration. Just as in the case of put options, it clearly shows that call options on the S&P 500 over the 10+ years of study underperform on a risk-adjusted basis. One-month calls that are in the money experience relatively moderate negative alphas, while those that are out of the money produce severe negative alphas. Twelve-month call options perform far better, particularly for those that are in the money. Those that are 10 percent in the money produced a negative alpha of just 0.2 percent per month, while those that are 10 percent out of the money suffer a 2.5 percent monthly negative alpha. Naturally, three-month calls display a performance that falls in between those displayed by the one and 12 month variety. In all cases, however, call options still produce unsatisfying results.

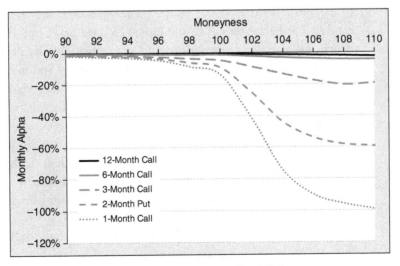

Exhibit 4.11 Historical Return Alphas on S&P 500 Index Call Options

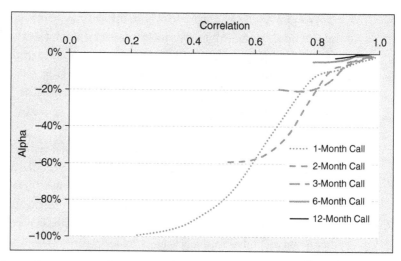

Exhibit 4.12 Historical Alpha versus Correlation

Exhibit 4.12 shows alphas on S&P 500 index calls as a function of correlation and time to expiration. Once again, correlation seems to play a role in the performance of call options much in the same way it does for put options. This analysis reveals that excess negative returns on call options are strongly related to the correlation of returns between call options and the underlying S&P 500 index. Specifically, as correlation falls, so does alpha. One-month call options exhibit the greatest variability with respect to correlation. As this short-dated option moves out of the money, its correlation to the underlying index falls rapidly. As a result, returns are driven by time decay and less by the movement of the underlying index. Longer-dated call options, such as those with 12 months to expiration, display far less sensitivity to correlation. Since time decay decreases as the time to expiration increases, this unique factor produces less systemic drag on option returns. Furthermore, out-of-the-money, longer-dated options have a higher delta, which makes them more sensitive to movements in the price of the underlying instrument. We would therefore expect longer-dated options to be more correlated with the returns on the underlying index relative to a shorter-dated option, all other things being equal. We might expect three-month call options to perform somewhere between that of a one-month and twelve-month option, and indeed this is the case for in-the-money calls. Interestingly, twelve-month options behave much more like their twelve-month brethren, than their one-month cohort. With a review of the charts above, we would rightly conclude that very-short-dated options display return characteristics that deviate from those with intermediate or long-term expirations.

Exhibit 4.13 shows the relationship between beta and moneyness for call options. Multiple curves are shown to control for time to expiration. Notice that for intermediate call options (three months to expiration) beta increases rapidly

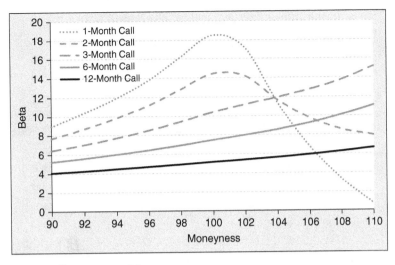

Exhibit 4.13 Call Betas versus Moneyness

for an increase in moneyness. Betas for longer-dated calls (twelve months to expiration) increase more slowly with moneyness. These monotonic relationships break down for short-dated calls (one and two months to expiration). Short-dated, deep-in-the-money calls display significant beta, and it rises like long-dated options as moneyness increases. As the strike price of the call goes out of the money, it deviates from this pattern and begins to fall. Beta approaches zero when the moneyness of the call exceeds 110. This can be explained by delta, which falls rapidly as it moves out of the money. In addition, these short-dated out-of-the-money calls only have time value, and this value declines rapidly as the option ages. Consequently, the price of the underlying instruments must rise sufficiently to overcome the time decay. This dynamic is what tears at the relationship between deep-out-of-the-money calls and the price action of the underlying index. Just like put options, it seems that the effect of price decay on short-dated options overwhelms an option's delta as it gets closer to expiration.

Conclusions about Option Returns

Most market observers and investors would not expect to find that both put and call options on the S&P 500 index would underperform the underlying index on a risk-adjusted basis. While investors might be expected to pay up at the margin for options to capture their asymmetric return characteristics, most would be surprised by the magnitude of negative alphas these index options produce. Nonetheless, investors should take these results at face value and come to some obvious conclusions:

■ Longer-dated options tend to outperform shorter-dated options.

- In-the-money options tend to outperform out-of-the-money options.
- Calls tend to outperform puts at the margin.

This suggests that to construct optimal option strategies, you should find a way to buy longer-dated in-the-money options, while simultaneously selling shorter-dated out-of-the-money options. This, of course, must be done in the context of one's investment objective. If you are constructing an option trade for either hedging or offensive purposes, you are looking to capture a certain delta, either positive or negative. Therefore, you need to mix and match individual options that will produce the desired return given the intended directional move, while minimizing the effects of negative alpha. Better yet, construct strategies that use an option's negative alpha to your advantage.

We know from the presentation of gamma scalping that there is a relationship between gamma (how much delta drifts with a move in the price of the underlying index) and theta (the measure of an option's time decay). Therefore, to minimize the drag due to theta, investors must give up the return kicker provided by gamma. This is not necessarily a bad trade-off. An investor usually needs a large volatility move for gamma to earn its keep. When hedging or trading for offensive purposes based on fundamentals, the buy-and-hold investor is concerned with how the option or combination of options will perform with a change in the underlying instrument over time. Unfortunately, most options strategies come with gamma the investor does not necessarily need, and time decay that the investor does not want. Therefore, buy-and-hold investors should look for strategies that are gamma neutral, as they will also be theta neutral, or nearly so. Later chapters, will discuss options strategies at length that capture these characteristics to produce better results than many of the common strategies followed by expert and novice investors alike.

If we knew how option-pricing models work and did not have data to test the result of that model, we would not expect to get the results presented above. Since the efficient market hypothesis tells us that the price of large and liquid securities should reflect all available information, we would expect that options on such securities would be fairly priced as well. After all, options are supposed to be priced in an arbitrage-free environment. So why do we witness big negative alphas? The following will go into this question more deeply and propose an answer to this question.

Why Do Options Behave as If They Are Overpriced?

To understand why options underperform for the buy-and-hold investor, we need to take a closer look at the characteristics of options. We showed in Chapter 2 that the performance of an option is driven by a number of components. The total differential is a decomposition of those components and reveals the true characteristic of a naked option.

$$\Delta C = Delta \times \Delta S + 0.5 Gamma \times \Delta S^2 + Vega \times \Delta \sigma$$
$$+ Theta \times \Delta t + Rho \times \Delta r + Phi \times \Delta q$$

The equation clearly shows that an option is a multidimensional financial product. For any given investment horizon, its return will be driven by the change in price of the underlying asset, the change in iVol, the passing of time, the change in interest rates, and the change in the dividend rate on the underlying instrument. Changes in interest rates and dividends on the underlying instrument have a negligible effect on the performance of an option, leaving a change in price, volatility, and time as the primary determinants of total return. As a result, for a buy-and-hold investor an option is both a directional and a volatility instrument.

The arbitrage condition that defines an option's price indicates that an option can be replicated by dynamically trading the underlying instrument. To synthetically create a call, simply buy the underlying instrument weighted by the delta of the option you wish to replicate. This is the foundation for gamma scalping. When the underlying instrument is sold against a call delta neutral, the resulting package of financial instruments is a pure volatility instrument. This tells us that the time premium of an option depends only on volatility. Since the price action of the underlying security can be hedged away, the market does not compensate option investors for price changes, only the volatility of those price changes. It does so because volatility, both implied and realized, is the only significant risk inherent in the delta-hedged option. When investors buy exposure to that risk, they pay for it with time decay. The following should help with the intuition.

When hedging, a trader is agnostic about which way the price of the underlying asset moves. If it goes up over an instantaneously small time period, so does the value of the call option. That gain is offset by a loss in the value of the hedge. If the price of the underlying asset goes down, the price of the call option will go down as well. That loss is offset by a gain on the value of the hedge. When purchasing an option delta hedged, traders are not agnostic about realized volatility, however. When purchasing an option delta hedged, an investor is buying a certain level of volatility. The direction of the price action is of no concern. It is the magnitude of the price action that matters. If realized volatility turns out to be higher than implied volatility, gamma will ensure the investor gains. If it turns out to be lower, the investor loses.

This is not the case for a naked option position. The future value of a naked call option has both a volatility component and a price direction component. In other words, the future value of a naked option is dependent in large part on the path of the price action of the underlying instrument. Holding iVol constant, the price of the underlying instrument must rise for a call to increase in price and the price of a put will only increase in value if the price of the underlying instrument falls. Options lose value as they age. For a call option to produce a positive rate of return, the price on the underlying instrument must move up to offset and exceed its daily price decay. If the price of the underlying falls, a call option suffers a double whammy. The delta effect will drive the price of a call down and time decay will compound the loss. Likewise, for a put option to increase in price, the value of the underlying instrument must fall enough to offset the loss caused by its price decay. If the price of the underlying increases, a put option suffers a double whammy as well. The delta will drive the price of a put down and time decay will compound the loss. This should make one point abundantly clear. When buying an option, success is dependent on both the direction of a price change and the magnitude of that change as well.

If the price of the underlying asset moves in the appropriate direction, that move must be large enough to offset time decay. For that move to be large enough, it must exceed the iVol used to price the option. One way to think about this is that the delta and gamma effect must exceed the theta effect. This assumes, of course, that there is no change in implied volatility, the risk-free rate, the dividend yield, or the cost of borrowing the underlying instrument. Gamma only has a significant role in the price change of an option for large moves in the underlying instrument. As a result, we can put it aside to get a sense of the price move needed by the underlying security to offset time decay for the buy and hold investor. To estimate a breakeven point, all we need to do, therefore, is to compare the delta effect to the theta effect. In the last chapter, we discussed gamma scaling the S&P 500. In that example, the price of the underlying was $1,600 and the strike price of the call was $1,600. The following is a numerical example.

$$\text{Change in call price} > 0 \quad \text{if Option delta } \Delta S > \text{Theta } \Delta t/365$$

Or

$$\text{One-day change in price of the underlying} > \frac{\text{Theta}/365}{\text{Delta}}$$

$$\text{One-day change in price of the underlying} > \frac{142/365}{0.46} = \$0.85$$

On the first day of this simulation, the price of the underlying must rise by $0.85 over a one-day horizon, just to break even. Anything less than that and the call option will decline in value over a one-day investment horizon. Since theta rises as an option ages, the rate of increase will have to accelerate over time. Over the life of the option, the price of the underlying must rise by $0.94 per day on average ([price of the option + [strike price − underlying price]/days to expiration, ([52.57 + {1632 − 1600}]/90) just for the investor to break even. Furthermore, to enjoy a gain on this option over its 90-day life, the price of the underlying would have to rise by $84.57, or 5.28 percent. This is a 22.88 percent move on an annualized basis, which is about twice the S&P 500 average annual rate of return for the past 100 plus years.

There are two basic ways for this option to manifest a positive rate of return over its life. Either the price of the underlying has to have a big jump in just a few days, or the price of the underlying must methodically rise day after day. In mathematical lingo, this is called autocorrelation, which is a statistical measure that indicates return dependency through time. An autocorrelation coefficient of 1.0 tells us that whatever happened today will definitely happen again tomorrow. A value between 0.0 and 1.0 tells us whatever happened today will *likely* happen tomorrow. In short, an autocorrelation coefficient greater than zero tells us there is a trend in place. An autocorrelation coefficient of 0.0 tells us that whatever happens tomorrow will be independent of what happens today. This is a tenant of the efficient market hypothesis. There is absolutely no trend and daily price action is purely random. An autocorrelation coefficient of −1.0 indicates the exact opposite will happen tomorrow as compared to what happened today. A value between 0.0 and −1.0 tells us whatever happened today will *likely not* happen tomorrow. Negative autocorrelation indicates mean reversion. This is a process where prices tend to reverse direction from extremes and drift back toward some long-term average.

The efficient market hypothesis suggests that price changes tomorrow are independent of price changes today. Tests of the efficient market hypothesis suggest this might be true over the long run, but the success of trend following as an investment strategy indicates that asset prices autocorrelate over short and sometimes intermediate time frames. We tend to see autocorrelation in the broad market averages and for some asset classes. Bull markets are characterized by positive autocorrelation and bear markets are associated with negative autocorrelation. What is important to recognize is that the more an option is out of the money, the more the price changes of the underlying asset need to autocorrelate in order for the option to increase in value over its life. We should think of autocorrelation as a descriptor of path dependence. One way to gain some intuition around path dependence is to examine a binomial tree of price action. (For those who are unfamiliar with the fundamental concepts of binomial tree construction, more detail is provided in the notes.)

Exhibit 4.14 shows an example of a 30-day binomial tree of price movements for the S&P 500 assuming 20 percent volatility, which is consistent with the example followed thus far. The far left of the chart shows the index value at each price node. To allow the tree to fit on a single sheet, each node represents the passing of three trading days. At each of these nodes there are two figures. The top figure indicates the value of the call option at that node. The number below it represents the probability the option will finish in the money. The figures on the far righthand side represent the probability the index will end between the particular values indicated on the left-hand side of the chart.

Days to Expiration

Underlying Price	30	27	24	21	18	15	12	9	6	3	–	Probability of Event	Cum Prob
1917.60											$285.60	0.1%	0.1%
1883.19										$251.46 / 100.0%		0.5%	0.6%
1849.40									$217.94 / 100.0%		$217.40	2.3%	2.9%
1816.21								$185.02 / 100.0%		$184.48 / 100.0%		7.4%	10.3%
1783.62							$152.83 / 99.3%		$152.16 / 100.0%		$151.62	16.1%	26.4%
1751.62						$122.03 / 95.9%		$120.64 / 98.8%		$119.89 / 100.0%		23.6%	50.0%
1720.19					$93.91 / 88.2%		$91.17 / 92.7%		$89.03 / 98.0%		$88.19	23.6%	50.0%
1689.32				$69.75 / 76.4%		$65.77 / 80.3%		$61.60 / 86.4%		$57.91 / 97.2%		16.1%	26.4%
1659.00			$50.21 / 62.6%		$45.65 / 64.4%		$40.42 / 67.5%		$34.06 / 73.9%		$27.00	7.4%	10.3%
1629.24		$35.18 / 48.8%		$30.74 / 48.6%		$25.66 / 48.3%		$19.46 / 47.8%		$10.59 / 46.3%		2.3%	2.9%
1600.00	$24.11 / 36.5%		$20.23 / 35.0%		$15.95 / 32.8%		11.09 / 29.3%		5.35 / 22.0%		0.00	0.5%	0.6%
1571.29		13.08 / 24.3%		9.79 / 21.5%		6.34 / 17.5%		2.87 / 11.4%		0.20 / 1.8%			
1543.09			5.96 / 13.7%		3.65 / 10.4%		1.59 / 6.1%		0.22 / 1.4%		0.00		
1515.40				2.10 / 6.1%		0.89 / 3.4%		0.16 / 0.9%		0.00 / 0.0%			
1488.21					0.51 / 1.9%		0.10 / 0.5%		0.00 / 0.0%		0.00		
1461.51						0.07 / 0.3%		0.00 / 0.0%		1.46 / 0.0%			
1435.28							0.00 / 0.0%		0.00 / 0.0%		0.00		
1409.53								0.00 / 0.0%		1.46 / 0.0%			
1384.23									0.00 / 0.0%		0.00		
1359.39										0.67 / 0.0%			
1335.00											0.00	0.10%	0.10%

Exhibit 4.14

A 30-day, 1,632-strike call option with the underlying index at 1,600 has a value of $24.11 and there is a 36.5 percent chance the option will expire in the money. If after three days the index falls by one standard deviation to 1,571.29, the value of the option falls to $13.08 and the probability of it finishing in the money falls by about a third to 24.3 percent. If the price of the underlying rises by one standard deviation to 1,629.24, its price rises to $35.18, and the probability it expires in the money increases to 48.8 percent.

The gray shaded areas shown at the upper end of the chart indicate the autocorrelated price paths that produce the maximum potential for the call option to finish in the money. Notice that if the price of the index follows one of the nonhighlighted paths, the probability that the option will finish in the money falls quite rapidly, and this is reflected in the option's price. This tells us that when buying an out-of-the-money option, price must move in the desired direction from the get-go, or the odds move quickly against the investor. If the price of the index follows one of these nonhighlighted paths, the price of the underlying needs to experience a large, multi-standard deviation up move sometime in one of the later periods. This, by definition, is a very low probability event, particularly for an index. If an extraordinary price jump does not occur, the option is destined to expire worthless. Since autocorrelation tends to be a temporary phenomenon, we can now understand why options, particularly those that are out of the money, tend to have negative alphas when analyzed on a term basis.

Final Thought

In this chapter, we showed that buying short-dated, out-of-the-money index options puts the investor at a disadvantage from a statistical perspective. While options across the moneyness and expiration spectrum are fairly priced, they behave as if they are ovepriced for the buy-and-hold investor. The reader should find this a very important and helpful insight. Few investors buy or sell options on a delta-neutral basis. This is the purview of volatility traders and market makers. Most investors buy options with a view that the price of the underlying security will move in a particular direction over a defined period of time. They usually choose options over the underlying instrument because they want leverage to support their conviction, or they are looking to limit their risk if their opinion turns out to be incorrect. As we have seen in earlier chapters, options have a number of attributes. While an investor might want a certain amount of delta to capture a directional move, many option strategies require the investor to buy gamma whether they want it or not. They pay for that gamma with time decay, as represented by theta. Option traders and investors who want to be successful in the long run need to find ways to shed or at least manage time decay. The first step in that process is to buy options whose negative alpha is small and sell another option with a larger negative alpha, while simultaneously capturing the delta needed to capture the directional view the investor possesses. In doing so, investors will find that they are reducing gamma or removing it all together. In the extreme, they might want to sell gamma at the margin to allow time decay to work in their favor. This is not altogether bad. Many option strategies allow the investor to construct spreads with the desired delta and carry little or no gamma and theta locally, but still retain limits on downside risk. We will talk about how to do this in the chapters ahead.

## CHAPTER 5

Fundamental Option Strategies

In Chapter 2, we presented the mathematics behind the price behavior of put and call options. A deep understanding of the Greeks is necessary for option traders to comprehend the risks they take and build an intuition about how their portfolio will behave as market prices change in real time. In Chapter 3, we presented an exhaustive discussion of volatility and how one can create strategies to take advantage of this important determinant of option pricing and behavior. With this theoretical foundation in hand, we examined the historical return characteristics of S&P 500 index options in Chapter 4, looking for clues that will lead the investor to make optimal choices when constructing single or multileg option strategies. Since most investors use options to express a directional view on individual stocks, stock indexes, commodities, currencies, or other assets, they need to know how an option's price will change as it ages. Few practitioners have delved into an analysis of historic option behavior, putting them at a disadvantage in their investing activity. In order to win in the options market, we must incorporate the critical insights uncovered in Chapter 4. By merging an understanding of the theoretical and historical return behavior of options, even the most seasoned practitioners will alter the way they structure their option trades to increase the probability of success and produce the desired results.

This chapter will discuss an array of option strategies that are used by professionals on a daily basis. Some of these strategies are simple and straightforward, while others might be a bit more complex. The ultimate purpose will be to give you a way of thinking about your investment objectives so you can select the proper option strategy, while tweaking expiration dates and strike prices to produce consistent and optimal results. Investors most commonly use simple option strategies for both hedging and directional price anticipation trades. This discussion will begin with the development of directional trades and finish with a dialogue of hedging strategies.

■ Single-Leg Puts and Calls

A single-leg structure characterizes the simplest directional strategy, where a single option is used to anticipate a directional move. If the price of the underlying is expected to rise, the investors will either buy a call or sell a put, depending on the magnitude of the rise expected. If a large move in price is expected, purchasing a call is the most appropriate way to capture the opportunity for a significant capital gain. If, on the other hand, moderate price movement is expected, an investor might sell a put option for the opportunity to capture time premium. It is important to remember that when going long an option, you are investing for capital gains. When selling options, you are looking to collect time premium as a yield play. While buying a call and selling a put both have similar price action for small changes in the price of the underlying security, they have very different risk and return characteristics for static and large price changes. It is very important to understand the different risk profiles these strategies have in order to select the one that is most appropriate for your expectation of future price action. You must consider risk tolerance as well. Buying a call often entails a high probability of losing some or all the option premium paid, for the chance of a large capital gain. Selling a put often entails a high probability of collecting and keeping premium with the potential risk of a large capital loss. To build a better understanding of the performance characteristics of these important derivative instruments, the payoff patterns for these strategies are presented in Exhibits 5.1 and Exhibit 5.2. We start with the static payoff pattern and quantify the Greeks along with the aging characteristics for a call and put option respectively.

Primary Characteristics

Current Price = $25.00

Strike Price = $25.00

Time to Expiration = 3 months

Risk-free Rate = 2.00%

Dividend Yield = 1.00%

Implied Volatility = 35%

Call Price = $1.77

Put Price = $1.71

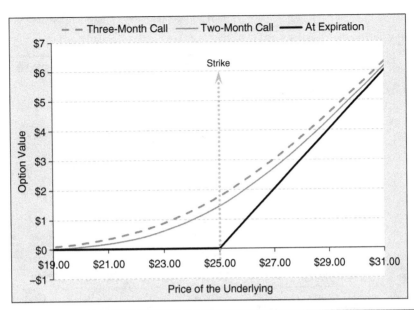

Underlying	$19.00	$21.00	$23.00	$25.00	$27.00	$29.00	$31.00
% Change	−24%	−16%	−8%	0%	8%	16%	24%
Price	$0.10	$0.34	$0.88	$1.77	$3.02	$4.56	$6.30
Change (%)	−94	−81	−51	0	71	158	256
Delta	0.071	0.185	0.353	0.539	0.704	0.827	0.906
Gamma	0.041	0.073	0.092	0.090	0.073	0.050	0.030
Vega	1.290	2.801	4.266	4.949	4.639	3.675	2.544
Theta	−0.915	−1.992	−3.050	−3.563	−3.377	−2.721	−1.936
Zeta	5.0%	14.2%	29.1%	47.1%	64.3%	78.1%	87.6%

Exhibit 5.1 Payoff Pattern of a Long Three-Month At-the-Money Call

Maximum gain = Unlimited

Maximum loss = Option premium

Breakeven at expiration = Strike + Premium paid

A long call is a leveraged play on the upside price action of the underlying instrument. Notice that if the price of the underlying security instantaneously rises 24 percent from $25.00 to $31.00 a share, the price of the call will rise 256 percent as its price goes from $1.77 to $6.30. The downside of this strategy is the risk of a loss in value due to a drop in the price of the underlying security, and price decay the investor suffers as time passes. The grey dashed line in Exhibit 5.1 shows the price pattern for a three-month call option given an instantaneous change in the price of the underlying security. The solid gray line shows the payoff pattern of that option after one month has passed. If the price of the underlying security does not change

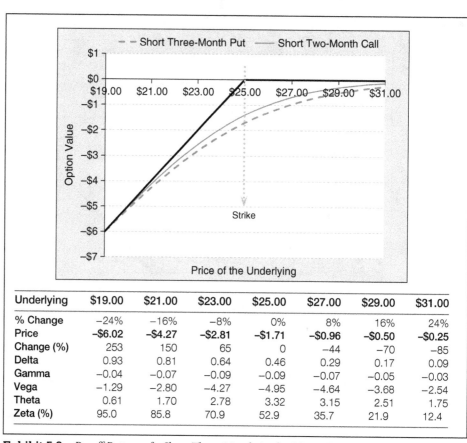

Underlying	$19.00	$21.00	$23.00	$25.00	$27.00	$29.00	$31.00
% Change	−24%	−16%	−8%	0%	8%	16%	24%
Price	−$6.02	−$4.27	−$2.81	−$1.71	−$0.96	−$0.50	−$0.25
Change (%)	253	150	65	0	−44	−70	−85
Delta	0.93	0.81	0.64	0.46	0.29	0.17	0.09
Gamma	−0.04	−0.07	−0.09	−0.09	−0.07	−0.05	−0.03
Vega	−1.29	−2.80	−4.27	−4.95	−4.64	−3.68	−2.54
Theta	0.61	1.70	2.78	3.32	3.15	2.51	1.75
Zeta (%)	95.0	85.8	70.9	52.9	35.7	21.9	12.4

Exhibit 5.2   Payoff Pattern of a Short Three-Month At-the-Money Put

$$\text{Maximum gain} = \text{Option premium}$$
$$\text{Maximum loss} = \text{Strike price} - \text{Option premium collected}$$
$$\text{Breakeven} = \text{Strike} - \text{Premium collected}$$

over a one-month time horizon, the call option will fall by 18 percent from $1.77 to $1.44. Naturally, losses will be compounded if the price of the underlying falls.

Even as the price of the underlying rises, time decay chips away at the investor's gains. For this at-the-money option, the price of the underlying must rise by the premium paid in order for the investor to break even at expiration. The advantage of owning an option is that the most the option holder can lose is the premium paid up front, which is a fraction of the price of the underlying security. In the final analysis, when purchasing call options, investors are buying a leveraged instrument with limited downside risk relative to the value of the underlying instrument. They pay for this limited downside risk by paying a time premium.

A short put position is a yield play on the price action of the underlying instrument. While there is about a 50 percent chance of an at-the-money option ultimately expiring worthless, it exposes the investor to a leveraged risk on downside price action. Like a call, it has an asymmetric payoff pattern, but with the opposite characteristics. Notice that if the price of the underlying instantaneously increases $6.00 from $25.00 to $31.00, the price of the put will fall by $1.46 from $1.71 to $0.25. The gain in dollar terms is limited to the premium collected for writing the put no matter how high the price of the underlying security rises. Fortunately, there is a better-than-even chance that this will occur for options that are at or out of the money. The downside to this strategy is that if the price of the underlying falls, the seller will be compelled to buy the underlying asset at the strike price, which might be substantially higher than the market price. If, for example, the price of the underlying asset falls by 24 percent, the value of the put will rise from $1.71 to $6.02 for a loss of $4.31, or 253 percent. This shows that investors can lose multiples of the premiums collected when writing a naked or unhedged option. In the case of a short put, the maximum an investor can lose is equal to the strike price minus the premium collected. When writing an uncovered call, the potential loss is unlimited as there is not an upper bound to an asset's price.

The dotted line in Exhibit 5.2 shows the price pattern of a short three-month put option for an instantaneous change in the price of the underlying security. The solid gray line shows the payoff pattern of that option after one month has passed. If the price of the underlying security does not change over a one-month time horizon, the value of the put option will fall 18 percent from $1.71 to $1.40. This will produce a gain of $0.31 for the option seller. Puts are very interesting derivative instruments, as they are a form of insurance. The writer of a put option is selling price insurance to the option buyer and collecting an insurance premium for taking the risk the price of the underlying security might fall. If the price of the underlying asset falls, the buyer will file a claim and collect on the insurance policy by exercising his or her right to sell.

When buying a call option, an investor has the potential for an open-ended gain but has to suffer time decay to capture that opportunity. When selling a put, the investor has the benefit of time decay but must take the risk of significant loss to get it. Under most circumstances, practitioners want to manage downside risk while getting exposure to the upside they desire. To do this, many sophisticated traders use spreads.

Vertical Spreads

The most common spread structure employed by professional investors is known as the vertical spread. A vertical spread can be either a bullish or bearish strategy and is constructed with two legs. A long vertical call spread is a bullish strategy, while a long put spread is a bearish strategy. Each leg references the same underlying security and has the same expiration date. The legs differ by employing differing strike prices. In a bullish call spread, the investor buys a call with strike price X and sells another call with a strike price higher than X. The return profile on this structure differs from that of single-leg call option in that the maximum gain is capped by selling the upside call. Vertical call spreads are generally preferred to buying a call outright because it requires less cash up front and suffers less return drag due to time decay. A vertical put spread has a similar structure, but the strikes are reversed. Specifically, an investor purchases a put option with a strike price of Y, and sells a put option with a strike price less than Y.

A trader can be long or short spread structures in order to take advantage of expected price changes in the underlying instrument. When purchasing a spread, investors are positioning their portfolios for a capital gain should the price of the underlying security move in the appropriate direction. Like selling an option outright, selling a spread is generally a yield play. The seller of the spread collects the premium up front with the expectation that both options will expire worthless. The risk the seller takes is that the price of the underlying moves against him and he suffers a limited capital loss. The following is the payoff pattern for a bullish call spread.

An examination of Exhibit 5.3 reveals a payoff pattern for a call spread that is remarkably different from the payoff pattern produced by simply buying a call option alone. Note the following differences:

- The upfront capital commitment for buying a call spread is $1.39, which is $0.38 less than buying a call outright.

- The potential price of a call spread is limited and hits its maximum value when the price of the underlying security rises to or above the upper strike price at expiration. In this case, the maximum price the spread can attain at expiration is $5.00. This occurs when the price of the underlying hits $30.00 a share or higher.

- Since the premium paid up front is less than purchasing a call on its own, time decay is substantially less for a call spread as well. In this case, theta for the call spread is −1.29 at the initiation of the trade versus −3.56 for a single-leg call. This indicates that the time decay is reduced by over 63 percent in the early days of the trade. Recall that theta increases as an option ages. In a static one-month holding period scenario, the call spread will have a value of $1.25, which is a drop of just $0.14. By contrast, time decay under the same scenario for a single-leg at-the-money call falls by about $0.33.

- As a give-up for reduced time decay, the call spread carries lower gamma than a single-leg call. In fact, gamma turns negative when the price of the underlying asset increases. In this example, it turns negative when the price of the underlying hits $27.00. This occurs because the upside potential of a call spread is capped at the upper strike. As the price of the underlying approaches the upper strike,

Long, Three-Month, Vertical (Bullish) Call Spread

Buy $25.00 Strike Call at	$1.77
Sell $30.00 Strike Call at	$0.38
Net Debit	$1.39

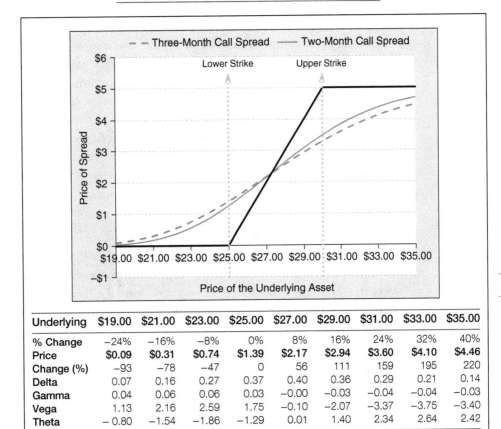

Underlying	$19.00	$21.00	$23.00	$25.00	$27.00	$29.00	$31.00	$33.00	$35.00
% Change	−24%	−16%	−8%	0%	8%	16%	24%	32%	40%
Price	$0.09	$0.31	$0.74	$1.39	$2.17	$2.94	$3.60	$4.10	$4.46
Change (%)	−93	−78	−47	0	56	111	159	195	220
Delta	0.07	0.16	0.27	0.37	0.40	0.36	0.29	0.21	0.14
Gamma	0.04	0.06	0.06	0.03	−0.00	−0.03	−0.04	−0.04	−0.03
Vega	1.13	2.16	2.59	1.75	−0.10	−2.07	−3.37	−3.75	−3.40
Theta	− 0.80	−1.54	−1.86	−1.29	0.01	1.40	2.34	2.64	2.42

Exhibit 5.3 Payoff Pattern of a Long Three-Month Vertical (Bullish) Call Spread

Maximum gain = Upper strike − Lower strike − Premium paid

Maximum loss = Premium paid

Breakeven = Lower strike + Premium paid

the rate at which the call spread increases in price slows down rapidly, until it reaches a point where it becomes relatively insensitive to the price of the underlying security.

■ If the price of the underlying asset rises toward the upper strike shortly after the initiation of the trade, the price of the short upper strike call increases faster on a percentage basis but slower on an absolute basis than the price of the lower strike call. This is what causes gamma to fall and eventually turn negative. As gamma turns negative, it causes the value of the spread to become less sensitive to changes to the underling security (i.e., it causes delta to fall). Since there is a trade-off between gamma and theta, theta turns positive and the structure will generate a yield. At this point, time works in favor of the call spread, and it will increase in price as it ages.

A call spread will outperform a single-leg call under most circumstances because the capital cost is lower, the time decay is less, and the probability that the price of the underlying goes above the upper strike at expiration is small at just 13.2 percent in this example. In other words, this call spread will outperform the naked call described earlier 86.8 percent of the time.

When structuring a spread trade, there are several factors to consider to ensure that there is enough reward for the risk taken. There are no free lunches, so we must make trade-offs when structuring a spread trade. The most important factor is the strikes used and, secondarily, the time to expiration selected. When constructing a call spread, we consider the following issues:

- Investors buy call spreads to capture a directional move. To make the payoff worthwhile, we try to select a combination of strikes that creates the potential for returns with a 3:1 payoff or better. In this example, we risk $1.39 for an opportunity to make $3.61 (5.00 − 1.39), for a 2.6:1 payoff. To increase the potential for a larger payoff, we would need to increase the upper strike by $1.00. There is a trade-off for doing this, however:

  - The capital required up front is higher because the price of the option sold is lower, time decay increases, as does gamma as well.

  - On the plus side, the band between the upper and lower strike is higher creating a higher upside potential.

- If the higher cost is unsatisfactory, we can increase both the upper and lower strikes. This has a number of trade-offs as well:

  - Increasing the two strikes reduces the upfront debt amount, which allows for a higher payoff ratio.

  - Since both options are further out of the money, there is a higher probability that the price of the underlying will not fall within the spread band at expiration. In the original structure, there was a 47.1 percent chance that the price of the underlying asset would be above $25.00 at expiration. By moving the lower strike up by $1.00, this probability falls to 38.3 percent. If the price of the underlying does not rise above the lower strike, the spread will expire worthless.

- The cash required to buy a call spread is a function of the volatility skew. In the most ideal case the implied volatility of the out-of-the-money option is greater than the in- or at-the-money call. This is the case when skew takes the shape of a "smile." This allows the investor to sell a more expensive upper strike call, which both minimizes the cash required up front while reducing time decay.

- The time to expiration must be long enough to allow a trade to fulfill its purpose. Investors can use shorter-dated options, as shown in this example, and roll the spread after a month to minimize losses due to time decay. Alternatively, investors can employ a longer-dated call spread. There is a trade-off with this second choice, however. A longer-dated call spread will require more capital up front and will have a lower delta than a shorter-dated one. Consequently, a longer-dated call spread will have less price sensitivity to an immediate change in the price of the underlying security.

A vertical put spread is a bearish strategy. We can take a bearish strategy and make it a bullish one by selling it short. If we expect the price of the underlying to remain stable or rise only marginally, we can write a vertical put spread to capture this expected price dynamic. This is a similar strategy to writing a naked put. One converts a short put into a short put spread by purchasing a downside put to eliminate the risk of runaway losses. Exhibit 5.4 displays the payoff pattern for a short put spread.

A short put spread gives the investor the opportunity to profit should they expect the price of the underlying instrument to stagnate or increase in price. Like a short single-leg put, it is in some sense a yield play. One gains as time decay does its job. That gain will accelerate if the price of the underlying security increases. The purpose of purchasing a downside put to complement a short at- or near-the-money put is to limit the losses should the value of the underlying instrument fall substantially. One way to think about a short put spread is to compare it to "first-loss insurance." In a first-loss homeowner's insurance policy, for example, the insurance company pays for damage to a home, but only to a point. The insurance company providing first-loss protection collects a premium for taking that risk. After the maximum benefit is reached, the homeowner or another insurance company picks up the remainder of the loss. In a short put spread, a trader sells price insurance at the money and buys price insurance out of the money. By selling first-loss price insurance, the investor collects a smaller premium as compared to the single-leg put, which would fully cover the put buyer for all losses. In this example, the investor collects $1.53, as opposed to a short put, where the investor collects $1.71.

The dashed gray line in Exhibit 5.4 shows the price behavior of a short put spread given an instantaneous change in the price of the underlying security. Notice it has the same shape as a long call spread. The solid gray line shows the payoff pattern of the same short put spread after one month has passed. If price of the underlying security does not change over a one-month time horizon, the value of the put spread will fall by 14 percent from $1.53 to $1.32. Since they are short this put spread, the investors will earn $0.21.

Short, Three-Month Vertical (Bearish) Put Spread

Sell $25.00 Strike Put at	$1.71
Buy $20.00 Strike Put at	$0.18
Net Credit	$1.53

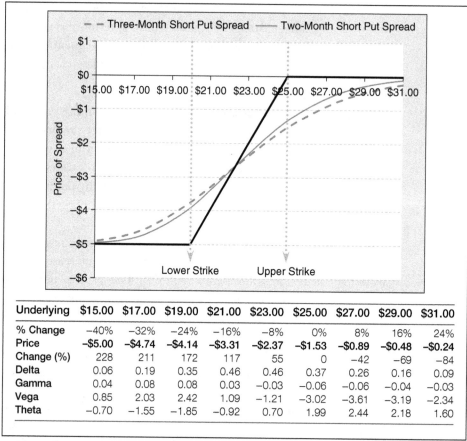

Underlying	$15.00	$17.00	$19.00	$21.00	$23.00	$25.00	$27.00	$29.00	$31.00
% Change	−40%	−32%	−24%	−16%	−8%	0%	8%	16%	24%
Price	−$5.00	−$4.74	−$4.14	−$3.31	−$2.37	−$1.53	−$0.89	−$0.48	−$0.24
Change (%)	228	211	172	117	55	0	−42	−69	−84
Delta	0.06	0.19	0.35	0.46	0.46	0.37	0.26	0.16	0.09
Gamma	0.04	0.08	0.08	0.03	−0.03	−0.06	−0.06	−0.04	−0.03
Vega	0.85	2.03	2.42	1.09	−1.21	−3.02	−3.61	−3.19	−2.34
Theta	−0.70	−1.55	−1.85	−0.92	0.70	1.99	2.44	2.18	1.60

Exhibit 5.4   Payoff Pattern of a Short Three-Month Vertical (Bearish) Put Spread

Maximum gain = Premium collected

Maximum loss = Upper strike − Lower strike − Premium collected

Breakeven = Upper strike − Premium

■ Ratio Spreads

In the typical spread structure, a trader buys and sells an equal number of options. Some practitioners look for ways to commit less cash up front as a way to get more bang for their investment dollar. Others simply look for ways to either minimize time decay, or, if possible, even profit from it. To implement these objectives, professionals often use ratio spreads. In a typical long ratio call spread, an investor buys a near- or at-the-money call option and sells multiple out-of-the-money options. A common ratio call spread is known as a 1 × 2 (one by two) ratio call spread. In this structure, an investor buys a single at-the-money call and sells two out-of-the-money calls. There is no magic to this ratio. Some professionals use 1 × 3s and even higher-order ratios if that suits their objective. A ratio call spread is really a mixed strategy. It is a bullish strategy, but only to a point. As the price of the underlying security increases, so will the price of a ratio call spread. Once the price of the underlying approaches the upper strike, the options sold begin to dominate the return performance of the spread. Since those calls are sold short, the delta of the spread turns negative and the spread loses value as the price of the underlying continues to increase. As a result, a ratio call spread is a useful strategy for investors who are bullish on the price of the underlying asset but not overly enthusiastic. The following example and Exhibit 5.5 show this graphically.

The gray dashed line in Exhibit 5.5 shows the payoff pattern for a 1 × 2 vertical call spread with three months to expiration given an instantaneous change in the price of the underlying security. The cash required to initiate this structure is just $1.01, which is far less than a single-leg call ($1.77) or a generic vertical call spread ($1.39). The reader should be aware that this is a levered option strategy and margin will be required to sell the additional upside call. Since one is selling multiple calls, the delta of this position is very small compared to a single-leg call (0.54) or a vertical call spread (0.37) at just 0.19. This occurs because when selling an upside call, the investor is selling delta at the same time. Consequently, this position will rise in value as the price of the underlying increases, but at a slower rate than the other two structures. Notice from Exhibit 5.5 that the gamma of this spread is negative. This tells us that the spread will lose upside sensitivity as the price of the underlying rises and does so at an ever-increasing rate. When the price of the underlying hits $28.00 the delta of this ratio call spread goes to zero. At this point, the ratio call spread is completely insensitive to small changes in the price of the underlying security. As it rises further, the delta actually becomes negative. At this point, the ratio call spread loses value as the price of the underlying trades above the delta inflection point. If the price of the underlying rises high enough, this structure will generate a loss for the investor. In theory, a ratio call spread can produce an unlimited loss, as the price of the underlying asset is unbounded.

A ratio call spread will produce the maximum return if the price of the underlying security rises to the upper strike at expiration. Under these circumstances, the price of the long at-the-money option rises from $1.77 to $5.00 and the two upper strike calls expire worthless. Since investors committed just $1.01 to this trade, the payoff is almost 5:1. Investors like this leveraged return potential creating a seemingly attractive risk/reward trade-off. But, trading ratio spreads is a particularly tricky affair. Not only does a trader have to get direction right, they must get the

Long, 1 × 2, Three-Month, Ratio Call Spread

Buy 1, $25.00 Strike call at $1.77	$1.77
Sell 2, $30.00 Strike call at $0.38	$0.76
Net Debit	$1.01

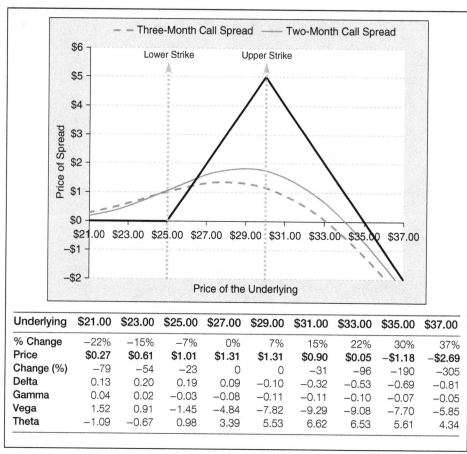

Underlying	$21.00	$23.00	$25.00	$27.00	$29.00	$31.00	$33.00	$35.00	$37.00
% Change	−22%	−15%	−7%	0%	7%	15%	22%	30%	37%
Price	$0.27	$0.61	$1.01	$1.31	$1.31	$0.90	$0.05	−$1.18	−$2.69
Change (%)	−79	−54	−23	0	0	−31	−96	−190	−305
Delta	0.13	0.20	0.19	0.09	−0.10	−0.32	−0.53	−0.69	−0.81
Gamma	0.04	0.02	−0.03	−0.08	−0.11	−0.11	−0.10	−0.07	−0.05
Vega	1.52	0.91	−1.45	−4.84	−7.82	−9.29	−9.08	−7.70	−5.85
Theta	−1.09	−0.67	0.98	3.39	5.53	6.62	6.53	5.61	4.34

Exhibit 5.5   Payoff Pattern of a Short Three-Month 1 × 2 Vertical Ratio Call Spread

Maximum gain = High strike − Low strike − Premium paid

Maximum loss = Unlimited

$$\text{Upper breakeven} = \text{High strike} + \left[\frac{\text{High strike} - \text{Low strike} - \text{Premium paid}}{\text{Ratio} - 1}\right]$$

Lower breakeven = Low strike + Premium paid

magnitude and timing of the move correct as well. It is hard enough to get direction right; adding timing and price to the mix makes the exercise significantly more challenging. Only the most nimble of traders should try their hand at these "thread the needle" trades.

What these ratio structures have going for them is that out-of-the-money options suffer from significant negative alpha. Ratio spreads capitalize on this fact by selling rapidly decaying options, so time tends to work in favor of these structures. This attribute does not come without risks, however, as any unforeseen event such as a company takeover can send the price of the underlying skyrocketing and the value of the ratio call spread plummeting resulting in a terrific loss.

Most individual investors should avoid highly levered ratio spreads and leave them to the professionals. This does not mean, however, that retail investors should avoid ratio spreads all together. One might want to use slight ratios under certain circumstances to take advantage of the negative alpha characteristics of out-of-the-money options. Small ratio call spreads give the investor the ability to capture the benefit of selling options with large negative alphas with a more manageable level of risk. The beauty of small ratio spreads is that gains come early when the price of the underlying rises and one only gives back a fraction of it as the price of the underlying continues to rise above the upper strike. In some sense, one can think of a small ratio spread as having a limited built-in hedge. In a 1 × 1.25, the price of the underlying has to rise far above the upper strike before an investor loses gains captured by the initial move in the price of the underlying security. As a result, losses on an upside move only occur under a super price spike scenario. The following shows the upfront cost of this structure. Bear in mind, that you cannot buy a quarter of an option, so the minimum size of the trade is 4 x 5. The numbers are provided as if one could buy a fraction of an option so that the numbers are easily comparable to previous examples.

Exhibit 5.6 shows the payoff pattern for a 1 × 1.25 ratio call spread. Contrast this to the payoff pattern for the 1 × 2 ratio call spread presented in Exhibit 5.5. Notice that like the 1 × 2 ratio call spread, the 1 × 1.25 ratio call spread reaches its maximum value when the price of the underlying instrument hits the upper strike at expiration. Bear in mind, however, that the 1 × 2 ratio call spread will produce a higher return as less premium is paid up front. While the payoff patterns for both of these ratio call spreads are similar when the price of the underlying instrument is below the upper strike, the payout patterns differ radically above that point. The 1 × 2 ratio call spread requires cash of about $1.01. If the price of the underlying security increases to $34 at expiration the value of this call spread will be $1.00. This is the upside breakeven point. As the price of the underlying continues to rise, the value of this call spread will fall resulting in a loss. The 1 × 1.25 ratio call spread has a great deal more headroom. This structure requires $1.29 in cash up front. If the price of the underlying security rises to $44.80 at expiration it will have a value of $1.29. In short, using a slight ratio moves the breakeven point out substantially.

Long, 1 × 1.25, Three-Month, Ratio Call Spread

Buy 4, $25.00 Strike call at $1.77	$7.08	or 1	= $1.77
Sell 5, $30.00 Strike call at $0.38	$1.90	× 1.25	= $0.48
Net Debit	$1.18		$1.29

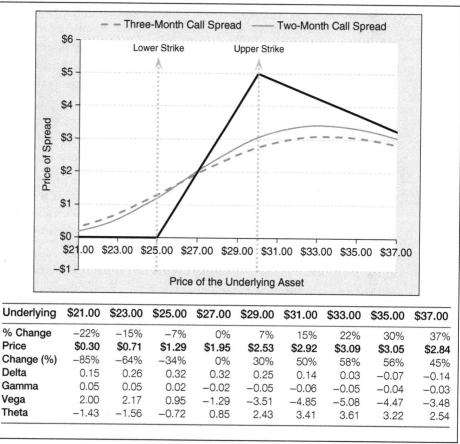

Underlying	$21.00	$23.00	$25.00	$27.00	$29.00	$31.00	$33.00	$35.00	$37.00
% Change	−22%	−15%	−7%	0%	7%	15%	22%	30%	37%
Price	$0.30	$0.71	$1.29	$1.95	$2.53	$2.92	$3.09	$3.05	$2.84
Change (%)	−85%	−64%	−34%	0%	30%	50%	58%	56%	45%
Delta	0.15	0.26	0.32	0.32	0.25	0.14	0.03	−0.07	−0.14
Gamma	0.05	0.05	0.02	−0.02	−0.05	−0.06	−0.05	−0.04	−0.03
Vega	2.00	2.17	0.95	−1.29	−3.51	−4.85	−5.08	−4.47	−3.48
Theta	−1.43	−1.56	−0.72	0.85	2.43	3.41	3.61	3.22	2.54

Exhibit 5.6 Payoff Pattern of a Short Three-Month 1 × 1.25 Vertical Ratio Call Spread

$$\text{Maximum gain} = \text{High strike} - \text{Low strike} - \text{Premium paid}$$

$$\text{Maximum loss} = \text{Unlimited}$$

$$\text{Upper breakeven} = \text{High strike} + \left[\frac{\text{High strike} - \text{Low strike} - \text{Premium paid}}{\text{Ratio} - 1} \right]$$

$$\text{Lower breakeven} = \text{Lower strike} + \text{Premium paid}$$

The reason why investors would want to use a small ratio call spread is that it will provide higher rates of return versus a standard call spread under any but the most extreme upside circumstances. This occurs because selling an option that is prone to generate negative alpha reduces return drag due to time decay.

■ Risk Reversals

The above strategies represent the most common option structures sophisticated investors use to position their portfolios to produce the gains desired by an anticipated move in the price of an underlying asset. There are other, more esoteric strategies professionals use to express their market opinion on the direction of the stock, stock index, commodity, currency, and so on, as well. The most notable of these strategies is the risk reversal. The structure for a bullish risk reversal is quite simple. One buys an out-of-the-money call and pays for it by writing an out-of-the-money put. In a typical risk reversal, the investor picks strike prices, which are equally out of the money. In other words, if the strike on the call is 5 percent out of the money, one typically sells a put that is also 5 percent out of the money. Investors use the strategy for a number of reasons not the least of which are those listed:

- The investor has a bullish opinion on the price of the underlying security, but wishes to take a position with the minimum amount of cash required. Ideally, one tries to establish a bullish position without spending any cash at all.

- While the investor might have a bullish opinion on the price of the underlying security, they may not be aware of any catalysts that will send the price of the stock higher in the short term. By committing little or no cash, the opportunity cost of putting on such a position is minimal. If the stock does not move up by the time the options expire, their position expires worthless. This is not an issue because little or no cash was put up in the first place.

- Every investor has had the experience of buying a stock, which seems to represent good value. Over time, the investor expects the price of that stock to rise, and yet its price falls instead. As the price the stock falls, the investor maintains the belief that the stock is a good investment and wishes he had bought it at the lower current price. Value investors who do their homework have a good handle on the value of the asset. As the price falls, they take the view that the stock is an even better value. Furthermore as the price falls, they have the view that risk is diminishing for further price declines. Risk reversal gives the value investor an opportunity to participate in the rise in the price of the stock if it occurs immediately, but also provides the opportunity to buy the stock at a lower price should it drop in the short term. In short, a bullish risk reversal allows an investor to participate in the immediate rise in the price of the stock, but also enables them to take a more significant position in the event the asset gets cheaper.

The following is an example of a typical risk reversal, along with Exhibit 5.7 showing its payoff pattern.

The gray dashed line in Exhibit 5.7 shows the payoff pattern for a three-month risk reversal given an instantaneous change in the price of the underlying security. The cash required to initiate this structure is just $0.20, which is far less than a

Three-Month, Risk Reversal

Buy 1, $29.00 Strike Call at $0.53	$0.53
Sell 1, $21.00 Strike Put at $0.33	$0.33
Net Debit	$0.20

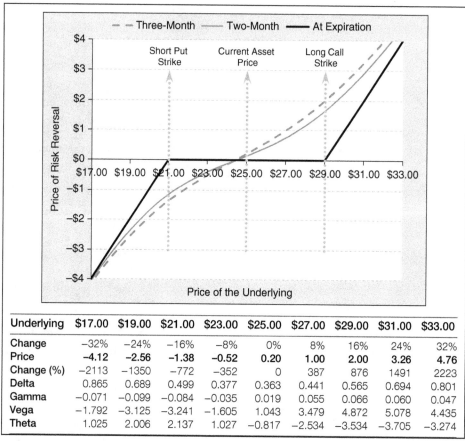

Underlying	$17.00	$19.00	$21.00	$23.00	$25.00	$27.00	$29.00	$31.00	$33.00
Change	−32%	−24%	−16%	−8%	0%	8%	16%	24%	32%
Price	−4.12	−2.56	−1.38	−0.52	0.20	1.00	2.00	3.26	4.76
Change (%)	−2113	−1350	−772	−352	0	387	876	1491	2223
Delta	0.865	0.689	0.499	0.377	0.363	0.441	0.565	0.694	0.801
Gamma	−0.071	−0.099	−0.084	−0.035	0.019	0.055	0.066	0.060	0.047
Vega	−1.792	−3.125	−3.241	−1.605	1.043	3.479	4.872	5.078	4.435
Theta	1.025	2.006	2.137	1.027	−0.817	−2.534	−3.534	−3.705	−3.274

Exhibit 5.7 Bullish Risk Reversal

Maximum gain = Unlimited

Maximum loss = Put strike + Premium paid

Breakeven = Call strike + Premium paid (if premium is a debit)

Breakeven = Put strike − Premium received (if premium is a credit)

single-leg call ($1.77) or a generic vertical call spread ($1.39). Since an unhedged short put is part of this strategy, margin will be required to implement this trade. Since both the put and call are 20 percent out of the money, their deltas are quite moderate. In combination, however, the delta of the overall position is similar to the long vertical call spread (0.37) at 0.36, and similar to the short vertical put spread as well. This occurs because the deltas are additive. If the price of the underlying security rises, the value of the short put will fall and the value of the long call will increase. Together, this risk reversal will rise in value as the price of the underlying increases at a similar rate to the spreads.

Notice that very little premium is committed up front, so naturally theta is very small. There will be very little price decay as the risk reversal ages. One can see this graphically as the solid gray line in Exhibit 5.7 shows the payoff pattern of the risk reversal after a month has passed. Notice that it lies almost on top of the dashed gray line, particularly around the price level where the trade was originally established. After one month, the position has decayed by only $0.03. Since theta is the price one pays for gamma, this trade has very little gamma initially. However, as the price of the underlying security rises, the gamma of the risk reversal increases as the increase in delta on the long call overwhelms the loss in delta on the short put. This causes the price appreciation of the risk reversal to accelerate as the price of the underlying rises. At the point where the underlying reaches the upper strike, the risk reversal takes on the characteristics of a long call as the price of the short put approaches zero.

The upside leverage of a risk reversal comes with costs other than a small time decay. As the price of the underlying security falls, the delta of the risk reversal increases. This makes the trade more sensitive to a change in the price of the underlying security. Once the price of the underlying falls to the strike on the downside put, the trade takes on the characteristics of a short put as the value of the call approaches zero. The upside is that this is the point of maximum theta. If the price of the underlying remains at the price of the downside put strike, the loss will decay as time passes. Since the risk reversal now has the return characteristics of a short put, the investor becomes vulnerable to large losses should the price of the underlying security continue to fall.

A key point to remember about a risk reversal is that it is a leverage strategy to instantaneous changes to the price of the underlying security, but it will ultimately expire worthless if the price of the underlying does not move very much and finds itself between the two strikes at expiration. This makes the risk reversal an interesting strategy for speculation while providing room for error. Risk reversals require extra monitoring after the trade is initiated as the character of the trade changes rapidly as the price of the underlying changes. One can observe this by reviewing the migration of the Greeks for instantaneous price changes. If the price of the underlying asset increases to the strike of the call, theta reaches an apex. At this point, the value of the risk reversal will decay at its most rapid rate and the investor takes the risk of giving back their hard fought gains. We can see this with simple numbers. When the price of the underlying moves instantaneously to $29.00 after the trade is initiated, its price will rise from $0.20 to $2.00. If the price of the underlying stagnates at that point, that $2.00 value will vanish over time. After one achieves a ten bagger, one needs to consider how much upside remains in the trade. If the big move one originally expected was achieved, one should close out the trade or roll the trade into new strikes to lock in the $1.80 gain and reestablish a position at higher strikes to minimize the effects of time decay. Since the risk and return characteristics of a risk reversal change rapidly with a change in the price of the underlying security, it must be actively managed.

In the strategy pairs described above, investors can create differing trade structures with puts and calls that start out with the same delta, but ultimately produce significantly different payoff patterns. For example, if one buys an out-of-the-money call, they have a moderate chance of a large gain and a high chance of a moderate loss. When selling an out-of-the-money put, one has a moderate chance of a large loss and a high chance of a moderate gain. Both are delta positive and will perform just fine in an up market. No such pair exists for risk reversals. A bullish risk reversal is constructed with a long call and a short put. A bearish risk reversal is constructed with a short call and a long put. Therefore a short bearish risk reversal is identical to a bullish risk reversal. If one wants to make a trade-off between delta, gamma, and theta, they must do so by adjusting the strikes and expiration dates of the risk reversal.

Finally, the cost of a risk reversal is very dependent on option skew. In the examples presented throughout the book, we assume flat skew for simplicity. That is to say, implied volatility is the same across moneyness. We know, however, that downside puts trade at a volatility premium to at-the-money puts virtually all the time for equities. This raises the price of out-of-the-money puts. Since puts are sold in a bullish risk reversal, their price will increase as skew increases. The net effect is to lower the price of a risk reversal and can even result in a net credit. As a result, there are times when the investor might prefer a risk reversal structure versus an outright purchase of the underlying asset. If skew takes the shape of a smile, instead, the price of the upside call will be higher erasing the advantage of skew.

■ Call Spread Risk Reversals

In Chapter 4, we show that out-of-the-money options suffer from large negative alpha, at-the-money options generate a moderate level of negative alpha, and in-the-money options displayed almost no negative alpha at all. With this information, we concluded that investors can gain an edge by selling out-of-the-money options whenever possible. By applying this principle, the structure of a bullish risk reversal can be modified to take advantage of the poor return potential of out-of-the-money options. To do this within the risk reversal structure, one moves the strike of the out-of-the-money call to one that is closer to an at-the-money call. This reduces the negative alpha on the upside leg the trade. This means of course, that the debit balance of the risk reversal increases sharply. To reduce the amount of cash needed up front, a far out-of-the-money call is sold. The strike on the out-of-the-money put is left unchanged. This new structure adds a call spread to a risk reversal, thus giving it the name of a call spread risk reversal.

The key points of the structure are that two options with heavy negative alpha are sold and one with moderate negative alpha is purchased. Just as importantly, the time decay of the short option positions puts time on the side of the investor. To give the structure the desired delta characteristic, all one has to do is select the appropriate near-at-the-money strike. The net effect of this structure is to create a risk reversal that has almost little or no theta (time decay) at the initiation of the trade. The beauty of this option strategy is that investors get the directional return characteristics they are looking for, without having time working against them, which is typical of option strategies. If there is a skew or a smile to the moneyness structure, this characteristic gets even better. Properly structured this spread can actually initially increase in price across the performance curve owing to accelerated time decay on the out-of-the-money options. The following example and Exhibit 5.8 show the return profile of a call spread risk reversal.

The gray dashed line in Exhibit 5.8 shows the payoff pattern for this call spread risk reversal given an instantaneous change in the price of the underlying security. The net debit of the structure is $0.91, which is more than four times higher than the debit on a straight risk reversal, so there is less leverage in the trade. The delta on the structure is very similar to the delta on a single-leg at-the-money call option. As a result, the price movement of the structure relative to small changes in the price of the underlying instrument is very similar to that which one would experience by simply purchasing a call. The downside of this structure is that potential gains are limited by the short upside call, whereas a single-leg call is unbounded. This loss in potential gains is offset by theta. The call spread risk reversal will experience little if any time decay initially. This is apparent by comparing the payoff pattern of the three-month call spread risk reversal with the same one that has two months to expiration. It is only after the call spread risk reversal ages by about 34 days that time decay begins to present a drag on performance of any significance. The single-leg call on the other hand will see its price fall rapidly from the get-go. In short, one is trading away the possibility for outsized gains to eliminate the loss in value due to the passing of time when prices might stagnate.

The strategy pair that goes with a long call spread risk reversal is a short put spread risk reversal. In a short put spread risk reversal, one sells an at-the-money put, buys an out-of-the-money put, and then buys out-of-the-money call. Both strategies will produce a gain if the price of the underlying security rises, but their returns differ markedly. This bullish strategy has the advantage over a call spread risk reversal in that it allows for unlimited upside gains, while limiting downside losses. In short, it's providing a return profile that is similar to a call option. The beauty of this structure is that is has less theta than a typical call option, and time decay turns from negative during the first two months of the trade to positive for the last month.

Long Three-Month, Call Spread Risk Reversal

Buy 1, $25.00 Strike Call	$1.77
Sell 1 $29,00 Strike Call	$0.53
Sell 1, $21.00 Strike Put	$0.33
Net Debit	$0.91

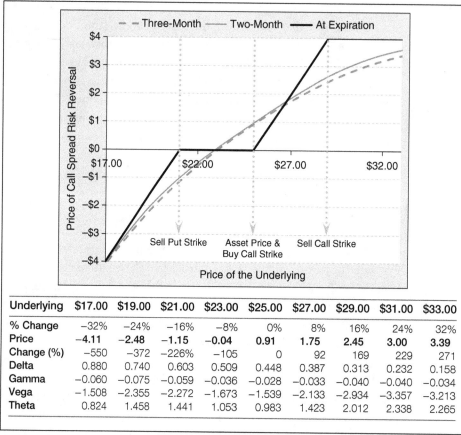

Underlying	$17.00	$19.00	$21.00	$23.00	$25.00	$27.00	$29.00	$31.00	$33.00
% Change	−32%	−24%	−16%	−8%	0%	8%	16%	24%	32%
Price	−4.11	−2.48	−1.15	−0.04	0.91	1.75	2.45	3.00	3.39
Change (%)	−550	−372	−226%	−105	0	92	169	229	271
Delta	0.880	0.740	0.603	0.509	0.448	0.387	0.313	0.232	0.158
Gamma	−0.060	−0.075	−0.059	−0.036	−0.028	−0.033	−0.040	−0.040	−0.034
Vega	−1.508	−2.355	−2.272	−1.673	−1.539	−2.133	−2.934	−3.357	−3.213
Theta	0.824	1.458	1.441	1.053	0.983	1.423	2.012	2.338	2.265

Exhibit 5.8   Call Spread Risk Reversal

Maximum gain = High call strike − Low call strike − Premium paid

Maximum loss = Put strike + Premium paid

Breakeven = Low call strike + Premium paid (if debt)

Breakeven = Put strike − Premium received (if credit)

Furthermore, one is able to take in a small credit at the time of execution instead of paying an option premium. As a result, the investor can actually earn a small profit in an unchanged scenario if the spread is held to expiration. Contrast this to a single-leg call where one would suffer a full loss of premium if held to expiration.

This characteristic is strongest when there is little volatility skew or smile. Under these circumstances, the out-of-the-money options become more expensive and the net credit collapsed toward zero. The following example and Exhibit 5.9 provide the return profile of a short put spread risk reversal.

Short Three-Month, Put Spread Risk Reversal

Sell 1, $25.00 Strike Put	$1.71
Buy 1 $21,00 Strike Put	$0.33
Buy 1, $29.00 Strike Call	$0.53
Net Credit	−$0.85

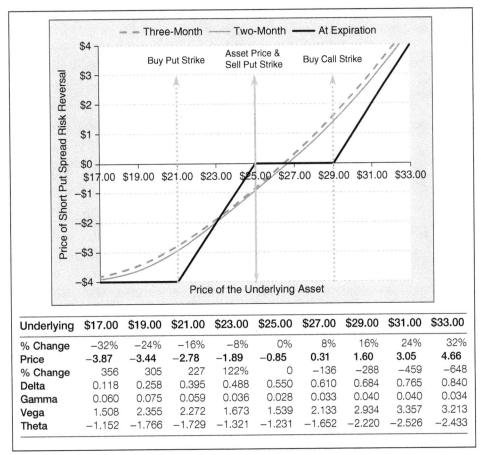

Underlying	$17.00	$19.00	$21.00	$23.00	$25.00	$27.00	$29.00	$31.00	$33.00
% Change	−32%	−24%	−16%	−8%	0%	8%	16%	24%	32%
Price	−3.87	−3.44	−2.78	−1.89	−0.85	0.31	1.60	3.05	4.66
% Change	356	305	227	122%	0	−136	−288	−459	−648
Delta	0.118	0.258	0.395	0.488	0.550	0.610	0.684	0.765	0.840
Gamma	0.060	0.075	0.059	0.036	0.028	0.033	0.040	0.040	0.034
Vega	1.508	2.355	2.272	1.673	1.539	2.133	2.934	3.357	3.213
Theta	−1.152	−1.766	−1.729	−1.321	−1.231	−1.652	−2.220	−2.526	−2.433

Exhibit 5.9   Short Put Spread Risk Reversal

Maximum gain = Unlimited

Maximum loss = Put strike + Premium paid

Breakeven = Call strike + Premium paid (if debit)

Breakeven = Upper put strike − Premium received (if credit)

■ Income-Generating Strategies

Covered Calls

The covered call trading strategy entails the purchase of an asset and writing an at- or out-of-the-money call option against it. This strategy also goes by the name of a buy-write or overwrite tactic. The covered call strategy is probably the most common technique investors use to enhance returns in stagnating markets for generating income. Given its simplicity it is often the first option strategy investors try when initiating an option-trading program. While one can simultaneously buy a stock and sell an option against it, the novice investor typically already owns shares of the underlying stock at the outset. To generate income, the investor will write an out-of-the-money call and collect a premium, which get deposited to their account at settlement.

When selling a call against a current stock holding, one is selling the right to buy their stock at some price, typically above the current price of the asset. If the price of the underlying asset rises, it will be called away and the investor will have to deliver their stock to the option buyer. The option is considered "covered" because the investor already owns the underlying asset for delivery and they will not need to make any cash outlay to satisfy their obligation. Writing a call limits the capital gains an investor can earn in a bull move. Since at-the-money options have more premium than out-of-the-money ones, one is implicitly making a tradeoff between the premium collected and the potential capital gain. Selecting the optimal strike price is critical for the success of this strategy. Ideally, the investor wants the price of the asset to rise up to the strike price of the call written so they can earn a gain on the stock while the options simultaneously expire worthless. Under this scenario, the investor keeps their stock and has the opportunity to repeat the process and sell another option and collect additional premium. If the stock is called away, the investor receives cash for their stock and they keep the premium as well. Once the stock is called away, they will have to repurchase the stock if they still want to own it or they will have to look for another investment opportunity. The following strategy and Exhibit 5.10 show the payoff pattern for a covered call transaction.

The gray dashed line in Exhibit 5.10 shows the payoff pattern for a covered call strategy with three months to expiration given an instantaneous change in the price of the underlying security. The stock is currently trading at $25.00 and the strike price of the call is set at $27.50, which is 10 percent out of the money or 110 percent moneyness. The cash required to initiate this structure is $24.14 ($25.00 for the stock less $0.86 option premium). The value of this trade will tend to rise over time as price decay accrues to the option writer. After one month, the payoff pattern will move up to the solid gray line. The solid black line represents the payoff pattern for the trade at expiration, which lies above the gray lines.

Covered Call Income Strategy

Buy 1 Share of Stock	$25.00
Sell 1, $27.50 Strike Call	$0.86
Net Debit	−$24.14

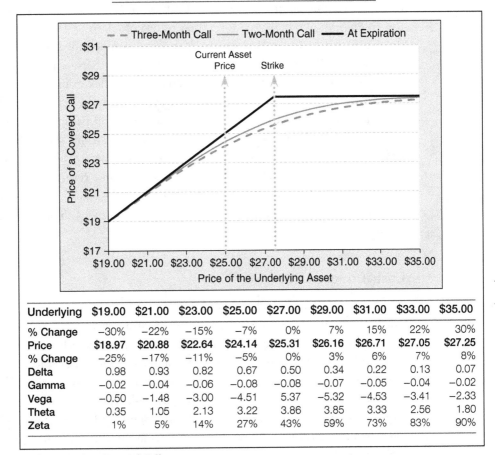

Underlying	$19.00	$21.00	$23.00	$25.00	$27.00	$29.00	$31.00	$33.00	$35.00
% Change	−30%	−22%	−15%	−7%	0%	7%	15%	22%	30%
Price	$18.97	$20.88	$22.64	$24.14	$25.31	$26.16	$26.71	$27.05	$27.25
% Change	−25%	−17%	−11%	−5%	0%	3%	6%	7%	8%
Delta	0.98	0.93	0.82	0.67	0.50	0.34	0.22	0.13	0.07
Gamma	−0.02	−0.04	−0.06	−0.08	−0.08	−0.07	−0.05	−0.04	−0.02
Vega	−0.50	−1.48	−3.00	−4.51	5.37	−5.32	−4.53	−3.41	−2.33
Theta	0.35	1.05	2.13	3.22	3.86	3.85	3.33	2.56	1.80
Zeta	1%	5%	14%	27%	43%	59%	73%	83%	90%

Exhibit 5.10   Covered Call

$$\text{Maximum gain} = \text{Strike price} - \text{Stock price} + \text{Premium}$$
$$\text{Maximum loss} = \text{Stock price} - \text{Premium received}$$
$$\text{Breakeven} = \text{Stock price} - \text{Premium received}$$

Since this is an income-producing strategy, the position rises in value as time passes and this is reflected in the position's positive theta. To capture this yield, one must "sell gamma." This exposes the investor to the risks of the covered call strategy. A covered call strategy using out-of-the-money options is ultimately a mildly bullish strategy as the initial delta of this position is 0.67. It possesses downside risk as delta increases just when the investor does not want it to. At the extreme, the investor can lose all the initial investment, which is equal to the value of the stock, less the premium collected. If the price of the stock rises, the investor enjoys a gain on their stock, but just to a point. The value of the position will never exceed the strike price of the written call. The very best outcome is for the price of the stock to rise to the strike price of the written call at expiration, which is $27.50 in this example. At this point, the investor captures a $2.50 capital gain in addition to the $0.86 premium collected for a total return of $3.36 or 13.44 percent over the three-month investment horizon (65.60 percent compounded annually).

By selling a 10 percent out-of-the-money option, there is a low probability the option will finish in the money, just 27 percent in this example. Since there is a 1 in 4 chance the stock will be called away, one should expect it to be done so just once a year. Practitioners will recognize the payoff pattern of a covered call is simply another way to express a short put, and indeed this should be the case. In Chapter 1, we introduced the concept of put–call parity. This arbitrage condition tells us that cash plus a call option will produce the same returns as stock plus a put. By rearranging this relationship, we find that stock less a call is equal to cash less a put. We can, therefore, replicate a covered-call strategy by simply holding cash and selling puts.

Cash-Covered Puts

As already explained, cash-covered puts is another way of executing a covered call strategy. In some sense, the risk in this strategy is more apparent than in a covered-call strategy. We know that if the price of the underlying security falls, the asset will be pushed onto the put writer and they will suffer a loss by paying the strike price of the put, which would be higher than the market price of the asset. In fact, many firms consider covered calls a low-risk strategy and cash-covered puts a high-risk strategy, when in fact the risks are identical. It is common for brokerage firms to allow customers to sell covered calls in their IRA accounts, but not allow cash-covered puts. This is unfortunate, as skew generally makes selling puts a higher yielding strategy than selling calls.

To execute a cash-covered put strategy, one sells a put option and holds cash equal to the present value of the strike price of the put option sold. In this day and age of extremely low interest rates on short-term securities, the cash requirement is essentially the strike price of the put. To make the comparison to a covered call readily apparent, the following example and Exhibit 5.11 show the structure and characteristics of a cash-covered put strategy, that is essentially equivalent to the covered-call strategy previously discussed.

Ultimately the investor needs to hold $27.36 in cash to cover the delivery risk of the put option. By investing this cash at the risk-free rate, the investor will have $27.50 at expiration, which is just enough to cover the cost of buying the asset if

Cash-Covered Put Income Strategy

PV Strike Price	$27.36
Sell 1, $27.50 Strike Put	−$3.29
Net Cash Required Upfront	$24.08

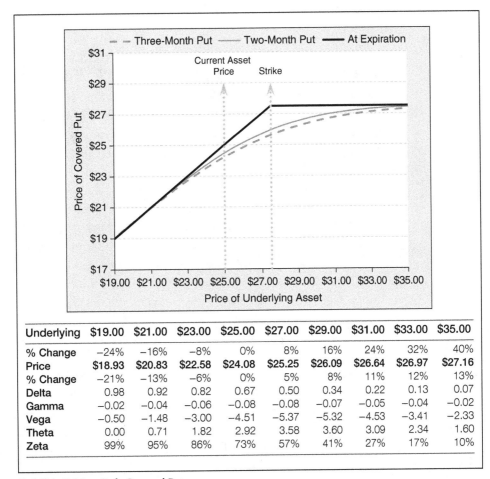

Underlying	$19.00	$21.00	$23.00	$25.00	$27.00	$29.00	$31.00	$33.00	$35.00
% Change	−24%	−16%	−8%	0%	8%	16%	24%	32%	40%
Price	$18.93	$20.83	$22.58	$24.08	$25.25	$26.09	$26.64	$26.97	$27.16
% Change	−21%	−13%	−6%	0%	5%	8%	11%	12%	13%
Delta	0.98	0.92	0.82	0.67	0.50	0.34	0.22	0.13	0.07
Gamma	−0.02	−0.04	−0.06	−0.08	−0.08	−0.07	−0.05	−0.04	−0.02
Vega	−0.50	−1.48	−3.00	−4.51	−5.37	−5.32	−4.53	−3.41	−2.33
Theta	0.00	0.71	1.82	2.92	3.58	3.60	3.09	2.34	1.60
Zeta	99%	95%	86%	73%	57%	41%	27%	17%	10%

Exhibit 5.11 Cash-Covered Put

$$\text{Maximum gain} = \text{Premium} + \text{Interest}$$
$$\text{Maximum loss} = \text{Strike price} - \text{Premium} - \text{Interest}$$
$$\text{Breakeven} = \text{Strike price} - \text{Premium} - \text{Interest}$$

they are compelled to do so. They do not need put up this entire amount however. Upon settlement, the investor will have $3.29 deposited into their account, which they can use as collateral to cover the option. As a result, they need just $24.08 in their account to execute the trade.

Notice that the payoff pattern of the cash-covered put option strategy is identical to that of the stock-covered call strategy, when both strategies employ options with the same strike price. (There is an ever-so-slight difference in the cost of the trade and the Greeks due to the effect of dividend payments.) In theory, investors should be indifferent between these two strategies. If one does not own the underlying asset, cash-covered puts have a slight advantage, as there is a transaction cost advantage. An investor does not have to buy an asset and then sell a call; the investor can simply write a put.

Getting Paid to Provide a Stop Loss to Another Investor

Most traders do not use cash-covered puts as a substitute strategy for covered call writing. They look at the proposition a bit differently. Consider an investor who wants to own this stock currently trading at $25.00, but only wants to pay $22.50 or less. Investors, who limit themselves to cash securities only, have no alternative but to place a limit order with their broker. Those that trade options can sell a put option with a $22.50 strike price instead. We can think of selling downside cash-covered puts as a strategy designed to give another trader or investor a hard stop loss, and get paid for doing so. If the price of the security falls below the strike price, which is the price they want to pay anyway, the stock will be put to them. If the stock does not fall below the strike price, the put expires worthless. In either case, the option seller gets to keep the premium. Furthermore, if the put expires worthless, the option seller can repeat the process and continue to collect premium, until the seller finally has the opportunity to buy the asset at the desired price. The following strategy and Exhibit 5.12 show the payoff pattern for a covered-call transaction.

Selling cash-covered puts at less than 100 percent moneyness is a mildly bullish strategy, as reflected by the very low but positive delta. So long as the share price stays above the strike price, the investor will capture a profit, which is equal to the premium collected. If the asset is delivered to the put writer, the writer now owns the asset at a price equal to the strike on the put option less the premium collected. Since in this example there is only a 30 percent chance that the put will finish in the money, there is a 70 percent chance that the put writer will have an opportunity to write another put when the current one expires. This is not a riskless transaction, however. The put writer will take a loss if the share price falls below the strike price less the premium paid and interest earned on the cash balance. Since this investor wants to own the stock anyway, the put writer is better off vis-à-vis the alternative of placing a limit order.

Iron Condor

Covered option writing is a process whereby the investor trades away some of the upside return potential on the underlying instrument in exchange for some cash

Cash-Covered Put Income Strategy: Getting Paid to Provide a Stop Loss

Cash	$22.39
Sell 1, $22.50 Strike Put	−$0.68
Cash Required Upfront	$21.71

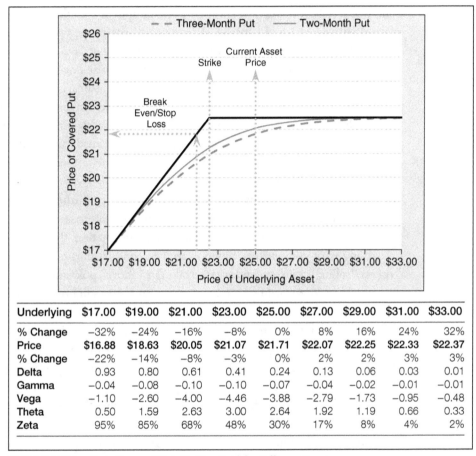

Underlying	$17.00	$19.00	$21.00	$23.00	$25.00	$27.00	$29.00	$31.00	$33.00
% Change	−32%	−24%	−16%	−8%	0%	8%	16%	24%	32%
Price	$16.88	$18.63	$20.05	$21.07	$21.71	$22.07	$22.25	$22.33	$22.37
% Change	−22%	−14%	−8%	−3%	0%	2%	2%	3%	3%
Delta	0.93	0.80	0.61	0.41	0.24	0.13	0.06	0.03	0.01
Gamma	−0.04	−0.08	−0.10	−0.10	−0.07	−0.04	−0.02	−0.01	−0.01
Vega	−1.10	−2.60	−4.00	−4.46	−3.88	−2.79	−1.73	−0.95	−0.48
Theta	0.50	1.59	2.63	3.00	2.64	1.92	1.19	0.66	0.33
Zeta	95%	85%	68%	48%	30%	17%	8%	4%	2%

Exhibit 5.12 Cash-Covered Put, Getting Paid for Selling a Stop Loss

up front. As these examples show, the investor will maximize their returns if the price of the underlying security stays within certain ranges or moves to a particular level. Although the probability of losses is moderate with these strategies, they do leave the investor exposed to the possibility of significant loss. If an investor takes a covered put or call position in a particular company that goes bankrupt, the loss will be close to if not 100 percent. Therefore, investors who are looking for income need to consider strategies that avoid the potential for devastating losses that might happen from time to time. The only way to capture income from options is to sell gamma. Generally, this means the trader must be net short options, but being short options leaves the door open to large losses. Therefore, an investor needs to be sure to hedge a short option position with a long position to cover tail risk. One of the ways investors who seek income do this is with the iron condor.

An iron condor is a four-legged trade constructed by combining a put spread and a call spread where one either buys both the put spread and the call spread, or sells both the put spread and the call spread. To use this structure to generate income, one would sell both vertical spreads. For example one could combine a bullish put spread with a bearish call spread. A near out-of-the-money put is sold and a further out-of-the-money put is purchased. The downside put is purchased to protect the position from a price collapse. Likewise, selling a near out-of-the-money call, and buying a further out-of-the-money call constructs a bearish call spread. The far out-of-the-money call protects the position from an extremely bullish event that would drive the price of the underlying security far higher. Since the bullish put spread has a small positive delta and the bearish call spread has a small negative delta, the trade is market neutral initially. Furthermore, delta tends to stay contained so long as the price of the underlying security stays in between the strikes of the two options sold. Since more premium is received than paid, the iron condor produces a net credit, and that premium will evaporate as time passes. One important note to readers is that there is some conflicting information that has been published regarding what constitutes "buying" an iron condor, thus taking a "long" position versus "selling" an iron condor, thus taking a "short" position. The important point we would make regarding iron condors is that if you sell both vertical spreads, you collect premium, and have a structure that generates income if the movement of the underlying is muted. On the other hand if you buy both vertical spreads you will pay a net debit and have a position that will decay over time, and will only see profits if the underlying moves through either the strike of the put you bought, or the call you bought by the total premium you paid. The following is an example of an iron condor, along with the chart in Exhibit 5.13 showing the payoff pattern changes in the price of the underlying asset.

The gray dashed line in Exhibit 5.13 shows the payoff pattern for an iron condor with three months to expiration given an instantaneous change in the price of the underlying security. The stock is currently trading at $25.00 and the near strikes are set 10 percent out of the money and the far strikes are set at 20 percent out of the money. The cash generated by this trade is $0.98. At its core, an iron condor is a realized volatility-selling strategy as a means of generating income. If the share price ends up between the near strikes at expiration, the investor will earn the premium collected. The solid black line represents the payoff pattern for this complex structure at expiration. Since this is an income-producing strategy, the position will rise in value as time passes, and this is reflected in the position's positive theta of 2.27. To capture this yield, the investor must "sell gamma." This shows up as tail risk, which is the risk inherent in the iron condor strategy. If the price of the

Generating Income with an Iron Condor

Sell 1, $22.50 Strike Put	−$0.68
Buy 1, $20.00 Strike Put	$0.18
Sell 1, 27.50 Strike Call	−$0.86
Buy 1, $30.00 Strike Call	$0.38
Net credit	−$0.98

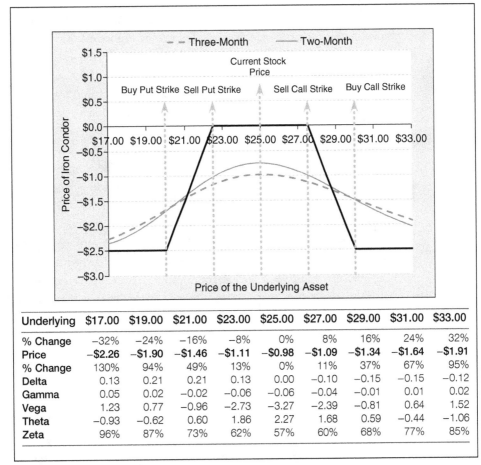

Underlying	$17.00	$19.00	$21.00	$23.00	$25.00	$27.00	$29.00	$31.00	$33.00
% Change	−32%	−24%	−16%	−8%	0%	8%	16%	24%	32%
Price	−$2.26	−$1.90	−$1.46	−$1.11	−$0.98	−$1.09	−$1.34	−$1.64	−$1.91
% Change	130%	94%	49%	13%	0%	11%	37%	67%	95%
Delta	0.13	0.21	0.21	0.13	0.00	−0.10	−0.15	−0.15	−0.12
Gamma	0.05	0.02	−0.02	−0.06	−0.06	−0.04	−0.01	0.01	0.02
Vega	1.23	0.77	−0.96	−2.73	−3.27	−2.39	−0.81	0.64	1.52
Theta	−0.93	−0.62	0.60	1.86	2.27	1.68	0.59	−0.44	−1.06
Zeta	96%	87%	73%	62%	57%	60%	68%	77%	85%

Exhibit 5.13 Iron Condor

$$\text{Maximum gain} = \text{Premium}$$
$$\text{Maximum loss} = \text{Maximum of upper loss or lower loss}$$
$$\text{Maximum upper loss} = \text{Upper call strike} - \text{Lower call strike} - \text{Premium}$$
$$\text{Maximum lower loss} = \text{Upper put strike} - \text{Lower put strike} - \text{Premium}$$
$$\text{Upper breakeven} = \text{Lower call strike} + \text{Premium}$$
$$\text{Lower breakeven} = \text{Upper put strike} - \text{Premium}$$

underlying security ends up outside the near strikes, the trade has the potential to lose value.

There is a fair amount of leverage in this transaction. To cash cover the potential for a loss up front, an investor needs to put up $1.52 in cash in addition to the premium collected. This is the maximum loss the investor could suffer. Notice that this strategy provides the potential for a very high yield. If the price of the underlying security were between the two near strikes, it would earn 64.5 percent (0.98/1.52) over the three-month holding period. This is 632 percent annualized! Such a large return does not come without significant risk. If the price of the underlying security trades beyond the outer strikes at expiration, the investor will lose the full $1.52 in cash put up to cover the trade plus the premium collected. There is a reasonable risk that the price of the underlying will be outside the near strikes. The B–S–M model tells us that there is a 57 percent chance this could happen. The probability that the price of the underlying security will fall outside the far strikes is a more modest 25 percent.

Since the iron condor is a short-volatility trade, we should take note of vega, which tells us how sensitive the trade will be to changes in implied volatility. If the implied volatility of the options that make up this trade change by 5 vol. clicks, the value of the iron condor will change by $0.16 (3.27 × 0.05), which is significant compared to the initial price of $0.98 (16.7 percent). Furthermore, a sharp rise in implied volatility would suggest the price of the underlying is more likely to break outside the strike bands, making this a more risky position. The best time to place such trades is when we expect implied volatility to remain stable or fall, along with the expectation that the price of the underlying will not trend over the life of the options. Under these circumstances, the iron condor can provide very high yields indeed.

Final Thought

In this chapter we introduced the foundational option strategies that professionals use when they anticipate directional price moves in the underlying security. In addition, we showed how options are used to create income. With these strategies, along with the volatility-trading techniques discussed in Chapter 3 and the alpha characteristics discussed in Chapter 4, the reader now has the underpinning necessary to trade options in a skillful manner. While most people think about using options for offensive or hedging purposes on individual assets, index options are very effective tools for hedging entire portfolios. In the following chapter, we will discuss techniques that are very useful for hedging both equity and high-yield bond portfolios.

## CHAPTER 6

Portfolio Hedging Producing Enhanced Returns

The Holy Grail of investing is to identify and implement a strategy that will generate alpha. Such a strategy will provide above-average rates of return with a below-average level of risk. Investors use many different approaches to achieve that goal. As a class, two basic techniques are used to find stocks or other opportunities that the investor expects to generate above-average rates of return with minimal downside risk. Those two techniques are fundamental/value investing and technical/momentum/trend following investing.

Value investors look for securities that are underpriced in the marketplace. In the case of equities, they evaluate a company's business strategy to determine its competitive position vis-à-vis the other participants in their economic sector. With the competitive analysis in hand, they have a basis for analyzing a company's historical financial performance and determining if that performance will continue into the future. The first step in that process is to focus on revenue generation. This tells the investor how successful a company might be in generating stable revenue growth in the future. Ultimately, the investor wants to know how successful a company will be in turning sales into free cash flow and earnings. To build that understanding, the value investor will analyze a company's cost structure vis-à-vis the other competitors in the marketplace. At one end of the quality spectrum, those companies that provide the highest-quality products and services can charge generous margins over their cost of production. Those companies that focus on the mass-market segments must be a low-cost producer to gain an advantage in the marketplace. They sacrifice quality at the margin and depend on economies of scale to compete on the basis of price. With this information in hand, the next step is to value the equity of the company. To do this, they use metrics such as enterprise value to earnings before interest, taxes, depreciation, and amortization (EV/EBITDA); price-to-book ratios; price to sales ratios; price to earnings ratios; and others metrics to value the firm, which may or may not agree with the market price of the company's securities. After determining the company's value, the value investor waits for an opportunity to buy the shares in that company at a price below his valuation estimate. This allows the value investor to build in a margin of safety, just in case there is a flaw in the valuation estimate. The ultimate goal is to find something worth the dollar and pay $.50 for it. Hedge funds use value-investing techniques to both go long and short. If the value investor identifies a stock that is overpriced in the marketplace, the investor might sell it short, hoping for the share price to fall in the coming days, weeks, and months.

Technical/momentum/trend following investors use entirely different techniques to identify investment opportunities. Pure technical traders do not consider valuation at all. They simply focus on price action. The price of financial assets changes continuously—some rise, some fall, and some move sideways in a choppy fashion. Long-only technical/momentum investors look for stocks whose price is trending higher and hold those issues. If the uptrend is broken, they will sell their longs and avoid issues in a down trend. They purchase the securities with the expectation that momentum will continue to push prices higher in the future. Their mantra is, "The trend is your friend." Their underlying premise is that there are too many fundamental factors to digest and that they cannot know more about an investment than all other investors buying and selling in the market place. So they simply try to interpret the information conveyed by the actions of other investors. To manage risk, they quickly sell the securities in their portfolios if the underlying price trend is broken. Hedge funds using momentum and trend flowing techniques take a more flexible stance also look for stocks, whose price are in a downtrend. They sell those stocks short with the expectation that the downtrend will continue. To limit losses on their shorts, they will buy back the shares if the downtrend is broken and the share price moves into a consolidation or an uptrend.

As investors pick investments one stock at a time, they ultimately build a portfolio. Properly constructed, investors will have a portfolio of assets spread out over multiple asset classes, and sectors within those assets classes. Fixed-income investors will diversify along quality lines, as well. Typical value investors will end up with a large number of positions, which they believe will rise over time. The same holds true for momentum investors. A critical element of the value investment style concerns measurement of risk. Value investors do not define risk as the volatility of returns over time. They consider risk as the potential for permanent loss. This represents the possibility that the price of an asset will fall and never recover. Value investors accept the daily fluctuation of market prices of assets held in their portfolio as a cost of doing business. They count on price fluctuations to provide an opportunity to buy good assets at temporarily low prices. Furthermore, they count on investment fads to drive the price of their portfolio holdings higher for an opportunity to sell at extreme valuations. Over time, these investors will ride the ups and downs of the market, with the hope that they will achieve higher rates of return than the market as a whole over some investment horizon. In short, these investors accept and experience market risk.

With the advent of derivative securities such as futures and options, investors have the tools to manage the market risk in their portfolios, which enables them to drive returns with their security selection skills. The beauty of options is that they provide leveraged returns as compared to the underlying instrument, so that an investor only has to dedicate a small amount of capital to capture the hedging benefits. Leverage, of course, is a double-edged sword. Options must be used correctly to achieve the risk management objectives and return-generating goals desired. Within the practice of portfolio hedging, there are two basic techniques. They are known as anticipatory hedging, and permanent hedging.

■ Anticipatory Hedging

Most investors, be they individuals or professionals, construct portfolios based on the belief that they can select individual investments that will outperform the market averages on a risk-adjusted basis. As a result, they rarely if ever hedge. They are willing to ride market cycles to capture the superior rates of return they believed their individual investments would provide. There are times, however, when investors fear that a large correction or bear market could be just around the corner. Under these circumstances, anticipatory hedgers might buy put options to protect the value of their portfolios. If the anticipated selloff manifests, the value of their portfolio will fall but this will be offset by an increase in the value of the put options. Once they believe the selloff is over, they will sell their puts and invest the proceeds into other investment opportunities they might see in the marketplace. Net-net, if the price of risk assets fall, they will experience an outsized rate of return when compared to the market as a whole. While their portfolio might fall in value, the hedge will reduce overall losses, allowing the portfolio to outperform the market averages. If, on the other hand, the anticipated selloff does not manifest, the put options will fall in value. The investors will either sell it at a lower price or let the options expire worthless, causing the portfolio to underperform in a stagnating or rising market.

At the end of the day, anticipatory hedging is really just an exercise in market timing. Value is created if and only if the price of the hedge increases over its limited holding period. Anticipatory hedging produces a similar result to selling a portion of one's stock portfolio and waiting for prices to fall. On the one hand, if prices do fall, cash outperforms equities and the overall portfolio will outperform the market. On the other hand, if risk assets continue to rally, the portfolio will be underinvested and thus underperform the market averages.

Hedging with Three-Month, 30-Delta Puts

Simply buying put options is the typical way investors purchase portfolio insurance. The most common put option employed by professional investors is the three-month, 30-delta put based on one of the market averages such as the S&P 500 or the Russell 2000 index. Options on broad market averages are used because they protect the portfolio from market risks and enable investors to keep their carefully selected portfolio of individual investments intact. A three-month, 30-delta put is one in which the strike price of the option is 5 to 10 percent out of the money depending on its implied volatility at the time of purchase. We saw in Chapter 2 that delta on out-of-the-money puts increases as implied volatility increases. When implied volatility is low, a put with 95 percent moneyness might have a delta of 30, whereas in a high-volatility environment, an option with lower moneyness will have a 30 delta. Many institutional investors favor 30-delta puts as their price tends to be nominal, and little capital is needed to purchase them. Furthermore, short-dated out-of-the-money puts on large market indices are very liquid. Institutional investors can transact in large volume without moving the market or suffering excessive transaction costs. Since these puts are out of the money, they provide little if any protection for a small drop in price that takes place over an extended period of time. Time decay eats up some or all of the gains due to price changes driven by the option's delta. They do however provide protection if the price drops swiftly and severely. In short, 30-delta puts really only provide insurance against "tail risk" even as investors who employ these options expect more robust protection from them. That tail risk protection comes from the option's gamma. Since moderately out-of-the-money options have a fair amount of gamma, the absolute value of delta increases as price falls. Most 30-delta put buyers may not realize it, but the real protection from these options comes from gamma, not delta, and gamma does not contribute to an option's returns unless price movements are large.

30-delta puts however are fraught with risks most investors don't appreciate. In Chapter 4, we discussed the historical return performance for options on indexes as a function of time to maturity and moneyness. In that analysis we showed that out-of-the-money options on indexes suffer significant negative alpha. As a result, we know upfront that these options destroy value if bought and held over an investment cycle. In addition, the analysis showed that short-dated options underperform the market more than long-dated options, as well. The typical investor usually finds out the hard way that purchasing three-month, 30-delta puts is a sub optimal method for permanently hedging market risk in their portfolio. Fortunately, there is a better way.

■ Permanent Hedging

Permanent hedging is the process by which the investor hedges their portfolio on a continuous basis without regard to market conditions. Hedging in this way makes risk management an integral part of the overall portfolio strategy. Properly executed, permanent hedging protects the investor's assets from any and all unforeseen market events. In 1987, the stock market was rising rapidly, and company earnings and the economy were growing nicely as well. With this very constructive macroeconomic backdrop, investors were confident that share prices would continue to increase, producing very high rates of return on investment. On October 19 of that year, a price crash began in the Hong Kong equity market, and spread to markets in the west. On that day, the Dow Jones Industrial Average fell by 508 points to 1,738, culminating in a one-day loss of 22.6 percent. This loss caught most investors by surprise, as virtually everyone believed the market could only go higher aided by an expanding global economy and higher corporate earnings. Many investors were so convinced that the equity markets would move higher that they held the majority of their assets in equity securities. Few, if any, investors who practice anticipatory hedging, took steps to protect their portfolios for downside risk at this time.

Booms and busts in asset prices occur more often than we might expect. In 1997, NASDAQ and Internet stocks began to rise very rapidly. Three years later, on March 10, 2000, the NASDAQ stock market index peaked intraday at 5,133. From that point forward the price of equity securities went on a two-year decline that took the NASDAQ index all the way down to about 1,100 on October 7, 2002. This was a crushing loss of 78 percent. Once again, in 1999 investors were enamored by the return potential provided by stocks in general and the technology stocks in particular. The Internet was a technological revolution not seen since the automobile. Most investors believed that this revolution would lead to new industries, new companies, and new ways of doing business. People thought the profit potential of these new companies was virtually unlimited in the long run, pushing confidence in stocks to an all-time high. While new companies and new industries did indeed spring from the technology revolution, profits did not, and investors suffered the consequence. Once again, with the promise of extraordinarily high capital gains just over the horizon, few if any investors were practicing anticipatory hedging at this time.

A more recent example was the stock market crash of 2008. In late 2001, the Federal Reserve eased monetary policy and the federal government went on a spending spree as a solution to the economic destruction caused by the bursting of the NASDAQ bubble. The general societal fears after the attacks of 9/11 compounded the economic malaise that was already in place. In the years from 2002 to 2007, the economy grew at a moderate pace, while the easy monetary policy by the Federal Reserve drove interest rates down to what was then historic lows. With the recent experience of a stock market crash in everybody's mind, individual and institutional investors alike switched their focus to investing in real assets. With credit easy to obtain, easy monetary policy found its way into the real estate market, both commercial and residential. Institutional investors, who need cash flow, have always had an affinity for fixed-income securities. With real estate promising a growing stream of cash flow over time, they heavily invested in this asset class as well. With interest rates falling, the value of bond portfolios was increasing rapidly, driving greater investor interest in these markets. With the promise of additional capital gains just around the corner, many institutional investors bought fixed-income securities with leverage through CLOs, CDOs, and other financially engineered products. Once again, with confidence high, the corporate bond markets peaked in 2007. At this point, prices of credit-risky assets fell swiftly and brutally as investors and financial institutions tried to deleverage their portfolios. Many were unsuccessful, and they saw the market value for their stock and bond portfolios fall by over 50 percent. By the time the bottom arrived in March of 2009, many investors were wiped out and a number of financial institutions went bankrupt. Just as with other periods of market turmoil, most investors did not take the steps necessary to protect themselves from unforeseen events. These three events should convince any rational investor that anticipatory hedging works only if an investor anticipates a bear market.

It is very difficult to identify a bear market before it starts. They generally begin when the economy is rosy and corporate profits are expanding. There are only a handful of investors skilled in the techniques of market timing. Therefore, investors should avoid leverage and consider continuous hedging as a fundamental element of their investment strategy. Fortunately, there are techniques for managing the market risk in a portfolio of stocks, bonds, or real estate that makes continuous hedging a viable part of a successful investment strategy.

■ Optimal Hedging Strategies

The most important use of options is their application to hedging individual positions or portfolios as a whole. There is a host of strikes and expirations, and an almost limitless number of multileg strategies from which investors can choose. In the remainder of this chapter, we will take up the challenge of portfolio hedging. Options on market and sector indexes are great tools for hedging market or sector risks contained in diversified portfolios of equity, corporate debt obligations, real estate, etc. But before evaluating various portfolio-hedging strategies, we must define what the perfect hedge looks like. The perfect hedge is one that allows investors to capture the expected returns of their individual investments in their portfolio, while reducing or eliminating the periodic ups and downs in its value. Such a portfolio will significantly outperform in down markets, as the hedges will offset portfolio losses. During these periods, fund managers will outperform their peers and appear to be extremely skilled. Unfortunately, a fully hedged portfolio will underperform in up markets. Professional investors who hedge in up markets will underperform their peers, making them look extremely unskilled relative to their competition. Most investors are reluctant to give up returns in the good times to avoid poor performance in bear markets. Most professional investors are judged based on how they perform relative to their peers or the market averages over relatively short periods of time, typically three months to two years. Consequently, they are judged by the short-term returns they produce on a relative, not an absolute, basis. Given this market structure, most investors are reluctant to run permanent-hedging programs. Nonetheless, we contend portfolio managers can outperform their peers over the long haul if they apply a hedging program that reduces volatility in the near term, without harming returns in the long term. With this thought in mind, Exhibit 6.1 shows our definition of a perfect hedge.

The black line in Exhibit 6.1 shows the performance of an idealized portfolio of risky assets. In a bull market, its value rises and in a bear market its value falls. The gray dotted line shows the performance of the same portfolio that is perfectly hedged. Notice that it does not suffer the ups and downs of the overall market. It simply captures a consistent return on the portfolio of assets over time. This is

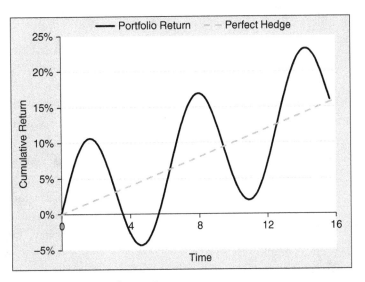

Exhibit 6.1 The Optimal or Perfect Hedge

the benchmark by which we should judge the effectiveness of a hedging strategy. In this idealized world, the optimal or perfect hedge is one in which the returns on a portfolio are preserved, while the volatility and fluctuations around those returns are reduced or eliminated. This, by necessity, means that a perfectly hedged portfolio will underperform in up markets, as indicated by the points where the solid black line is rising faster than the dashed gray line. It also means the hedged portfolio will outperform in down markets, as indicated by the areas where the solid black line is falling relative to the hedged portfolio. It goes without saying that eliminating all risk while preserving returns is beyond the realm of possibility, but it should not eliminate it as a goal. Capital market theory tells us that risk and return are intimately related. To capture the high returns available from risky assets, we must expose our portfolios to either equity or credit risk. So hedging these risks often reduces returns over an investment cycle. Nonetheless, it is important to optimize the hedge to get as close to perfection as possible.

When initiating a hedging program, the first step in the process is to compare the historical relationship between the return characteristics of the portfolio under consideration and potential hedging instruments and techniques. It is very important to understand past performance in different scenarios to build expectations about what is possible in the future. In the following pages, we will walk through a number of steps to build the intuition necessary to construct optimal hedges for both high-yield and equity portfolios. By the end of this process, we will be able to create customized hedges for any portfolio of risk assets that will produce returns that are superior to the return profile of those assets on a standalone basis.

■ Hedging High-Yield Debt with Equity

The asset value of any corporation will fluctuate, depending on its financial performance along with market and economic conditions. Those asset values are reflected in the price of the debt and equity securities issued by the firm. In their theorem of capital structure, Franco Modigliani and Merton Miller reminds us that in the absence of taxes, bankruptcy costs, agency costs, and asymmetric information, the value of a firm is unaffected by the way a firm is financed. Some firms are composed entirely of equity, while most are capitalized with a combination of debt and equity. Investment-grade companies tend to have nominal levels of debt, while below-investment-grade companies tend to capitalize themselves with high levels of debt. There is not one perfect capital structure for all companies. Service firms that are asset light and technology companies that have high levels of business risk tend to employ moderate levels of debt. Asset-heavy companies such as utilities, manufacturers, and pipeline companies typically have steady cash flows and collateral to pledge, enabling them to take on higher levels of debt. In the final analysis, companies select a capital structure that maximizes the expected rate of return to the company's owners. In the case of companies with high debt loads, a large proportion of the asset-value risk is borne by the bondholders. Under these circumstances, it's fair to say that high-yield debt carries a significant level of equity risk. As a result, we can think of high-yield bonds as equity in drag. How investors capture returns is different, however. Equity holders tend to capture returns primarily through rising share prices, whereas bondholders tend to capture their return primarily through interest payments. Nonetheless, credit-risky debt pays a rate of return that is, at least in part, a reflection of the amount of equity risk bondholders carry. Consequently, we think of corporate debt securities as some combination of a risk-free asset and equity. The lower the credit rating on a bond, the more equity risk it carries. Therefore, it is natural to assume that there is a relationship between the returns provided by equity and the returns provided by credit-risky debt.

To examine the validity of this assertion, it is useful to compare the total return of an index of high-yield bonds with an index of equity securities. By using indexes, we eliminate company-specific issues, which allows for a comparison of the market risk in credit-risky debt with the market risk in equities. Exhibit 6.2 makes such a comparison using the IBOXX high-yield index as a proxy for credit-risky debt and the Russell 2000 index as a proxy for equities. The IBOXX high-yield index represents a portfolio of investable debt securities, issued by companies spread across the universe of industries, with ratings in the range of BB and lower. The average time to maturity on the portfolio is 4 to 5 years, and the vast majority of the securities in the index mature in less than 10 years. Since most institutional fund managers benchmark themselves against the IBOXX high-yield index, this is a great index to use as a proxy for a typical high-yield bond portfolio. The S&P 500 index and

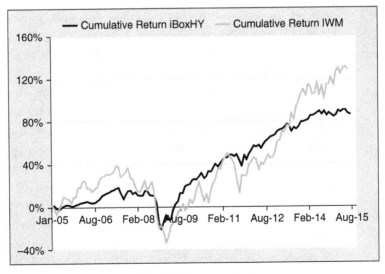

Exhibit 6.2 Total Returns on High-Yield Debt versus Equity

the Russell 2000 index are two broad-market indexes that investors use to evaluate the performance of the equity market overall. Most fund managers use the S&P 500 as a benchmark for evaluating their individual performance, as most institutional investors focus on large-capitalization blue chip stocks. These companies dominate the economic activity that takes place in the United States and they have a significant presence in international markets as well. The Russell 2000 index is a market-capitalization-weighted portfolio of stocks issued by 2,000 medium- to large-size corporations. Since many of the companies in the IBOXX high-yield index are also represented in the Russell 2000, this is a good equity index to use to compare returns on high-yield debt. As a result, when we compare equity returns with high-yield bond returns, we chose the Russell 2000 as a proxy for equity markets. Bear in mind, however, that comparing the performance of high-yield bonds to the S&P 500 gives similar results.

The black line in Exhibit 6.2 shows the total return (price change plus coupon payments) for the IBOXX high-yield index. The gray line represents the total return (price change plus dividend payments) for the Russell 2000 index. Notice that the historical total returns on these two indices tends to rise and fall together. Naturally, the returns generated by the Russell 2000 index rise and fall faster than the returns on the index of high-yield bonds. We should expect equities to have more volatility than high-yield bonds as they lie at the bottom of a company's capital structure and are therefore more risky. Furthermore, we postulate that only a portion of the risk in high-yield bonds is equity risk, so they should be less volatile. This is the first bit of evidence to suggest the returns on high-yield bonds are driven, at least in part, by equity risk.

The next step in the process is to employ statistical methods to measure the correlation of returns between equities and corporate debt. To do this, we need to compare periodic returns between these two indices to see how well they track each other in the short run. Exhibit 6.3 shows a comparison between the monthly returns on the Russell 2000 index and the IBOXX high-yield index from June 2005 through August 2015.

The black line in Exhibit 6.3 represents a regression line between the monthly returns of these two indexes. We can see visually that the correlation is quite high, and the r-squared of the linear regression confirms this with a reading of 50 percent. Since high-yield bonds are not pure equity instruments, we would expect them to have a lower rate of return and volatility relative to equities themselves. The regression line tells us that this is indeed the case, as a 1 percent monthly return from equities translates into a 0.62 percent return on high-yield bonds. Thirty-nine basis points of return is attributable to return on stocks and the remaining 23 basis points of return is independent of returns on equity. This suggests that if we wanted to eliminate the equity risk from a portfolio of high-yield bonds, we would sell equity in an amount equal to 39 percent of the market value of the bond portfolio.

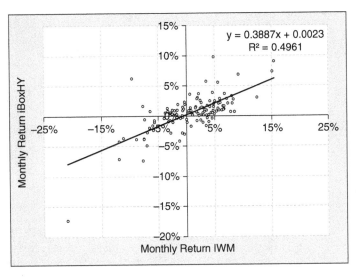

Exhibit 6.3 Monthly Return Comparison, January 2005 to July 2015

$$R_{IBOXX} = \underset{(10.3)}{0.39} R_{Russell\ 2000} + \underset{(1.2)}{0.00283}, \qquad R^2 = 0.50$$

Over time, we would expect to earn the 0.23% per month on average over the long haul.

Although some might argue that hedging is an exercise in minimizing risk, we believe hedging is an exercise in managing risk while maximizing return. Therefore, to get the best results we must find a hedge ratio that enables the investor to maximize returns per unit of risk. To do this, it is useful to plot the efficient frontier of risk and return for a series of portfolios with differing hedge amounts.

Each point on the black line in Exhibit 6.4 represents a portfolio of high-yield bonds and some amount of an equity hedge. The point at the upper-right-hand corner of the efficient frontier represents the risk and return characteristics of the IBOXX high-yield index on a standalone basis. As we add a hedge, portfolio return falls and so does the standard deviation of returns. We should expect this result as equity risk is being removed from the high-yield bond portfolio. This process continues until the minimum risk portfolio is reached, which is found at the tip of the efficient frontier. The hedge ratio for this portfolio is equal to the slope of the regression line in Exhibit 6.3. As weight is added to the hedge, return continues to fall but risk rises. This occurs because at the bottom half of the curve, the portfolios are net short equity risk, which increases portfolio volatility. Since the expected return on equity is greater than the expected return on high-yield bonds, the expected returns of an over-hedged portfolio will fall as the hedge ratio rises.

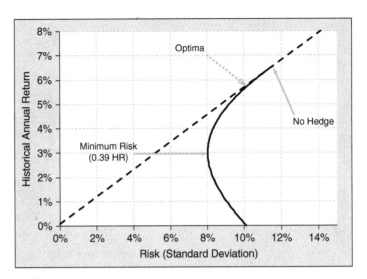

Exhibit 6.4   Efficient Frontier

To find the optimal portfolio, a line is drawn connecting the return on a risk-free asset to the highest point on the curve of potential portfolios. This is known as the borrowing and lending line. The portfolio on the solid black curve that is tangent to the dashed black line is the unique portfolio that is superior to all others. If investors can borrow or lend at the risk-free rate, any portfolio on that line is superior to any on the efficient frontier. If some investors want to take more risk to capture a higher expected rate of return, they are better off buying the optimal portfolio with leverage than picking a portfolio further up on the efficient frontier. If others want to take less risk, they are better off buying a mix of the optimal portfolio and a credit-risk-free asset. This analysis suggests that the best portfolio is one that removes some but not all of the equity risk in the high-yield bond portfolio.

We mentioned earlier that many fund managers typically use three-month. 30-delta puts to hedge their portfolios. A good way to test the effectiveness of a hedge is to apply it on a permanent basis. Exhibit 6.5 compares the total rate of return on the IBOXX high-yield index on a standalone basis with a portfolio that is hedged by three-month, 30-delta puts using a 17 percent hedge ratio. (The optimal hedge ratio is a function of the expected returns, volatilities, and correlation of returns between the high-yield bonds and the Russell 2000 index. Naturally, volatility and correlation estimates will vary depending on the time period chosen, and expected returns are a subjective estimate made by the investor. A hedge ratio of 0.17 was chosen as estimates have a tendency to drift toward this figure.)

The results of this analysis are not particularly satisfying. In fact, they are downright frightening. The return on the hedged portfolio of high-yield bonds is less than a tenth of the return earned by high-yield bonds on a standalone basis.

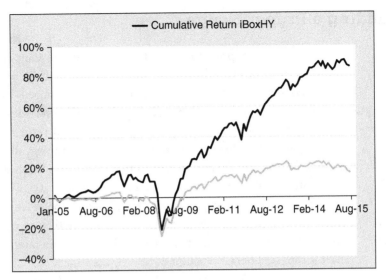

Exhibit 6.5   Performance of High-Yield Bonds Hedged with Three-Month, 30-Delta Put

	High-Yield Bonds	Hedged High-Yield Bonds	Difference	% Difference
Annualized Return	6.09%	0.51%	−5.58%	−91.6%
Risk	10.59%	7.72%	−2.87%	−27.1%
Return/Risk	0.58	0.07	−0.51	−88.4

Exhibit 6.6   Return Comparison

This would be okay if there was an enormous reduction in portfolio volatility. This, unfortunately, is not the case.

The data in Exhibit 6.6 clearly show why investors are not very successful in hedging their high-yield bond portfolios by using three-month, 30-delta puts on an equity index. This analysis of historical returns shows that hedging with these options cuts returns by 91.6 percent, while reducing risk by only 26 percent. After reviewing the data found in Chapter 4, we should not be surprised by the excessive return drag. That data revealed that three-month, 30-delta puts on market indexes typically suffer from negative alpha of as much as 17 percent a month. This is the source of the return destruction with this hedging method. With out-of-the-money puts producing very poor results, investors need a better alternative. The question is, "Can we construct a hedge that adds value to the investment process?" The following is a presentation of how we think about and construct a hedge that will both preserve returns and reduce risk.

Building a Proper Hedge

In Chapter 2, we presented the B–S–M option-pricing model, along with an explanation of the Greeks that reveal an option's price behavior for changes in market conditions and/or model inputs to predict sources of returns in a scenario analysis. In our experience, how an option's characteristics change as it ages is a very important but often overlooked driver of total return as well. Theta tells us how fast an option loses value as time passes, assuming all other factors are held constant. A close look at theta reveals that all options lose value as time passes, but short-dated options decay at an extraordinarily fast rate, while long-dated options decay at a more modest pace. Exhibit 2.8 shows the relationship between option time decay and time to expiration. It reminds us that an option loses value at an exponentially faster rate as it approaches its expiration date. For convenience, that chart is repeated here in Exhibit 6.7.

What the B–S–M option model does not predict is the large negative alpha our analysis in Chapter 4 uncovers. Not only do short-dated options decay at a very rapid rate, historical performance tells us that, in practice, they tend to destroy value on a risk-adjusted basis. Longer-dated options, on the other hand, decay at a far slower rate, resulting in an alpha that is only marginally negative.

Out-of-the-money options suffer the same fate only worse, compounding the return drag. We know that out-of-the-money options only have time value, which reflects the possibility the option might one day trade in the money and have value at expiration. The price decay in *absolute* terms is fastest for at-the-money options as these options have the greatest time value. The B–S–M option-pricing

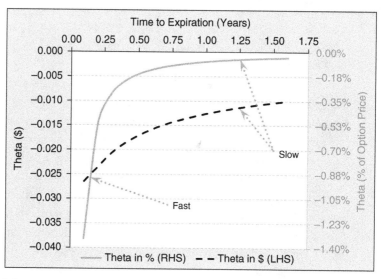

Exhibit 6.7 Option Decay for At-the-Money Options versus Time to Expiration

model predicts that out-of-the-money options will decay faster on a *percentage* basis. Furthermore, the more an option is out of the money, the faster its price will fall as time passes. This occurs because the probability of expiring in the money diminishes quickly as time passes. To hold this probability constant, the price of the underlying security must move rapidly toward the option's strike price. We showed this phenomenon in Exhibit 4.14. In Chapter 4, we also learned that negative alpha increases as an option moves out of the money and decreases as it moves in the money. This results from the interplay between theta and autocorrelation or lack thereof in the price action of the underlying security. For convenience, we represent Exhibit 6.8, which shows the rate of decay of an option in both absolute terms and as a percent of premium options versus moneyness.

The analysis presented in Exhibits 6.7 and 6.8, along with our understanding of an option's alpha, tells us everything we need to know to explain why three-month, 30-delta puts provide a very poor hedge against any portfolio. This analysis suggests that short-dated out-of-the-money puts should be cast aside as a viable alternative for hedging market risk in portfolios of risky assets. While not providing a solution to the hedging problem, knowing what not to do presents a powerful clue to finding a solution. The above analysis suggests that an option's time decay is the killer. Buying an option that decays rapidly in a stagnant or nontrending market is a lead weight around the single put hedging technique. Therefore, we need to find a solution that minimizes time decay. To minimize theta and still get the downside protection we are looking for, it is better to buy long-dated at- or in-the-money options, while simultaneously selling short-dated out-of-the-money options. This way, the decay we suffer on the long-dated option is offset by the decay on the short-dated option,

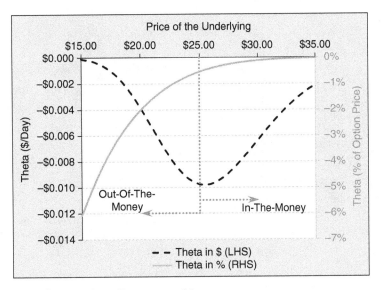

Exhibit 6.8 Call Option Price Decay versus Moneyness

and by adjusting the strikes appropriately we can get the delta needed to provide an effective hedge. This is a description of a long diagonal put spread. Properly structured, a diagonal put spread can eliminate time decay and under most market conditions it will even generate income.

■ Diagonal Put Spreads

A diagonal put spread is a combination of both a horizontal (time) and vertical (price) spread. Nonetheless, to construct a long calendar put spread, an investor buys a long-dated put at a given strike, and sells a shorter-dated put with a different strike. When hedging high-yield debt, we suggest purchasing a 12-month, at- or near-the-money put and selling a 3-month out-of-the-money put. When the value of the underlying asset falls, the value of the long put increases in value faster than the out-of-the-money put. Recall the absolute value of delta on out-of-the-money options is smaller than the absolute value of delta for at- or in-the-money options. As a result, a long calendar put spread is net short delta, which is precisely what the hedger wants. The calendar put spread will reach its maximum value when the price of the underlying security falls to the strike price of the shorter-dated, out-of-the-money put at its expiration. This is a unique scenario where the long-dated put achieves its maximum value while the short-dated put, which is sold, expires worthless.

The beauty of a diagonal put spread is that it can be constructed so that its value will hold steady or even increase should the price of the underlying security remain unchanged. This insight turns the table on the portfolio hedging challenge. With this technique an investor can hedge portfolios of high-yield bonds or equity securities without suffering the pain of option decay. Properly structured, an investor can even profit from it.

The following is an example of the typical structure, mechanics, and return characteristics of the diagonal put spread. Since we are using the Russell 2000 Index as a proxy for the performance of the equity market, we will use it as the underlying instrument. Since the most common method used to hedge by both retail and institutional investors is the 30-delta puts, the characteristics of that single-leg trade are provided for comparison purposes. To keep the comparison on a consistent basis, the strikes incorporated into the diagonal put spread were chosen to create a delta of 30 as well.

The table in Exhibit 6.9 shows the price and attributes of this diagonal put spread, along with that of a 30-delta put. The capital required to purchase this diagonal put spread is $6.774 per spread. The capital required for a three-month, 30-delta put is far lower at $1.958. The lower initial capital required up front is one of the reasons why even sophisticated investors use 30-delta puts to hedge their portfolios.

	At the Money	Out of the Money	Diagonal Put Spread	30-Delta Put
Price IWM	$100.00			
Dividend Yield	1.73%			
Strike Price	100	91.4		95.1
Time to Exp	12 Months	3 Months		3 Months
Risk-free Rate	0.10%	0.05%		0.05%
iVol	18%	21%		19.5%
	Buy	Sell		
Price	$7.943	$1.169	$6.774	$1.958
Delta	−0.492	−0.192	−0.300	−0.300
Gamma	0.022	0.026	−0.004	0.036
Vega	39.21	13.62	25.59	17.34
Theta	−4.322	−6.040	1.718	−7.266

Exhibit 6.9   Diagonal Put Spread Characteristics versus Three-Month, 30-Delta Put

This occurs because many investors misinterpret the capital outlay as the cost of the hedge. This view has grown over the years as those who purchased 30-delta puts as a hedge found that this instrument expires worthless most of the time. We think investors should define cost differently. To our way of thinking, the cost of a hedge is the loss of time value as the option ages, assuming there is no change in the price of the underlying security. With this definition, there is a clear distinction between cost of capital and capital commitment. Exhibit 6.10 shows how the price of a diagonal put spread changes in a scenario where the price of the underlying security does not change compared to that of a three-month, 30-delta put.

Exhibit 6.10 shows that there is a remarkable distinction between the performances of the diagonal put spread and the 30-delta put in a scenario where the price of the underlying does not change. The value of the diagonal put spread actually rises by $0.14 or 2.1 percent. Not only does the diagonal put spread not fall in value, it actually increases in price as it ages by a month. Contrast this to the 30-delta put, which falls by $0.441 or 22.5 percent. This highlights the enormous expense of using short-dated 30-delta puts and the extraordinary attractiveness of

	12-Month, 100 Mny Put	3-Month, 91.4 Mny Put	Diagonal Put Spread	3-Month, 30-Delta Put
Price in 1 Month	$7.576	$0.661	$6.915	$1.517
Initial Price	$7.943	$1.169	$6.774	$1.958
Change	−$0.376	−$0.508	$0.140	−$0.441

Exhibit 6.10   Aging of a Calendar Put Spread

using a diagonal put spread. It is worth noting that this distinction becomes more pronounced as volatility rises, skew rises, or the term structure of volatility inverts. Recall that theta increases as iVol rises. Under all of these cases, the price decay on the 30-delta put increases and price accretion on the diagonal put spread increases as well. Increasing skew is particularly beneficial as the price of the downside put sold decays in value faster relative to the at-the-money put causing the rate of accretion on the spread to increase. An inversion of the term structure does the same thing.

A close examination of the Greeks tells us why this result occurs. Recall that in the dialogue on volatility trading in Chapter 3, we discussed the relationship between gamma and theta. To purchase gamma (accelerating price action), the option investor must pay for it with theta (time decay). More to the point, as gamma increases, so does the rate of option price decay. We know that gamma for a 30-delta put is positive, as the absolute value of its delta will increase when the price of the underlying falls and decrease when the price of the underlying increases. This is without question a good attribute. Exhibit 6.9 reveals that gamma for the calendar put spread is actually negative. This means the investor is actually paid to hold the position. In this example, theta is 1.718 (it is normally negative), and gamma is −0.004 (it is normally positive). Contrast this to the characteristics of the three-month, 30-delta put. Theta is highly negative at −7.266 and this pays for gamma of 0.036.

The diagonal put spread gets the property of positive theta (increasing price with time) by trading away gamma. At first blush, we might think this is a poor tradeoff. After all, investors who hedge are often concerned about a large move in price. It is important to remember however, that large moves are the exception and not the norm. Buying a 30-delta put is really a strategy designed to protect against tail risk. Since tail risk events only occur once every 5 to 10 years, purchasers will rarely collect on such insurance. Since moderate bear markets occur on a more regular basis, more consistent returns are likely by designing a hedge to protect against slow-grinding bear markets. Even as the calendar put spread makes a trade-off between theta and gamma, the strategy captures the characteristic needed for an effective hedge, namely negative delta.

Exhibit 6.11 shows the profit or loss earned on this diagonal put spread for changes in the price of the underlying securitiy. Notice that both upside potential and downside risk are limited, which is typical of a spread structure. The chart explicitly shows that the spread reaches its maximum value when the price of the underlying hits the lower strike at expiration of the short-dated option. Prior to expiration, the value of the spread increases as the price of the underlying falls, but slows as it approaches the lower strike. This is the characteristic of an option strategy with negative gamma. This causes the delta of the spread to decrease as the price of the underlying falls. Offsetting this phenomenon is a rise in theta. As the price of the underlying falls to the lower strike, delta moves toward zero, gamma becomes more

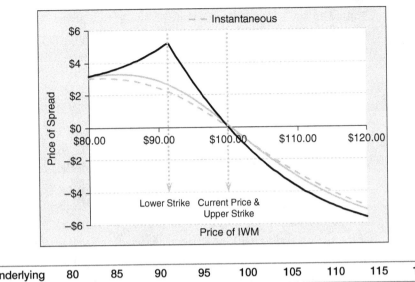

Underlying	80	85	90	95	100	105	110	115	120
% Change	−20%	−15%	−10%	−5%	0%	5%	10%	15%	20%
Price	$9.817	$9.737	$9.212	$8.176	$6.774	$5.265	$3.876	$2.732	$1.860
% Change	45%	44%	36%	21%	0%	−22%	−43%	−60%	−73%
Leverage	−2.246	−2.915	−3.599	−4.139	N/A	−4.456	−4.278	−3.978	−3.627
Delta	0.014	−0.055	−0.158	−0.252	−0.300	−0.296	−0.256	−0.201	−0.148
Gamma	−0.009	−0.018	−0.021	−0.015	−0.004	0.005	0.010	0.011	0.010
Vega	7.32	8.75	12.01	18.21	25.59	31.12	32.99	31.34	27.39
Theta	1.793	3.606	4.570	3.789	1.718	−0.469	−1.934	−2.524	−2.489

Exhibit 6.11   Profit/Loss for a Calendar Put Spread

$$\text{Maximum gain} = \text{Value of Long Dated put} - \text{Premium}$$
$$\text{when price of underlying} = \text{Strike of Short Dated put at its expiration}$$
$$\text{Maximum loss} = \text{Premium}$$
$$\text{Breakeven} = \text{Initial share price} + \text{Avg Theta} \times \Delta t$$

negative, and theta becomes more positive. As a result, the rate at which the price of the spread drifts increases, allowing time to cure some of the performance drag caused by negative gamma.

In structuring a hedge, we cannot emphasize enough the importance of managing the price decay that accompanies a typical option strategy. In static scenarios, the value of an option decreases as time passes. This can be true for spread structures as well. It is important to choose a combination of strikes and expirations that is at least theta neutral. Some might argue that spreads do not provide enough protection in a crash scenario. This is indeed the case, and the profit and loss chart reveals this weakness. It is worth repeating that if the price of the underlying index crashes, the protection from this diagonal spread will provide a moderate benefit, which is limited to the difference between the two strike prices less the premium paid up front. It is important to note that the frequency of market crashes compressed into a time period of a few days or a week is quite rare. As a result, hedging to gain crash protection is a losing strategy almost all the time. The analysis in Chapter 4 reminds us of this fact. What is more likely is the slow-grinding bear market which this strategy addresses nicely.

Since spread trades, by their very nature, present limited gains and losses, it is important to manage the position. Investors should consider rolling the hedge on a monthly basis if the price of the underlying security has changed. A change in the price of the underlying security along with the passing of time causes the delta of the spread to drift away from its original level. Therefore, in order to maintain the desired delta and price decay characteristics, we must adjust the strikes on both legs of the spread and extend the expirations as well. Even if the price of the underlying does not change, we might want to tweak the spread around the edges. This might be necessary because delta on a diagonal put spread will rise as it ages. Furthermore, fluctuations in the volatility surface will cause delta to drift as well.

Performance Simulation: Hedging High-Yield Bonds Plus a Diagonal Put Spread

Theory is one thing, and application to the real world is quite another. It is important to test the effectiveness of this hedging technique under real-world conditions. To do this, we performed a simulation of this hedging technique using the historical performance of high-yield bonds and index options. Furthermore, investors are faced with transaction costs in the form of commissions paid to brokers and bid/off spreads paid to market makers on listed options. It is important to consider transaction costs in the analysis, as the value of the hedge must overcome this source of performance drag. After all, if transactions costs eat up all the hedging benefits, what is the point?

To that end, the following is a presentation of the effectiveness of the calendar put spread referencing a broad market equity index for protecting the value of a portfolio of high-yield bonds. In this historical simulation, we use the IBOXX high-yield index as a proxy for a diversified portfolio of high-yield bonds. In addition, we use listed options on IWM, which is an ETF designed to mimic the performance of the Russell 2000 index. Before we get started, it is important to understand the elements of the simulation. Listed below are all the characteristics that define the historical simulation. It defines the indexes used and expresses the option structure employed and transactions costs incurred, along with criteria for how the hedge is managed.

Underlying Portfolio and Hedging Structure

Underlying high-yield portfolio = IBOXX high-yield index

Underlying equity index = Russell 2000 index (IWM)

Upper strike on long-dated (12-month option) = at the money

Lower strike on short-dated (3-month option) = 8.6% out of the money

Hedge Amount

Value of high-yield portfolio = $1 million

Hedge Ratio = 0.17

Notional amount of IWM to sell = 0.17 × $1,000,000 = $170,000

Initial delta on the put spread = Delta of upper leg − Delta on lower leg

Delta on put spread = −0.492 − (−0.192) = −0.300

# of spreads = Notional Equity/(Delta × Price IWM × 100 shares/option)

# of spreads = −$170,000/(−0.300 × 100 × 100) = 57 spreads

Capital required = # of spreads × Price/spread × 100 shares/contract

Initial capital required = 57 × $6.774 × 100 = $38,612

Transactions Costs

Commission = $3/spread

Bid/Offer iVol of 12-month ATM option = 0.25% ($0.094)

Bid/Offer iVol of 3-month 8.6% OTM option = 0.10% ($0.008)

Transaction cost = # of contracts × (Commission + Bid/offer spread)

57 × (3 + (0.094 + 0.008) × 100) = $752

Roll Criteria

Roll after 1 month if IWM moves more than 3%

Mandatory roll after 2 months

The simulation assumes we start out with a $1,000,000 bond portfolio. To hedge that portfolio, we apply a hedge ratio of 17 percent. This means we short $170,000 notional of the Russell 2000 index. A diagonal put spread is purchased to create that hedge. The upper strike selected is at the money and has a life of 12 months. To get the same price performance as the 30 delta put, we chose a strike price that is

8.6 percent out of the money with three months to expiration for the downside put. At the end of each month, a test is made. If the price of IWM has moved by 3 percent or more, the diagonal put spread contracts are rolled into a new longer-dated spread and the strikes are reset to the structure stated above. If not, the position is held for an additional month. This is done to minimize transactions costs.

Exhibit 6.12 shows how this hedging technique would have performed from January 2005 through July 2015. To be clear, the time to expiration and moneyness of the two options is held fixed during the simulation. There is no tweaking of the structure over time. By keeping the structure constant, this will provide a true test of the diagonal put spread as a permanent investment strategy. Furthermore, it will allow us to witness the performance of this strategy across an investment cycle and certain market events. At the beginning of the simulation, 57 spreads are purchased to provide the appropriate hedge. The reader should be aware that the delta of the spread would fluctuate with changes in the volatility term structure, the level of the underlying index, and interest rates. This causes the number spreads and cost of the hedge to fluctuate with market conditions to keep the hedge ratio fixed at 17 percent.

Exhibit 6.12 shows a comparison of the historical returns of high-yield bonds with a hedged portfolio. The light gray line shows the total return path of the IBOXX high-yield index on a standalone basis. The black line shows the total return path of the IBOXX high-yield index hedged with a diagonal put spread on IWM using the hedge ratio of 0.17 established earlier. The reader can see that during the first few years, the unhedged portfolio outperforms. Once high-yield bonds enter a bear market in 2007, the hedged portfolio outperforms the IBOXX high-yield index in a

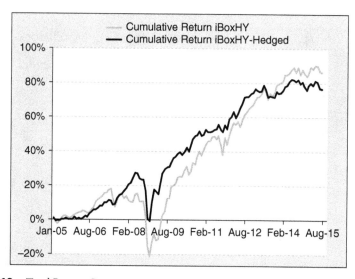

Exhibit 6.12   Total Return Comparison

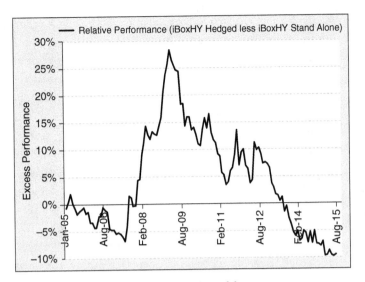

Exhibit 6.13   Relative Performance of the Hedged Portfolio

big way. As the high-yield bond market recovered after the crash of 2008, the hedge portfolio begins to lag once again. This becomes apparent in Exhibit 6.13, which shows the relative performance of the hedged portfolio versus high-yield bonds held on a standalone basis.

What investors should find very interesting about these results is that over the investment cycle, the hedged portfolio produces a very similar cumulative total rate of return as the unhedged portfolio, but produces those returns with far lower volatility. Said another way, return per unit of risk increases substantially and this is just as valuable as increasing returns at the same level of risk. To capture those higher returns, an investor could have leveraged up the hedged portfolio to match the risk level of the unhedged portfolio. This leveraged portfolio would have handily outperformed the high-yield bonds on a standalone basis. Exhibit 6.14 summarizes the risk and return characteristics in numerical form.

This hedging strategy, after transactions costs, reduces the risk of the high-yield bond portfolio by a whopping 287 basis points, or 27.1 percent, while reducing

	IBOXX Unhedged	IBOXX Hedged	Absolute Differential	Difference in %
Annualized Return	6.09%	5.57%	−0.53%	−8.7%
Volatility	10.59%	7.72%	−2.87%	−27.1%
Return/Volatility	0.58	0.72	0.15	25.3%

Exhibit 6.14   Risk versus Return Statistics

return by just 53 basis points a year, or just 8.7 percent. Remember, our goal is to capture the returns of high-yield bonds over the investment cycle without suffering the heart-wrenching fear that comes along with a severe bear market. The diagonal put spread provides a huge improvement in the lifetime return and risk characteristics, proving it is a viable choice for portfolio hedging. Furthermore, it is an infinitely better solution than simply using three-month, 30-delta puts.

This strategy, as with all hedging methods, comes with opportunities and challenges. In Chapter 2, we explained that the delta of out-of-the-money options are particularly sensitive to implied volatility. To recap, as implied volatility rises, so does the absolute value of delta and theta. So in the case of hedging with diagonal put spreads, the delta of the put spread falls as volatility rises if we hold absolute moneyness constant. To maintain the proper hedge, one needs to purchase more spreads, requiring the investor to tie up more money at the margin to maintain the hedge. This phenomenon occurred during the financial crisis of 2008. It is very important to understand this dynamic, as it can affect the capital required to maintain the hedge in real time. This is not an entirely troubling artifact of this tactic. As skew increased and the term structure inverted, the yield of the spread increased. Even though this meant committing more capital to the hedge, the yield provided by that capital increased, adding to the total return of the portfolio. Exhibit 6.15 shows how the characteristics of this diagonal put spread changes with a doubling of implied volatility.

Notice that if volatility doubles, the absolute value of the delta on the 12-month, at-the-money option falls at the margin from 0.492 to 0.439. At the same time, the absolute value of the delta on the downside put rises from 0.192 to 0.303. This causes the absolute value of the delta on the spread to fall by 55 percent

	At the Money	Out of the Money	Calendar Put Spread	30-Delta Put
Price IWM	$100.00			
Dividend Yield	1.73%			
Strike Price	100	91.4		91.8
Time to Exp	12 Months	3 Months		3 Months
Risk-free Rate	0.10%	0.05%		0.05%
iVol	36%	42%		38%
Price	14.977	4.548	10.429	4.003
Delta	−0.439	−0.303	−0.136	−0.299
Gamma	0.011	0.017	−0.006	0.018
Vega	38.856	17.410	21.445	17.321
Theta	−7.694	−15.131	7.437	−13.664

Exhibit 6.15 Calendar Put Spread Characteristics in a High-Volatility Environment

(1 − 0.136/0.300). This means we would have to almost double the amount of diagonal put spreads purchased to maintain a consistent hedge and would have to pay more per spread as well. In this high-volatility environment, capital commitment to the hedge would have to increase from $38,612 to $130,363.

$$\text{\# of spreads} = \$170,000/(0.136 \times 100 \times 100) = 125$$
$$\text{Capital required} = 125 \times \$10.429 \times 100 = \$130,363$$

There is a benefit of purchasing a diagonal put spread in a high-volatility environment. As volatility rises, so does the "yield" on the spread. The theta on the base case example was 1.718. Theta in this high-volatility environment jumps by a factor of 4.3 to 7.437. This means that we would earn a very high yield on the hedge creating a significant return boost. Recall that in Exhibit 6.9 the price of the spread would increase by about $0.14 over a month if the price of the underlying security did not change. Contrast that to a high volatility environment. Exhibit 6.16 shows us that if volatility were to double, the price of the spread would rise by about $0.702 over the same period, resulting in about a fivefold increase in price appreciation per spread.

The relationship between the delta and theta of an option is not as mysterious as it might seem at first blush. Most of us think about how much an option is in or out of the money on an absolute dollar basis. So a put option with a $91.4 strike price on an asset with a value of $100 is $8.6 out of the money. A better way to think about how much an option is in or out of the money is in terms of volatility. In our base case scenario, the $91.4 strike put is about 40 percent of a standard deviation out of the money. This is determined by the following equation:

$$\text{Moneyness in vol. terms} = \text{Moneyness}/i\text{Vol}$$
$$\text{\# of Vols} = 8.6\%/21\% = 0.41 \text{ standard deviations}$$

Now if volatility doubles, the option is half as far out of the money in terms of expected standard deviation of returns. We know from our study of the Greeks in Chapter 2 that theta in dollar terms increases as an out-of-the-money option move closer to at the money. Naturally, the absolute value of delta rises as well.

	12-Month, 100 Mny Put	3-Month, 91.4 Mny Put	Calendar Put Spread	3-Month, 30-Delta Put
Price in 1 Month	14.322	3.191	11.131	3.327
Initial Price	14.977	4.548	10.429	4.003
Change	−0.655	−1.357	0.702	−0.676

Exhibit 6.16 Aging of a Diagonal Put Spread in a High-Volatility Environment

The end result is for the absolute value of delta on the spread to fall, and theta to increase.

If an investor has a limit on how much capital is available to commit to a hedge, there are a few choices available to reduce the number of spreads to purchase and the amount of premium the investor must put up:

- The first and most obvious alternative is that the investor sells a downside put that is more than 8.6 percent out of the money. This will increase the net delta on the spread, reducing the number of spreads that must be purchased, which is partially offset by a higher cost per spread. Net-net, if a downside put sold is 15 percent out of the money, the capital commitment for hedging high-yield bonds in the high-volatility scenario will fall from $130,363 to $87,276. This does, however, reduce theta by about a 44%, reducing the ability of the structure to provide a yield push at the margin.

- The second alternative is to buy an in-the-money put. This will increase the absolute value of delta and preserve the positive theta. While this approach will also reduce the number of spreads required, the increase in the cost per spread almost completely offsets the savings. Replacing the upper strike option with one that is 5 percent in the money only reduces the capital commitment by about $10,000. This change in structure does little to address the constraint.

- The third alternative is to add a "risk reversal" feature to the calendar put spread by selling an out-of-the-money call along with the diagonal put spread. This solution will increase the absolute value of the spread's delta and reduce the capital outlay as well. For example, if we were to write a 10 percent out-of-the-money call and add it to the diagonal put spread, the cash commitment would fall to just $23,450. Furthermore, since we are writing an out-of-the-money call, we know from the analysis in Chapter 4 that these options have a negative alpha, making them a good security to short. Selling another decaying asset to the spread helps preserve the return push from the hedge. The downside is that the hedge will perform very poorly should the IWM rally through the strike on the call option. One of the benefits of using a put spread is that the hedge loses sensitivity as the price of the underlying rises. As a result, the hedge loses potency just when you want it to. By selling an upside call the limited risk feature of a put spread falls away and the hedge increases potency at just the wrong time.

As a final note, capital commitment to a hedge is generally not a problem for institutional managers such as hedge funds. These investors can borrow from their prime brokers to fund their hedges and use their existing portfolio of assets as collateral. These fluctuations in capital commitment only affect those long-only investors who do not have access to borrowing against their portfolio holdings.

1 × 2 Ratio Put Spreads

Some practitioners use ratio put spreads to hedge a specific asset or underlying portfolio of securities, particularly in low- to moderate-volatility environments. In a long ratio put spread, more downside puts are sold than at-the-money puts. Typically, the practitioner sells two downside puts for every at-the-money put, both having the same time to expiration. At first blush, a 1 × 2 ratio put spread, which is the most common ratio used, appears to be a reasonable method of hedging portfolios or individual securities while reducing the capital outlay upfront. After all, if the price of the underlying security falls, but not by enough to exceed the downside put strike, a capital gain is earned on the long put position and the downside puts expire worthless, producing a handsome gain overall. We believe the ratio put spread is a poor structure to use when constructing a hedge and the reason for this view will become clearer in a moment. Exhibit 6.17 summarizes the capital outlay and characteristics of a typical ratio put spread in an average volatility environment.

The capital outlay for each spread is $1.451, which is less than the amount needed for the diagonal put spread or even a 30 delta put. However, we should also note that the delta on this ratio put spread is just −0.115, which means we need almost three times as many spreads to get the same delta as in the 1 × 1 diagonal put spread, which means more transactions costs. The big selling point of this structure carries a highly positive theta, which tells us that the value is the structure will increase faster than a traditional diagonal put spread. Notwithstanding its positive attributes, we believe the 1 × 2 ratio put spread is a very poor solution to the hedging problem. Exhibit 6.18 shows why.

Price IWM	$100.00		
Dividend Yield	1.73%		
# of Contracts	Buy 1	Sell 2	
	At the Money	Out of the Money	1 × 2 Put Spread
Strike Price	100	91.4	
Time to Maturity	3 Months	3 Months	
Risk-free Rate	0.10%	0.05%	
Implied Volatility	18%	21%	
Price	$3.788	$1.169	$1.451
Delta	−0.498	−0.192	−0.115
Gamma	0.044	0.026	−0.008
Vega	19.861	13.616	7.371
Theta	−7.958	−6.04	4.122

Exhibit 6.17   Characteristics of a Three-Month 1 × 2 Ratio Put Spread

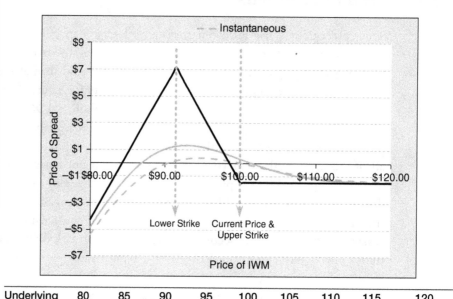

Underlying	80	85	90	95	100	105	110	115	120
% Change	−20%	−15%	−10%	−5%	0%	5%	10%	15%	20%
Price	−3.932	−0.565	1.338	1.824	1.451	0.856	0.402	0.156	0.051
% Change	−371%	−139%	−8%	26%	0%	−41%	−72%	−89%	−97%
Leverage	18.553	9.261	0.776	−5.149	N/A	−8.197	−7.228	−5.952	−4.825
Delta	0.794	0.536	0.227	−0.012	−0.115	−0.111	−0.069	−0.032	−0.012
Gamma	−0.040	−0.061	−0.059	−0.035	−0.008	0.007	0.009	0.006	0.003
Vega	−13.70	−23.51	−26.42	−19.06	−7.371	0.866	3.458	2.781	1.463
Theta	6.914	10.886	12.026	8.988	4.122	0.537	−0.823	−0.816	−0.454

Exhibit 6.18   Profit and Loss, 1 × 2 Ratio Put Spread

The solid black line shows the payoff pattern for this 1 × 2 ratio put spread at expiration. Note that it provides a significant benefit when the Russell 2000 index falls by 8.6 percent or less. The maximum benefit is captured when the index falls exactly to the downside strike. In this example, we would earn about $7.149 before transactions costs on this hedge if the value of the Russell 2000 index falls exactly 8.6 percent to $91.4. This is a terrific result, but somewhat deceptive. Anyone who tries to time the market knows how difficult it is to predict the price of an asset or an index over any time interval. It is even more difficult to predict the price of an asset at a specific point in time. Equally deceptive is that the strategy works nicely when the markets are well behaved. If markets rise modestly, investors lose a small fraction of their premium by the time they roll the hedge and reset the strikes. If, on the other hand, the market falls moderately, the value of the hedge rises in response to that market action and the positive theta acts as a kicker resulting in an additional boost to the hedge's performance.

An effective hedge will provide some level of protection to the value of an asset or portfolio under all circumstances. Notice that this is not the case with the 1 × 2 put spread. The problem is that the value of the hedge hits an inflection point as the price of the underlying asset approaches the downside strike. At some point, the delta of the hedge collapses to zero eliminating its effectiveness for a further drop in price. Even worse, as the value of the index continues to fall, the delta on this structure turns from negative to positive, causing the value of the hedge to fall in price adding to the losses taking place in the high-yield bond portfolio. This is very problematic as the investor is adding risk and leverage to their portfolio just at the time when they want to reduce risk and leverage. So instead of being long high-yield bonds and short equities as in a hedge, one is long high-yield bonds and long equities after a significant downside move.

While we believe investors should avoid 1 × 2 or more highly leveraged ratio put spreads as a solution to the hedging problem, one should not discount the concept altogether. Slight ratios can improve the risk / return performance of a high-yield bond or equity portfolio over an investment cycle. This occurs because using a slight ratio has only a moderate impact on the spread's delta, which can be addressed by layering on a few more spreads. We showed in Chapter 4 that downside puts suffer from negative alpha. Therefore, selling a few more of these options increases the yield or return push of the hedge. Furthermore, statistical theory tells us that there is only a 2.5 percent chance that returns will be worse than two standard deviations to the downside. So the risk of running past the inflection point is nominal, and even if it does, returns on the hedged portfolio will only be reduced nominally. With this in mind, testing various ratios against historical experience indicates using a 1 × 1.2 ratio diagonal put spread is an optimal long-term solution that provides the protection needed to stabilize returns on a high-yield bond portfolio while adding additional yield. Exhibit 6.19 shows the characteristics of a 1 × 1.2 ratio diagonal put spread. Exhibit 6.20 shows the profit-and-loss pattern for this structure.

Notice that even under a crash scenario, this slight ratio put spread still produces a payoff pattern that provides some protection to the underlying portfolio. It's important to remember that while a slight ratio spread structure will not provide the same level of protection as a 1 × 1 put spread under this scenario, it will outperform that structure 97.5 percent of the time. So over an investment cycle, additional returns are there for the taking by incorporating a slight ratio into the diagonal put spread structure. To show this phenomenon, Exhibit 6.21 combines a 1 × 1.2 to

Price IWM	$100.00		
Dividend Yield	1.73%		
# of Contracts	**Buy 1**	**Sell 1.2**	**1 × 1.2**
	At the Money	**Out of the Money**	**Put Spread**
Strike Price	100	91.4	
Time to Maturity	3 months	3 months	
Risk-free Rate	0.10%	0.05%	
Implied Volatility	18%	21%	
Price	$3.788	$1.169	**$2.386**
Delta	−0.498	−0.192	**−0.268**
Gamma	0.044	0.026	**−0.013**
Vega	19.861	13.616	**3.522**
Theta	−7.958	−6.04	**−0.710**

Exhibit 6.19   Characteristics of a 1 × 1.2 Ratio Put Spread

$$\text{\# of spreads} = \$170,000/(0.268 \times 100 \times 100) = 63$$

$$\text{Capital required} = 63 \times \$2.386 \times 100 = \$15,032$$

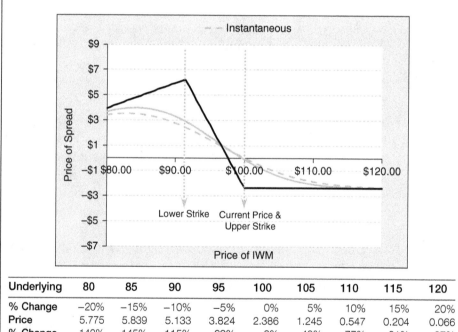

Underlying	80	85	90	95	100	105	110	115	120
% Change	−20%	−15%	−10%	−5%	0%	5%	10%	15%	20%
Price	5.775	5.839	5.133	3.824	2.386	1.245	0.547	0.204	0.066
% Change	142%	145%	115%	60%	0%	−48%	−77%	−91%	−97%
Leverage	−7.10	−9.65	−11.51	−12.06	N/A	−9.56	−7.71	−6.10	−4.86
Delta	0.081	−0.063	−0.214	−0.292	−0.268	−0.184	−0.099	−0.043	−0.016
Gamma	−0.023	−0.032	−0.025	−0.005	0.013	0.019	0.014	0.008	0.003
Vega	−7.92	−12.78	−12.25	−5.02	3.52	7.72	7.06	4.41	2.10
Theta	3.535	5.530	5.410	2.645	−0.710	−2.470	−2.393	−1.520	−0.730

Exhibit 6.20   1 × 1.20 Ratio Put Spread

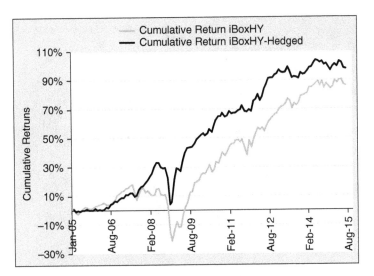

Exhibit 6.21   Hedging with a 1 × 1.2 Calendar Put Spread

the diagonal put spread structure analyzed above as a hedging method and compares its performance to the total rate of return of the IBOXX high-yield index.

Exhibit 6.21 shows a comparison of the historical returns of high-yield bonds with a hedged portfolio incorporating a slight ratio into the diagonal put spread. The gray line shows the total return path of the IBOXX high-yield index on a standalone basis. The black line shows the total return path of the IBOXX high-yield index using the same hedge ratio of 0.17 determined earlier. This analysis shows that a slight ratio improves the performance of the hedge portfolio substantially over the time period studied. Exhibit 6.22 shows the relative performance of the hedged portfolio versus high-yield bonds held on a standalone basis.

Investors should find these results very interesting. The hedged portfolio substantially outperforms the IBOXX high-yield index in bear markets, which is what it is designed to do. When the equity market rallies, the hedged portfolio lags, but to a lesser extent than incorporation of a 1 × 1 ratio diagonal put spread. Since the value of high-yield bonds are higher over the time period studied, this tells us that over a market cycle, the sale of additional short-dated, downside puts at the margin provides more than enough yield over the long haul to offset the return lost during market distress. Not only does it produce higher returns, but this structure produces those higher returns with far lower volatility. This is a very nice improvement in the return earned per unit of risk endured. Exhibit 6.23 summarizes the risk-and-return characteristics in numerical form for the time period studied.

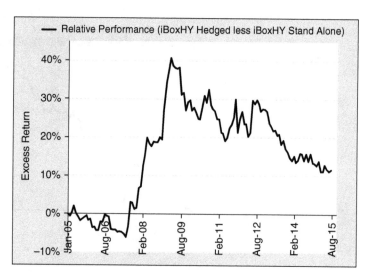

Exhibit 6.22   Relative Performance of the Hedged Portfolio

	IBOXX Unhedged	IBOXX Hedged	Absolute Differential	Difference in %
Annualized Return	6.09%	6.71%	0.62%	10%
Volatility	10.59%	8.45%	−2.04%	−20%
Return/Volatility	0.58	0.79	0.21	36%

Exhibit 6.23   Risk versus Return Statistics of the Ratio Calendar Put Spread

After transactions costs, the portfolio hedged with a ratio calendar put spread produces a total return that is 62 basis points a year higher than the IBOXX index on a standalone basis. This is a remarkable 10 percent improvement. In addition, volatility of those returns is 204 basis points lower, which is a 20 percent reduction. This is alpha generation at its finest.

■ Hedging Equity Portfolios with 1 × 1.1 Ratio Diagonal Put Spreads

The traditional method of hedging an equity portfolio in some sense is a more straightforward process. One simply takes the dollar-weighted beta of the portfolio to be hedged and sells short an equivalent amount of dollar-weighted beta of the hedge instrument. This hedge instrument might be an ETF on the S&P 500 index (SPY), an ETF on the Russell 2000 index (IWM), or a futures contract on any leading market index. By rearranging that relationship, the notional value of the hedge instrument we need to sell is simply the market value of the portfolio multiplied by the ratio of the portfolio beta divided by the hedge instrument beta.

$$\text{Value of ETF needed for hedge} = \text{Market value portfolio} \times \frac{\beta_{Portfolio}}{\beta_{ETF}}$$

We know from capital market theory that the return on an individual equity or equity portfolio is a function of the risk-free rate, the beta of the asset, and the return on the market portfolio.

$$R_{Portfolio} = \text{RFR} + \beta_{Portfolio} \times [R_{Market} - RFR]$$

As a result, the return and risk on a portfolio of equities is linearly related to the return and risk provided by the equity market. The trouble with a straight beta hedge is that reducing market risk reduces return by a fixed proportional amount for any level of hedge. If we reduce beta of the portfolio to zero by hedging, we should expect to just earn the risk-free rate. Such a position would have basis risk, as the composition of the portfolio is not likely to be the same as the hedge instrument. Unfortunately, the market does not compensate the investor for this risk. If we do not want to take any risk, we are better off simply investing in a portfolio of short-term government securities. The only way to create alpha using a strategy of shorting a market index against the portfolio of specific equity investments is through superior security selection. The ultimate objective of hedging is to identify a strategy in which the hedge itself creates alpha over an investment cycle. In principle, we know how to do this by employing a diagonal put spread on a market index incorporating a slight ratio.

With this in mind, the investor needs to find the appropriate hedge ratio. To find the optimal hedge ratio, we recreate the efficient frontier of hedged portfolios just like the exercise performed in Exhibit 6.4. In this instance, we need to apply mean variance analysis a little bit differently. In this application, we examine the risk/return tradeoff using two assets. The portfolio itself is used as one asset and instead of using a market index, we use the ratio diagonal put spread as the second asset. Even though equities are more volatile than high-yield bonds, we chose to sell a short-dated downside put that is 8.6 percent out of the money while still using a long-dated at-the-money put. By using the spread directly in the optimization process, we incorporate the nonlinearity in the hedge into the optimization process. Specifically, when using a diagonal put spread, the hedge tapers off as the price of equities increases and holds relatively stable as the price of equities fall up until

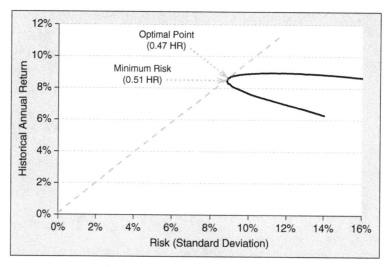

Exhibit 6.24   Efficient Frontier of Hedged Equity Portfolios

it reaches the lower strike of the spread. To apply this approach, one performs a statistical analysis on the historical returns to determine mean, variance, and correlation of these two assets. We then plot the performance of theoretical portfolios that incorporate differing hedge ratios in mean-variance space, just as we did in Exhibit 6.4. Once again, one draws a borrowing and lending line to a point that is tangent to the efficient frontier of potential portfolios to identify the one that is superior to all others. The following chart shows this graphically. By the way, we employ IWM in this example as a proxy for an actively managed portfolio of equity securities. Options on IWM are used to construct the ratio diagonal put spread.

To produce Exhibit 6.24, we assumed the same transaction costs incorporated in the debt-hedging exercise and a slightly less levered ratio of 1 × 1.1 is used. This small ratio helps create additional positive theta, which adds the return derived from the hedge over time while still providing the protection desired. The results of this analysis are really quite intriguing. The lowest point on the frontier of potential portfolios represents an fully hedged portfolio. The highest point found on the upper-right-hand side represents an unhedged portfolio. Notice that the top of the efficient frontier is relatively flat. This tells us that adding a hedge reduces risk and has little impact on returns. This phenomenon continues until we reach the optimal portfolio. Getting to the numbers, this analysis tells us that the minimum risk portfolio is constructed by purchasing a 1 × 1.1 diagonal put spread with a notional value equal to 51 percent of the market value of the underlying portfolio.

The optimal portfolio incorporates a slightly heavier hedge at 47 percent.

$$\text{\# of spreads} = \$470,000/(0.281 \times 100 \times 100) = 167$$
$$\text{Capital required} = 167 \times \$6.657 \times 100 = \$111,172$$

For every million dollars of equity portfolio market value, an investor buys 167 spreads, which requires a capital commitment of approximately $111,000 or 11.1 percent of the underlying portfolio. To show the historical performance of this hedging strategy, Exhibit 6.25 compares the total rate of return of IWM with one that is optimally hedged with a slight ratio diagonal put spread.

Exhibit 6.25 shows a comparison of the historical returns of IWM with that same ETF optimally hedged incorporating a slight ratio diagonal put spread. The gray line shows the total return path of IWM on a standalone basis. The black line shows the total return path of this index hedged at the 47 percent level. This analysis shows that the hedge portfolio substantially outperforms the unhedged portfolio over the time period studied. To get a closer look at the short-term tracking error, Exhibit 6.26 shows the relative performance of the hedged portfolio relative to IWM held on a standalone basis.

Once again, investors should find these results very interesting. The hedged portfolio substantially outperforms the IWM in bear markets, which is what it is designed to do. When the market rallies, the hedged portfolio tends to lag, which is to be expected. Over a number of years, the hedge does not seem to damage returns as the yield on the hedge tends to offset the loss due to delta. But over a full

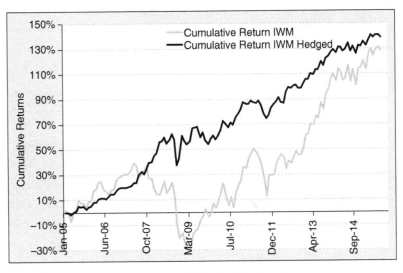

Exhibit 6.25　Hedging IWM with a 1 × 1.1 Calendar Put Spread

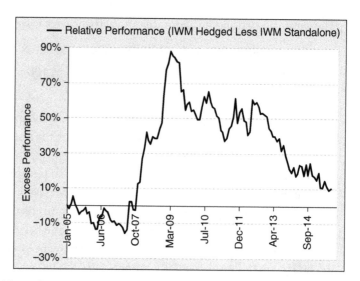

Exhibit 6.26 Relative Performance of the Hedged Portfolio

	IWM Unhedged	IWM Hedged	Absolute Differential	Difference in %
Annualized Return	8.18%	8.65%	0.74%	9.1%
Volatility	19.19%	8.94%	−10.25%	−53%
Return/Volatility	0.43	0.97	0.54	126%

Exhibit 6.27 Risk versus Return Statistics of the Ratio Calendar Put Spread

investment cycle, not only does the hedged portfolio produce higher returns; it does so with far lower volatility. This is a very nice improvement in the return earned per unit of risk endured. Exhibit 6.27 summarizes the risk-and-return characteristics in numerical form for the time period studied.

After transactions costs, the hedged equity portfolio produces a total return that is 0.74 basis points a year higher than the IWM on a standalone basis. This is a 9 percent improvement. In addition, volatility of those returns is 10.25 basis points lower, which is a notable 53 percent reduction in risk. This exercise shows that incorporating a 1 × 1.1 ratio diagonal put spread as a hedge is a strategy that will generate alpha over an investment cycle.

Final Thought

Many investors avoid using options as an integral part of their portfolio strategy. They avoid options because single-leg strategies produce too much return drag and damage returns over time. The analysis in Chapter 4 showed that short-dated, out-of-the-money puts generate negative alpha. Those that attempt to hedge using these instruments generally walk away disappointed. Unless their timing is perfect, these options tend to expire worthless. In this chapter, we showed that investors could enhance their returns and reduce risk by employing a more sophisticated strategy that is relatively simple to execute. Listed options on the major equity indexes are very liquid and are tradable at moderate cost. Given the depth of the market for these instruments, even institutional investors who manage billions of dollars will find they can employ the proposed strategy without moving the market. Since these instruments trade continuously throughout the day, individual investors are able to get the same quality of execution as the big guys do. Slight ratio diagonal put spreads are a hedging strategy fit for most if not all investors.

## CHAPTER 7

Option Strategies for Special Situations

Price action of risky assets in capital markets is anything but predictable with certainty. Companies announce changes in sales, profitability, products, policy, strategy, and capital structure all the time for example. Sometimes an investor doing his homework might be able to predict the probability of certain events occurring, but many if not most news events are a surprise catching the investor flatfooted. These corporate actions not only have an effect on the share price of the underlying stock, they have an effect on the price of options associated with those shares. Consequently, it is important to build intuition concerning option-pricing behavior in unusual circumstances. With this understanding, traders and investors will find opportunities from time to time that others will miss. Just as importantly, investors will avoid some of the pitfalls that cause unexpected but predictable losses with hindsight. The first situation discussed below concerns companies whose shares are heavily shorted. Stocks or other assets that are heavily shorted by speculators often behave differently than those that are not. In particular, they have the potential to become more volatile vis-à-vis historical experience and the distribution of potential returns can become skewed. Furthermore, it can cause the market to price options differently apart from a shift in implied volatility. With this knowledge, we can structure an option strategy to put the odds of success in the investor's favor to capitalize on this unique and temporary condition.

Second, we will also discuss skew more deeply. Skew changes the price and performance characteristics of certain options relative to their cohorts. These changes reveal shifts in investor sentiment concerning near-term price action of the underlying asset. The "signal" of stress or lack thereof expressed through the shape of the volatility surface often creates directional opportunity. To take advantage of that signal, we present a strategy designed to take advantage of this indicator of market stress.

Third, it is important to remember that the standard listed option in the United States allows for exercise at any time. While this does not affect the price behavior most of the time, it does so often enough to be an issue that must stay on our radar screen. One of the strategies institutional investors use to add value is called "dividend capture." In theory, when a company pays a dividend, its price is supposed to fall by the amount of dividend paid. Academic studies show that stocks often fall less than the dividend paid. As a result, tax advantaged institutional investors like pension funds will buy a stock before the ex-dividend date, and flip the stock after the dividend is paid. (Tax laws require owners of stocks paying qualified dividends to hold the asset unhedged for at least 61 days out of a 121 day required holding period to enjoy favorable tax treatment of the dividend paid. So taxable entities usually do not participate in this activity.) For protection during this holding period, investors buy puts or sell calls to reduce or eliminate market risk from the strategy. With heavy demand for liquidity, price dislocations pop up from time to time, allowing speculators to get paid for providing liquidity to investors willing to pay for protection. Owners of calls do not have the right to the dividend paid by a company. To capture the dividend, the investor must exercise the option and settle the trade before the ex-dividend date. When a company pays a large special dividend, it might pay for the owners of an in- or at-the-money option to exercise their right early. Option sellers need to be aware of this phenomenon to avoid unexpected losses.

◾ Option Strategy for Stocks under Heavy Short Interest

When companies falter (think Best Buy in 2011 and 2012) or are perceived to be way overpriced by some investors (think Tesla in the second half of 2013), they attract short sellers who want to take advantage of a potential fall in the price of a company's shares. Hedge funds do this by selling the company's shares short, which requires them to borrow stock. If too many hedge funds get the same idea, the amount of stock sold short becomes large relative to the total number of shares issued by the company. The measure of the quantity of shares that investors have sold short but not yet covered is known as the **short interest**. By itself, the number of shares sold short is not particularly meaningful, as the number of shares issued from one company to another differs. A more meaningful measure is known as the **short interest ratio**. It reveals the percentage of stock outstanding that is sold short. When the short interest ratio hits an extreme, there is the potential for a **short squeeze**. A short squeeze manifests as a sharp rise in the price of the asset sold short. It usually starts with a small rise in price. Short sellers, by their very nature, invest with a short time horizon. As they see price start to rise, they quickly get nervous and some will begin to cover their short position. As they do so, they push the price of a stock higher. Eventually, other short sellers panic and buy back their position at virtually any price. The end result it that the company's share price increases violently until the short sellers are *squeezed* out of their positions. Sometimes, other aggressive investors see the price spike and attempt to sell short at these higher prices. If the price continues to rise, these investors eventually exit their position at a loss before an even greater loss is suffered. At the extreme, this self-feeding loop can cause the price of an asset to rise far beyond a rational investor's view of value. This process continues until there are few if any short sellers or potential short sellers left.

Short squeezes represent a unique situation. Most investors do their homework and decide to buy an asset because they believe it is underpriced in the market place. They deliberately invest in the asset with the expectation that the price will rise to the value they place on the asset. Large institutional investors buy carefully, sometimes using trading algorithms to minimize their impact on price. When a short squeeze gets underway, short sellers buy for the exact opposite reason. They do not buy to take advantage of expected higher prices in the future; they buy to hide from higher prices. This makes the purchase an emotional one and the execution price is secondary to asset valuation.

Options provide a good way to play a potential short squeeze, as we can construct a strategy that has the potential for large gains with limited risk. One of the best strategies to capitalize on a potential price spike brought on by a short squeeze is to construct a *short ratio call spread*. To structure a short ratio call spread, sell an at-the-money call and buy two or more out-of-the-money calls. Don't be confused by the name. A short ratio call spread has both bullish and bearish implications. If the share price rises moderately, this spread will perform with bearish repercussions, as it will lose value. If the share price rises substantially, it will perform with bullish implications, and it has the potential to produce significant gains. There is always the possibility that a stock in a bearish trend will continue. The beauty of this strategy is that if it is properly structured, this strategy can allow for a nominal gain should the price of the stock stagnate or drift lower. As the options approach their expiration date, this allows the investor to reset strikes and expirations to new levels without suffering a loss due to time decay while awaiting the anticipated short squeeze and the outsized gains that come with it.

Consider company XYZ, whose stock exists with a heavy short interest that is currently trading for $25.00 a share. Exhibit 7.1 is an example of how we might want to structure a short ratio call spread to capitalize on a price spike resulting from a short squeeze. In this structure, we sell a three-month, at-the-money call, and buy two, three-month 12 percent out-of-the-money calls. Since a stock that is

	Sell	Buy	Net Credit
Number of Options	1	2	
Strike	$25	$28	
Risk-free Rate	2.00%	2.00%	
Dividend	1.00%	1.00%	
Time to Expiration	0.25	0.25	
Volatility	35%	35%	
Call Price	$1.77	$1.48	$0.29

Exhibit 7.1   Short 1 × 2 Ratio Call Spread, Stock Trading at $25 a Share

falling might continue to do so, we chose strikes and a ratio to enable the trade to profit if the stock price stagnates or trades down over the life of the spread.

With this structure, the investor collects a $0.29 credit at the time the trade is initiated. This is the profit the investor will earn if the share price stagnates or falls, and the position is held to expiration. This is an important part of the structure as stocks that are heavily shorted are often in a downtrend, which usually continues until the selling stops. To attain this attribute, there is a trade-off between the ratio selected and the strike prices chosen, while still creating the opportunity for significant upside gains should a short squeeze manifest. The beauty of this structure is that it has a high probability of success. Probability theory tells us that there is a 66 percent chance the stock will be trading below $25.29 or above $30.71, which are the two breakeven points. Like any trade, this one is not guaranteed to be a winner, but the risk of loss is quite moderate if managed properly. Under the worst-case scenario, the price of the underlying increases to $28.00 a share at expiration. Under these circumstances, the trade loses $2.71. This return dynamic is revealed in the following chart showing the payoff pattern of this structure. But we should not hold the spread to expiration. The profit and loss dynamic indicates it should be rolled into new strikes and expirations each and every month.

The gray dotted line in Exhibit 7.2 shows the profit or loss we would experience given an instantaneous change in the price of the underlying security. Since the structure has positive delta, a gain will result if the price of the underlying asset rises. Furthermore, the structure has a very high gamma. This causes the delta to disappear quickly if the price of the underlying falls. If the price drop is significant, the delta of this structure turns negative and a gain occurs as well. The trade will suffer a very small nominal loss should the price of the underlying asset fall by a dollar or two.

How this structure ages and how the price of the underlying moves is very important to the way it should be managed to minimize the potential for loss. Since the structure has positive gamma, the theta of this structure is negative (i.e., it will suffer time decay) when the trade is initiated, even though it starts out with a net

Underlying	$20.00	$22.50	$25.00	$27.50	$30.00	$32.50	$35.00
% Change	−27%	−18%	−9%	0%	9%	18%	27%
Price	$0.10	$0.25	$0.29	−$0.06	−$1.02	−$2.55	−$4.52
Change (%)	−283	−517	−583	0	1583	4167	7450
Delta	−0.052	−0.057	0.045	0.257	0.505	0.713	0.851
Gamma	−0.014	0.015	0.066	0.098	0.095	0.069	0.042
Vega	−0.483	0.683	3.623	6.503	7.452	6.415	4.501
Theta	0.346	−0.470	−2.553	−4.622	−5.348	−4.671	−3.358

Exhibit 7.2   Profit/Loss on Short Ratio Call Spread

credit. The process of decay turns to accretion after about a month or so, if the price of the underlying security does not change. To manage the trade, it is important to focus on the performance after a one-month holding period. The breakeven points over a one-month horizon are $23.00 and $27.75. Only a small loss occurs if the shares reside between these points over a one-month time horizon. Of note, the maximum loss we might suffer is just $0.24 a share. If the share price rises modestly, it is important to recognize that the time decay (theta) speeds up as the spread ages. Therefore, we should roll the spread by extending the expiration into new three-month options and adjust the strikes after a one-month holding period. If this is done, the investor eliminates the chance of a loss of any significance. If we let the position ride to expiration, we take the risk of suffering the maximum loss scenario. This analysis shows that there is no reason to take that chance. By holding the spread to expiration, we would lose if the share price trades above $25.00 a share and stays below $30.70 a share. Furthermore, we risk a substantial loss of $2.71 if the share price finds itself at $28 a share. Rolling avoids this potential.

Beginning Values						Ending Values				Gain	Cumulative
Price	Sell Strike	Buy Strike	Sell 1	Buy 2	Net Credit	Price	Sell 1	Buy 2	Net Credit	Loss	Gain/Loss
25	25	28	1.77	0.74	0.29	27	2.72	1.13	0.46	−0.17	−0.17
27	27	30	1.91	0.85	0.21	26	1.08	0.34	0.40	−0.19	−0.36
26	26	29	1.84	0.80	0.24	25	1.02	0.30	0.42	−0.18	−0.54
25	25	28	1.77	0.74	0.29	24	0.97	0.27	0.43	−0.14	−0.68
24	24	27	1.70	0.68	0.34	35	11.05	8.10	−5.15	5.49	$4.81

Exhibit 7.3 Waiting for the Squeeze

The insight to this strategy is that it is a winner if the stock eventually has its big move. While waiting for this event, the investor is likely to suffer a string of small losses. To build some intuition around this phenomenon, it would be useful to walk through an example.

Exhibit 7.3 shows the results of a simulation of performing a monthly roll on this short 1 × 2 ratio call spread. In the first four months, the share price bounces around in a moderate trading range as the share price bleeds lower. Since these are small moves, time decay plays its part and a loss is suffered in these periods. In month 5, the share price reflects the short squeeze and a big gain is recorded. Over this five-month period, this strategy produced a total profit of $4.81. This is extraordinary, given the maximum expected monthly loss is just $0.24. The only scenario in which we suffer a loss is one where the short squeeze never takes place. While not a likely event, it certainly could happen. Given that one winner covers multiple small losers by many factors, a portfolio of these positions should be a winning strategy over time.

To find stocks with short squeeze potential, investors should filter through a list of stocks with liquid listed options and identify the 10 to 20 companies with the highest short interest ratios and construct trades with structures similar to the one just presented. There is one caveat to keep in mind when employing this strategy: Do not overpay for volatility. The higher the iVol on the options traded, the lower the expected rate of return, as the investor needs a bigger move in price to capture a gain. Second, the item to keep an eye on is skew. In a "normal" situation, the iVol of the upside calls is lower than the at-the-money calls. If this is the case, the trade has a higher chance of succeeding than indicated above because the trader buys volatility at a lower price than he sells it. If, on the other hand, the skew takes the form of a volatility smile, this trade requires an investor to buy volatility more expensively than she sells it. This will work to dampen returns and reduce the probability of success. In short, this strategy works best when iVol is low and volatility skew has a normal shape for equities. This strategy will fight against significant headwinds when iVol is high and skew takes the form of a smile.

There are other filters we can use to improve the potential for success. For example, we might look at the valuation metrics of stocks with high short interest to identify the candidates that are more likely to enjoy a turnaround. When good news comes out on a company whose shares carry a high short interest ratio and whose shares trade with cheap valuation metrics, it is an elixir for explosive upward price movement.

Equities with high short interest are not the only situation for ratio spreads. This trade structure is applicable to other situations, such as when a biotech company is waiting for approval for a new drug that would substantially change the fortunes of the company. It is important to keep a creative mind when looking at unique situations to create option strategies that will maximize returns and minimize the risk of loss. Performance charts like the one in Exhibit 7.2 can be used to test strategies and manage time decay.

◾ Opportunities in Skew

Option skew is best represented by the difference between the implied volatility for at-the-money put and call options and out-of-the-money puts or in-the-money calls. It is natural for options with moneyness of 80 or 90 percent to have a higher implied volatility than those with 100 percent moneyness. This is the market's way of expressing observed market dynamics in which prices tend to fall faster than they rise.

Most of the time, skew has little predictive power as an indicator for future price movements of an asset. However, when it hits a historical extreme, it can provide a strong clue that a change in trend might be at hand. When prices are in a downtrend, iVol tends to rise as investors look to put options to protect their existing positions. Some investors do not want to risk much premium, so they select out-of-the-money puts, which pushes up their price and skew. As a result, very high skew is associated with extremes in investor fear, and fear is associated with price bottoms. When markets are in an uptrend, investors are generally confident that prices will continue to rise. Consequently, they shy away from buying insurance. Option sellers participate in that confidence by freely offering put options for sale. They particularly like to sell downside puts as they expect stable or higher prices to cause those puts to expire worthless. This process drives down the absolute value of skew and lowers the volatility surface, as well. Thus, extraordinary low skew indicates complacency by market participants. When traders and investors become overconfident that a bull market will continue, they tend to act on feelings

Exhibit 7.4   Price of Gold versus Skew

of greed, and buy without regard to price. This is the kind of market sentiment that is associated with a top in price.

Directional investors often seek out assets where volatility skew is at an extreme, as these are situations where the options market usually provides opportunity. Exhibit 7.4 is a chart of the price of gold overlaid on top of the corresponding historical skew for options on gold. Notice that skew was very low in August 2011 and this phenomenon occurred just at the time when the price of gold hit a peak. During the next nine months, skew fluctuated around its historical norm and the price of gold fluctuated randomly while falling during this period. In August 2012, skew once again collapsed during an uptrend in price. Depressed skew indicated a top was at hand. Predictably, the price of gold fell. This time prices fell in a relentless down trend that took the price of gold down 25 percent in a matter of just six months. In April 2013, skew moved to a record high, indicating investors were afraid the bear market would continue. Investors who follow skew would be on the lookout for a change in trend. The bottom was confirmed by a reduction in skew as prices began to move higher.

So how should an investor structure a trade when skew moves to an extreme high and they expect a change in price trend at any time? We know from the above analysis that skew will revert to the mean at some point. So we know iVol for options with moneyness less than 100 will fall more than options with moneyness of 100 or more. This tells us we definitely want to be a seller of options with moneyness less than 100 and a buyer of options with moneyness of 100 or higher. This way if the skew curve flattens, the price of the options sold will fall and the price of the options purchased will be relatively unaffected. Since the price of gold is depressed and skew is signaling a bottom could be at hand, we want the trade to profit from a rise in price. To do this, the resulting structure must be delta positive. iVol across the board is elevated and it is expected to fall as the price of gold rises. Therefore, we want the trade to be profitable as iVol falls and reverts to the mean as well. This tells us we are looking for a structure that is short vega. It often takes longer for a scenario to manifest than one expects. Option decay can kill the best-laid plans, so we need a structure that is either theta neutral and positive if possible. A potential trade structure that captures all these attributes is a call spread risk reversal. In this option structure, one buys an at-the-money call. To pay for that call, one simultaneously sells an out-of-the-money call (creating the call spread) and an out-of-the-money put (creating the risk reversal).

Exhibit 7.5 shows the valuation and performance metrics of this call spread risk reversal. This strategy meets all the criteria just outlined: positive delta, negative vega, and positive theta. The same amount of premium is collected on the options sold relative to the call purchased, resulting in no net debit or credit. Since April 2013 was a time of fear with respect to the gold market, downside puts traded with a significant skew. At-the-money options were priced with a 19 percent iVol, while 94.8 moneyness puts were priced at 22 percent. This volatility differential makes these puts relatively expensive allowing a seller to collect a relatively high premium. At the same time, skew drives down the iVol on upside call options, making them somewhat less expensive than at-the-money calls. At the end of the day, this structure allows the investor to buy options with 19 percent volatility and sell others with an average volatility of 20 percent.

The selection of expiries depends on our expected price action, the level of implied volatility, and skew in the future. In this example, we selected a three

	Buy	Sell	Sell	Net
Option Type	Call	Call	Put	
Strike	$115	$121	109	
Moneyness	100	105.2	94.8	
Risk-free Rate	0.10%	0.10%		
Dividend	0.00%	0.00%		
Time to Expiration	0.25	0.25	0.25	
Volatility	19.00%	18.00%	22%	
Call Price	$4.37	$1.90	2.47	$0.00
Delta	0.52	0.30	−0.29	0.51
Vega	22.91	20.07	19.78	−16.94
Theta	−8.76	−7.26	−8.67	7.17

Exhibit 7.5 Call Spread Risk Reversal on GLD Trading at $115/Share

month time to expiration, for consistency with the numerical examples presented throughout the book. However, one should look to longer expirations when the situation warrants. If we hold the opinion that volatility and skew will fall as the price of gold rises, we might want to use a longer-dated structure to gain from a drop in implied volatility. If we were to employ six-month options with the same strikes as above, the trade turns into one with a $1.62 credit. If the price of gold stays above $109 at expiration, the investor gets to keep that premium. If the iVol instantaneously falls by 200 basis points, skew falls from 9.5 percent to 4.75 percent, and the price of gold does not change, the net credit will fall to $0.78. This will allow the investor to exit the trade early and pocket the $0.84 per spread. Not only can the investor earn a return by a likely change in price, but by skew and iVol returning to normal levels as well.

Exhibit 7.6 shows the total return profile of this longer six-month call spread risk reversal. This structure has positive theta initially so it will tend to rise in value over time. If the price of gold rises, the positive delta of 0.49 ensures this structure will be a winner immediately. Since the investor is writing an upside call, the maximum

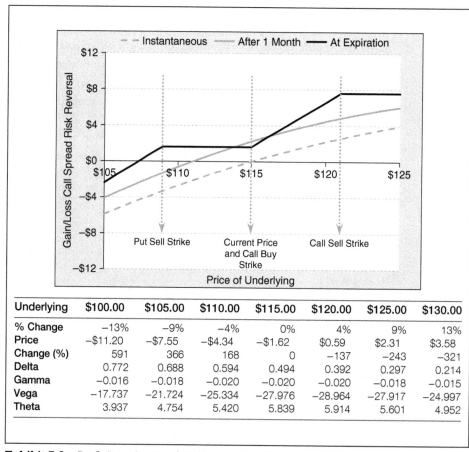

Underlying	$100.00	$105.00	$110.00	$115.00	$120.00	$125.00	$130.00
% Change	−13%	−9%	−4%	0%	4%	9%	13%
Price	−$11.20	−$7.55	−$4.34	−$1.62	$0.59	$2.31	$3.58
Change (%)	591	366	168	0	−137	−243	−321
Delta	0.772	0.688	0.594	0.494	0.392	0.297	0.214
Gamma	−0.016	−0.018	−0.020	−0.020	−0.020	−0.018	−0.015
Vega	−17.737	−21.724	−25.334	−27.976	−28.964	−27.917	−24.997
Theta	3.937	4.754	5.420	5.839	5.914	5.601	4.952

Exhibit 7.6 Profit/Loss Six-Month Call Spread Risk Reversal on GLD

amount one can earn is $7.62 (call upper strike-call lower strike-premium) per spread. As long as the price of GLD does not fall below $107.38, which is the strike of the downside put less the premium collected, the trade will generate a gain. Below that point, the investor will suffer a loss. In the final analysis, the risk/reward of this trade is attractive. So long as the price of GLD does not fall more than 6.63 percent at expiration, the investor will be rewarded for the risk taken. A drop in iVol and/or skew before expiration provides another way the investor can profit from this structure.

There are other strategies investors can use, of course. One could simply sell a six-month, $109 strike put and hope the price is above this level at expiration. In this case, the investor would keep the $4.33 premium collected. The breakeven point of this trade is $104.67, which is 9.0 percent less than the going price of GLD. Investors who are more risk averse might select a lower strike. Naturally, they would have to accept a lower premium. Those who are more risk tolerant might choose a higher strike and collect a higher premium.

Exhibit 7.4 shows that there are times of extremely low skew, as well. August 2011 and July 2012 is a perfect examples of a time when skew went far below its historical norm—in fact, it briefly went negative in 2011. This represents another special situation that option investors can capitalize on. So how should an investor structure a trade in gold options when skew is severely depressed? Skew is a mean reverting variable so, the investor should expect it to increase over time. As a result, iVol for options with moneyness less than 100 will rise more than options with moneyness of 100 or more. This tells us we definitely want to be a buyer of options with moneyness less than 100 and a seller of options with moneyness of 100 or higher. This way, if the skew curve steepens, the price of the options purchased will rise and the price of the options sold will stay the same or fall. Since the price of gold is elevated after a sharp bull move and skew is signaling a change in trend, we want the trade to profit from a fall in price. To do this, the resulting structure must rise when the price of GLD falls (i.e., possess a negative delta). iVol across the board is depressed and it is expected to rise as the price of gold falls. Therefore, we want the trade to be profitable as iVol increases and reverts to the mean as well. This tells us we are looking for a structure that is long vega. We want to avoid time decay, and profit from it if possible, so we need a structure that is either theta neutral or, better yet, positive. A trade structure that captures all these attributes is a short ratio put spread. In this option structure, the investor sells an at-the-money put and uses some or all of the proceeds to purchase downside puts.

Exhibit 7.7 shows the valuation and performance metrics of this 1 × 3 short ratio put spread. This strategy meets the primary criteria outlined, namely, negative delta and positive vega. Theta is problematic, at least initially, as it starts out negative. Far more premium is collected than spent, resulting is a credit of $1.79. This will cause theta to eventually become positive, as the spread ages under the scenario where the price of gold stagnates or continues to rise. Be aware, however, that it

	Sell	Buy	Net
Option Type	Put	Put	
Number of Options	1	3	
Strike	$170	$156	
Moneyness	100	91.8	
Risk-free Rate	0.10%	0.10%	
Dividend	0.00%	0.00%	
Time to Expiration	0.25	0.25	
Volatility	18.00%	18.50%	
Call Price	$6.08	$1.43	–$1.79
Delta	–0.48	–0.16	–0.00
Gamma	0.03	0.02	0.03
Vega	33.87	21.02	29.19
Theta	–12.11	–7.75	–1.51

Exhibit 7.7　　Short 1 × 3 Ratio Put Spread with Gold at $170/Ounce

becomes increasingly negative should the price of gold fall. Since September 2012 was a time of euphoria with respect to the gold market, downside puts trade at a significant discount. At-the-money options were priced with an 18.0 percent iVol, while 91.8 percent moneyness puts were priced at just 18.5 percent. At the end of the day, this structure allows the investor to buy volatility cheap and sell it expensively on a historical basis. As a final thought, extending the time to expiration from three months to six months turns this trade from a net credit of $1.79 to a net debit of $1.17, making it more costly to put on. This structure has a bigger negative delta and more vega, which is good, but it comes with more time decay. At the end of the day, how one structures a trade is a personal choice. While it may not appear that the investor are compensated for the additional time decay by extending time to expiration. However, the loss in a worst case scenario is less, so there is an offsetting benefit.

Exhibit 7.8 shows the total return profile of the three-month short 1 x 3 ratio put spread. This structure has negative theta initially so it will tend to fall in value over the initial phase of the trade. Since the structure pays a net credit, theta eventually become positive and introduces a slight boost to returns. If the price of gold falls, the negative delta and positive gamma make this trade a winner immediately. The beauty of this structure is that the investor still earns a profit if they are too early, which happens quite often in manias. If held to expiration, the investor will keep the premium collected in a bullish scenario. Nonetheless, investors should probably roll the structure to new strikes and expirations after a month should the price of gold rise. Remember, if investors are expecting a sharp drop in price, they should have an optimal structure to capitalize on it.

There are other strategies investors can use, of course. One alternative is to simply sell a 180-strike call and hope the price of gold stays below this level at expiration. In this case, we would keep the $2.52 premium. The breakeven point

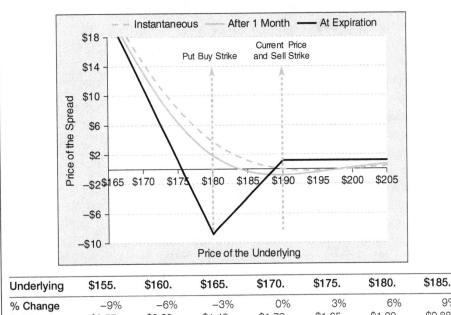

Underlying	$155.	$160.	$165.	$170.	$175.	$180.	$185.
% Change	−9%	−6%	−3%	0%	3%	6%	9%
Price	$2.57	−$0.09	−$1.43	−$1.79	−$1.65	−$1.29	−$0.88
Change (%)	−244	−95	−20	0	−8	−28	−51
Delta	−0.689	−0.386	−0.157	−0.011	0.061	0.082	0.074
Gamma	0.066	0.054	0.037	0.021	0.008	0.001	−0.003
Vega	73.580	64.650	48.046	29.185	12.886	1.704	−4.187
Theta	−27.307	−24.121	−18.069	−11.137	−5.106	−0.931	1.308

Exhibit 7.8 Profit/Loss Short Three-Month 1 × 3 Ratio Put Spread on GLD

of this trade is $182.52, which is 6.9 percent higher than the going price of GLD. Those who are more risk averse might select a higher strike. Naturally, they would have to accept a lower premium. Those who are more risk tolerant might choose a lower strike and collect a higher premium. This is a very dangerous trade, however, as huge price moves can accompany a mania before it ends. This is the lesson learned from the dotcom bubble of 1997 to 1999 and the real estate bubbles for 2000 to 2007. We recommend investors stay with risk-limiting structures like the one suggested above.

Dividend Capture

Investors who purchase common stock are entitled to the dividend, if any, paid by the company. Investors in call options, on the other hand, are not entitled to the dividend because they do not own the stock yet. If the owner of a call wants the dividend, they must exercise their option and take ownership of the shares before the ex-dividend date. This being the case, the market prices of puts and calls reflect the market's expectation of the stream of dividends the company pays over the life of the options. Taking into account discreet dividends is a bit tricky, as the investor must have a sound estimate of the dividend to be paid and the date on which it will be paid.

The B–S–M model is a method of pricing a European option, which cannot be exercised early. Listed options on stocks of individual companies that trade in the United States are American-style options, which are exercisable at any time before the option expires. Most of the time, the B–S–M will price American options correctly, as an option always has time value. Therefore, it is usually better to sell an option than to exercise it early. This condition can break down the day before the ex-dividend date. If the dividend is large enough, such as when a special dividend paid as part of a corporate financial restructuring, it might be optimal to exercise in-, at-, or near-at-the-money options before their expiration date.

Setting aside the issue of early exercise for a moment, we can modify the B–S–M option-pricing model to take into account discrete dividends payable on specific dates. The most common technique practitioners' use is called the *dividend escrow method*. This method assumes that the dividends are known in advance and when they will be paid with certainty. Using this approach, we simply replace the current price of the stock S, with S minus the present value of the dividend stream expected over the life of the option. Now that the dividends have been accounted for in a discrete fashion, the dividend yield is no longer part of the mathematical relationship. By making these substitutions, the following are the formulas we should use when pricing options that pay discreet dividends.

Black–Scholes–Merton Option-Pricing Model for a Company or Index Paying Discrete Dividends

$$C = S^* N(d_1) - Ke^{-rt} N(d_2)$$

with the boundary condition that $C = \text{Max}(0, \ S - K)$ at expiration.

$$P = Ke^{-rt} N(-d_2) - S^* N(-d_1)$$

with the boundary condition that $P = \text{Max}(0, \ K - S)$ at expiration.

$$S^* = S - \sum_{td=0}^{N} \frac{D_t}{(1 + r_{td})^{td}}$$

$$d_1 = \frac{Ln\left(S^*/K\right) + (r + \sigma_S^2/2)\,t}{\sigma_S \sqrt{t}}$$

$$d_2 = d_1 - \sigma_S \sqrt{t}$$

where:

C = Price of a call option
P = Price of a put option
S = Current price of the stock or index
K = Strike price of the option
D_{td} = Dividend paid at time td
r = Risk-free rate
t = Time to option expiration
td = Time to dividend payment
σ_S = Standard deviation of asset returns
$N(\ )$ = Cumulative standard normal distribution function

To price the option correctly using the escrowed dividend model, we must value the option in two distinct ways. We must value the option on the day before the stock goes ex-dividend and repeat the process by valuing the option to its expiration date. The true value of the option is the higher of these two figures. Take the following example where a three-month option goes ex-dividend the day before option expiration.

The analysis in Exhibit 7.9 shows that the B–S–M option model incorporating discrete dividends would price the call at $3.44. If the option could not be exercised early, this would be a fair price as the owner of the option could not exercise their right and collect the dividend. If the option is priced as if it expires the day before the dividend is paid, its value is $5.12. It is higher, because the owner of the option could exercise and capture the dividend if it made sense to do so. Therefore, the fair value of an American option is equal to $5.12, as it can be sold or exercised anytime before the dividend is paid. Said another way, the difference between the value of an American and European option is $1.68.

	Value to Expiration	Value Day Before Ex-Dividend Date
Stock Price	$100	
Strike Price	$102	
Interest Rate	1%	
Volatility	30%	
Time to Dividend	89 days	
Time to Expiration	90 days	89 days
Dividend	$4.00	0.00
Value of a Call	$3.44	$5.12

Exhibit 7.9   Valuing a Call Option with Discreet Dividends

When applying the escrow method, we are implicitly making the assumption that the dividend payments are known in advance with certainty. As we all know, companies change their dividend payments all the time. When companies are doing well and management believes that their prosperity will continue, they will increase their dividend. We know from option-pricing theory that for a given share price, an increase in the dividend will reduce the value of a call option and increase the value of a put option because the price of the stock falls by the dividend amount when the stock goes ex-dividend. But a permanent increase in the dividend is a signal to investors that management expects good times to continue and for earnings to grow. This entices investors to push up the price of the stock, which drives up the price of a call and pushes down the price of a put. This is generally not the case when the company pays a special one-time dividend.

Special one-time dividends are rare, but there are unique situations where a company might choose to do so. One reason for a special dividend occurs when market actors believe there will be a change in the tax law applied to dividend payments. In 2012, for example, dividend payments were taxed at the long-term capital gains tax rate and not the personal tax rate on ordinary income. This means that when a company paid a dividend, investors would have to pay an income tax of no more than 15 percent of the dividend amount, which was far less that the rate on ordinary income of 39.6 percent. The law that established the preferential tax treatment of dividends was set to expire at the end of the year. When it did, dividends for 2013 and beyond would be taxed at the marginal tax rate for ordinary income, which could be as high as 39.6 percent. Since dividends paid to shareholders are not tax deductible at the corporate level, they do not reduce a company's income tax liability. As a result, shareholders were better off getting paid dividends sooner rather than later. At the same time, many large capitalization companies were holding a great deal of cash on their balance sheet. Others had little or no debt on their books. As a result, many companies had the ability to pay dividends out of cash on the balance sheet. Super low interest rates allowed companies without excess cash to borrow and payout the proceeds.

When these companies announced a special dividend to be paid before year-end, it did not have a permanent effect on the company's stock, as it did not represent a signal about rosier future prospects of the company. It could, however, have a material effect on the value of listed options. Take the situation where an investor holds a 90-day option on a company that usually pays a $1.00 per share dividend, and the company announces that it will accelerate $2.00 per share of future dividends into the current dividend payment of $1.00 scheduled for payment in 30 days.

Exhibit 7.10 shows that if investors were holding a European at-the-money call option on the day the accelerated dividend was announced, they would have suffered an immediate loss of $0.96 (5.53 − 4.57). This analysis points out the importance of monitoring the political landscape for potential changes in tax laws that can

	Value to Expiration	Value Day Before Ex-Dividend Date
Stock Price	$100	
Strike Price	$100	
Interest Rate	1%	
Volatility	30%	
Time to Dividend	30 days	
Time to Expiration	90 Days	
Dividend	$1.00	$3.00
Value of a Call	$5.53	$4.56
Value of a Put	$6.28	7.32

Exhibit 7.10 Change in Valuation of a Call Option Incorporating a Special Dividend

temporarily change a company's dividend policy. Buyers of calls also need to pay close attention to management's propensity to give excess cash back to shareholders on a one-time basis as part of a financial restructuring as well. If we anticipated this change, the optimal strategy would be to sell calls and buy stock on a delta-neutral basis. With this strategy, the investor would be hedged against random movements in the price of the underlying stock while capturing a potential windfall from a sharp drop in premium. The effect on the price of a put is equally dramatic. By lowering the forward price of the underlying instrument, the value of an at-the-money put would increase by $1.04 (7.32-6.28). In the end, a special dividend could result in a wealth transfer from call buyers to put buyers, and from put sellers to call sellers. The loss above could be avoided if the owner held an American-style option and they exercised early. So options traders must be aware of when it is appropriate to exercise early.

While the math of special dividends is straightforward, the regulations around that special dividend are more complicated. As a result of this episode with accelerated dividends, regulators in the United States have changed the rules concerning accelerated dividends. Currently in the United States, if the amount of the special dividend is more than $12.50 per contract ($0.125 per share for most option contracts), the strike price will be reduced by the amount of the special dividend. This eliminates the effect of the special dividend on the price of an option. It is important to remember that the rules concerning special dividends differ by country and they change over time. To stay abreast of these rules, investors should visit the website of the local regulatory bodies. For U.S. investors, that would be the OCC.

Listed options that trade on U.S. exchanges are American-style options that give the owner the opportunity to exercise anytime before or at expiration. It is rarely if ever optimal to exercise an option early on a stock that does not pay a dividend. For options on stocks that do pay a dividend, there are circumstances when the investors should exercise early to capture the dividend and avoid losing money. As already shown, cash dividends affect the price of an option because the price of the stock is expected to fall by the dividend amount on the ex-dividend date.

The question is, "When should we exercise an option early?" In option speak, we should exercise an option early when the theoretical value of the option is at parity (i.e., there is no time value) and the option's delta is 1.0. While this might not be particularly helpful for the novice, an example should add clarity. For simplicity in Exhibit 7.11, we will look at an deep in the money call option with two days to expiration and one day to the ex-dividend date.

The value of this call option the day before the ex-dividend date is $10.00. This must be the case because we could buy the call for $10.00, immediately exercise the option at $90.00, sell the stock immediately for $100.00, and be left with $0.00. If the option had a lower price, an arbitrage opportunity would exist. Even though the option is fairly priced at $10.00 and an arbitrage opportunity does not exist, this is a situation where an existing owner of the call would find it in their best interest to exercise the option anyway.

If the owner of the call does nothing, the stock would fall by $2.00 on the ex-dividend date and so would the price of the option. In this case, the owner of the call would lose $2.00 overnight. If the owner of the call exercises early, they now own the stock at a cost of $100.00, and could sell it for the same price. When the stock goes ex-dividend the next day, it will trade for $98.00, resulting in a $2.00 capital loss. This loss, however, is offset by the $2.00 dividend and the owner retains a total value of $100.00. The investor is not better off because he makes a profit, he is better off because he avoids a loss. If, for some reason, the option were trading at $9.50, which is below parity, the investor should immediately buy the call and exercise it. Under this scenario, we would pocket $0.50 (100 − 90 − 9.50). Bear in mind that options rarely trade at or below parity because the arbitrageurs

	Value to Expiration	Value Day Before Ex-Dividend Date
Stock Price	$100	
Strike Price	$90	
Interest Rate	1%	
Volatility	30%	
Time to Dividend	1 days	
Time to Expiration	2 days	
Dividend	$2.00	$0.00
Value of a Call	$8.00	$10.00
Delta	1.00	1.00

Exhibit 7.11 Valuing of a Call Option the Day before a Special Dividend

and market makers step in and push the price of the option to at least parity. If the option were trading slightly above parity at $10.50, the investor would lose $0.50 $(100 - 90 - 10.50)$ if they did exercised early. This, however, is a better choice than holding the option and suffering a $2.50 loss.

This might seem like an interesting theoretical artifact of the option market, but this has real-life implications. Market makers and institutional investors often write call options on stocks that pay big dividends hoping some fraction of the option buyers do not exercise their right before the ex-dividend date. When this happens, this results in a windfall profit for the option seller. Many option buyers who forgot to exercise their options before the ex-dividend dates in late 2012 suffered a heavy price.

Final Thought

Active investors find that interesting situations come up all the time. If they have a good idea of how a situation will play out, they can combine options in many different ways to take advantage of their insight. We think it is very important to look at scenario analysis like those shown in the charts above to see the potential gains and losses given various structures. This way, they can make an educated judgment concerning risk and return. Options are complicated instruments and one must be cognizant of the intricacies concerning their mechanics particularly as it concerns dividends. As a result, investors must be deeply aware of actions management might take concerning one-off events like takeovers and capital restructurings. With a proper understanding of these issues, the investor will reduce the chances of getting blindsided and if they are nimble enough, profit from special situations.

## CHAPTER 8

Extracting Information from Options Prices

The strong form of the efficient market hypothesis suggests that asset prices reflect all available information in the marketplace. Under this interpretation, we can think of the capital markets not as a venue of asset prices but as a setting for the pricing of information. New information continuously enters the market, causing prices to change endlessly. This information flow takes many forms. The most obvious and direct information flow comes from news releases by companies. These news releases typically discuss past financial performance in their regulatory filing and press releases. Earnings conference calls are another avenue in which management disseminates information such as business strategies they might pursue going forward. The government collects a myriad of macro economic and industry data with the intent of sharing it so people understand the status of a particular industry or the economy as a whole. Political representatives also use it as the foundation for establishing government policy and regulation. There are private-sector organizations that collect, analyze, and publish information as well. Journalists and the media interview senior management of leading companies, consultants, and industry specialists to inform their viewership about what is taking place in both the political and economic landscape. Brokerage firms employ teams of analysts who examine industry-specific factors and individual companies to publish reports and establish a basis for making forecasts and valuation estimates in pursuit of investment recommendations distributed to their clients. Consultants perform many of these same tasks as they advise corporations on business strategy, mergers, acquisitions and divestitures, competitive threats, and capital investment opportunities just to name a few.

If the information flow has positive implications, investors will bid up the price of the affected asset or security to a point where that news is fully captured in the asset's price. If, on the other hand, the information has negative implications, investors will sell the affected asset or security, pushing its price down until it reaches a point where price fully reflects the consequences of that news. This process tends to be fairly transparent to market participants. News reports are released to the public for all to see and investors react accordingly.

Market prices also incorporate information that may not be well distributed and therefore less transparent to the marketplace. Individual investors and institutional investment firms seek out information that is unknown to the marketplace by performing their own proprietary analysis. They do not publish the results of their work. Instead they monetize their work by making the appropriate investment decisions, which impacts the value of the securities traded. If their efforts suggest the current market price of an asset or security is less than their valuation estimate, they will buy the security pushing its price up. Information wants to be free, and it eventually comes out. Transactions occurring in the marketplace are one way that information is released, albeit with limited transparency. Some investors make their decisions based on what other "smart money" investors are doing. These folks buy the affected security over time until its price reflects all available information. Once that objective is met, early investors who made decisions based on their proprietary work sell their asset and look for other opportunities. If their efforts suggest that the market price of the security is too high, they will sell the security if they have it in inventory. More aggressive investors, such as hedge funds, will sell the asset short and cover the position when the market price falls to their estimated valuation level. Investors who are uninformed are often confused by what appears to be random price movements or extreme price levels. There are many times when the price of a stock, currency, commodity, or bond rises or falls for no apparent reason. But it's important to recognize that asset price behavior reflects the actions of large investors who are acting on the proprietary information they have uncovered or analysis they have performed.

There are other reasons why asset prices fluctuate on a continuous basis. The investment public as a whole, or any particular investor, might change the way they interpret information that is already captured in market prices. While bullish news might push the price of the security up, investors might come to the conclusion that prices have been pushed too far based on a closer examination of the data. When this occurs, prices will fall a bit, reflecting the reevaluation of information that is already captured in asset prices. It is important to remember that price is subjective. Some investors will value assets higher or lower than others based on their view of the economy, monetary policy, government action, management performance, and other factors. These differences might be driven by different risk tolerances, methods of valuing assets, or ways of thinking about information already captured in the marketplace.

Experienced market professionals know that people go through waves of optimism and pessimism. When people are optimistic, they will tend to view news through rose-colored glasses. They will see good news and act accordingly, but are prone to pushing prices up too high. Investor optimism tends to show itself with the release of bad news. Under normal circumstances, we would think that negative news would result in a fall in price. But when investors as a group are optimistic, they tend to shrug off bad news with the expectation that good news is just around the corner, or that bad news will catalyze the government or the central banks to act in a way that is bullish for asset prices. Waves of optimism can last just a few days or extend for years. When people are pessimistic, they tend to take a darker view of the news. When bad news about a company or the economy hits the market, investors tend to sell assets more aggressively than they otherwise might under other circumstances. Furthermore, when investors are emotionally pessimistic, they tend to discount good news. While good news might cause an asset's price to increase, it usually does so less than it would under a more optimistic environment or the blip in prices may quickly reverse.

Since asset prices capture all information available to the marketplace, the proprietary work of expert investors, and the mood of people as a whole, it is very difficult to look at an asset's current price or its price action to gain an edge. The efficient market hypothesis indeed suggests that since all available information is captured in market prices, future price action is dependent upon future news flow. Since few people can predict the future with consistent accuracy, price action is random. Thus, the efficient market hypothesis argues few investors can beat the returns of the market averages through actively trading individual assets or securities over the long run. As with most things in life, there are exceptions to the rule and there are a small handful of professional investors that consistently beat the market averages over time.

Options are leveraged instruments on asset prices. Consider a $20 stock, whose price increases by $2. This represents a 10 percent increase in price. A $2 option on that stock with a 50 delta will move by approximately $1 under these circumstances. This represents a 50 percent move in the price of the option. Since options are leveraged financial instruments that limit downside risk, you can see why an investor who has a strong view based on proprietary information or analysis might use the options market to capitalize on that view. Instead of risking $20, the investor only has to risk $2 to take advantage of his work. If, for some reason, the investor's analysis is incorrect or new information hits the market that overwhelms the implications of past work, the price of the stock price could fall 10, 20, or 30 percent. If the investor were to express his views by purchasing the underlying stock, he could lose $2, $4, or $6 on his $20 investment. The option buyer on the other hand, limits her loss to just the premium paid, or $2 in this example.

As a result, investors in general and institutional investors in particular, such as hedge funds, often use the options market to express their investment views. If they get it right, they can earn multiples of their capital commitment, while limiting their loss to a fraction of the value of the underlying instrument. Since the options market is small relative to the underlying instrument, the actions of large sophisticated and informed investors leave a footprint exposing what they are doing. This footprint may not tell you why they are doing what they are doing, but there is value in simply knowing that significant levered investments are taking place. If an individual investor is bullish on a particular stock, it's important to look at activity in the options market, because if large sophisticated investors are taking bearish positions with put options for example, they might know something that you do not. This should give individual investors pause, and they might want to either rethink their thesis or do more investigation before acting on their analysis.

The theory of option pricing is dependent on a number of factors, the most important being the price of the underlying security and implied volatility. As a valuation model, option prices are dependent on a probability distribution of potential outcomes. Those outcomes are dependent, at least in part, on a company's strategic plan, financial performance, dividend policy, and the cost of borrowing stock, in addition to the level of interest rates. Given the variety of factors that affect options prices, we can look at each of those factors to glean some insight into what important market participants are thinking, and what outcomes they expect to occur. In the balance of this chapter, we will discuss a number of methods that an investor can use to extract information from option prices quoted in the public markets. The first technique we will explore is a method designed to uncover where investors in the option market believe the price of the underlying security is likely to go. We will do this by looking at the option-implied distribution of future prices.

Option-Implied Distribution of Expected Future Price

The efficient market hypothesis, and indeed option pricing theory, suggests that the best estimator for the price of an asset tomorrow is its price today. It draws this conclusion because it assumes that the current price of an asset reflects all relevant information about the asset. Therefore, it is fairly priced. Information coming into the market is random and it is just as likely to have bullish implications as bearish ones. Putting aside a moment the fact that prices will drift, depending on market rates of interest and the company's dividend policy, it is just as likely for the price of an asset to rise in the future as it is to fall. Therefore, the efficient market hypothesis submits that prices in the near future will have a random normal distribution. This is the bell-shaped curve you may have learned about in statistics class in school. Bullish option traders believe that price is more likely to rise than fall at the margin. Bearish option traders on the other hand, hold the belief that price is more likely to fall than it is to rise. To the degree in which there are more bullish or bearish market participants, we should expect the options market to exhibit skew in the distribution of potential future prices relative to the standard normal distribution. We might also expect the same if a limited number of well-capitalized investors are more confident in their expectation of future price. If these investors express their view by trading options, they will have an influence on the price of the available series of options outstanding. Savvy options investors recognize this phenomenon and use option-pricing theory to uncover the market's expectation for the distribution of expected future asset prices.

To estimate the probability that an asset's price will rise or fall to some level or beyond it is useful to employ zeta. Recall from Chapter 2 that zeta tells us the probability that a particular option will expire in the money. To estimate the probability that an asset will be in a certain price range at expiration, we simply take the difference between zeta for two options with differing strike prices and the same time to expiration.

$$Zeta_{Call} = P(S_{t+\Delta t} \geq K)$$

$$P(K_1 \leq S_{t+\Delta t} \leq K_2) = Zeta_{Call, K_1} - Zeta_{Call, K_2}$$

or

$$P(K_1 \leq S_{t+\Delta t} \leq K_2) = P(S_{t+\Delta t} \geq K_1) - P(S_{t+\Delta t} \geq K_2)$$

Consider a stock trading at $25.00 a share. What is the probability that its price will trade between $29.00 and $30.00 a share in three months? See Exhibit 8.1.

The best and most direct way to calculate the probability that an asset will trade within a specific range at expiration is to compute zeta for options with strike prices of $29.00 and $30.00. The probability the share prices will trade between $29.00 and $30.00 is simply the difference between the two zetas. In this example, the probability that the price of the stock will trade between $29.00 and $30.00 at expiration is 4.6 percent (17.8% − 13.2%).

We do not necessarily have to use the Greeks and higher math of option-pricing theory to estimate this probability. By observing the price of a call spread in the marketplace, we can make a "back of the matchbook" approximation of zeta. In the example above, we see that a 30/29 call spread has a price of $0.154. If the price of the stock at expiration is $29 or higher, this call spread will have value that falls somewhere between $0.00 and $1.00 (the difference between the two strikes).

	Call #1	Call #2	Call #3	#1-2	#2-3
Share Price	$25.00				
Strike Price	$29.00	$30.00	$31.00	$1.00	$1.00
Dividend Yield	2.00%				
Risk-free Rate	1.00%				
Time to Expiration	0.25				
Implied Volatility	35.0%				
Priced of Option	$0.530	$0.376	$0.263	$0.154	$0.113
Zeta	17.8%	13.2%	9.6%	4.6%	
Implied Zeta	15.4%	11.3%		4.1%	

Exhibit 8.1   Probability Price in Three Months Is Between $29.00 and $30.00

Since the window between $29.00 and $30.00 is small, relative to a window of $29.00 and above, the expected value of the spread is very close to but somewhat less than $1.00, if the spread is in the money at expiration. (The exact figure is $0.862 in this case.) As a result, we can say there is at least a 15.4 percent (0.154/1.00) chance the stock will trade above $29.00. If we repeat this process, we find the value of a 30/31 call spread is $0.113. This implies that there is a 11.3 percent chance the share price will be $30.00 or higher at expiration. If we take the difference between these two figures, we find the probability that the share price will be in the $29.00 to $30.00 range at expiration is 4.1 percent (15.4% − 11.3%), which is very close to the more precise probability estimate determined by zeta.

Experienced option traders will recognize the difference between the two call spreads as a call butterfly. In a call butterfly, a trader is long a call with strike $Y − X$, and long one with a strike of $Y + X$, while being short two calls with strike Y. The value of a call butterfly is directly related to the probability that the asset price will be between Y and X at expiration.

$$Price_{Call\ Fly} = P_{Call}(K = Y - X) + P_{Call}(K = Y + X) - 2xP_{Call}(K = Y)$$
$$Prob(K_1 \leq S_{t+\Delta t} \leq K_2) = Price_{Call\ Fly}/X$$
$$Price_{Call\ Fly} = \$0.53 + 0.263 - 2x\$0.376 = \$0.041$$
$$Prob(K_1 \leq S_{t+\Delta t} \leq K_2) = \frac{\$0.041}{1.00}x100 = 4.1\%$$

In short, it is most accurate to use zeta to compute the probability that the price of the underlying asset will be at some level or within a range on a certain date. Barring the computing power needed to make this calculation, we can use prices observed in the marketplace to get a first-order approximation. Bear in mind that the accuracy of this "back of the matchbook" method will improve as the difference between the strike prices on the options selected decreases.

The value of this analysis does not end here. If we compute zeta across a strip of strike prices, we can produce a chart that displays the distribution of potential outcomes implied by prices in the options market. This is very powerful analysis, as we can see if option traders have a bullish or bearish bias, anticipating an explosive move up or down, or simply anticipating stagnant price action. This bias is revealed when the market implied distribution is compared to the theoretical distribution of future prices based on the efficient market hypothesis.

Exhibit 8.2 continues the example started above and compares the distribution of future prices derived from option prices with one derived by the efficient market hypothesis. The gray dotted line shows a lognormal distribution of future prices assuming the stock in our example has a current price of $25.00 and an expected volatility of returns of 35 percent. This is a distribution pattern that is consistent with the efficient market hypothesis, which states that future prices are unknowable with precision, but will fall somewhere above or below the current price adjusted for the cost of carry. We would expect an outcome within this distribution if we did not have any special knowledge that would improve our ability to predict the future price of the stock. The dark black line is a distribution of expected future prices implied by the options market. We can draw four conclusions with a close look at this chart:

1. Investors are putting a higher probability on a crash in price than the efficient market suggests.

2. At the same time, investors are putting a higher probability of a mild increase in price as compared to a random walk.

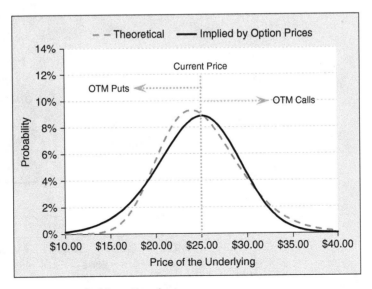

Exhibit 8.2   Option Implied Price Distribution

3. Investors are putting a lower probability on a mild decrease in price than a random walk predicts.

4. Investors believe the probability of a huge rally in price is close to but somewhat less than the probability suggested by a random walk.

A skew chart is directly related to a distribution of potential outcomes. When the market prices downside options with a higher implied volatility than at-the-money options, the left-hand tail of the distribution becomes fat, for example. As a result, when examining a skew chart, one is looking at parameters that drive the distribution chart. Exhibit 8.3 shows the volatility skew captured in the analysis above.

In this example, out-of-the-money put options are priced with an implied volatility that is significantly higher than those puts with strikes that are either at or in of the money. Option traders take this stance when they believe there is significant downside risk in the price of the underlying instrument, which exceeds the risk implied by the efficient market hypothesis. In a case like this, put buyers are willing to pay a higher premium to protect the value of their asset for an extreme downside event, while sellers of insurance are demanding a higher price to compensate for crash risk.

The beauty of distribution analysis is that it gives the investor an excellent way of understanding what other investors are doing and how they are pricing risk. There will be times when the implied distribution has very fat tails. This might occur for a biotech company awaiting approval on a new drug. At an extreme, it could even be bimodal. Other times, the distribution may have a bigger peak in the middle, suggesting the option traders expect low volatility and no trend in

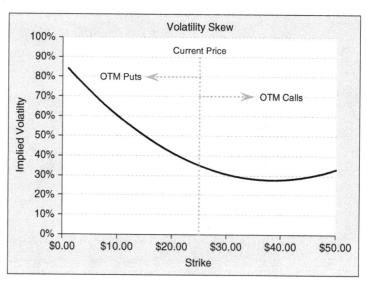

Exhibit 8.3 Volatility Skew

price action. In short, examining the implied distribution of expected future prices tells us something about market expectations in general, and potentially what large investors believe is a more likely outcome.

The previous analysis is a snapshot of the distribution of the market's price expectation at a particular point in time. In this case, the focus is on an investment horizon of three months. It is natural to assume that market expectations could differ across different time horizons. Investors might believe prices will be stable for a period of time and get more volatility later on, or vice-versa. They might expect near-term headwinds in price, but expect a greater upward price movement as a new factory comes online, or a potential acquisition is made. Higher earnings might lead investors to expect a change in dividend policy sometime in the future, or a large share buyback to take place at a specific point in time. All these factors and more can affect the volatility surface and how the market prices near-dated options versus long-dated ones.

Another way to apply the expected distribution of forward price analysis is to examine how the expected distribution of future prices morphs over time. To do this, we would repeat this process at each of the option expiration dates available, which generally go out 9 to 12 months. For those issues that have LEAPS (Long-term Equity AnticiPation Securities) outstanding, data might be available to look out as long as two or three years. To put this data in a usable form, we can chart price in terms of standard deviation away from the forward price relative to time. This creates an envelope of potential outcomes. This analysis reveals how the distribution is expected to change as the investment horizon increases.

Exhibit 8.4 shows a two-dimensional representation of the expected future share prices over differing investment horizons. The solid black line shows the expected

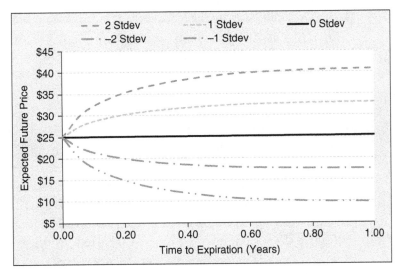

Exhibit 8.4   Envelope of Option Implied Expected Price Distributions

futures price. (With short-term interest rates near zero and a moderate dividend yield, the drift in forward prices is close to zero.) The gray dashed lines, above the black line show the expected forward price given a one and two standard deviation upward move, respectively. The gray dotted/dashed lines below the black line shows the expected forward price for a one and two standard deviation drop in price, respectively. Notice that in the near-term, the price envelope widens quite rapidly, but then it flattens out. Since volatility increases with the square root of time, we would expect the envelope to widen monotonically as the investment horizon increases, only the rate of increase would slow down as the investment horizon increases. However, after about 0.6 years in this example, the envelope of potential prices becomes extremely contained. As the investment horizon lengthens beyond this point, the distribution of potential prices no longer widens. This is a unique result. This analysis indicates option traders expect prices to be volatile short terms and more confined longer term. We might expect this pattern to emerge when the term structure of volatility is inverted.

When viewed in this manner, we can uncover an optimal trading strategy. With a rapidly widening envelope short term and a flat envelope long term, we should consider buying a calendar spread, which entails buying a long-term option and selling a short-dated one. Both options should use the same strike price, and it does not matter if a put or call is used. The delta of a calendar spread using the same strikes is very close to zero. Since this envelope is abnormally tight, any reversion to a random walk creates an opportunity to capitalize on that shift. This process will manifest itself by a normalization of the volatility surface. Specifically, short-dated volatility is more likely to fall than rise, and long-dated volatility is more likely to rise than fall. We have discussed at length that calendar spreads enjoy positive theta, and in this case this phenomenon is compounded by the term structure inversion. The high volatility driving the price of short-term options will result in price decay at a far faster rate than the long-term option. With this positive yield, there are two ways to win. Either the term structure normalizes for a capital gain, or time passes producing income yield. Exhibit 8.5 shows the specifics of an appropriate trade using call options.

Exhibit 8.5 shows an example of a long calendar call spread when the terms structure of volatility is inverted. This spread costs $0.90 and is essentially delta neutral. This is desirable because the trade is designed to capitalize on a normalization of iVol term structure over time, not a shift in the price of the underlying asset. The structure does have negative gamma, so delta will increase as the price of the underlying falls and fall when the price of the underlying rises. As a result, the structure will have to be rebalanced should price trend in one direction or the other. Notice that the structure is vega positive. This tells us that the spread will increase in value if there is an upward shift in the term structure of volatility. Since this trade is short, short-term volatility and long, long-term volatility, the trade will

	Sell	Buy	Net Debit
Number of Options	1	1	
Strike	$25	$25	
Risk-free Rate	2.00%	2.00%	
Dividend	1.00%	1.00%	
Time to Expiration (yrs)	0.25	1.00	
Volatility	45%	31%	
Call Price	$2.26	$3.16	$0.90
Delta	0.55	0.57	0.02
Gamma	0.07	0.05	−0.02
Vega	4.94	9.70	4.77
Theta	−4.53	−1.58	2.95

Exhibit 8.5   Long Calendar Call Spread

also increase in value as the term structure normalizes to an upward slope from an inverted one. It does not matter if long-term volatility rises or short-term volatility falls, a capital gain will follow.

To gain greater appreciation concerning the performance of this structure over time, it is useful to examine a total return analysis. This will uncover where the returns come from, and how much we might expect to earn. In addition, it will show where the risk is found. Exhibit 8.6 provides this analysis.

The solid gray line in Exhibit 8.6 shows the total return characteristics of this calendar spread, given an instantaneous shift in the time price of the underlying security. Calendar spreads are typically gamma negative. In this case, it is −0.02. Consequently, the total return pattern takes an upside-down U shape. The absolute value of gamma is relatively small, so the downside risk is small compared to the upside potential. The dashed gray line shows the payoff pattern of the spread over a one-month time horizon if the term structure of volatility flattens to 35 percent across all expirations. The flattening of the curve adds a significant kick to returns as volatility falls on the short-dated option sold, and volatility rises on the long-dated option purchased. We can estimate the return attribution by taking a close look at the Greeks for a scenario where the price of the underlying does not change:

$$\text{Change in price} = \text{Vega } \Delta_{iVol} + \text{Theta } \Delta t$$

$$\text{Price change} = -4.94\,(35\% - 45\%) + 9.70\,(35\% - 31\%) + 2.95\left(\frac{1}{12}\right)$$

$$\text{Change in price} = \$1.13$$

The solid black line shows the payoff pattern of the spread on the expiration date of the short dated, three-month option. All of the returns are attributable to price decay less the returns driven by gamma. Since the spread is negative gamma, we

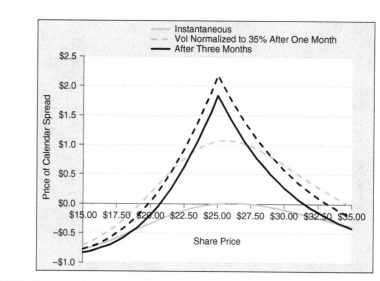

Underlying	$17.50	$20.00	$22.50	$25.00	$27.50	$30.00	$32.50
% Change	−30%	−20%	−10%	0%	10%	20%	30%
Price	$0.304	$0.558	$0.781	$0.896	$0.890	$0.795	$0.657
% Change (%)	−66	−38	−13	0	−1	−11	−27
Leverage	2.202	1.886	1.288	N/A	−0.071	−0.567	−0.891
Delta	0.094	0.102	0.071	0.021	−0.023	−0.050	−0.058
Gamma	0.011	−0.005	−0.018	−0.020	−0.014	−0.007	−0.001
Vega	3.150	4.125	4.565	4.766	4.900	4.913	4.709
Theta	0.393	1.385	2.435	2.952	2.774	2.144	1.399

Exhibit 8.6   Profit/Loss on Short Calendar Spread

see that the shift in the price of the underlying asset causes the spread to lose value. If the shift is large enough, an absolute loss can occur. The black dotted line shows the return pattern at the end of three months, including the effect of a flattening of the volatility term structure to 35 percent for all expirations. This reversion to the mean adds returns across the spectrum of share prices.

It is important to remember that options of various strikes and expirations discount different volatilities. But at the end of the day, the underlying asset will realize a single unique volatility. This suggests that over time the yield surface will normalize or "revert to the mean." Taking advantage of a temporary dislocation in the yield surface should produce alpha over time. In this example, there is just a 28 percent chance the value of the underlying will trade above or below the breakeven points. Even if it does, the total return chart in Exhibit 8.6 above suggests the loss will be less than $0.90. Said another way, there is a 72 percent chance this trade will be a winner. If it is a winner, the trade is likely to make a profit of about $1.10. As a result, there is an expectation for a "statistical" arbitrage of $0.54 (72% × $1.10 − 28% × $0.90).

There are two potential risks of this strategy. First, there is a risk that volatility could fall sharply across the board, resulting in a mark-to-market loss on the spread. That loss, however, is likely to be temporary as it becomes even less likely the price of the underlying will trade outside the breakeven points at expiration. With price decay working in favor of the position, the yield on the structure will offset at least some of the loss and potentially result in a gain. That gain will simply be smaller than originally expected. The second risk is that the volatility curve continues to invert. This will also result in a mark-to-market loss and a higher probability that the price of the underlying will trade outside the breakeven bands. Offsetting this drag on returns is the opportunity to place the trade again at expiration, this time at even better prices and a higher yield. In other words, the statistical arbitrage for the second swing of the bat is even greater than the first. If we simply repeat this trade enough times, the gains are almost assured and substantial. In the final analysis, when the envelope of option-implied expected price distribution is flat, there is a clear opportunity to make outsized gains with moderate risk.

Implied Borrowing Cost on the Underlying Security

In earlier chapters we discussed the important issue of borrowing costs on the valuation of puts and calls. Specifically, as the cost of borrowing the underlying security increases, the value of call options falls, and the value of put options increases. Under most circumstances, there is little or no cost of borrowing a stock. Brokers usually have ready access to shares they can lend to short sellers and those who need them to hedge option positions. Because of this dynamic, it is important to know if borrowing costs are affecting the price of an option the investor wants to trade. Furthermore, if borrowing costs are high enough, it becomes advantageous for institutional call buyers to exercise early, take delivery, and lend the shares out and collect lending income. Fortunately, finding stocks that are expensive to borrow is relatively simple. We should only expect stocks with high short interest ratios or very small floats to have high borrowing costs.

A strong clue that a stock is expensive to borrow is revealed by an examination of put–call parity. If the price of a call is depressed and the price of a put is heightened by borrowing costs, options prices will *appear* to violate put–call parity. When we run across such a situation, we should look to borrowing costs to explain the discrepancy. But how can we find out what the borrowing costs are for an underlying issue? Self-clearing broker/dealers have their own lending desks that actively lend out the firm's inventory for either funding and/or income-generating reasons. At the same time, they are responsible for borrowing securities when the firm's traders need them to hedge their option or other proprietary/market-making positions. Under these circumstances, traders can find out the cost of borrowing a security by contacting their lending department. Hedge funds that want to sell a security short as part of their investment strategy get the details from their prime brokers. They regularly provide their customers with quotes on the cost of borrowing securities, how many shares might be available, and the term over which those shares are available.

Most individual investors do not enjoy such luxuries. Individual investors must contact their broker, who may or may not be able to provide this information on a timely basis. But all is not lost. Since the prices of puts and calls are impacted by the cost of borrowing the underlying security, investors can use option prices to determine an implied borrowing cost. If option prices do not reflect the cost of borrowing the underlying security, then all is well and good. But if the options market indicates significant borrowing costs, individual investors might need to modify their investment strategy accordingly. Since borrowing costs push down the price of calls and push up the price of puts, they would want to implement strategies that make them a seller of puts or a buyers of calls, all other things equal. This will allow retail investors to capture returns at the margin as if they were lending out the securities from their portfolio. (Retail investors do not earn income from lending fees on the securities they own. The brokerage firm keeps these revenues as part of their business model and compensation for providing securities safekeeping services.)

In addition to the price action of the underlying security, there is an additional danger in selling calls when borrowing costs are rising. As borrowing costs rise, the time premium on a call option falls. Should borrowing costs drive option premiums on in-the-money calls down to or below the intrinsic value, the buyer of that option has a financial incentive to exercise the option early. If option writers sold naked calls, they will have to deliver stock, which they do not own. At this point, option writers have two choices. The first choice is to go into the market, buy the stock, and deliver it against their call. The second is that the call writers can borrow shares from their broker and deliver them. This is possible of course only if the broker has access to shares, which it can lend to the option writer for delivery to the option buyer. If the broker is able to borrow stock, the call writer is short common stock. Under these circumstances, the investor has to pay borrowing costs on those shares, as long as the short position is outstanding. Needless to say, borrowing for an extended period of time can become quite expensive if the borrowing rate is high. The only good scenario that can occur is that the price of the shares fall over time by an amount greater than or equal to the borrowing cost. The one-time call writer who is now short shares profits on the decline of the stock, and is able to repurchase the stock at a lower price and return it to the stock lender.

Short sellers can borrow stock in one of two ways. They can borrow stock overnight and pay the cost of borrowing for just one day. This process continues day after day until the short seller voluntarily covers his position. Short sellers who borrow stock on a spot basis run the risk that the stock gets called back. This might occur because the lenders have sold their shares, which are needed for delivery to the new owner. Alternatively, lenders might decide they no longer want to lend their shares at the going overnight rate and prefer to retain physical possession of the stock certificate unless they can get a higher rate.

To eliminate this risk, a borrower might contract with a lender to borrow shares for a specific period of time. This is known as *term borrowing*. Term borrowing has advantages for both the borrower and lender. From the borrower's perspective, contracting with a lender to borrow shares for a specific period of time guarantees that the borrower will have access to those shares. The borrower does not have to worry about the shares being called in before they want to cover the short. From the standpoint of the lender, there is a guaranteed stream of income for a specified period of time. Term lending is less work, as the lender does not have to find a borrower day after day and continually negotiate a borrowing rate.

Computing the option's implied borrowing cost is relatively straightforward. To do this, we go back to the fundamental relationship between puts, calls, the underlying asset, and cash defined in Chapter 1 known as put–call parity. Put–call parity tells us that purchasing calls, selling puts, and holding an appropriate amount of cash replicates the price performance of stock. With this relationship, we can compare the cost of synthetic stock with the price of real stock. The difference will tell us the borrowing cost implied by option prices. The following is an example of how to use put–call parity to extract the term borrowing costs implied by option prices.

	Call
Price of Stock (S)	$25.00
Strike Price (K)	$25.00
Risk-free Rate (r)	2.00%
Dividend Yield (d)	1.00%
Borrowing Cost (b)	12.00%
Implied Volatility (σ)	35.0%
Price Call (C)	***$1.395***
Price Put (P)	***$2.069***
Without Borrowing Costs	
Price Call (C)	$1.767
Price Put (P)	$1.705

The example above continues the example started in Chapter 2. Recall that the price of the call is $1.767 and the price of the put is $1.705 in the absence of borrowing costs. Assume for a moment that the borrowing cost of 12 percent is known with certainty. If we incorporate that cost into the B–S–M option-pricing model, we find the price of a call is $1.395 and the value of a put is $2.069. The borrowing cost drives the cost of a call down $0.372 and pushes the value of a put up $0.364 relative to the no-borrowing-cost scenario. (*Note:* Using the B–S–M option-pricing model to determine the implied borrowing rate is challenging exercise because we must solve for both implied volatility and borrowing costs at the same time.)

$$\text{Cost of synthetic stock} = SS = C - P + PV(K)$$

$$PV(K) = Ke^{-rt}$$

$$\text{Borrowing rate} = \frac{\ln\left(S/SS\right)}{t} - d$$

$$PV(K) = 25.00e^{-0.02 \times 0.25} = \$24.875$$

$$\text{Synthetic stock} = \$1.395 - \$2.069 + \$24.875 = \$24.20$$

$$\text{Borrowing rate} = \frac{\ln\left(25.00/24.20\right)}{0.25} - 1.00\% = 12.00\%$$

Now assume the only information we have is the prices we observe in the market place. Given these prices, we can create the underlying stock synthetically by applying put–call parity. Using these three-month at-the-money options we find that the price of synthetic stock trades at $24.20, which is a $0.80 discount to the quoted price of the stock observed in the marketplace. Now we can buy stock synthetically for $24.20 instead of real stock for $25.00. This discount will produce a continuously compounded yield of 13 percent rate of return. The owner of this synthetic stock does not have rights to the dividend, only a shareholder has this right. To determine the borrowing cost, we must subtract the dividend yield from the return provided by the discount associated with the synthetic stock. This return less the dividend yield not received tells us that the borrowing cost is 12 percent.

We can create stock synthetically using options of any expiration. The beauty of the method described above is that it is useful in determining the borrowing rates for any term, at any point in time. There is no reason for borrowing rates to be the same for differing tenors. Consequently, there is information in knowing how term borrowing costs differs over various time horizons. Borrowing costs might rise, fall, or remain flat, depending on the demand for shares by arbitrageurs who are attempting to capture price discrepancies or hedge other positions. To glean more precise information from term borrowing rates, it is useful to extract the forward borrowing rates from the term borrowing rates. The concept of term structure of borrowing rates is similar to the term structure of interest rates that fixed income investors use to help make valuation assessments and duration decisions. The forward spot rate curve reveals the exact point in the future where borrowing

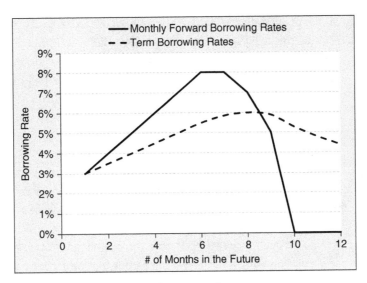

Exhibit 8.7 Term Structure and Forward Spot Rate Curves

costs hit an inflection point. Exhibit 8.7 is an example of the term structure and associated monthly forward rates extracted from the data.

The dashed black line in Exhibit 8.7 shows the term structure of borrowing costs for a stock that is in demand by short sellers. These rates are extracted from call/put option pairs with different times to expiration just like the example computation above. The solid black line represents the monthly forward rates extracted by decomposing the term-structure curve into a series of forward rates. As the cost of borrowing rises, the monthly forward rates rise even faster. In this example, those rates eventually peak in months 6 and 7. This provide investors with a clue that short sellers are positioning their portfolios for some event expected to occur six to seven months out into the future. With this information investors are directed to focus on what is likely to happen at that time.

One example could be the announcement of earnings for a company domiciled outside the United States, where companies are only required to report semi-annually. If a hedge fund, for example, expects a disastrous earnings report, it might sell short shares now under a term borrowing arrangement with the expectation that prices will fall due to a preannouncement before the official earnings date. At the same time, it has the ability to maintain a short position with a known cost until the company provides its earnings report.

Examining forward borrowing rates is useful in handicapping the approval date of an important new drug by the FDA. Hedge funds employ PhDs to assess the probability the FDA will approve a drug. Furthermore, they make assessments of market size and market share for the drug. With this information, along with the cost of producing and marketing the drug, they will have a solid estimate of its profitability should it be approved. Alternatively, preliminary data may suggest the drug is more likely to be a failure. Either way, biotech hedge funds often take large positions in either the company's stock or options to capitalize on their work and expertise. The term structure of borrowing costs provides a clue to investors who do not have access to pharmaceutical experts. If, as in this case, the term structure of borrowing costs is a hint that big money is betting against approval along with an estimate of when that realization will be delivered to the market.

A third example could be a company takeover. When company A announces a stock tender offer for company B, risk arbitrageurs buy the shares of company B and sell those of company A. Their goal is to profit from the price differential between the shares of the two companies. If the risk-arbs believe the transaction will go through, they will put on a convergence trade with a great deal of leverage. This entails taking a large short position in company A. If the borrowing costs on company A are high, it indicates the smart money believes the deal will probably go through. The peak in the forward rate curve tells investors when the deal is likely to close. If, on the other hand, borrowing rates are modest, the option market is signaling that the deal will probably not go through in its current form. It might be telling investors that a higher offer might be forthcoming from another suitor or white knight, or the deal will fall apart altogether.

In the final analysis, it is important to monitor the implied borrowing rate before making an investment decision to take a position in a company's stock or its associated options. Furthermore, do not be fooled by a depressed price of a call option. It just might be option traders handicapping an event the retail investor is not aware of or an event that is unappreciated by the market as a whole.

◼ Put/Call Ratio

Just as it is important to find information in option prices and activity, it is important to avoid methods that do not provide clear and precise information. The put/call ratio is such a statistic. The put/call ratio is a technical indicator used by many individual and professional investors alike. It is computed by taking all the put open interest and dividing by the call open interest. Some people calculate it on a trading volume basis. They divide the volume of puts traded by the volume of calls traded. When applied to the overall market, many see it as a gauge of market sentiment. When applied to an individual asset, many believe it is both a sentiment indicator and a time-to-event indicator by examining the put and call activity parsed by expiration dates. When puts or calls are bought or sold outright, professional and individual investors are taking a position in anticipation of a directional change in the price of the underlying security. If this was all options were used for, the put/call ratio might be a useful market-timing tool. However, people trade and hold options for reasons other than making directional bets.

When combined with the underlying asset on a delta-neutral basis, option investing turns from a directional bet to a volatility bet. Volatility traders are usually expecting a change in implied or realized volatility. They buy volatility if they think realized volatility will be higher than implied volatility. They sell volatility if they believe the opposite will manifest.

Option trading can facilitate income-generation strategies. An investor who owns an asset can sell a call option against it and collect a premium for doing so. If the asset price does not rise above the strike price of the option written, the option expires worthless and the investor can repeat the process. The investor can also write cash-covered puts to generate income. In this strategy, interest is earned on the cash held and additional income comes from the premium collected. If the price of the asset stays above the strike price of the put written, it expires worthless and the investor can repeat the process all over again. This is functionally equivalent to buying an asset and selling a call.

Herein lies the problem with trying to glean information from open interest and trading activity in the options markets. We do not know *why* trades are taking place. If calls trade on the offered side, someone is stepping up to buy. If puts trade on the bid side of the market, someone is stepping up to sell. In either case, someone is probably making a bullish bet. Likewise, if calls trade on the bid side, someone is stepping up to sell. If puts trade on the offered side of the market, someone is stepping up to buy. In either case, someone is probably making a bearish bet. At the end of the day, to properly interpret outright trading activity, we need to know if the transactions take place on the bid or offered side of the quoted market. This tells us the intention of the more aggressive participant.

Investors use options to manage volatility. They can sell calls and buy the underlying stock as a means of selling volatility. Alternatively, they can sell puts and sell the underlying asset. In either case, the investors are not making a directional bet. They are attempting to profit from a drop in implied or realized volatility. To buy volatility, they can buy calls and sell the underlying asset. Alternatively, they can buy puts and buy the underlying asset. In this way, investors will profit if implied or realized volatility increases. Since either puts or calls can be used to create a long or short position in volatility, there is no directional information to be gleaned from simply looking at trading activity or open interest.

In the final analysis, call trading can be either bullish or bearish, depending on the intent of the originating investor. The same can be said for trading in options. Furthermore, trading activity in either puts or calls can have nothing to do with

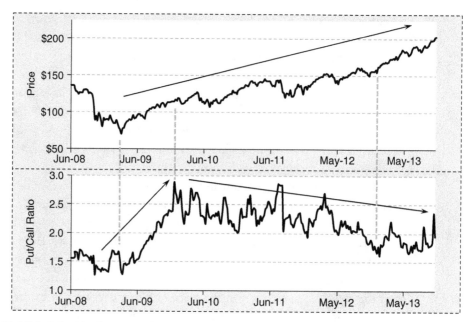

Exhibit 8.8 Total Returns of S&P 500 versus Put/Call Ratio

directional expectations by market participants. We think it is important to leave the put/call ratio out of one's toolkit. Without a strong fundamental argument backed up by statistical analysis of historical experience, this indicator of market action does not have the chops to systemically and repeatedly improve one's trading activity. Exhibit 8.8 should convince you that the theory about information provided by the put/call ratio is not necessarily backed up by market experience. In it we find a graph of the price performance of SPY. SPY is the SPDR ETF Trust designed to track the performance of the S&P500. Below is a chart of the put/call ratio based on the open interest of options on SPY.

Notice that in Exhibit 8.8 the S&P 500 increases steadily from March 2009 through October 2013. There was very little if any relationship between the performance of large-cap stocks and the put/call ratio. Interestingly, the put/call ratio was depressed for most of 2009. Market folklore suggests this means market participants are complacent, so we might expect share prices to fall. But share prices rose instead. Notice that if this indicator is low or high, rising or falling, share prices seem to simply march higher. This suggests to us that there was little information, if any, conveyed by the put/call ratio over this five-plus-year time period. This is not just an issue with this index of large-cap stocks. We see the same thing with gold.

In the third quarter of 2008, the put/call ratio became depressed in the second half of 2008 as the price of GLD had fallen by about 25 percent during the financial

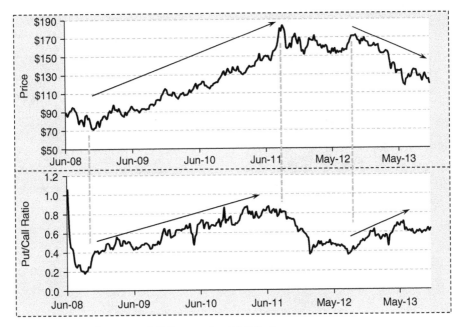

Exhibit 8.9   Total Return of GLD versus Put/Call Ratio

turmoil experienced from 2007 to 2009. From the low, it rose steadily until mid-2011. Concurrently, the put/call ratio rose and it peaked at the same time the price of gold did. While the shine came off the price of gold, it did not enter a bear market. But the put/call ratio fell sharply. In the third quarter of 2013, the put/call ratio was, suggesting complacency. One might have thought the price of gold would rise. Instead, it fell sharply. This time, the price of gold fell into a downtrend as the put/call ratio entered an uptrend. This conflicts with the relationship experienced earlier. Once again, the put/call ratio was of little use in helping investors determine the next move in the price of the associated asset. The most important lesson from this analysis is that you must always verify theories with historical data. If historical data does not back up theory, the theory must be changed or discarded altogether.

Final Thought

Option pricing models give us a way of pricing options given market conditions. Since it provides a discipline about how options are priced in the marketplace, we can combine market observations with mathematical models to expose information that is hidden with in the data. Since options are levered financial instruments and tend to be less liquid than the cash equity counterparts, institutional investors tend to leave noticeable footprints in the marketplace. Clever analysts and option traders can use option-pricing theory to extract information from the markets that is not available to the casual observer. With this information, investors who use options can find trading ideas and adjust their strategies accordingly.

The markets provide all kinds of time series data and technical indicators that investors often use to help make decisions. It is important to back test any indicator you might use to time your entry and exit decisions. The objective of back testing is to verify one's theory with data. A good indicator will point you in the right direction most if not all of the time and improve the odds of exceptional returns. A poor indicator will appear to work sometimes and not work at other times. One should stick to a discipline that produces repeatable results. Otherwise, one is really just flipping a coin when the trader believes they are making an informed decision. Such a method is sure to end in tears.

## CHAPTER 9

Synthetics

In earlier chapters, the discussion was put forth showing how investors use options to manage the volatility of individual positions or a portfolio of positions. These are powerful techniques investors can use to obtain their investment objectives while managing downside risk. The other broad category of uses for options is the creation of synthetic positions. A synthetic is simply a derivative contract or combination of contracts, which replicates the return performance of a particular asset, security, or market index. Options enable the creation of synthetic positions because there is a deterministic relationship between puts, calls, and the underlying instrument. This relationship, by definition, must be arbitrage free, as a violation of this condition would allow investors to combine positions in the underlying asset along with their associated options in a way that would guarantee a riskless profit. The relationship between the security and its associated options is defined by put–call parity, which is discussed in detail below.

Put–Call Parity

Put–call parity defines the relationship between the prices of a European call, a European put, the underlying security, and the risk-free asset. For this relationship to hold, the strike price and the time to expiration of the put and the call must be identical. In addition, the risk-free asset that is typically defined as a U.S. Treasury bill must have the same maturity date as the expiration date of the two options. In the case of equity securities, the equation for put–call parity is defined below. Put–call parity does not just apply to stocks and their related options. It governs the relationship between the price of any asset and its associated options.

$$\text{Stock} + \text{Put} = \text{Cash} + \text{Call}$$

The intuition behind this equation should be very clear. The left-hand side of the equation describes a stock with a married put having the same payoff pattern as holding cash plus a call option. Given this identity, if the price of the stock rises by the expiration date of the put, the investor can sell the stock for a gain while the put expires worthless. If the price of the stock falls below the strike price of the put option, the investor can exercise her right and sell the stock to the put writer at the agreed upon strike price. This will minimize investor loss, which is equal to the starting stock price less the option's strike price less the premium paid on the put option.

The right-hand side of the equation is another way of describing the same payoff pattern. Instead of buying stock and a married put, the investor buys a call option, keeping the rest of her assets in credit and interest rate risk-free cash equivalents. If the price of the underlying stock is above the strike price by expiration, the investor exercises the call and sells the stock purchased for a gain. If, on the other hand, the price of the stock falls, the call expires worthless, leaving the investor with cash. All that is lost in this scenario is the option premium on the call.

The beauty of put–call parity lies in its simplicity, requirement for minimal assumptions, and ease of implementation. Put–call parity allows for the static replication of any of its four elements. In addition, with the assumption that traders can freely borrow and lend at the same rate, cash on hand is not necessary to structure a trade. In theory, borrowing funds for the term of the options can finance the underlying asset and the relationships still holds. Furthermore, it does not require the existence of a forward contract, although one can be created synthetically. In addition, put–call parity presents the relationship of static replication. In a static replication, the reference asset and the replicating portfolio have the same cash flows. By contrast, dynamic replication does not have the same cash flows as the reference asset. A good example of dynamic replicating is gamma scalping. The payoff pattern of a call option is created dynamically by purchasing the underlying asset as its price rises and selling it as its price falls. The end result is a payoff pattern that looks identical to the final payoff pattern of a call option, but the cash flows are different.

One way to think about the right-hand side of the equation is that it is akin to a cash-covered call. To ensure that the buyer of the call can pay for the stock in the event the call is exercised, the buyer must hold enough cash to purchase the stock. Therefore, the quantity of the risk-free asset the seller must hold is equal to the present value of the strike price of the call option.

$$Cash = Ke^{-rt}$$

In this relationship, K represents the strike price of the options, r is the interest rate on the risk-free asset, and t is the time to expiration of the put and call options, which must be the same as the maturity date of the Treasury bill. The implication of put–call parity is quite profound. It tells us that there is equivalence between puts and calls even though they have very different payoff patterns. As a result, we can replicate any delta-neutral portfolio. If a call has a delta of D, for example, then buying a call and selling D number of shares of stock is equivalent to selling a put and buying $(1 - D)$ shares of stock. This is a very important relationship and market makers use it regularly to manage the price risk of their inventory.

Synthetically Replicating Stock

By rearranging the equation of put–call parity above, we can see that we can replicate the return characteristics of stock by purchasing a call, selling a put with the same strike price and time to expiration, while holding the appropriate amount of cash.

$$S = C - P + Ke^{-rt}$$

Since the relationship between the four elements that make up put–call parity exists in an arbitrage-free environment, the advantage of holding synthetic stock versus real stock is not entirely obvious. There are times, however, where it is cheaper to buy stocks synthetically than buying the security outright. One example is the situation where there is heavy short interest on a stock, and as a result it is expensive to borrow. Since market makers borrow stock and sell it short against their long call positions, they must pay the stock lender a fee to do so. This affects the price of a call by driving down its price. Since the market makers must pay a fee to hedge their call position, the call is worth less to them. By the same token, if a market maker buys put options, they purchase stock as a hedge. Now that they own stock, they can take advantage of the high cost of borrowing by lending the stock to short sellers, who have to pay them a fee. Since they can make a return on their stock holdings, the puts have more value to them. As a result, they can pay a higher price for puts. In short, a trader can buy cheap calls and sell expensive puts while holding cash, and in doing so, own synthetic stock at a lower price than the quoted price of the shares in the marketplace.

To see how much we could improve returns by synthetically creating stock versus purchasing stock outright, it's useful to walk through a numerical example. To do this, we will continue with the example presented in Chapter 8, where we walked through the mathematics of computing the implied borrowing cost extracted from option prices. All the factors of those numerical examples are the same, and we will assume there is a 12 percent borrowing cost to the underlying stock. In making this assumption, we get the following results:

Stock Price = $25.00

Strike Price = $25.00

$$\text{Risk-free Rate} = 2.00\%$$

$$\text{Dividend Yield} = 1.00\%$$

$$\text{Stock Borrowing Rate} = 12.00\%$$

$$\text{Time to Expiration} = 0.25 \text{ years}$$

$$\text{Implied Volatility} = 35.0\%$$

$$\text{Call Price} = \$1.396$$

$$\text{Put Price} = \$2.069$$

$$\text{Cash Required} = \$25.00 \, e^{-0.02 \text{x} 0.25} = \$24.875$$

$$\text{Price of Synthetic Stock} = \$1.395 - \$2.069 + \$24.875 = \$24.20$$

$$\text{Amount Saved} = \$25.00 - \$24.20 = \$0.80$$

This analysis shows that the cost of creating stock synthetically is $24.20. This is a 3.2 percent discount to the price of the underlying stock. This is a direct savings to an investor who might want to own the stock, but chooses to buy it synthetically instead of buying it outright. The reason why this apparent arbitrage exists is due to industry structure. Individual investors do not have the opportunity to lend their stock holdings and collect a fee. Most people are under the impression that brokerage firms only make money by the commissions they charge their customers to transact securities. But brokerage firms have other very important sources of revenue that cover their cost of doing business. One is lending money to investors who buy securities on margin. The second is through securities lending. When an investor buys a security, the brokerage firm holds that security in their name. When a short seller needs a stock, she must borrow it first and then sell it into the marketplace. The lender of stock wants to be sure that it eventually bets the stock back. For protection against a default on the stock loan, the broker-dealer demands cash in an amount equal to the value of the stock lent out. The broker-dealer invests that cash in short-term securities to earn a return. Most stocks are not hard or expensive to borrow. Under these circumstances, the only revenue the broker-dealer earns is interest on the cash collateral. But there are situations where there is a high demand to borrow a stock and the broker-dealer can charge stock borrowers a premium to do so. When they do, this creates an additional revenue source for the broker-dealer. Broker-dealers, however, do not share this revenue with their retail clients. This is not the case for institutional clients, such as corporate pension plans. Firms performing securities safekeeping for these large institutions have programs where they share the revenue generated from securities lending with the owners of the securities. For these folks, there is a far smaller advantage of owning synthetics versus the actual securities as they get a portion of the securities' lending revenue. Since retail investors do not capture the returns provided by securities lending, they can greatly benefit by using synthetics.

Synthetically Replicating a Call

Not only can an investor replicate stock with a combination of puts, calls, and cash, but put–call parity allows the investor to create a call synthetically as well. By rearranging the standard equation of put–call parity, we can replicate a call by purchasing stock, buying a put, and financing those positions by borrowing the present value of the strike price of the underlying options.

$$C = S + P - Ke^{-rt}$$

Just as investors can arbitrage the difference between a synthetic stock and a reference stock, investors can arbitrage the price difference between the call and the synthetic call. In the previous example, the opportunity to do so might occur when a stock is expensive to borrow or when there is a dislocation in price due to a large buyer or seller of a particular option with a specific time to expiration and strike price. Continuing with the example, the following shows the price of a call option with one created synthetically:

$$\text{Synthetic call} = \$25.00 + \$2.069 - \$24.875 = \$2.194$$

$$\text{Savings} = \text{Market price} - \text{Synthetic price}$$

$$\text{Savings} = \$1.395 - \$2.194 = -\$0.80$$

The comparison shows there is an $0.80 cost advantage of buying a call in the market versus creating one synthetically. We might be tempted to believe there is an arbitrage opportunity to be had by selling a synthetic call for $2.194 and buying a real one for $1.395. This would leave us with $0.80 in our pocket. But this apparent arbitrage is just an illusion. The exercise of creating synthetic stock shows us that the cost of borrowing was worth $0.80 a share. So if we bought the option and sold a synthetic one, the $0.80 up-front advantage would be eaten up by the cost of borrowing stock when creating the synthetic call. So a long real/short synthetic pair trade would only earn a profit if the borrowing rate fell during the life of the trade. This would reduce the cost of carrying the synthetic call and increase the price of the real call. This, however, is a far more difficult arbitrage for the individual investor to capture. This is true for two reasons. The first impediment to capturing this arbitrage is that individual investors cannot borrow at the risk-free rate. They have to pay the broker loan rate to borrow cash, which typically runs 6 percent or more in today's market. To figure out the breakeven broker loan rate, we need to determine the point where higher cash borrowing costs offset the stock borrowing. This is done by setting the synthetic call price equal to the quoted call price in solving for the cost of carry.

■ Synthetically Replicating a Put

Just as a stock or call option can be created synthetically, a put option can also be created synthetically as well. This is done by purchasing a call, selling a stock short, and holding the present value of the option's strike price in a credit and market risk-free cash equivalent security. We can see this by rearranging the equation of put–call parity solving for the value of a put:

$$P = C - S + Ke^{-rt}$$

By continuing with our example, we see that the value of a synthetic put is equal to $1.27. By selling a put option available in the marketplace and purchasing an equivalent put synthetically, we will capture $0.94 advantage:

$$P = \$1.395 - \$25.00 + \$24.875 = \$1.27$$

$$\text{Savings} = \text{Market price} - \text{Synthetic price}$$

$$\text{Savings} = \$2.069 - \$1.270 = \$0.80$$

This comparison shows that there is a $0.80 cost advantage of buying a synthetic put, versus one trading on an exchange. Once again, we might be tempted to believe there is an arbitrage opportunity to be had by purchasing a synthetic put for $1.27 and selling a real one for $2.069. This would also leave the investor with $0.80 in his pocket. Like the case of a synthetic call, this apparent arbitrage is just an illusion, and it goes back to the discount on creating synthetic stock. The process of creating a synthetic put entails shorting stock. The cost of borrowing that stock will consume the $0.80 advantage over the life of the trade. So a long synthetic/short real pair trade would only earn a profit if the borrowing rate fell during the life of the trade. This would increase the value of the synthetic put and decrease the price of the real put. In the end, like the situation of a pairing a real and synthetic call, this is really just a method for trading the borrowing rate.

■ Synthetically Replicating Cash

Since put–call parity governs the relationship between the underlying security, its options, and cash, we can use the relationship to synthetically borrow or lend cash. This is a tactic that is used by institutions from time to time to generate liquidity and/or invest in a high-yielding synthetic asset whose return is driven, at least in part, by the cost of borrowing. To create an investable asset, someone buys stock, sells a call, and buys a put to hedge it. We can see this by rearranging the equation of put–call parity solving for cash. Within the framework of put–call parity, the cash required to buy stock purchased is perfectly hedged with an option structure that has a delta of −1.0. The long stock and option structure leaves the investor with a position that is perfectly hedged.

$$\text{Cash required} = Ke^{-rt} = S - C + P$$

To generate cash, we do just the opposite. The appropriate structure is to sell stock, buy a call, and sell a put. In this example, this structure would generate $25.675 in cash up front and would earn an additional $0.129 by investing the proceeds in the risk-free asset at 2 percent a year for three months.

$$\text{Cash generated} = -Ke^{-rt} = -(\$25.00 - \$1.395 + 2.069) = -25.675$$

$$\text{Return generated} = \text{Cash generated} - \text{Cash required}$$

$$\text{Return generated} = 25.675 - 24.875 = \$0.80$$

There is no real advantage for pursuing this approach, as it is a yield strategy. Yield strategies depend on the passage of time to collect income. In this case, the investor would collect $25.675 up front, invest that sum to earn interest, but give it all back in the borrowing cost of the stock sold short. While this is not a viable strategy for the individual investor, it might be available for a broker-dealer whose customers might own the underlying stock. Under these circumstances, the broker-dealer can borrow the customer stock at no cost and implement the strategy, capturing the $0.80 advantage per share of stock. Furthermore, a broker-dealer could use this as a cheap source of funding to cover the cash needed to pay for other positions in their trading book.

In this section we discussed the traditional ways option professionals create options and securities synthetically. We show that when there is a heavy cost of borrowing in the underlying security, individual investors can take advantage of this circumstance by creating the asset synthetically. In doing so, they can capture the implied lending income reflected by the discount available from the synthetic security. The beauty of this strategy is that investors do not have to lend their securities, so anyone can take advantage of the opportunity. Furthermore, the synthetic security will automatically be converted to a real one at expiration. If the price of the underlying is above the strike, the investors exercise their call and take delivery of the stock. Alternatively, if the price of the underlying stock is below the strike price of the two options, stock will be put to them. Either way, the investors now own stock. If the cost of borrowing remains at expiration, the trade can be rolled and repeated over until such time that the implied borrowing rate ceases to exist.

Synthetics go beyond simply replicating stock with puts, calls, and cash, or any of the other permutations suggested by put–call parity. Corporate finance theory tells us there is a relationship between the values of the firm's assets and the claims on those assets. The primary claims on corporate assets are debt and equity securities. In the following section, we will present a discussion about how we might synthetically create corporate debt securities by using options on the company's equity securities.

Creating Corporate Debt Synthetically

Corporations raise both debt and equity capital to fund their operations. The equity capital in private firms comes from their owner/operators, other individual investors and/or institutional investors such as private equity firms and venture capitalists. Public companies raise their equity in the capital markets. Capital market investors are individuals who purchase stock directly or indirectly through mutual funds and their retirement plans. Institutional investors, such as insurance companies, pension funds, and hedge funds participate in these markets as well. Insurance companies for example, purchase stocks and bond in public companies with the insurance premiums they collect from their customers. These funds are invested with the intention of earning a return until the day comes when the insurance company needs to make good on its promises.

The capital structure of most companies' equities tends to be quite simple, as a good number of companies only issue common stock. Some companies such as banks and utilities also issue preferred stock, as they have a shareholder base that looks to dividends for their cash-flow needs. Most companies borrow money to fund their operations in addition to sourcing equity capital. That tends to be a more complex aspect of the firm's capital structure. It is not uncommon for firms to borrow money from a bank collateralized by receivables, inventory, real estate, and/or equipment. At the same time, they might borrow money from an insurance company or the capital markets on an unsecured basis. Since unsecured lenders get paid in bankruptcy only after the secured lenders are paid, these loans are more risky and companies have to pay a higher rate of interest to compensate investors for that risk.

Some firms look for more esoteric ways of raising capital that meets their funding and cash flow needs. These firms might issue "quasi-equity" securities in the form of convertible bonds, which allow the investors to convert their loan into the equity of the issuing firm at their discretion. Companies like to issue these securities, as the conversion feature of the imbedded call option has value. By selling an imbedded call, which has value, it allows the issuing company to offer these securities at a lower rate of interest. Investors like convertible securities because it allows them to earn equity rates of return should the company do extremely well. At the same time, it provides some cash flow while they wait. Furthermore, they get the added benefit of owning a security that resides higher in the capital structure relative to equity, giving the convertible securities investor some downside protection in a bear market or bankruptcy scenario. Some companies are tight on cash flow in the short to intermediate term because they are making large investments in plant and equipment, for example. These companies often issue *pay in kind* (PIK) bonds. Issuers of PIK bonds have an option of sorts. PIK bonds give the issuer the flexibility of paying interest with additional bonds instead of cash. Highly levered capital-intensive firms often issue this type of bond. These firms value the flexibility to issue additional bonds to conserve cash in the short run and to match their operating cash flow with their debt service requirements.

Companies issue debt securities when they want to expand their businesses, buy back stock, or pay off other existing debts. When firms issue additional equity, they increase the balance of the existing equity securities outstanding. When firms issue debt they usually create a new security in the company's capital structure, as the terms of the new issue are usually different from older outstanding issues. Over time, firms may issue a large number of different tranches of debt, making each issue somewhat illiquid. Some tranches may not be particularly large. More often than not, small debt issues are "put away" by institutional investors who plan to hold them to maturity. These factors serve to limit liquidity in the debt issues of many companies. Investors who might want to buy those outstanding issues may not be able to find sellers or may not be able to find securities in sufficient size to satisfy their needs. As result, these investors must find debt securities issued by other companies that meet their investment objective and risk profile. The alternative that few investors pursue is to create debt securities synthetically. It is possible to create debt securities synthetically because there is a relationship between the value of a firm and the value of the financial claims on that firm's assets.

Depending on the operational risk of a business and/or the risk tolerance of investors and managers, companies will pursue different capital structures. High-risk companies, such as development-stage biotech companies, often finance themselves entirely with equity. Companies that are somewhat less risky, such as mature technology companies, often finance themselves with modest amounts of debt. Companies borrow as an alternative to issuing equity as a means of creating financial leverage designed to increase returns to shareholders. Since interest payments are tax deductible for a company, financial leverage lowers a company's income tax liability as well. This tax shield has value to shareholders by increasing after-tax cash flow. Companies with low business risk, such as regulated utilities, produce steady cash flow. With steady cash flow and hard assets to pledge as collateral, debt service is more assured. As a result, electric utilities are often financed with high levels of debt. Other times, investors and managers finance manufacturing companies with high levels of debt to retain ownership, while minimizing their equity contribution at risk. High levels of debt are used simply for the purpose of maintaining control of the enterprise.

When a company is capitalized purely with equity, all the asset price performance risk is born by shareholders. Under these circumstances, asset risk and equity risk are identical. When some portion of the company is capitalized with debt, some of the asset price risk is shifted to the lenders. If debt levels are low, the asset price risk transferred to the lenders is quite small. This is the situation common to investment-grade corporate bonds. These loans are relatively safe and pay a low yield premium relative to U.S. Treasury securities, which are thought of as credit risk-free. If the debt levels are high, the asset price risk shifted to the lenders is relatively high. This is the situation common to high-yield bonds, often referred to "below-investment grade" or *junk bonds*. Having more risk, these corporate obligations pay a higher rate of interest vis-à-vis investment-grade corporate bonds. At the end of the day, the yield premium companies must pay over a U.S. Treasury note to issue debt securities is a reflection of how much asset risk has been transferred to lenders. At the end of the day, asset risk does not change by the way a company is capitalized. It only changes how much risk each claim holder must carry (see Exhibit 9.1).

Option-pricing theory allows us to think about a company's equity as a call option on the value of a company's assets. If the value of a firm's assets exceeds the value of its liabilities, equity investors can exercise their option to buy the company's assets. Upon exercise, the investor can sell the company's assets, repay the debt, and keep the residual. If the value of the company's assets falls below the face value of its liabilities, the equity investor lets the firm go into liquidation. This is akin to allowing their call option to expire worthless. The lenders now have control of the assets, which they sell as repayment for some or all of the company's debt. Notice that when shareholders let their call options expire, this is equivalent to "putting" the company's assets to the lenders. Thought of in this way, we can think of lenders as put sellers on the value of a company's assets. The strike price of that put is equal to the face value of the company's debt. The time to expiration on that put is equal to the tenor of the debt security issued. Since the company can file bankruptcy at any time, that put the lenders sell is an American-style option.

In a default scenario, it is very rare that the value of a company's assets will fall to zero. Secured lenders have first claim on the assets pledged against the loan. Unsecured lenders capture value that is left over after the secured lenders are

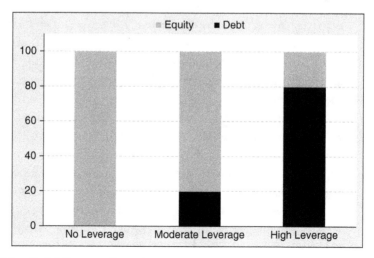

Exhibit 9.1 Capital Structure Examples

made whole. Take, for example, a company that has two loans outstanding. One loan is secured by the company's manufacturing plant. The second loan is unsecured. When the company is liquidated in a bankruptcy proceeding, the funds received by selling the facility are used to repay the secured lender. If there is something left over, that value will accrue to the unsecured lenders. As a result, even unsecured lenders are likely to recover some value when a company defaults on its debt. Naturally, secured lenders will recover more than unsecured lenders since they have first claim on company assets. Since lenders have effectively sold a put on the company's assets to the shareholders, we can recreate the investment performance of debt securities by selling a put option on the company's assets with a strike price equal to the face value of the company's debt, and a time to expiration equal to the tenor of the loan. At the same time, lenders effectively own a put on the company assets, as they have the right to sell those assets they take control of in a bankruptcy proceeding. The strike price of this option is equal to the expected value of the company's assets in a bankruptcy scenario. The strike price of this put is equal to the value of the company's assets in a quick, distressed liquidation. In essence, lenders are not really short a naked put. They are short a put spread with the upper strike equal to the loan amount and the lower strike equal to the corporation's expected liquidation value which is the same as the amount the lender expects to recover on a defaulted loan.

Credit rating agencies such as Moody's and Standard & Poor's have done historical studies of corporate and sovereign defaults. With this data, they are able to estimate default rates by credit rating and loan recovery rates parsed by industry and where the loan resides in a company's capital structure. Since these are the result of real-life situations, they also provide a good foundation for estimating the strike price of the recovery option.

Putting these two elements together, we can synthesize the return performance of a corporate loan by selling a put with a strike price equal to the face value of a company's debt and buying a put with the strike price equal to the expected recovery amount on a defaulted loan. The return on this short put spread captures the effects of a *change* in company assets on the value of corporate debt. It does not capture the returns driven by credit risk-free rates. To capture those returns, we must buy a credit risk-free instrument, a U.S. Treasury bond with a maturing date equal to the maturity of the corporate bond being replicated.

Synthetic credit-risky debt = Credit risk free bond − Put spread

Synthetic credit risk debt = Treasury − $\text{Put}_{K=FV\ Debt}$ + $\text{Put}_{K=Recovery\ Amount}$

These equations describe the conceptual formulation for understanding the behavior of credit-risky corporate debt. Creating a short put spread on a company's assets is problematic, as markets for options on company assets do not exist. Fortunately, there are liquid markets for options on a public company's equity securities. Since the value of a company's equity is directly related to the value of its assets, equity options are a less than perfect but usable instrument to replicate the performance of options on assets. To build an understanding of how this process works, it is useful to walk through an example.

Assume, we want to replicate a five-year unsecured corporate bond that is currently priced at $94.00 paying an annual coupon of 7.00 percent. The market value of this hypothetical company's assets is $10 billion; 80 percent of the company's market value is financed with debt and 20 percent is financed with equity. The company has 100 million shares outstanding so the shares trade at $20 a piece. Should the company find itself in financial distress, an in-depth recovery analysis and historical experience suggests that the lenders will recover 55 percent of the face value of loan. As a point of reference, a five-year U.S. Treasury security pays a 1.60 percent coupon with the same yield to maturity. Since the yield to maturity is the same, this five-year security trades at par.

Exhibit 9.2 summarizes the details of the corporate bond under review. Since this company has a high level of debt, its credit rating falls in the high-yield spectrum. With a market price of $94.00 and a semiannual coupon of 7.00 percent, it pays a yield to maturity of 8.50 percent. With five-year Treasuries paying 1.60 percent, the credit spread paid by the corporate obligation is 6.90 percent. To recreate this bond synthetically, we combine a U.S. Treasury note with a short put spread on the company's equity securities. The number of spreads sold and strikes selected are identified in Exhibit 9.3.

Exhibit 9.3 reveals the structure, price, and delta of the put spread designed to replicate the performance of the corporate obligation. Since the synthetic bond is replicating a five-year cash bond, the time to expiration chosen for the options is five years. Selling this put spread at the strikes indicated on 10.42 shares of stock while purchasing $100 worth of five-year government notes would create a synthetic

Current Price	$94.00	
Coupon (%)	7.00%	
Maturity	5 years	
Yield to Maturity	8.50%	
Yield on 5-Year Treasury	1.60%	
Credit Spread	6.90%	
Recovery Rate	55%	
Enterprise Value	$10 billion	
Debt	$8 billion	80% Debt
Equity	$2 billion	20% Equity
Share Price	$20.00	
# of Shares	100 million	
Rating	Ba3/BB-	

Exhibit 9.2   Bond Description

	Short Put	Long Put	Put Spread
Stock Price	$20.00	$20.00	
Strike Price	$16.52	$9.71	
Risk-free Rate	1.60%	1.60%	
Div. Rate	1.00%	1.00%	
Expiration (Yrs.)	5.00	5.00	
Volatility	35%	35%	
Price	3.523	0.872	2.651
Delta	(0.238)	(0.084)	(0.175)
Gamma	0.019	0.010	(0.009)
Theta	(0.388)	(0.214)	0.175
# of Spreads			10.42

Valuation

Time	Buy Treasury	Sell Put	Buy Put	Net
0.00	−$100.00	$36.71	−$9.08	−$72.37
0.50	0.80			0.80
1.00	0.80			0.80
1.50	0.80			0.80
2.00	0.80			0.80
2.50	0.80			0.80
3.00	0.80			0.80
3.50	0.80			0.80
4.00	0.80			0.80
4.50	0.80			0.80
5.00	$100.80			$100.80
Internal Rate of Return				8.50%
Credit Spread				6.90%

Exhibit 9.3   Synthetic Corporate Bond

security with the same internal rate of return as the corporate bond it seeks to replicate. Since we want to put the same amount of money to work, we prorate the synthetic structure by a ratio of 94.00/72.37.

Since the performance characteristic of equity has a nonlinear relationship to the value of a company's assets, there is not a direct way to determine the best strike prices to incorporate in the spread. Furthermore, there are two moving parts. Creating the bond synthetically requires a trade-off between the strikes used and the number of spreads incorporated in the trade. As the difference between the strike prices on the two put options increases, the net credit increases and the delta of the spread becomes more negative. As delta becomes more negative, fewer spreads are needed, which reduces the net credit. As a result, we determined the optimal structure in this example through linear optimization. In this optimization process, we minimized the tracking error of the synthetic bond relative to the cash bond, while ensuring the cash flow generated by the synthetic bond matches the cash bond as close as possible. (In practice, we would have to round the strike prices to ones

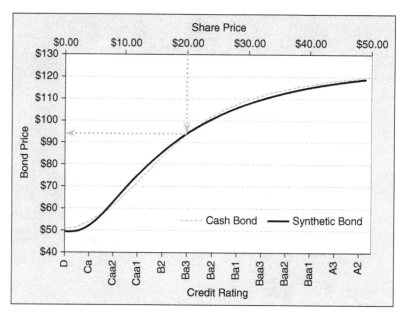

Exhibit 9.4 Synthetic versus Cash Bond

that are available in the marketplace. To eliminate any confusion in this numerical example, we do not round the figures in this analysis.) Exhibit 9.4 shows how well the synthetic bond tracks the cash bond, as a function of the company's credit rating and share price.

At this stage you are probably wondering how we determine the pricing relationship between a company's debt and its equity. We think about this relationship in the following way. The market value of a company's stock and bonds reflects the market value of a company's assets. When the price of the company's stock falls, the equity markets are signaling that the value of the company assets have fallen. Since the face value of debt remains unchanged, the firm becomes more levered on a market value weighted basis. As a result, the credit risk of a bond increases, and its price and credit rating falls. Therefore, there is a direct relationship between the market price of a company's stock and the market price of its debt. (For more on the technique used to derive this relationship, see the book *Quantitative Analytics in Debt Valuation and Management* listed in the reference section.) The gray dashed line in Exhibit 9.4 shows how the price of the five-year, 7 percent coupon bond changes as the price of the company's stock changes. The solid black like shows the same relationship for the synthetic bond. Notice how well the value of the synthetic bond tracks the cash bond. This shows that by selecting the appropriate strike, and number of spreads, a synthetic bond can provide an excellent substitute for the real thing, when none are available in the marketplace.

If we think of equity as a call option on a company's assets with a strike price equal to the face value of debt, we can extend that analogy and posit that an asset can be valued as a zero strike call on the company's assets. The performance characteristics of an option are dependent in part by the option's strike price. As a result, the performance characteristics of the cash bond and the synthetic bond will change differently as time passes. All other things being equal, the delta of a put spread will rise over time. Since the options used to replicate the cash bond are close but not perfect surrogates, the rate of drift in the delta of the options used to create the synthetic bond might move away from the delta of the options imbedded in the cash bond. As a result, the structure must be reoptimized from time to time. At a minimum, you should do this rebalancing as each coupon payment is made. This will ensure the tracking error between the cash bond and the synthetic bond is held to a minimum. While this analysis assumed volatility surface did not change over the investment horizon, a shift in the term structure or skew might allow you to restructure the synthetic bond to improve returns as well.

In this example, we showed that we are able to create a high-yield bond synthetically by purchasing Treasury notes and selling a put spread. Prices and market factors were chosen to show that you should be indifferent from owning a cash bond or a synthetic one. Returns over time will be the same. It is important to recognize that prices in the equity and options markets do not always agree with the price of risk in the bond market. This gives rise to the potential for arbitrage opportunities. With respect to the options market, this analysis shows that if the implied volatility associated with the company's stock is 35 percent, we can recreate this corporate obligation with the same expected yield to maturity. The iVol of the associated equity is a key ingredient to the valuation of the synthetic corporate bond. If the iVol used to price options for the underlying equity were more than 35 percent, the synthetic bond would cost less relative to the cash bond. If the iVol used to price long-dated options of the underlying equity is less than 35 percent, the cash bond would cost less than the synthetic bond.

The solid black line in Exhibit 9.5 shows the sensitivity of the yield to maturity of the synthetic bond to changes in implied volatility of the underlying stock. Notice that as iVol rises, the yield to maturity for the synthetic bond rises. In this example, for an increase of one vol. click, the yield to maturity of the synthetic bond would increase by 21.5 basis points. Likewise, if iVol falls by 1 percent, the yield to maturity on the synthetic bond falls by 21.5 basis points. This change in yield to maturity is equivalent to a $0.83 change in price.

This is the setup for arbitrage opportunities between these two distinct markets. We can look at bond prices to determine how the fixed-income portfolio managers and traders are pricing volatility relative to those priced by the equity options markets. This is very important for hedge funds that invest across asset classes and a company's capital structure. Since most market participants focus on just one asset

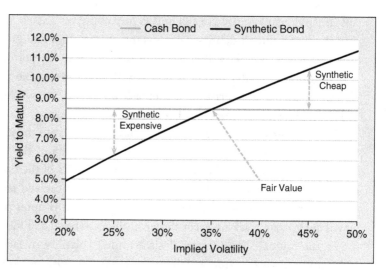

Exhibit 9.5   Valuation Comparison

class, there are times when there is a divergence of opinions between these two markets. When the bond market is discounting a lower volatility than the options markets, cash bonds will be more expensive than synthetic bonds. Under these conditions, we should sell cash bonds and buy synthetic bonds. When corporate bond investors are more fearful than the equity and option investors, they will incorporate higher volatility into their securities valuation by demanding higher yields. Under these circumstances, we should sell their synthetic bonds and buy traditional cash bonds. This is a distinct method for long-only investors to add alpha to their portfolio returns and outperform their index benchmarks. Hedge funds that seek to eliminate market risk can buy cash bonds when these markets reflect higher risk than the options market, and hedge them by buying put spreads, leaving nothing but interest rate risk. To eliminate that risk, they could sell T-note futures. This will result in a pure alpha-generating strategy, as returns will be independent of general market action. Shorting cash bonds is a bit more problematic as they tend to be harder to borrow. However, you might look to single-name CDS (credit default swaps) and buy put spreads if credit is pricing in a lower volatility than the options market.

There are some pragmatic issues that need further discussion. The typical option series for single names have an expiration cycle of 3, 6, 9, and 12 months. Corporate debt obligations typically extend for years. Industrial and financial companies often issue debt securities with 5- to 10-year maturities. It is not uncommon for telecom and utility companies to issue debt with tenors as long as 30 years. This makes using listed options somewhat problematic when creating debt securities synthetically. LEAPS (Long-Term Equity AnticiPation Securities) are a type of listed option with expirations that extends for up to three years. These options provide a viable alternative for synthetically creating short-term debt. Institutional investors who want to create debt synthetically with maturities longer than two or three years have to look to the over-the-counter market for these financial products. Since these markets are less liquid and fungible, we should expect to pay higher transaction costs to both initiate and close positions. This makes short-term arbitrage trades more difficult. These markets would be more useful for those who want to initiate positions with a longer-term time horizon.

As a final thought, you might want to use synthetic bonds for pricing bonds that trade very infrequently. Since you are simply pricing bonds and not trading synthetic bonds, one can model options with expiration dates that more closely align with the maturity of the bond. You can do this by extending the volatility surface based on what is priced in the marketplace. This way, you are matching long-term volatility expressed by the options market with that of the corporate bond in question. The term structure of volatility is generally upward sloping. It is the long-term volatility in equity prices that is priced into long-term bonds.

Final Thought

Creating hedges and synthetic securities are some of the powerful features of derivatives products in general and options in particular. In this chapter, we wanted to introduce you to the concept of synthetics which most individual investors typically do not think about in their investment activities. With the basics of synthetics under your belt, you can use your imagination to tackle investment and hedging challenges that usually go unsolved.

## CHAPTER 10

Home Runs

The preceding chapters discussed theory, application, and strategy concerning methods to improve returns and manage risk with options. While theory is great, we need to see how some of these strategies are applied and work in the real world of investing. In this chapter, we will provide a number of real life examples of investments that are either directly expressed with options or contain imbedded options that drive the risk/return equation. Since options are leveraged investment vehicles, assets with option characteristics have the potential to generate outsized gains. Furthermore, listed and OTC options enable investors to structure investments to limit risk and create the potential for very high returns. As a good way to show the potential offered by the listed option market, we will discuss a specific example of how skilled investors structured a multileg option trade in the oil markets to make huge gains without taking much, if any, risk.

■ The Oil Trade

In the years after the dotcom crash and 9/11, the federal government increased spending in an attempt to increase the rate of economic activity in the United States. At the same time, the Federal Reserve eased monetary policy by significantly lowering short-term interest rates by increasing their purchases of U.S. Treasury securities for the same reason. From 2002 to 2008 the Western economies recovered modestly, while the big winners were the BRIC (Brazil, Russia, India, China) countries. Up to this point, these countries were modest consumers of oil as compared to the United States and Western Europe. With trade barriers falling, these and other emerging markets increased their manufacturing output and domestic consumption. These products were sold into the international markets and these BRIC countries grew their GDP at very high rates, some in the range of 7 to 10 percent. With manufacturing growing and international trade increasing, transportation of goods (shipping, rail, and trucking) also became a big area of growth. To transport the goods produced in Asia to buyers in the Western economies, the global fleet of container ships, oil tankers and dry bulker carriers exhibited spectacular growth. Manufacturing and transportation of raw material and manufactured goods, of course, are very energy-intensive business activities.

Twenty years ago, only a small portion of the population in developing countries owned their own cars. As local development and international trade brought fast growth in wealth in these countries, many people bought cars. The explosion in automobiles for personal transportation was particularly acute in China, for example. It was not long before traffic jams in the major cities of developing countries became legendary. At the end of the day, with an increase in manufacturing and international trade, compounded with staggering growth in local transportation, the demand for energy, particularly liquid energy, went to record levels. This brought on a boom in oil prices (see Exhibits 10.1 and 10.2).

The demand for oil has grown steadily since its discovery. Exhibit 10.2 shows how global consumption of oil grew steadily since 1965. The recession of the late 1970s caused by a spike in interest rates in response to high inflation rates resulted in a reduction in economic activity and demand for energy. But once the global economy started to grow in the early 1980s, the global demand for oil has grown steadily and has not looked back. With demand for energy growing by leaps and bounds, many analysts and investors believed that investments in oil and gas would be the way to riches. For a time, this was indeed the case. Exhibit 10.1 shows

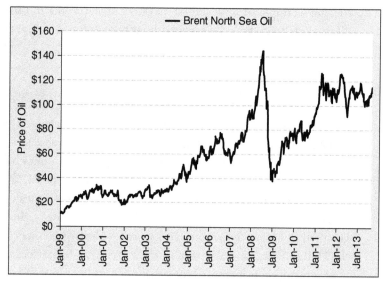

Exhibit 10.1 Historical Price of Crude Oil

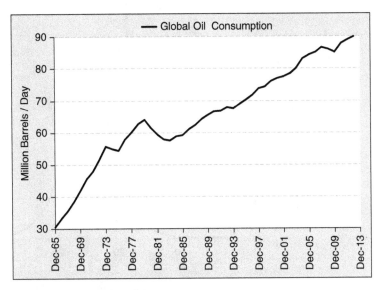

Exhibit 10.2 Historical Crude Oil Consumption

the price of oil going back to 1999. Notice that the price of oil might fluctuate significantly more than consumption, but at the end of the day, they both follow a rising trend.

With demand growing rapidly along with a dearth in significant discoveries of new sources of oil, many believed that an oil shortage was just around the corner. Rising prices seemed to support that proposition. This gave rise to what became a widely followed investment theme known as *peak oil*. Peak oil is a concept introduced by M. King Hubbard in 1956. This theory states that every oil field goes through a life cycle. It starts with exploration, which leads to discovery. Once a field is discovered, huge investments are made to develop the production infrastructure to develop the resource. This entails drilling production wells and building a pipeline infrastructure to take oil from the fields to the refineries. As more wells are drilled on an existing field, oil production increases. It is important to remember however, that pockets of oil, while sometimes very large, ranging in the billions of barrels, are limited in size. At some point, additional wells will not increase production. As production takes oil out of the ground, pressure that once pushed oil out of the ground falls. At some point natural pressure falls away, the oil must be pulled out of the ground. From that point forward, production declines until the resource is depleted and the field produces no more oil. In short, oil production starts at zero and rises until it hits a peak, then falls back to zero. Since all fields go through this process, it is logical to conclude that the sum of all oil fields around the globe will follow the same path (see Exhibit 10.3).

Peak oil became a particular concern as oil production was far outdistancing new discoveries. If new discoveries were not going to keep up with production, it is

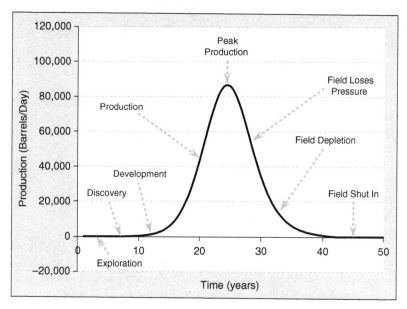

Exhibit 10.3 Oil-Field Production Cycle

logical to conclude that supplies would run out someday. To add weight to this theory, investors had seen peak oil theory play out first hand in the United States. There was a time when the United States was the largest oil producer in the world. Massive discoveries in the Middle East quickly moved North America into second place. By the mid-1970s, production in the United States reached a peak of almost 10 million barrels a day. From that point to the late 2000s, oil production fell by half, hitting just 5 million barrels a day by 2008.

This was not just a problem for production in the United States. In 1976, a fisherman by the name of Rudesindo Cantarell discovered a super-giant oil field off the southeast coast of Mexico. Experts estimated the field held 35 billion barrels of oil and held the expectation that about half of it was recoverable. Its development grew rapidly after discovery. By 1981, 40 wells were producing 1.1 million barrels a day. Well pressure fell rapidly and by 1994, production was down to 0.9 million barrels a day. To extract the remaining oil, 26 offshore platforms were put to work drilling nitrogen-injection wells to increase the pressure in the field. With additional production wells, PEMEX, the Mexican oil company, brought the field to peak production of 2.2 million barrels a day in 2004. While secondary recovery techniques can maintain or even increase production in the short run, doing so is the equivalent of putting the oil field on life support. It is just a matter of time before the last bit of oil is squeezed out of the field and production runs out. With the fields approaching depletion, production from this field has now fallen to less than 0.4 million barrels a day. Optimists looked to the Middle East for additional production, and they were able to do so at the margin. It takes many years of lead time and a significant investment of capital to increase the production of any field. In addition, increase Middle East production for local consumption. Since the Middle Eastern economies were growing rapidly, energy consumption in these countries was growing just as fast, if not faster, than the world as a whole. In the end, oil supplies appeared to become tighter. With this backdrop, the psychology was in place for the price of oil to move sharply higher, and it did.

Purchasing stock in exploration and production companies handsomely rewarded many investors. Oil service firms that helped develop the existing inventory of oil fields earned healthy profits as well. Since exploration and production companies own oil in the ground, buying stock in these companies is like buying a call option on the price of oil. The strike price of that option is the cost of extracting that oil and sending it to market. The cost of producing oil varies from field to field driven by unique geological and infrastructure challenges and regulatory hurdles as well. Furthermore, there are different grades of oil that affect the cost of production and refining, and the different modes of transportation have their own cost structures. So every field has a different strike price. What makes it different from a traditional option is that the time to expiration is undefined. Oil in the ground does not go away, of course. The oil company has the option to exercise it and develop an oil field whenever it thinks it can sell its oil at a price higher than the production costs. This is the point where the option goes in the money.

Assume for a moment that a company owns 1 billion barrels of recoverable oil in the ground and the estimated cost to extract and deliver that oil to market reflects the costs indicated in Exhibit 10.4.

Further assume this company has no debt and there are 1 million shares outstanding. In January 2005, the market price of Brent North Sea oil, which is a global benchmark for the price of high-quality oil, was $43 a barrel. At this price, the low-cost reserves are an in-the-money option. The E&P firm can produce the oil at $30/BBL and sell it for the going rate of $43/BBL. The difference of $13/BBL goes to the company's bottom line. Given this operating leverage, the E&P firm will earn higher profits on a greater than one-for-one basis when the market price of oil rises. If for some reason the market price falls below the cost of production, the E&P firm will lose money on every barrel of oil produced. Instead of suffering this

	Reserve (millions of BBLs)	Production Cost/BBL
Low Cost	500	$30
High Cost	500	$50
Total	1,000	

Exhibit 10.4   Reserves & Estimated Cost of Production

loss, the E&P firm can stop or reduce production and wait for higher prices. (One should be aware of the limits of halting production. Halting production can change the geology of an oil field, reducing its ability to produce at the same rate once the field is put back into production. For the sake of this analysis, we will ignore this complexity.) The high cost of oil represents an out-of-the-money option on oil prices. At current prices, it is not economical to bring these fields into production. Being an out-of-the-money option, once the price of oil rises sufficiently, the value of the option rises rapidly and the firm can produce very levered returns by bringing the field into production. Exhibit 10.5 is a chart of the payoff pattern of these options (gray lines) without time value. Combining these options and incorporating time value (black line) results in an estimate of total enterprise value.

Since these oil fields represent options on the price of oil, we can use option-pricing theory to value the company. All we need to do is input the appropriate variables into an option-pricing formula as they relate to the oil fields and oil price behavior. To do this we apply the historical volatility of returns on oil prices of 16 percent. The next important variable is time. Engineering reports might tell us that it will take five years to produce all the oil from these fields once they are put into production, and that a field awaiting production is expected give up its reserves sometime over the next 10 years.

If oil is at $43/BBL, as it was in January 2005, the value of this company is about $10.31 a share. Options always have value. If the price of oil falls $13.00/BBL to $30, the cost of production would equal revenues. A cash-flow analysis would show that the company would not make any money by producing oil. It suggests this company does not have any value. But the option to produce has value. If we value the company as an option on oil prices, we find the value of this company falls

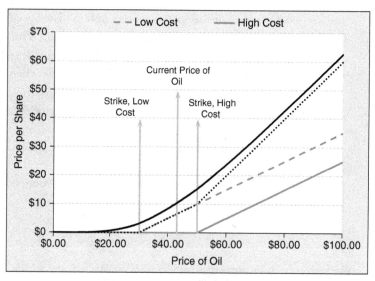

Exhibit 10.5   Equity Value Based on Imbedded Option

by $7.16/share to $3.15. While the company does not make money at this price, a rational buyer would pay $3.15 for the option to produce oil. The option becomes apparent when we examine the skewness of returns. If the price of oil increases by $13/BBL to $56, the value of the firm increases by $10.03/share to $20.34. The investors make more on the way up than they lose on the way down.

This analysis uncovers a viable investment strategy. If one is bullish on the price of oil, one could buy cheap call options on oil with undefined expirations by investing in exploration and production companies that have reserves that can be brought into production relatively quickly when prices rise. Since these reserves do not produce free cash flow at current prices, they only have time value. Since they have essentially an infinite time to expiration, they will be cheaper and more flexible options than call options on oil itself. This is not just a theoretical exercise. Exhibit 10.6 is a list showing the returns on a smattering of E&P stocks, all of which showed incredible performance.

At the close of trading on January 3, 2005, the price of oil was $43.00/BBL. By the end of trading on July 1, 2008, it rose to $131.00/BBL, for a gain of 205 percent. At the same time, the price of natural gas, which is a substitute for crude in some uses, rose 119 percent. Exhibit 10.6 shows us that the typical exploration and production company rose by over 400 percent. Natural gas is a byproduct of oil production. As a result, most oil producers also produce natural gas, so one should compare the performance of E&P companies with the price of hydrocarbon energy. On this basis, equities outperformed the commodity by a factor of 2.6:1. These equities did indeed behave like options on the price of oil.

Company	Initial Price	Ending Price	Return w/Dividends Reinvested
Cabot Oil & Gas	3.58	16.93	385%
Range Resources	12.73	65.54	433
Comstock Resources	20.77	84.43	310%
Chesapeake Energy	15.47	67.36	346
Southwestern Energy	5.59	48.53	724%
Quicksilver Resources	11.71	39.2	235%
Ultra Petroleum	23.08	98.59	327%
Noble	14.56	51.40	260%
Contango Oil & Gas	6.92	92.05	1230%
Suncor	16.94	57.22	242%
Crescent Point Energy	16.85	40.38	283%
Average			434%
Oil	43.00	131.00	205%
Natural Gas	6.16	13.51	119%
Average			162%

Exhibit 10.6 Returns on E&P Companies from January 3, 2005, to July 1, 2008

Contango Oil & Gas, the best-performing equity, represented an out-of-the-money option, as the company was not producing at all in 2005. By 2008, it had put a field into production and had a revenue run rate of $117 million a year. Bear in mind these companies have compound option features that go beyond the option to produce oil. Many of these companies employ financial leverage by issuing debt. In the discussion on synthetics in Chapter 9, we explained that when a company issues debt, equity becomes an option on company assets. In some sense, the equity of an exploration and production company is an option on a portfolio of oil call options. This expresses itself in the highly levered returns displayed above. When investing in E&P companies, one must be very careful to understand both the cost of producing reserves and the company's capital structure. When the price of oil falls, the price of E&P stocks will fall just as fast as they rise.

Although this is an excellent example of how equity in an E&P stock is like a call option on the price of oil, an example of equal interest centers on the action of oil options before and during the oil price crash that occurred in the six months after its peak. In 2008, the term structure of volatility was inverted. This is a natural occurrence after a very volatile movement in the price of an asset. Investors expect volatility to continue in the near term, but at the same time expect volatility to revert to the long-term mean over time. One of the interesting aspects of all commodities is that the inflation-adjusted price reverts to the long-term average over time as well. Historical experience tells us that volatility on all asset classes exhibits a mean reverting property. The only question is how long it will take for the mean reversion to take place. Exhibit 10.7 is a chart of the term structure of implied volatility on oil options in the months before the price of oil peaked.

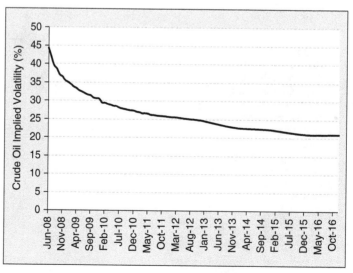

Exhibit 10.7   Crude Oil Volatility Term Structure, May 2008

The typical term structure of volatility is upward sloping. Investors tend to have a better understanding of risk in the short term relative to the long term. When the term structure inverts, the market provides an opportunity for those who want to carry a volatility arbitrage trade through a calendar spread. In this trade, the investor sells short-dated volatility high and buys long-dated volatility more cheaply. When the trade is weighted on a delta-neutral basis, the investor earns a profit if short-dated iVol falls relative to long-dated iVol. How this occurs is important, however. We showed in Chapter 4 that this structure is long vega. As a result, the investor will gain if the volatility curve flattens with an upward shift in volatility across all expirations. The investor will also enjoy a profit if short-dated volatility falls while long-dated volatility holds steady. Losses will be suffered if volatility falls across all expirations or the curve inverts further. The structure is also short gamma. As a result, if the price of the underlying trends in one direction or another, the investors will suffer a loss. Since the structure is short gamma, it will be long theta. Therefore, the structure will increase in value as time passes, should the price of the underlying security and implied volatility stagnate.

With so much uncertainty about the future price of oil, the skew chart of oil took the shape of a "smile." Options that are out of the money are priced at a higher iVol than those close to or at the money. The smile shape in the skew chart generally occurs when speculators and option writers expect big price movements, but are uncertain about which way that price jump will go.

Exhibit 10.8 shows the skew chart for 3-month and 24-month options on crude oil. When presented with a volatility smile, one can sell iVol expensively by selling out-of-the-money options while buying at-the-money options on a delta-neutral

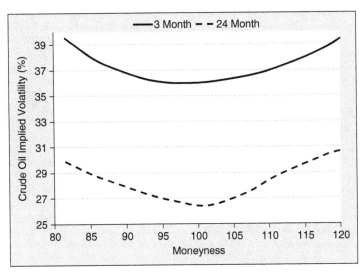

Exhibit 10.8 Crude Oil Volatility Skew, May 2008

basis. One way to do this is to sell out-of-the-money put and call spreads. If skew flattens, this strategy will be profitable. This strategy carries positive theta so time is our friend in this strategy. To offset theta, the trade is short gamma, so the trade will show a loss if the price of the underlying trends in one direction or the other.

The combination of an inverted term structure along with a volatility smile presents an opportunity to create a very cheap and even free straddle. The options on crude oil provided such an opportunity in the months before the oil price peak and eventual crash. The clues to create a free straddle in May of 2008 were revealed above. To buy volatility cheap, buy long-dated at-the-money puts and calls on a delta neutral basis. This is the lowest point on the volatility surface. At the same time, sell short-dated out-of-the-money put and call spreads. These are the highest points on the volatility surface. These out-of-the-money spreads offset the time decay one suffers on the long-dated options. Exhibit 10.9 shows the structure of this multileg trade.

At first blush, one might say this is not a free straddle. After all, one has to pay $19.33 up front. But remember, the cost of an option is not necessarily the amount of money you pay up front. The cost of an option is the value it loses as it ages. There is an interesting aspect to this structure. It starts out gamma neutral and nearly theta neutral, so one should not expect the structure to lose value over a short investment horizon. Furthermore, one is able to take advantage of rolling up the inverted term structure as time passes. The vega of the long-dated options is far higher than the short out-of-the-money put and call spreads. Consequently, the value of the spread will rise as it moves toward the forward volatility surface.

Exhibit 10.10 shows a total return analysis of this multileg trade. The solid black line shows the return profile for an instantaneous change in the price of crude oil. Since the structure is initially delta and gamma neutral, the return profile is flat

Type	Put	Put	Put	Call	Call	Call	Combo
# Buy or Sell	1	−1	1	0.57	−1	1	
Strike Price	95	102	110	119	134	145	
Risk-free Rate	1.80%	1.80%	2.50%	2.50%	1.80%	1.80%	
Dividend	0%	0%	0%	0%	0%	0%	
Time to Exp. (Mth)	3	3	24	24	3	3	
Volatility	37.10%	36.30%	26.65%	26.75%	37.10%	39.00%	
Price	$1.50	$2.96	$11.88	$17.77	$2.65	$1.45	$19.33
Delta	(0.13)	(0.23)	(0.33)	0.59	0.23	0.14	0.00
Gamma	0.010	0.014	0.008	0.009	0.014	0.010	0.00
Vega	12.1	17.2	59.0	63.1	17.5	12.6	84.9
Theta	(8.70)	(11.96)	(2.67)	(5.46)	(13.44)	(10.12)	0.80

Exhibit 10.9 Crude Oil Trade Structure, May 2008, Crude at $114.56

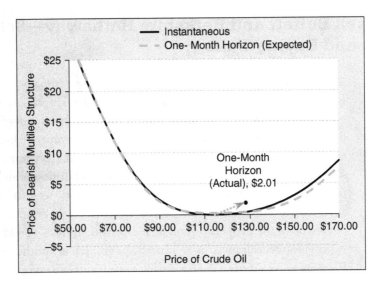

Exhibit 10.10 Total Return Analysis

for a moderate change in the price. As it drifts further away, gamma becomes positive, creating the return characteristic of a straddle. The gray dotted line shows the expected return for the structure, assuming volatility moves toward the implied forward volatility surface. Since the structure is vega positive and iVol is expected to rise due to the inverted term structure, this multileg trade is expected to increase in value by $0.26 at a minimum. After transaction costs, this is a free straddle.

The black dot on the chart above shows the actual profit one would have earned by holding this trade for a one-month time horizon. It performed even better than expected as the iVol for long-dated at-the-money options actually increased by two vol. clicks. Remember, a free straddle does not mean a riskless straddle. Once delta was hedged out, this became a volatility trade. It would perform best if either iVol increased or the price of crude oil trended in one direction or another.

This is not just a theoretical trade discovered after the fact. In our market-making activities, we witnessed a large hedge fund put this trade in the second quarter of 2008. The fund making this trade was a bit early, and they had to roll the position for a few months. But rolling up the volatility term structure meant they were being paid to wait for a bearish resolution to the oil price spike. When investors recognized that peak oil was not at hand, the price of crude oil finally cracked. The gains captured by this trade were ultimately enormous. This is a terrific example of the power of a free option. Since one does not have to suffer time decay, sophisticated professional investors can place a trade "in size," without the risk of significant loss if they have to wait for the market to move in their direction. The moral of this story submits that if you can find a free option or straddle, take it.

Warren Buffett and Berkshire Hathaway—Selling Puts and Buying Calls

Many think of Berkshire Hathaway as a holding company that possesses a number of wholly owned subsidiaries that engage in a wide variety of business activities. From the standpoint of organizational structure, this is indeed the case. At its core, Berkshire is a property and casualty insurance company. In its primary insurance activities, it assumes the risk of loss for people and organizations that are directly subject to certain risks. P&C insurance protects businesses and people against losses to their business, home, car, or other assets and personal heath as well. It also covers these entities against legal liabilities that might result from personal injury to people or to the property of other individuals. In its secondary insurance business, it provides reinsurance. A reinsurance contract is another form of risk transfer. Reinsurance is simply a contract where one insurance company, the direct insurance provider, offloads some or all of the risk of an insurance contract to another insurance company. In addition, Berkshire provides financial protection through life insurance and financial guarantees. Insurance companies protect themselves through diversification. They write insurance contracts against a wide variety of risks to a large number of customers who are spread out by both geography and industry. By diversifying across type of risk, customer, geography, industries, and so on, losses within any given time period are predictable and do not put the enterprise at risk of excessively large losses or insolvency.

The beauty of P&C insurance is that the customer pays a premium up front for protection against a future event. While this creates a liability for Berkshire, it also provides cash that it can invest to produce additional revenue. Warren Buffett has proven himself to be one of the best investors of all time, and this has been a key to the success of Berkshire. Mr. Buffett likes stocks for the long term, so much so that he typically buys companies outright. These investments become permanent subsidiaries of the enterprise. We are not aware of any company that Berkshire has purchased outright that was later sold.

If we look at Berkshire from the perspective of options theory, we see that Berkshire is in the business of both selling and buying options, and collecting and paying premium. At its core, insurance is a put option. This put option, however, is one unlike the typical option discussed in this book that pays if the price of an asset falls. The put option sold by a P&C insurance company pays if something breaks. By writing insurance, Berkshire collects premiums to cover the costs of catastrophic events that might occur in the future. Think of homeowner's insurance as a put option on the risk that the house is burned down or a tree falls through the roof. With that premium collected by selling insurance, Berkshire buys call options in the form of common stock. As discussed in Chapter 9, common stock is a call option on the assets of a corporation. If the value of the assets rises, the value of the stock rises.

If, on the other hand, the value of the company's assets falls below the face value of the company's debt, the company goes bankrupt. The owners of common stock lose everything. This is another way of saying that the option expires worthless. This has happened at Berkshire. When Mr. Buffett purchased Berkshire Hathaway, it was a textile company. As time passed, it became clear that it was a dying business so Mr. Buffett wound down that enterprise and eventually closed it as he repositioned the enterprise into what eventually became a holding company.

At the end of the day, Berkshire Hathaway is an enterprise that sells puts and buys calls as its core, fundamental business strategy. Berkshire has been successful in this endeavor and provided shareholders with outsized returns by purchasing underpriced call options and selling overpriced put options. From this perspective, the secret of Mr. Buffett's success is that he only sells puts when he believes they are expensive and buys calls when he believes they are cheap. In the reinsurance business, for example, there is a clear premium cycle. If there are no hurricanes in Florida or no earthquakes in California, competitors in the P&C space become complacent and succumb to the pressure of growing earnings in the short term. As a result, reinsurance premiums fall. At this point in the pricing cycle, Berkshire does not write reinsurance. Mr. Buffett goes so far as to continue to pay the reinsurance staff well during these periods to remove the incentive to do business for business sake. Nature does what it will and hurricanes strike and earthquakes hit. Those companies that sold insurance too cheaply suffer outsized losses relative to the premium collected when those events occur. With a drop in their capital base, they lose the ability to write new insurance policies and become insignificant competitors in the marketplace. Furthermore, companies who maintain a strong capital base become more fearful of natural events and cut back on writing new insurance policies. This is the point where Berkshire becomes an aggressive seller of reinsurance policies. Other companies run swiftly to remove risk from their books and are willing to pay a high price to do so. In the world of options, this is the same as selling puts when implied volatility is high. At the end of the day, Berkshire only sells puts when iVol is high and does not participate when iVol is low.

Berkshire follows the same philosophy with regard to its investments. Stock prices rise and fall with the economy and investor sentiment. When investors are feeling good, they push stock prices up to extremes to the point of overvaluation. At this point in the cycle, Mr. Buffett will reduce his holdings of common stocks and let cash build up on the balance sheet, keeping it available for the day when prices are more reasonable. Since stock is an option on company assets, and the value of that option is dependent on iVol, high share prices imply high risk. On the flip side, when share prices are depressed, the iVol implied by a company's equity is low. This is the point where Berkshire buys options on company assets (i.e., equities).

At the end of the day, Berkshire sells insurance (i.e., puts on catastrophe) when iVol is high and shows the discipline to stand aside when iVol is low.

Likewise, Berkshire buys equities (i.e., call options) when iVol is low. In this way, Mr. Buffett systematically sells volatility high and buys it low. The importance of this strategy goes further and speaks to diversification. There is no statistical relationship between the cost of insurance and the value of financial assets. As a result, there is no connection between when insurance benefits will have to be paid and the performance of equities. Since there is no correlation between the financial performance of the puts written and the call purchased, risk is reduced.

There is another way Berkshire buys calls on company assets. It sells naked puts outright. Between the years 2004 and 2008, Berkshire sold out-of-the-money put options on the S&P 500, FTSE 100, Euro Stoxx 50, and the Nikkei 225. According to the 2012 10-K, the notional value of those options is close to $34 billion. It is difficult to tell what iVol was used to price the individual contracts or times to expiration when selling these puts, but we estimate Berkshire took in approximately $7.25 billion in premium (give or take a billion) when they originally made the sale. It is our understanding that Berkshire sold out-of-the-money puts. If they took advantage of skew, which we are sure they did, they would have sold those options with an iVol in the low 20s. Since realized volatility on large-cap stocks in developed countries runs in the mid-teens, it looks like Berkshire was able to sell expensive puts, which expire between 2018 and 2026. Bear in mind that Berkshire is selling puts on a buy-and-hold basis. The regulatory filings stated that Berkshire expects these index puts to decay in value over time and potentially expire worthless. In short, they are selling price insurance with the hope and expectation that a claim will never be filed against the insurance contracts.

Put–call parity tells us that selling cash covered puts is like buying a covered call. We see this by rearranging the equation presented in Chapter 9.

$$\text{Cash} - \text{Put} = \text{Stock} - \text{Call}$$

If, for some reason, markets fall dramatically, Berkshire has the financial resources and liquidity to take ownership of the underlying stocks that populate the indexes, so it is reasonable to assume the puts are covered with cash or equivalents. Since this is equivalent to a covered call strategy, Berkshire is selling covered calls to produce income. Since it looks like they were able to do so with an iVol higher than historical rVol, the strategy should produce excess returns. This is precisely what Berkshire has done as it sells put options. Remember that Berkshire is selling puts on a sell and hold basis. As a result, one should expect this trade to produce positive alpha as the analysis in Chapter 4 suggests.

The moral of the story is this: We can describe Berkshire Hathaway as a portfolio of options. The company systematically sells expensive options and buys cheap ones. Over time, this is a winning strategy.

The Louisiana Purchase—The Greatest LBO of All Time

We know from corporate finance theory that equity is akin to owning a call option on the underlying asset. If there is no debt associated with an asset, the option is deep in the money and one can value that asset as a zero strike call. If there is debt associated with the asset, the strike price of the call is equal to the value of the debt used to finance the purchase of the asset. Most companies have debt levels that are a fraction of the value of the asset. Equity in these firms is simply a deep in-the-money call. If the value of debt is equal to the value of the asset, the equity represents an at-the-money call on those assets. There are times where the face value of debt is greater than the market value of the asset. Prior to the financial crisis in 2008, there were many lenders who would provide mortgages on houses that exceeded the value of the property by as much as 20 percent. In this case, the homeowner held an out-of-the-money call option on the property they lived in. Other times, a business will languish and the value of the company's assets will fall below the face value of the company's debt. The company will be able to remain in business and continue operations so long as they can make their debt payments. In these circumstances, equity in the real estate or business described earlier represents an out-of-the-money option on the value of the asset with an undefined expiration date. To keep that option alive, the owner of equity must continue to service the debt. One can think of this debt service payment as option premium. Thought of in this manner, the Louisiana Purchase was the greatest LBO and cheapest option purchased of all time. The story of this transaction is quite interesting and investors should keep it in the back of their minds when allocating capital.

The land covered by the Louisiana Purchase encompasses an enormous parcel of land that represent what are now 15 states in the United States. Specifically, the Territory of Louisiana covered all of present-day Arkansas, Missouri, Iowa, Oklahoma, Kansas, and Nebraska. The territory also covered parts of what are now Minnesota, North Dakota, South Dakota, New Mexico, Texas, Montana, Wyoming, Colorado and Louisiana. A small portion of the land extended into what are now the Canadian provinces of Alberta and Saskatchewan. This territory covered a grand total of 828,000 square miles, a very serious piece of property in deed.

From 1699 to 1762, the government of France owned a vast area of land that was then called the Territory of Louisiana. At the end of the Seven Years' War, France gave the territory to Spain, a key ally of the state. The city of New Orleans is located at the mouth of the Mississippi River, making it a key shipping port for agricultural products that were transported to other parts of the United States. In 1795, Spain and the United States signed the Pinckney's Treaty, which gave U.S. merchants the "right of deposit." The right of deposit gave U.S. merchants the right to freely navigate the Mississippi River and store goods, such as flour, tobacco, pork, feather,

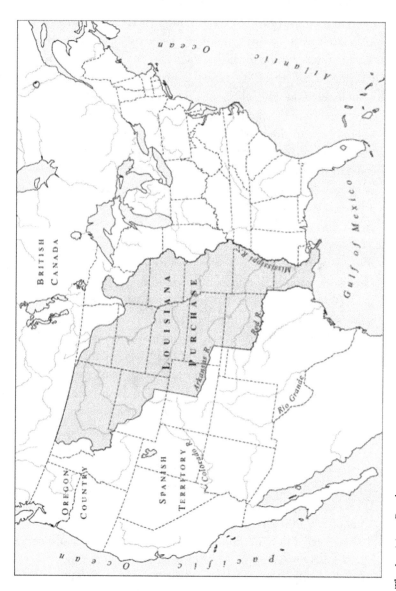

Exhibit 10.11 The Louisiana Purchase

Source: The History of American Business, historybusiness.org

cider, butter, cheese, and so on for export. This treaty was short lived and Spain revoked it in 1798, greatly upsetting relations between the two countries. In 1801, the right of deposit was restored.

But in 1800, Napoleon Bonaparte signed the Treaty of San Ildefonso with Spain to take back the territory as he set his sights on building an empire in North America. This treaty was kept secret until November 3, 1803, which was just three weeks before France and the United States ultimately cut a deal to transfer ownership.

Getting a deal done was anything but certain. Thomas Jefferson, who was president at the time, recognized the geographic significance of New Orleans, and in 1801 he sent representatives to Paris to make an offer to buy the city and port of New Orleans from the French government. Given Napoleon's ambitions, it was no surprise that he rejected the idea. In 1803, negotiations began anew. Pierre Samuel du Pont de Nemours, a French nobleman, facilitated negotiations with France at Jefferson's request. It was at this time that the idea of a larger Louisiana Purchase was put forth. At the same time, France was under financial pressure as Napoleon began preparations to invade Britain in 1803. Furthermore, there was a slave revolution going on in Saint-Domingue (modern-day Haiti). Napoleon had sent more than 20,000 troops to reconquer the territory and reestablish slavery. But yellow fever and the revolutionaries destroyed the French army, in what became the only successful slave revolt in the Americas. Without the revenues from the sugar trade, Louisiana was not so attractive to the French empire. Even though Spain had not completed the transfer of Louisiana to France, Napoleon decided to sell the entire territory to the United States. Napoleon liked the idea of selling something that was not his yet, and the sale would also serve to raise cash to fight the imminent war against Britain. The Americans were prepared to pay $10 million for New Orleans and the surrounding area, but were pleasantly surprised when France offered the entire territory for $15 million.

Complicating the deal still further, many in the United States, led by House Majority Leader John Randolph, as well as some historians, believed that this purchase was either unconstitutional or simply unjust. Jefferson's political adversaries made hay of the fact that a strict constructionist would appear to play fast and loose with the constitution. James Madison, one of the authors of the U.S. Constitution was thrown into the same camp. The House even went so far as to hold a vote to deny the purchase, but it failed by two votes, 59–57. The Federalists feared that the Louisiana Purchase would alter the balance of power. They felt the purchase was a potential threat to Atlantic seaboard states, merchants, and bankers, shifting power and influence to the Western merchants and farmers. Furthermore, an expansion of the number of slave-holding states would inflame already existing divisions between the northern and southern states. Jefferson argued that such a purchase was constitutional under the power granted to the president to negotiate treaties. Finally the question of citizenship was an issue. The treaty between France and the

United States granted citizenship to the French, Spanish, and free black people living in New Orleans. Critics of the deal felt that foreigners, who were unacquainted with the U.S. style of democracy posed a risk to the political system. In the midst of all this, the government of Spain argued that Napoleon did not have the legal authority to sell the territory. They argued the Third Treaty of San Ildefonso forbade it and that France promised Spain it would never sell or alienate Louisiana to a third party. Furthermore, Spain argued that if the property were to be transferred, it must be transferred to them. But in the end, the Spanish prime minister had authorized the United States to negotiate with the French government for the acquisition of territories, which suit U.S. interests. But in the end, the path was cleared for the federal government of the United States to purchase the territory, the Senate ratified the treaty and the two houses of Congress authorized the funds needed to close the deal.

Not surprisingly, the federal government did not have cash on had to close the deal. As a result, the Louisiana Purchase was a highly leveraged deal. The federal government allocated $3 million of gold to the transaction and borrowed $12 million by issuing bonds underwritten by Francis Baring and Company and Hope and Company of Amsterdam. Recall that equity is an option on the underlying asset. By issuing a high degree of debt, Jefferson created an option that was slightly in the money with an indeterminate time to expiration. The U.S. government could keep this option alive by simply making its debt service payments as contracted. When the debt came due, they could simply roll over the loan and keep its option alive. Should for some reason, the government decide the territory was of little value, they could default on the loan and transfer the property to the lenders. This is akin to letting the option expire.

The moral of this story is quite simple, but one that is often forgotten. Napoleon's warmongering put him in a financial bind. In some sense he was facing the mother of all margin calls. To meet this margin call, he had to sell assets. Jefferson recognized a distressed seller of an asset that would be of tremendous value to the United States for both economic and national security reasons. Since he did not have enough money to purchase the property outright, he purchased an real option with an infinite life on the asset. It turns out the $3 million option turned into an asset worth trillions. Move over Warren Buffett, Benjamin Graham, and George Soros. It looks like Thomas Jefferson was the greatest investor of all time.

■ Bitcoin

Bitcoins are a new phenomenon that is just starting to get the attention of the general population. The concept of Bitcoin is quite interesting. It is a digital or virtual currency that employs peer-to-peer technology, implemented over the Internet, to facilitate instant payments. This is similar to how traditional currency works when people buy products over the Internet and pay with a debit card. To ensure transactions take place in a safe and secure manner, the sender encrypts the payment messages, which are then decrypted by the receiving entity. Anyone who intercepts the message will be unable to decipher its contents. What makes a Bitcoin transaction unique is that the workings of the system are decentralized. Traditional financial institutions do not facilitate the transaction in any way. Since a third party cannot monitor transactions, these digital transactions are anonymous, much like a traditional cash transaction with paper currency.

Bitcoins are held in a program/file that resides on one's computer. The owner of this program makes payments by sending the digital currency to the payee. Processing a Bitcoin transaction takes place on secured servers called Bitcoin miners. These servers confirm transactions by adding them to an encrypted global ledger. The payee receives his Bitcoins when his electronic wallet accesses the Bitcoin peer-to-peer network and synchronizes with the ledger. Once the Bitcoins are stored in one's wallet, they are immediately ready for use.

Bitcoin miners are paid a fee for participating in this process. In theory, anyone with the proper software can act as a Bitcoin miner and facilitate a transaction. To earn the right to process a transaction, the Bitcoin miner must perform a very difficult mathematical task. The miner who completes this task first generates a sequence of numbers that provides proof the miner solved the mathematical task. This sequence of numbers is known as "proof of work" and is attached to the transaction message. In this process, some Bitcoins, or fractions thereof, are created and deposited into the wallet of the Bitcoin miner. This is how Bitcoins are created. One does not necessarily have to perform work or sell a product to obtain Bitcoins. Like any currency, one can buy Bitcoins by exchanging their traditional currencies (U.S. dollars, euros, yen, etc.) for them. This is where a traditional financial institution comes into play. To buy Bitcoins, you need to wire money to a Bitcoin exchange. They will buy Bitcoins on your behalf at the market price and send them to your electronic wallet. If you want to sell your Bitcoins, you send them to an exchange where they are converted to traditional currency, which is wired to your traditional bank account.

To be sure, Bitcoins are a form of currency. As a result, they represent a financial asset. The value of that asset is difficult to determine, as they are not backed by anything real. Bitcoins only have value to the extent that someone will take them as payment for the delivery of a particular good or service, or to the extent someone is willing to buy them with a traditional currency. This, by the way, is true of all traditional fiat currencies. If Bitcoins are a currency, how can they have option value? To understand the option value in Bitcoins, we need to introduce the idea of a "real option."

In this book, we discussed at length options as financial assets. There is another broad type of option known as a **real option**. Real options are characterized by a choice that is only available to a particular business or person in the real economy. They are not derivative instruments per say, as they represent an actual option to change course in the real world. Real options get the name "real" because they usually pertain to tangible assets (e.g., capital equipment), not financial assets.

The definition of a real option is similar to the definition of a derivative instrument. It is the right, but not the obligation to acquire the present value of a stream of cash flows by making an investment on or before the opportunity ceases to exist in an uncertain environment. This definition might be confusing. Think of it as buying an asset and deciding how best to monetize that investment sometime later. The potential for choice creates an asymmetry in potential outcomes, which creates the option's value. The following are examples of real options:

- Building a new, highly efficient manufacturing plant. When a company builds a new plant, they have the option to expand production or to close down an older and less efficient plant. By doing so, the company is well positioned to address an increase or decrease in demand, or compete more aggressively on the basis of price.

- Building a power plant that has the ability to deliver electric power to more than one electrical grid. Most power plants are connected to just one grid. They have to sell electricity at whatever the going rate is for that market. If a plant is able to locate close to a node between grids, they have the option to deliver power to the grid that pays the highest price. This choice increases the profitability of the power facility.

- A computer manufacturer designing its products to use generic off-the-shelf components enables them to have multiple suppliers of logic and memory chips, microprocessors, and other components, is a real option. It allows them to buy parts from whoever can deliver them most cheaply, at the highest quality, and in the timeliest manner.

While it may not be readily apparent, in its infancy, Bitcoins were clearly a real option in the currency space. In 2008, an unknown person by the name of Satoshi Nakamoto published a paper over the Internet describing the Bitcoin protocol. At this stage, Bitcoin was just a concept. In 2009, the concept started to take shape when a network came into existence by the release of the first Bitcoin client and the issuance of the first coins. The client was open source, which allowed anyone interested in viewing and improving the code to do so. An important feature of open-source software is that it technically does not have an owner. Anyone can work with some or all of the code to make new software. Like the original software and source code, this new and improved software is then made available to anyone for free. At the end of the day, the open-source platform allows the ecosystem of freelance developers to make and improve software for the good of the community.

There are no owners, sponsors, or monopolies to extract economic rents from the universe of users.

This environment is the perfect backdrop for a real option as it is an asset with an unknown value and potential but unknown use. If someone buys a Bitcoin, she is taking advantage of an investment opportunity today in a highly uncertain environment, which may or may not have any value in the future. In 2009, Bitcoins were nothing more than an interesting theoretical currency experiment. Nobody knew what a Bitcoin was worth, if Bitcoin would become accepted as a medium of exchange in the future, or if they would represent a store of value. Since Bitcoins were in their infancy, formal exchanges did not exist where one could trade goods, services, or other traditional currencies for Bitcoins. The first transactions were negotiated in 2010 on talk forums. In these forums, those who wanted Bitcoins expressed an interest to buy them and those who had them expressed an interest in selling them. With a little give and take, they agreed on a price and an amount and transactions took place. This all took place without a controlling financial institution or controlling authority. In August 2010, a mammoth vulnerability in the protocol was identified and exploited. Over 184 Bitcoins were generated and captured by two addresses on the network. With the ability to generate (i.e., counterfeit) great numbers of Bitcoins, they would have no value. Fortunately, this flaw was identified within hours and erased from the transaction ledger. Technical changes were made to the network protocol to ensure this flaw was fixed permanently. This event added more uncertainty to the concept of a cryptocurrency. There are millions of very clever people out there who will challenge any system that attracts their attention.

The total value of an option is equal to the sum of its intrinsic value and its time value. It is fundamentally clear that if Bitcoins are vulnerable to counterfeit, then their intrinsic value is questionable. Furthermore, it was unclear if anyone in 2010 would accept them in exchange for goods and services, or for traditional currencies. It was entirely possible that Bitcoin would have nothing more than a small cult following, never making it to the mainstream. One of the first notable transactions took place when someone bought a pizza for 10,000 BTCs. Bitcoin began to gain traction in 2012 when Wikileaks began to accept Bitcoins as donations. As other organizations joined the bandwagon, the Electronic Frontier Foundation stopped accepting Bitcoins because of legal concerns. This threw additional uncertainty into the market and Bitcoin could have died then and there before it ever got off the ground. Adding additional resistance was Jim Cramer, the widely followed host of CNBC's *Mad Money* TV show. In an episode of *The Good Wife* he played himself in a courtroom scene where he stated that he did not believe that Bitcoin was a legitimate currency. With all these headwinds, it was clear that Bitcoins probably did not have any intrinsic value.

The other source of value that contributes to the price of an option is time value. While it was unclear that Bitcoin would become anything more than an interesting curiosity, there was always a chance it could become something. With time, the imperfections and resistance to a cryptocurrency might be overcome. It is time value that makes an option different from other financial assets. With respect to a financial option, one can buy an out-of-the-money option to have the right to buy or sell something for a small premium within a given period of time. With respect to a real option, one has the right to make a choice to do something sometime in the future. The significant difference between the two pertains to time to expiration. Real options do not necessarily expire. After investing in an asset with an uncertain value in an ever-changing environment, the investor retains a strategic option to change course over the life of the investment.

Take, for example, a company that buys a large piece of land and puts a small factory on that property. If demand stagnates, it has the option to do nothing. If demand increases, it has the option to expand capacity to fulfill that demand. That option will never expire so long as the company owns the land.

Back in 2008 to 2012, Bitcoins represented a deep out-of-the-money option. In the fourth quarter of 2010, you could have bought a Bitcoin for a tiny premium of about $0.08. If you held that coin, you would have had the option sell it at a later date or exchange it for a good or service if—and it was a big if—other economic actors decided to accept Bitcoins as payment. If the whole idea of Bitcoins faded away, those options would fade away, and the Bitcoin would simply become worthless. Since there was no formal exchange to trade a Bitcoin to someone else for a traditional currency, and traditional retailers did not accept Bitcoins for payment of goods and services, there was no intrinsic value to this option. But there was always the chance those mechanisms could develop in the future. If they did, you could exercise that option by trading your Bitcoins.

As it turned out, there was another option that Bitcoin proponents advertised. That was the option to hold purchasing power outside the banking system. This option does not have any value if an exchange does not develop or Bitcoins do not become a medium of exchange for goods and services. Think of this as a barrier option. Once a barrier is breached, the option can be exercised. This may not seem important, but this option became valuable at the onset of the second phase of the European banking crisis, which began in 2011. At this time, the Greek economy was falling into depression and it was becoming clear that the central Greek government was bankrupt. Greek banks were the biggest lenders to the local government, bankrupting these institutions as well. Since the Greek government could not bail out the banks, it became fundamentally clear that depositors were in trouble. This caused a run on the banks as depositors took their money out of local institutions and placed them in banks domiciled in the United Kingdom, France, and Germany. At the margin, some people took their money out of the banking system by exchanging their euros for Bitcoins. A few keen observers saw this phenomenon as well and bought Bitcoins. This caused the price of Bitcoins to rise to the $30 range by June of 2011. This was made possible because by this time, there were a number of exchanges available that would facilitate the purchase and sale of Bitcoins. Investors were putting value on the opportunity to take money out of the banking system for safekeeping as the traditional financial system was teetering on insolvency.

The established intergovernmental and monetary authorities were able to stabilize the Greek banking system and the fear of a collapse of the banking system went away. Since there was not a well-defined economic ecosystem for people to exchange their Bitcoins for goods and services, owners of Bitcoins had to sell them to buy the things they needed. As a result, the price of Bitcoins fell to just a few dollars a coin. The option to keep money out of the banking system had lost much of its luster. This did not last long.

In 2013, the banking system in Cyprus collapsed. Instead of a government sponsored bailout of banks and the banking system, the monetary regulators opted for a *bail-in*. This was a process in which depositors were forced to convert some portion of their deposits into the stock of worthless banks. In this process they lost money. Fearing the banking system once again, many people in Cypress tried to get their money out of local banks and, indeed, the country. Some took their money out of the banking system by purchasing gold and silver and tried to get those precious metals out of the country. Once again, there were some people who took a different approach to get money out of the banking system. They bought Bitcoins. This time, the price of Bitcoins rose to a price of $230 in April 2013. As the crisis in Cypress began to resolve itself and the need to get money out of the banking system subsided, the price of Bitcoins once again fell into the mid-$70 range. As of August 2013, Bitcoins were trading around $120.

The market price of Bitcoins is not likely to fall to the price they held in their early days because a number of issues have been resolved. Barriers have been crossed and the barrier option is now exercisable and in the money. There are now close to 40 online exchanges where people can convert traditional currency into Bitcoins. Regulators are taking a kinder eye to the currency alternative as well. Many exchanges are registering with FinCEN, the Financial Crimes Enforcement Network, which is a bureau of the U.S. Department of Treasury. This is giving regulators confidence that these important participants are taking their fiduciary responsibility seriously. In addition, more companies are beginning to accept Bitcoins as payments. As this system of cryptocurrency gains wider acceptance, it will become increasingly difficult to ban it altogether.

At the end of the day, Bitcoins turned out to be one of the great options trades in modern time. One could have bought Bitcoins in 2011 at $0.08 apiece as an option on a new currency system and shield from a shaky banking system. With perfect timing, one could have sold that option for $230 a Bitcoin. This would have provided a return of over 287,000 percent. Said another way, if you bought $100 of Bitcoins, you could have sold them for \$287,500. These returns are the dream of every option traders. As of November 2015, Bitcoins change hands at about \$400 a virtual coin.

Final Thought

In this chapter, we showed a few examples of how one can generate tremendous wealth by understanding the options imbedded in various securities or by simply purchasing underpriced options and selling overpriced ones. This is how many traditional businesses such as insurance companies make their money. Businesses that maximize flexibility are, in fact, buying cheap real options that enable them to change course on a dime to maximize cash flow and profits. Every once in a blue moon, a huge investment opportunity comes around that contains a very cheap option. Understanding that option is key to recognizing the opportunity. The lesson from this chapter is quite simple. Analyze businesses and individual investment opportunities as if they were options. This will reveal their true character. If there is an investment that does not have optionality imbedded in it, find a way to structure the transaction to limit downside risk while enjoying unlimited gains. Make your own option.

## CHAPTER 11

Strike-Outs

Investors pursue a never-ending search for investment strategies that will produce high rates of return with manageable levels of risk. Some investors trade options, buy low P/E stocks, or buy momentum stocks. Some investors buy zero coupon bonds, or high-yielding debt. A rational investor intuitively knows that every strategy has its day in the sun, even if it's a bad one. Even great strategies and great investors suffer losses, even when they follow a time-proven strategy. Everyone in the equity markets but short sellers lost money in 2000–2002 and they lost again in the 2008 bear markets, for example.

Blow-ups are particularly intriguing to those who follow the financial press. These stories often start out innocently enough. Someone finds a strategy that produces outsized profits for a few years, and the people who discover said strategy are often hailed as financial geniuses. Whether it is a good idea or a bad one, Wall Street cannot keep a secret, and it does not take long for copycats to come out of the woodwork. Some of these copycats know what they are doing and many do not. One of the many paradoxes of investing tells us that the potential for a major blowup increases markedly when a particular strategy becomes popular. When this happens, too much money chases a particular investment strategy and the underlying asset or class of assets inevitably becomes overvalued. This occurs because people throw caution to the wind and pay any price just to get in the game. In this process, asset prices inevitably become divorced from economic reality. When this occurs, a price collapse is guaranteed, only the timing is uncertain.

Sophistication has little to do with it. Some investors jump in and knowingly buy into a mania. They believe they are clever enough to get out before the inevitable collapse occurs. Alternatively, they might construct a financial model to justify why a particular strategy will produce outsized gains indefinitely. Others blindly fall into a trap and get on board the latest investment fad because a trend has been in place for some time or their friends are convinced they have found a sure thing. The investment landscape is littered with investment strategies that did not pan out over the long run. In this chapter, we will discuss the details of some high-profile blow-ups and a few that did not hit the front page of the *Wall Street Journal*. One of the biggest causes of blowups is put writing. Most investment strategies entail writing a put option, only it is not apparent that one is doing so. Mix in a little financial leverage and you have the potential for a spectacular train wreck.

■ The Carry Trade

One of the most common strategies that investors in general, and hedge funds in particular, employ to earn higher rates of returns is the "carry trade." Carry trades are very simple: Look for a high-yielding asset and find a way to finance it at a lower rate. At a minimum, the expected return is equal to the yield differential between the high-yielding asset and the cost of financing that asset. An example of this might be the purchase of a long-term mortgage-backed security that yields 4 percent, which is financed in the repo market. A repo financing entails the investor selling a long-term asset and agreeing to repurchase it at another date at a fixed price. The cost of this financing is simply the difference between the prices of the security sold and the agreed-upon repurchase price plus coupon interest or dividends. In this case, the investor is buying a long-term asset at a high yield and financing it at short-term at a low yield. Trades like this have interest-rate risk, as the price of the long-term asset is generally very sensitive to fluctuations in long-term interest rates. To hedge this risk, these investors might sell an interest rate futures contract on U.S. Treasury securities. But oftentimes, investors do not hedge and bear the risk of the trade to earn the highest return possible. Other carry trades entail the purchase of a high-yield security, while simultaneously short-selling a low-yield security. An example of this might be purchasing high-yield debt and selling U.S. Treasuries against it, or just as common, buying an emerging-market government bond while simultaneously selling a developed-market government bond. An example of this includes buying 10-year Brazilian government bond while selling 10-year Japanese government debt, or buying 10-year Greek government debt while selling a 10-year German government bond. Other times, investors develop complex trading strategies that are designed to produce a specific payoff pattern. This type of strategy often requires frequent trading, and its success is dependent, in part, on the liquidity of the securities traded. What is important to recognize is that in most carry trade or active trading strategies, there is an option embedded somewhere in the process. Many times, investors do not realize that they have sold an option hidden somewhere in their investment strategy or in the securities used to implement the strategy, which gives rise to a risk that goes unrecognized. It is this unrecognized risk that provides a high rate of return over certain periods of time, but also plants the seeds of eventual destruction. In this chapter, we discuss a number of investment strategies followed by sophisticated investors who took risks they did not understand. We share these stories by decomposing the strategy to highlight the hidden option embedded in those strategies. Generally, it is a hidden option sold that makes a portfolio manager looked like a genius for years, only to later show that the star portfolio manager is simply a modern-day emperor with no clothes. Other times, investors create strategies that have an embedded option that is recognized by the investor, but these folks simply underestimate how far prices can move away from their estimate of "fair value." Other times, they do not understand the true nature of the option written, which might have risk characteristics that are far different from the typical exchange-traded option. One of those strategies is known as portfolio insurance.

■ Portfolio Insurance

Portfolio insurance was a strategy developed in 1976 by a couple of academics named Hayne Leland and Mark Rubinstein. Portfolio insurance was an outgrowth of traditional opion-pricing theory, which was becoming a more important component to portfolio management techniques at the time. At its core, portfolio insurance is an active strategy designed to replicate the payoff pattern of a call option. It became popular because one could, at least in theory, synthetically create a call option without paying a premium up front with a very simple strategy. Recall that the delta of an at-the-money call option is about 50. As the price of the underlying security rises, the delta of the call increases, allowing the investor to capture a larger share of the gain in the price of the underlying security. If, on the other hand, the price of the underlying security falls, the delta on the call decreases, reducing the portfolio sensitivity to the underlying asset. Since the call option investor earns more in an up market than they lose in a down market, they must pay a premium to capture this asymmetric return pattern.

In the early days of option trading, many investors believed the premium one had to pay for listed options was too high. As a result, institutional investors were hungry to find a way to capture the asymmetric returns provided by options without seemingly paying a premium. Portfolio insurance looked like a very simple way to do just that. Portfolio insurance is a mechanical trading strategy in which investors buy more of the underlying asset as its price rises. Reducing cash and increasing exposure replicates the effect of increasing delta in a trending bull market. If the price of the underlying asset falls, some of that asset is sold. The exposure to risky assets falls and cash holdings increase. This has the effect of reducing delta in bear markets. In the 1980s, the biggest participants in portfolio insurance programs were institutions like corporate pension plans and insurance companies. These funds held large diversified portfolios of stocks. Actively buying and selling entire portfolios was both cumbersome and expensive. However, with the advent of futures contracts on stock market indexes, one could synthetically buy or sell a basket of stocks by purchasing or selling a single futures contract. Due to the simplicity and low cost, this became the preferred way of implementing a portfolio insurance program.

The ongoing cost of an option is clearly observable. It is simply the rate of price decay of the option. Investors measure this cost with the Greek variable theta. The cost of a portfolio insurance program is opaque. As market prices rise, investors buy the appropriate number of futures contracts *after* the price rise has occurred. If market prices then fall, the appropriate number of futures contracts is sold *after* the price drop has occurred. As a result, when running a portfolio insurance program, the investor buys high and sells low in a choppy market. Therefore, when creating a synthetic call through portfolio insurance, the premium paid is reflected by realized volatility. If volatility turns out to be high, the cost of the synthetic call will be high. If volatility turns out to be low, the cost of the synthetic call will be low. Just as important, in the process of buying futures contracts high and selling them low, investors do not know the true cost of the option they have purchased.

The stock market crash of 1987 exposed a serious flaw in this strategy. When investors purchase calls or puts, they purchase a certain level of volatility for the life of those options. If investors continuously delta hedge options, they will enjoy a gain if realized volatility turns out to be higher than the implied volatility used to price an option. Likewise, the investors will lose if realized volatility turns out to be lower than implied volatility incorporated into the option price. The critical factor to remember is that a level of volatility is locked in *before* a price move. This is not the case for the portfolio insurance program. To replicate a call option, the portfolio is rebalanced *after* a price movement takes place. Therefore, in this or any other dynamic option replication strategy, an investor pays realized volatility for the option and not the implied volatility associated with the listed option. As it turns out, this distinction is very important.

The S&P 500 peaked on August 25, 1987, at 336.77, and implied volatility for at-the-money options on the S&P 500 was running about 20 percent. By early September, the S&P 500 had fallen to about 310. This was a 9 percent drop in price in about half a month suggesting an annualized volatility of at least 44 ($9\% \times \sqrt{12/0.5}$) percent for this brief time period. This crack in the market was the first sign that portfolio insurance as a portfolio protection scheme was beginning to fail. One of the ways portfolio insurance was validated was through Monte Carlo simulation. Based on this analysis, one could predict the performance for a portfolio insurance program for various market conditions. Unfortunately, the returns for equity funds using portfolio insurance were less than the models were predicting. In other words, the strategy did not provide the downside protection investors expected. Prices bounced in the first two weeks of October and investors breathed a sigh of relief. The bounce in price, however, was almost as violent as the previous price drop. Once again,

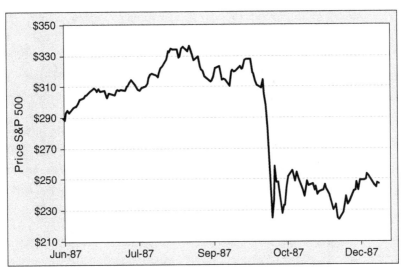

Exhibit 11.1   1987 Stock Market Crash

portfolio insurance programs were underperforming predicted results, but this time
it was underperforming on the way back up. In short, portfolio insurance programs
underperform on the way down, and then, just as importantly, underperform on the
way back up. This is not a way to "make friends and influence people." This brief
period of violent price action exposed a problem with the strategy. Unfortunately,
many believed that this was a statistical anomaly that should be expected on rare
occasions, but it was unlikely to be repeated with any regularity.

Remember, to recreate an option, one must continuously rebalance the allocation
to cash and the exposure to the market index. Doing so, however, is quite impractical
and extremely expensive. Transaction costs in terms of commissions and bid/offer
spreads would destroy returns. In practice, the plan was to rebalance portfolios
at the end of the day or after a certain price movement as a way of managing
transaction costs. This approach worked well in simulations, as the models reflected
capital market theory, which assumed that volatility was well behaved over time. It
is important to understand that tracking error increases the longer the time period
between rebalancing. As a result, portfolio returns did not keep up with those
enjoyed by investors who actually purchased married puts on the way down and
those who purchased calls and cash on the way up.

Wells Fargo, Bankers Trust, Morgan Guaranty, and Leland O'Brian and Rubinstein were the biggest fund managers running portfolio insurance schemes in one
form or another. By the time the stock market crash of 1987 took place, these and
other managers were running portfolio insurance programs of as much as $60 billion.
When equity prices started to fall in October 1987, portfolio insurance programs
required managers to sell futures contracts aggressively. Since prices were falling

very rapidly, investors were forced to pay an extraordinarily high volatility for the synthetic option they were attempting to replicate. Implied volatility for options on the S&P 500 historically fluctuated around 20 percent before the crash. On that fateful day, the S&P 500 fell by 20.5 percent. In a world of constant volatility, this was a 16 standard deviation move, which on a statistical basis is supposed to be essentially impossible.

The one-day realized volatility during the crash increased to 325 percent ($20.5\% \times \sqrt{252}$). Just before the market crashed, the S&P 500 was trading at about 310. At that time, the fair price of a one-day option was about $1.50. The fair price of a one-day option during the market crash (assuming realized volatility) was about $25.00. Said another way, on the day before the crash, investors implementing a portfolio insurance program thought they were going to pay $1.50 for one-day protection. Instead, they ended up paying $25.00. The S&P 500 fell by about 64 points on that fateful day, and if they bought a one-day at-the-money option, they would have lost $1.50. Instead, they lost $25.00. If they could not trade during the day when their rebalancing triggers were hit, they lost even more. Not the protection they were looking to capture. Furthermore, unbeknownst to most participants, the very existence of portfolio insurance programs increased the expected volatility. With $60 billion of portfolio insurance programs buying when the markets rise, and selling when markets fall, price movements increased in both directions compared to a world without portfolio insurance. Investors implementing these programs unwittingly sowed the seeds of their own self-destruction.

This analysis shows how the underlying premise of the strategy was flawed, but the problem goes beyond the theoretical. The portfolio insurance strategy assumes one could implement a portfolio insurance program rebalancing periodically or throughout the day by selling futures contracts at a fair price relative to the cash price of the S&P 500. The price of the futures contract is a function of the spot price of the underlying asset or index plus the cost of carry. It is defined by the following equation, assuming dividends are continuously paid.

$$\text{Futures price} = \text{Spot price} \times e^{(r-d)t}$$

In this case, r is equal to the risk-free rate, d is equal to the dividend yield paid by the stocks that make up the market index, and t is the time between the valuation date and the date the future contract expires. It is important to remember that the futures market is smaller than the cash market for equities. As a result, the depth of the futures market was and still is far less than the cash market. As institutional investors scrambled to hedge their portfolios, speculators piled on with shorts during the market decline. At the same time, there were few buyers prepared to absorb the intense selling. With the imbalance between buyers and sellers, prices in the futures market were pushed far below fair value relative to the cash market. As result, portfolio managers attempting to implement their portfolio insurance programs were selling futures at discounted prices, making the cost of insurance even more expensive. Furthermore, given the chaos in the market, many investors were placing orders and could not find out if their orders were filled, and if they were filled, at what price they transacted in a timely manner. In short, portfolio managers were flying blind. Compounding the problem, many found that even if they were filled, markets were so chaotic that they transacted at prices below the depressed quoted prices. These are not the characteristics of a reliable hedging program.

While many investors lost a substantial portion of their wealth during the crash, very few bankruptcies resulted from the market calamity. Headlines in the days and weeks after did not focus on famous portfolio managers who "blew up," as there were few hedge funds in existence at the time. Furthermore, investment strategies did not incorporate the kind of leverage we see in the marketplace today. Portfolio insurance strategies did not create leverage, but it did change the attitude of institutional investors with regard to asset allocation and risk management. Since market wisdom suggested portfolio insurance was a way to tame return volatility, institutional investors, primarily pension funds, increased their allocation to stocks. These investors typically did not use leverage to enhance returns at the time.

Since there were few salacious headlines about the once-great portfolio managers falling from grace, the discussion by investors, the media, and regulators focused on the causes of the crash. Many have speculated that portfolio insurance caused the crash. This assertion is based on the premise that portfolio insurance programs forced portfolio managers to sell as prices fell. Their selling caused prices to fall more, forcing additional selling. But was this the real problem? What started the initial price decline to start the crash in the first place? This is a question still left unanswered.

Dotcoms Were Just Out-of-the-Money Calls

From the early 1980s through the year 2000, investors enjoyed terrific gains on their stock portfolios. One did not need to be particularly adept at picking stocks. All one had to do was buy an equity mutual fund and go for a ride. To fulfill investor demands for equity returns, new mutual funds were introduced daily. To differentiate themselves from existing financial products, these funds focused on different stock-selection strategies or targeted companies in particular sectors. By the last half of the 1990s, tech stocks were all the rage, personal computers were becoming more powerful, and the Internet began to take shape. The Internet created a new way for people to communicate and share information. Entrepreneurs saw the opportunity this new technology had to offer and pundits said the Internet would change the world, and people who invested in new businesses that used the Internet as the core of their operational infrastructure would become enormously wealthy. Well, the Internet did change the world, but few people beyond company insiders and venture capitalists became wealthy. Internet companies went public and the stocks for many companies jumped hundreds of percent in the first days and weeks of trading. While Internet stocks had enormous gains from 1998 to the year 2000, few retail investors were able to hold onto their gains. In early 2000, the NASDAQ stock market index reached its apex. In the following few years, it fell by about 80 percent, more than erasing the gains retail investors captured in the preceding years. To make matters worse, those once high-flying dotcom stocks crashed and many of them went out of business, leaving investors with nothing but a worthless piece of paper.

The typical investor who looked at the tech and dotcom bubble would interpret market action as an exercise in "irrational exuberance," to use the words of former Fed Chairman Alan Greenspan.* This interpretation is indeed correct. Optimism ran wild and people bought any dotcom stock their broker, newsletter, writer, or market pundit brought to their attention. The option trader would look at that period of history a little differently. Most dotcoms stocks did not produce earnings. In fact, many barely produced any revenue. People who believed in the technology revolution were really buying deep-out-of-the-money call options on companies that might restructure the way companies did business in the future. We have explained in earlier chapters that equity is a call option on company assets. If the company does well, the value of company assets accrues to the equity holders. If the company does poorly, the company goes bankrupt. Since equity is an option, it expires worthless and lenders take control of company assets. This concept should not be lost on dotcom companies, even though most did not carry any debts. Dotcom equities were not in-the-money options, but deep-out-of-the-money options. The price of a dotcom company's shares was simply reflecting triple digit implied volatilities. This is so because these companies did not produce earnings and had to fund their operations out of cash raised in their IPOs. It was very uncertain if and when earnings would actually roll in.

The massive losses suffered by investors would not surprise anyone who read Chapter 4. In this chapter we showed that *fairly priced* long-dated options historically produce a return close to zero. Since investors put multi-billion dollar valuations on companies with no revenues, the prices investors were paying were anything but fair. This alone would tell the option investor that dotcom stocks would produce nothing but losses. Those losses came swift and severe when cash on company balance sheets ran low. Dotcom companies in this condition morphed into short-dated call options. As we pointed out in Chapter 4, the expected return on deep out-of-the-money short-dated options is close to a full loss. The savvy investor might have used fundamental analysis to find an opportunity, but the savvy option investors would

---

*Remarks by Chairman Alan Greenspan at the Annual Dinner and Francis Boyer Lecture of the American Enterprise Institute for Public Policy Research Washington, DC December 5, 1996.

have known what to pay. At the end of this fiasco, hundreds of billions of paper wealth disappeared. Hundreds, if not thousands, of companies went bankrupt and many individual investors were wiped out.

■ Credit Blowup: Subprime Mortgage-Backed Securities

The crash of technology, NASDAQ, and dotcom stocks had a profound effect on the psyche of individual investors. Many wrote off the stock market and began to look at other opportunities for the savings they had left. It was not long before people took a shine to real estate. Investors noticed that real estate was not affected by the crash of NASDAQ stocks and at the same time, it became a national priority of the federal government for people to own their own homes. Furthermore, real estate is a hard asset that provides protection from inflation and many believed that housing prices "always rise in the long run." In an attempt to get the economy going after the NASDAQ bubble popped, the Federal Reserve lowered interest rates so that companies could borrow more cheaply to expand productive capacity. These low interest rates made it easier for people to afford homes, cars, and consumer goods like furniture and home improvements as well. All these factors laid the foundation for the upcoming boom and eventual bust in real estate.

At this time, most people secured a mortgage on their house through a bank, saving and loan, or mortgage company. These firms originated and underwrote these loans and sold them to one of the GSEs (government sponsored enterprises). These GSEs (Federal National Mortgage Association, Federal Home Loan Mortgage Corporation, Government National Mortgage Association) would buy these mortgages, wrap them with a guarantee for timely payment of principal and interest, and sell them to investors. Investors found that these MBSs (mortgage-backed securities) paid a higher coupon than U.S. Treasury securities and they were well received by the marketplace. Mortgages sold to FNMA and FHLMC could only be made to qualified buyers. A qualified home buyer is one who could make a down payment of at least 20 percent of the home value and had gross income in excess of three times principal, interest, homeowner's insurance, and property taxes. Those who did not meet these requirements were required to buy mortgage insurance, which would protect the lender from loss should the homeowners default on their mortgages. Since most homeowners had a lot of "skin in the game," few people historically defaulted on their mortgage.

Studies showed that people historically paid their mortgage first because this was where they lived and they did not want to lose the place where they lived or the equity in their home. They paid their other bills second should money get tight. Some mortgage lenders took note of the low default rate on mortgages and began to lighten the income and down payment required to buy a home. This broadened the market for potential customers. Since these are lower-quality borrowers, there is a higher risk of default. Since there was more risk of nonpayment, mortgage lenders could charge higher rates of interest and additional closing costs. These less-creditworthy borrowers became known as *subprime borrowers*. Since these loans could not be resold to the GSEs, these mortgage lenders needed to find someone else to buy these mortgages. Fortunately for them, investors were hungry for yield as the Fed's easy monetary policy designed to lower mortgage rates also lowered rates of return on U.S. Treasury, agency, and corporate securities. To satisfy investor demand for higher-yielding investments, the major Wall Street banks purchased these subprime mortgages and bundled them together in what became known as private-label, residential mortgage-backed securities (RMBSs). Investors wanted some assurances of repayment of principal and interest from these lower-quality borrowers. To meet this requirement, RMBSs were structured to protect some lenders while passing credit risk to investors who were willing to take it. In return, they received a higher rate of interest.

While defaults on home mortgages were historically few and far between, they did occur. The structure of an RMBS needed to take this credit risk into account. It is important to remember that the default risk in a pool of subprime loans, or any pool of loans for that matter, cannot be eliminated. Risk can be redistributed, however, and there are investors willing to take that risk for the possibility of a higher rate of return. Exhibit 11.2 shows a very simplified version of a RMBS. In this example, we assume that thousands of loans are pooled together into a diversified portfolio of loans. This pool is broken into a series of *tranches*, which are sold separately to different investors. Some investors value protection of principal over high returns. To minimize their risk of credit loss, they are given priority in a cash flow waterfall. The highest-quality tranches were rated "AAA" by the credit rating agencies that reviewed the deal's structure. When homeowners pay their mortgage, these investors are paid first. There are other investors who are willing to take on a

		P&I Paid	% of Deal	$90 Available	
Senior	AAA	1st	80%	$80	Paid in Full
	AA	2nd	5%	$5	Paid in Full
	A	3rd	8%	$5	Partial Payment
Mezzanine	BBB	4th	3%	$0	None
	BB	6th	2%	$0	None
Equity	Unrated	Last	2%	$0	
	Total		100%	$90	

Exhibit 11.2 Simplified Residential Mortgage-Backed Securities Deal Structure

little more risk to get a slightly higher rate of return. These tranches were typically rated "AA" and get paid after the "AAA" tranche gets paid. There are still other investors who are willing to take on even more risk to get a higher rate of return. These tranches were typically rated "A" and get paid after the "AAA" and "AA" tranches gets paid. This theme continues down the credit spectrum. In the end, there are a series of tranches each with their own unique risk and return characteristics. The most risky tranches are found at the mezzanine level. These tranches enjoy very little credit protection, as there is just a thin layer of "equity" (a residual tranche) protecting them in the capital structure. With seemingly high-quality collateral backing an RMBS deal, investors flocked to these securities for their high yield, as most perceived the default risk in MBS as moderate.

Ideally, the homeowners pay the principal and interest on their mortgage, as the loan agreement requires. These principal payments are allocated to the senior tranches first. In more complicated structures, there is a sharing of principal with a number of the tranches designed to keep the original cash flow waterfall intact. In any event, after the most senior tranche is paid off, principal payments are allocated to the next highest tranche in the structure. This continues until all the loans packaged into the RMBS are paid off.

In the discussion of synthetics in Chapter 9, we show that a secured loan is a combination of a risk-free asset and a put option on the underlying asset. In this case, should the value of the property fall below the face value of the loan, the homeowner can choose to walk away from the loan and the house. The lender is now the proud owner of a depreciated asset. The more the value of the property has fallen, the greater the loss the lender will suffer. In the case of an RMBS, the mechanics of settling that put option is different than an exchange-traded option. When a borrower defaults, the financial institution that services the loan takes over management of the property on behalf of the owners of the RMBS. RMBS investors are in the business of financing homes, not owning them. The loan servicer does what is necessary to fix the property and make it presentable for sale. At this point, the servicer hires a real estate broker and sells it back into the market. As compensation for doing work above and beyond the normal course of business (collecting mortgage payments and distributing them to the RMBS), the loan servicer collects a fee, which is deducted from the proceeds of the sale. This is an additional cost of bankruptcy. The remaining funds left over after all costs of disposing the property are paid, are passed on to the RMBS and distributed to the various tranches, as the deal structure requires. Since there is usually a loss on the property in a foreclosure proceeding, the loss suffered is absorbed by the last tranche in the capital structure. This protects the more senior tranches from the occasional default in the loan portfolio. If many defaults and foreclosures occur, the equity tranche will be wiped out. At this point, the lowest mezzanine tranche in the capital structure will absorb the next round of losses if any, protecting the more senior tranches above it in the capital structure.

While it may not seem obvious at first, investors who lend money to homeowners are writing put options on the value of the underlying house. To make this assertion clear it is useful to go back to the example of a corporation. One can think of an investor who owns stock in a company as owning a call option on the company's assets. Through put–call parity, this is the same as owning cash plus a put option on those assets. If the value of the company's assets rises, shareholders enjoy most of the gain. If on the other hand, the value of the company's assets falls below the face value of the company's debt, the call option falls out of the money. At this point, the value of liabilities exceeds the value of assets and the company goes into bankruptcy. Shareholders lose everything as the value of their call option expires worthless. In a bankruptcy, the lenders take over the asset. In option speak, the company's assets are *put* to the lender. The lenders suffer a loss, which equals the difference between the face value of the company's debt (the strike price of the put) and the market value of the company's assets.

This analogy holds true for the real estate market as well. The owners of real estate hold a call option on the value of that property. This is the same as owning the house and a put option on the house. If the value of the property rises, that gain accrues to the homeowners. Likewise, if the value of the property drops, the homeowners suffer a loss. If the value of the property falls below the face value of the mortgage, the homeowners are now underwater. At this point, they can choose to continue to hold on to the property and services the mortgage or they can stop paying and *put* the property to the lenders. If they choose the latter, the lender becomes the new owner of the property and it becomes the lender's responsibility. Now that the owners of the put option have exercised their right, the lender will suffer a loss that is equal to the difference between the market value of the house and the face value of their mortgage, which is the strike price of the put option.

Most people who lend money are not aware that they are writing put options. They see themselves as taking on the credit risk of the borrower, mitigated by the collateral they hold against that loan. These risks, however, are one and the same. The value of the put option sold is equal to the credit risk the lender takes. With this framework in mind, one can analyze RMBS securities to determine if lenders were pricing risk correctly during the heyday of the real estate bubble.

Before the real estate bubble took hold, lenders required would-be homeowners to put 20 percent down on the value of the house. With a significant equity stake, these new homeowners would have a financial incentive to take care of their property and service their loan. If they did not have 20 percent of the value of the property to put toward the price of the house, they could put 5 or 10 percent down and pay for mortgage insurance, which makes the lender whole in the event there is a default on the mortgage. Homeowners insurance was not tax deductible at the time but it is now, while interest enjoyed this tax benefit. This was part of the appeal of subprime mortgages. Lenders charged a higher rate to earn a higher return. Borrowers paid a higher rate of interest instead of mortgage insurance, so they received a greater income-tax benefit. Since there was a long history of very low default rates on mortgages, and recoveries on those defaulted loans was quite high, lenders expected losses, if any, to be moderate. Option theory confirms that lenders in the pre-subprime days priced credit risk in mortgage loans correctly. The following is an application of option-pricing theory to the valuation of credit risk in a typical mortgage.

$$\text{Price of a House} = \$100,000$$
$$\text{Amount Borrowed} = \$80,000$$
$$\text{Risk-Free Rate} = 5\%$$
$$\text{Time to Expiration} = 1 \text{ year}$$
$$\text{Volatility} = 10\%$$
$$\text{Price of the Put Option} = \$8.33$$
$$\text{Probability of Default} = 0.37\%$$

The above analysis shows that there is minimal credit risk in a traditional conforming mortgage where the borrower puts 20 percent down and borrows just 80 percent of the value of the house. With this structure, lenders are selling a put option, which is 20 percent out of the money. There's a fair amount of evidence to suggest that the volatility of returns on unlevered residential real estate is about 10 percent. Using this as an estimate for future volatility to price the embedded put on a traditional mortgage, one finds that it is just $8.33 against a loan value of $80,000, or just 0.01 percent. The probability that the borrower defaults on this loan over a one-year time horizon is equal to the probability that this put option will expire in the money. Option-pricing theory suggests that there is only a 0.37 percent annual probability the borrower will default on the mortgage. This analysis shows why mortgage lending was a good business for decades. It is worth noting that the interest rate on fixed-rate mortgages is 50 to 100 basis points higher than a U.S. Treasury security with the same average life. This difference is a reflection of the cost of originating and servicing a mortgage, and the cost of the prepayment option. Borrowers have the option to prepay a mortgage and take out a new one (i.e., refinance). Most homeowners exercise this option when interest rates fall. The only impediment to refinancing is the income requirement and the current value of the underlying real estate.

Since the default rate on mortgages was very low, lenders began to offer mortgages on less-restrictive terms. One of the ways they did this was by offering little or no down payment loans. Instead of requiring mortgage insurance, they took on the added credit risk and charged a higher interest rate. To eliminate interest-rate risk, they offered these loans with a variable rate. If interest rates fell, so would the monthly payment. If interest rates rose, the borrower would pay a higher interest rate. To make loans even more affordable at the time of origination, they usually offered subsidized rates for the first few years of the mortgage. These changes made it possible for virtually anyone to buy a home. Since these loans did not conform to the standards of the GSEs, these subprime loans were packaged into private-label RMBSs and sold to investors. The flaw in this loan arrangement is that the character of the credit risk of these loans was much different than those on the traditional conforming loans. The subprime lender is writing an at-the-money put instead of an out-of-the-money put. This becomes clear when one prices the credit by applying option-pricing theory.

$$\text{Price of a House} = \$100,000$$
$$\text{Amount Borrowed} = \$100,000$$
$$\text{Risk-free Rate} = 5\%$$
$$\text{Time to Expiration} = 1 \text{ year}$$
$$\text{Volatility} = 10\%$$
$$\text{Price of the Put Option} = \$1,928$$
$$\text{Probability of Default} = 32.6\%$$

The analysis above shows that the price of credit risk in a subprime loan is 231 ($1,928/$8.33) times higher than an equivalent conforming loan, and it is about 88 times more likely to default. Bear in mind that this analysis assumes one is paying a fair price for the property. With little or no money down, people often bid the price of real estate up quite rapidly creating a bubble in prices. Leverage did what it often does. It pushes the price of the underlying asset up beyond where it would be without cheap credit, while increasing volatility in the process. Under these circumstances, price is more likely to fall than history suggests. If anything, the options valuation analysis underestimates the price of the embedded put option in a world with zero money down mortgages.

The vast majority of investors in RMBS wanted high-quality securities that paid a reasonable rate of interest. Since 85 percent of a typical RMBS is rated AAA or AA, there was plenty of demand for these securities. The probability one could lose money on an AAA– or AA-rated corporate security is a very small fraction of a percent. There was a yield kicker in there as well. RMBS securities paid interest at a higher rate than equivalently rated corporate securities. Given the perception of low risk and high yield, hedge fund managers believed they could produce equity rates of return by using leverage to magnify returns. Unfortunately, they did not understand that by investing in the senior tranches of RMBS, they were selling put options far below their true value. This becomes apparent when one looks at the strike price of these embedded puts. The typical AAA tranche has protection against a 20 percent loss on the underlying pool of RMBS. Therefore, if 40 percent of the loans went bad and the loss on those loans were 50 percent that 20 percent of credit enhancement disappeared. At this point, the AAA tranche would suffer real cash flow losses.

The analysis above tells us the annual probability of default on a subprime mortgage is at least 32.6 percent. This is the average annual default rate one should expect in the pool of loans over a business cycle. In year two, one should expect 32.6 percent of the remaining loans to default. This process continues until all the loans are repaid or defaulted on. Over a two-year investment horizon, one should expect a cumulative default rate of 54.6 percent ($[1 - 32.6\%] \times 32.6\% + 32.6\%$). At the end of the day, an investor in an AAA tranche with a long time to maturity should expect to lose all credit protection and lose money. In the final analysis, investors in senior tranches (AAA or AA) were selling at-the-money puts and charging for out-of-the-money puts. A proper analysis using option-pricing theory shows that homeowners would be exercising their put option on the senior tranche holders of the RMBS pool within just a few years. This was a prescription for disaster and precisely what happened.

Leverage at the investor level compounded the problem as well. If a hedge fund was lucky enough to invest in RMBS pools with lower-than-average default rates, or higher-than-average recovery rates, it was still put out of business by mark-to-market losses. As the support tranches disappear, the credit quality of the senior tranches will fall. As credit quality falls so does the price. It would not take long before the hedge fund's equity was wiped out. Consider the typical mortgage hedge fund.

Typical Hedge Fund Structure

$$\text{Investor Capital} = \$10.00$$
$$\text{Borrowed Funds} = \$90.00$$
$$\text{Portfolio Assets} = \$100$$

With the typical hedge fund levering 10:1, it took only a 5 percent loss or less before a margin call and a 10 percent loss before investors were completely wiped out. The power of option-pricing theory shows us that there was a 100 percent chance that leveraged mortgage funds would ultimately go bankrupt. Selling $2,000 put options for $10 does not a business model make. Many sophisticated investors made this mistake. There were a host of funds that followed this strategy of levering up highly rated RMBS securities, not the least of which were the following:

- Bear Stearns High Grade Credit Fund
- Dillon Read Capital Management
- Caliber Global Investment
- United Capital Markets Holdings Inc.: Horizon Funds

- Galena Street Fund

- Parvest Dynamic ABS

- BNP Paribas ABS Euribor

- BNP Paribas ABS Eonia

Since 2006, a host of hedge funds famously blew up because they overleveraged their capital, while they underestimated the risk they were taking and therefore undercharging for risk. A list of firms that blew up during the financial crisis of 2007 to 2009 can be found at hf-implode.com. While some of these funds were closed down due to investors' withdrawals or "accounting irregularities," most crashed due to imprudent risk management. If one builds a strategy based on selling put options, one must understand those options and charge appropriately for them. Unfortunately, few if any, credit investors who use traditional fundamental analysis employ guidance from option-pricing theory for pricing and managing risk. This example suggests that investors should use option-pricing theory as a tool for pricing and managing risk.

■ Convergence Trades

Convergence trades are very popular strategies with hedge funds. Convergence trades are a subset of a carry trade where an investor buys a high-yielding asset and simultaneously sells a low-yielding asset as a hedge. The objective of the convergence trade is to not only capture that yield differential, but to capture a capital gain as the price of the high-yielding asset rises relative to the price of the low-yielding asset. Hedge funds that employ these strategies typically use a great deal of leverage as the market risk in long/short pair trade is minimized. Properly constructed, the only risk that remains in a convergence trade is the unique price action between the two assets.

The European Union was formed to enhance trade among members of Western and Eastern Europe. Every country had its own currency. Politicians and economists argued that trade between countries could be improved if everyone shared a common currency. With a common currency, losses due to friction (i.e., currency transaction costs) would be eliminated, allowing consumers to buy goods from other countries more cheaply. The cost of doing business would be reduced as well, making the economies of member countries more competitive. Manufacturing companies could source parts and raw materials from the lowest-cost producers, as currency valuation would not play a role in a producer's competitiveness and currency conversion fees would be removed from the cost of doing business.

Since every country had its own currency, each had different rates of interest and inflation. To become part of the European Union, interest rate and inflation rates had to be "normalized" between the member states. This means that everyone who wanted to be part of the Union would have to have the same interest rates and inflation rates to minimize the shock of moving to a new currency regime. Investors recognized that local politicians and central banks would pursue policies that would make them eligible to join the union. To join the EU, countries with large budget deficits would shrink the government sector, and central banks in countries with high inflation rates would slow the expansion of money and credit to bring inflation rates down. Investors saw this as an opportunity to earn low-risk profits by buying long-term bonds in countries with high interest rates and selling bonds issued by governments with low interest rates. As inflation comes down, so would interest rates, increasing the price of high-yielding bonds. This looked like an easy way to make a buck as the value of the currencies and financial assets converged.

The fundamental strategy behind Long-Term Capital Management was the convergence trade. LTCM bought government bonds from high-yielding issuers and sold government bonds from low-yielding issuers. Since membership to the common currency was a popular political objective, LTCM believed the glide path to eligibility was certain. With this perceived certainty, it perceived a low-risk, high-return opportunity in the eventual union of the various countries in Europe. To maximize returns on their convergence trades, it employed a great deal of leverage. On a cash basis, we believe it held leverage of 25 to 1, or just 4 percent equity. When executions in the cash markets became saturated, it placed equivalent trades in the derivatives market, making its leverage an order of magnitude higher.

What is useful to remember about markets is that just because politicians and central bankers want something to happen does not mean it will. While they might be able to move markets in the short run, at the end of the day, markets are stronger than any government or central bank. Even if their objectives are successfully achieved eventually, it does not mean they will get there in an orderly manner. Markets are chaotic by nature and have minds of their own. In 1997, the Asian debt crisis took hold. Currencies and stock markets crashed throughout Asia. Governments were financially overextended, and companies that borrowed in foreign currencies found that they could not repay lenders as the local currencies crashed and business declined. Shortly thereafter, Eastern European governments found themselves in the same soup. Russia outright defaulted on its government debt. As investors rushed for safety, they sold risky emerging market and Eastern European assets and purchased the financial obligations of high-quality Western governments. This caused prices of high-yield assets to fall and the price of low-yielding assets to rise. This is the exact opposite of what the managers and investors of LTCM wanted and expected. In the end, the losses mounted and margin calls rolled in. With bankruptcy all but certain, their goose was cooked. Financial regulators took note of their predicament because of their excessive use of leverage. They were afraid that if LTCM defaulted on their obligations to financial intermediaries, the financial system would be deeply harmed. To address their problems, the Federal Reserve brought all the counterparties together to orchestrate an orderly liquidation of their positions.

The interesting part of LTCM is that it brought together the best academic minds and practitioners with the objective of creating the most successful hedge fund ever. Members of LTCM's board of directors included Myron S. Scholes and Robert C. Merton, two of the inventors of the Black–Scholes–Merton option-pricing model. With their understanding of financial markets and the pricing of derivatives instruments, who would think that such a spectacular blow-up could occur under their watch? Was it simply too much leverage, or was something else at work? To see how this could happen, it is useful to look at a simpler situation.

MF Global was a major derivatives and commodities broker with a global presence. It was very active in listed derivatives instruments such as futures and options. In addition, it provided transaction services for over-the-counter derivatives products such as swaps, foreign exchange, and other sophisticated financial products. MF Global also dabbled in traditional debt and equity securities and its broker/dealer subsidiary was a primary dealer in U.S. Treasury securities. Primary dealers have regulatory permission to trade with the Federal Reserve Bank directly, and participate in the auction of new debt offered by the U.S. government. The firm employed skilled and knowledgeable individuals who not only executed complex transactions for customers, but advised customers on strategy as well. Given its sophisticated operation and a deep understanding of the financial products it traded for customers and the house, we might conclude that MF Global ran a tight ship. We would be wrong, of course, as it somehow found a way to blow up.

MF Global had a history of risk management problems before it became insolvent. In February 2008, the CFTC fined MF Global $10.4 million for failures in proper risk supervision. One of the firm's traders, Evan Brent Dooley, lost $141 million trading wheat. Dooley was fired and is now serving time in prison. In March 2010, Jon Corzine, who was once CEO of Goldman Sachs, governor, and Senator of New Jersey became CEO of MF Global.

Corzine was under pressure to improve the fortunes of the firm, as it had not reported a profit since 2007. Corzine had plans to make MF Global a smaller version of the great trading platform he once ran. To improve profitability quickly, Corzine put his vision into action and took a more aggressive stance in committing the firm's capital. The financial debt crisis of 2007 to 2009 knocked people off their feet. The popping of the real estate bubble in the Western world, along with high private-sector debts, left economies damaged. Weakened banks did not help. These economic stresses made investing in government debt attractive as interest rates rose on these financial instruments and government debt is thought to be much less risky than private-sector debt. Given this perception, financial institutions can easily finance their purchases of government debt at moderate rates of interest.

Corzine's big idea was to use the firm's cheap cost of capital to put on a number of carry trades. While MF Global's trading positions may have started out small, early success in the strategy gave the firm confidence to build a position in European government bonds issued by some of the more indebted countries in Europe, totaling $6.3 billion. While these countries had issues, nobody thought the central governments in Italy, Spain, Portugal, or other European nations would have any problem servicing their debts. The European sovereign debt crises made people rethink that possibility.

An investment in a government bond is a bet on the solvency of the issuing entity. In the case of governments in the European Union who share a common currency, the risk of that insolvency is reflected in the interest rate any particular government pays over the credit risk-free rate. The credit risk-free rate is a bit more difficult to define in Europe, as the European Central Bank (ECB) is not associated with any particular government. The closest instrument to a risk-free asset is one issued by the strongest government, in this case Germany. This is no different than an investment in the debt securities in a private company. The credit spread of a corporate bond is a reflection of the credit risk of that company. Since a lender takes over the company assets in a default, lenders are writing a put option on the company assets. The situation is quite similar with respect to a government bond issued by a European government. In the case of a government loan, the underlying asset is not plant and equipment, as in the case of a corporation. For a government loan, the asset to be captured is a stream of tax revenue the government collects from its citizens. If an economy falls into recession, tax revenue falls. As a result, the risk of default rises and the potential recovery falls as well. At the end of the day, someone who buys a government bond is selling a put option on the solvency of a sovereign entity and its ability to collect taxes.

When the government debt crisis hit Europe, owners of government debt found their put options, which were sold far out of the money, approached in or at the money. In the case of Greece, the option moved into the money and the government exercised that option and defaulted on its obligation. Recall that MF Global bought $6.3 billion of bonds issued by various governments in Europe. The company only had $1.5 billion of capital, most of which was needed to back their brokerage business. At the end of the day, MF Global only had a sliver of equity to back these bonds. As the price of the bonds fell, the value of the puts rose commensurately. When an uncovered option is written, the writer must put up more collateral to back those puts as the value of those puts rises due to a fall in the value of the underlying asset. At the same time, the value of the investor's equity is disappearing as the investor takes mark-to-market losses on those puts. The gamma effect only makes the problem worse. As the value of the government's revenue stream falls, the value of the puts rises and does so at an ever-increasing rate. These effects serve to push a leveraged owner of government bonds into bankruptcy. Such was the case of MF Global. It is worth noting that none of the governments that MF Global lent to actually went bankrupt. If it could have held on long enough, the bonds would have been repaid in full. Had the managers of MF Global used option-pricing theory to compute their risk, they would have sized their investment appropriately and would be in business today.

With the analysis of MF Global in mind, one can now understand what happened at LTCM. LTCM had a massive number of these positions in its portfolio, which was also highly levered. Managers of LTCM felt they could take on high leverage as they diversified their convergence trades. If just a few of those positions suffered the kind of losses suffered by the sovereign debt portfolio held by MF Global, it would have been able to hold on and wait for its convergence trades to get back on track. In addition to leverage, LTCM's problem was the illusion of diversification. While it might have had hundreds of different convergence trades, those did not protect it from systemic risk. As the Asian and Russian debt crisis took hold, correlation of returns on risky assets increased markedly. The price of all high-yielding assets fell (this is what LTCM was long) and the price of all low-risk, low-yielding assets rose (this is what LTCM was short as a hedge). Said another way, the value of all the puts it wrote increased in tandem. Its investment performance was no different than if it held just a few different trades. Skilled index volatility traders are hyperaware of correlation. Volatility traders focus on major indexes like the S&P 500. Sometimes it is better to buy or sell options on all the constituents of an index instead of the index itself.

The lesson here is clear. If one is going to sell put options, do not use excessive leverage, and be aware of fluctuations in correlation. Correlation always rises when markets are in financial distress. This is precisely when put options move in the money.

The Howie Hubler Trade (Short, Ratio Put Spread)

Howie Hubler was an icon on Wall Street. In his heyday, which stretched over a decade, he was a successful and well-regarded trader at Morgan Stanley. With success came rank and he held the position of head of asset-backed securities trading. Asset-backed securities are bonds backed by other financial assets like bank loans, credit cards, auto loans, and mortgages. In 2004, the market for subprime mortgage-backed bonds was growing fast and furious. Anything and everything in this space was getting securitized, and Hubler started to become skeptical of some of the subprime mortgage deals constructed and sold to the market.

The cleanest way to express a bearish view on an asset is to sell it short. In this way, the investor captures a gain as the asset's price falls. Generally speaking,

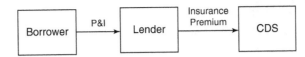

Exhibit 11.3 Cash Flows for a CDS

it is difficult to sell fixed-income securities short. This is the case for a number of reasons. The primary challenge is the availability of a large, liquid issue that institutional investors can easily move in and out of without impacting its market price. If an investor is prepared to deal with liquidity issues, it is often difficult to find the desired security to borrow so that it can be sold short. Luckily for Howie, there was a growing market in a relatively new financial instrument known as a credit default swap (CDS). Howie was very familiar with this financial product, as he and other traders used this instrument to hedge the mortgages warehoused in the securitization underwriting process. CDS is essentially an insurance policy that protects the investor in the event that borrowers default on their financial obligations. When a borrower defaults, the lender suffers a loss on the loan held in its portfolio. Upon default, the lender files a claim with the writer of the CDS, who then covers the investor's loss.

Recall that put options are a form of insurance. Put options protect the owner of an asset from a drop in the price of that asset. It is important to recognize that traditional insurance can only be purchased if the buyer has an insurable interest. This means that one must own a house to buy insurance on that house. Your neighbor, for example, cannot buy insurance on your house in the hopes of it someday burning to the ground. The same holds true for life or automobile insurance. Investors, however, can buy put options to protect the value of a financial asset (i.e., hedge) or they can buy puts to capitalize on the price of an asset falling, even if they do not own the asset. It is useful to think of CDS in these terms. CDS allows an investor to protect the value of a loan in the event there is a default by the borrower on that loan. Like a put, one can use CDS to profit from a default event or even financial distress. It shares the characteristic of an option in that it has a limited life and exercise criteria. It is economically beneficial to exercise an option at expiration if the price of the asset falls below the exercise price. A CDS becomes exercisable when the borrower defaults. Since CDS is an insurance product, the investor who is hedging a bond would simply put that bond to the CDS writer who then pays the bond investor par value for their bond. But like a put option, one does not have to have an insurable interest to buy this financial product. If one does not own the bond, a cash settlement is made in an amount equal to the loss a bondholder would have suffered.

$$\text{YTM bond} = \text{Credit risk-free asset} + \text{Credit spread}$$
$$\text{YTM bond} = \text{YTM treasury} + \text{CDS notional yield}$$

When investors loan money, they face the risk that the borrowers might not repay their loans. This might occur because of fraud or it might occur because of financial hardship. Therefore, the yield to maturity on credit-risky debt is a function of the rate that could be earned on a credit-risk-free note (usually defined as a U.S. Treasury note) plus a credit-risk premium. The price of a CDS is a reflection of the perceived credit risk of the borrower. In theory, the notional yield on a CDS contract should be equal to the credit spread on the loan. In practice, this is not the case because the price of a CDS is a function of counterparty risk, benchmark interest rate (usually LIBOR and not a US Treasury rate), capital requirements, liquidity issues, and so on, in addition to the underlying instrument's credit risk.

In 2006, many high-profile traders were jumping ship to start their own hedge funds. To keep Mr. Hubler and his team of asset-backed securities traders happy, Morgan Stanley created the Global Proprietary Credit Group (GPCG). This was an internal Morgan Stanley–sponsored hedge fund that someday might become an independent money management business. GPCG provided the platform for taking a significant position in CDSs on subprime mortgages. Luckily for Howie, there were a number of institutional investors willing to write CDS contracts on subprime mortgages. At the same time, a number of investment banks came together to design a standardized contract, with the objective of making the product more transparent and liquid. All the pieces came together for hedge funds and other high-powered investors to actively trade and invest in these derivative instruments.

At this time, the subprime mortgage market was performing quite nicely, as real estate prices were steadily increasing. Market expectation was for prices to continue to increase for the foreseeable future. As a result, if homeowners got into financial trouble, they could easily sell their property and repay their mortgages. This made the riskier tranches of residential mortgage-backed securities (RMBS) look rather safe. Some investors wanted to buy RMBS on a levered basis to increase returns. Selling CDSs was an alternative method for doing just that. One could capture the high yield offered by RMBS and collateralized debt obligations (CDOs) without having to borrow money to do so.

We do not know the exact date, nor do we know the precise terms and price of the CDS contracts Mr. Hubler entered into to structure his subprime bets. But we believe we have a conceptual understanding of what took place, the order of magnitude of the swaps entered into, and the economics of the underlying trade. The following is our interpretation of the strategy pursued and the events that followed.

To take advantage of Mr. Hubler's expectation that default rates on subprime mortgages would rise, he looked to the CDS market to "buy protection," and he did so by purchasing CDSs on the BBB-rated tranche of a CDO that was collateralized by BBB-rated tranches of RMBS. Exhibit 11.4 shows a simplified CDO deal put together and sold in 2006. A quick look at the table reveals that as soon as the credit losses on the underlying collateral exceeded 3.5 percent, the BBB-rated tranche

| | | | BBB RMBS | BBB RMBS | BBB RMBS | BBB RMBS | BBB RMBS | BBB RMBS | BBB RMBS | BBB RMBS | BBB RMBS | BBB RMBS | BBB RMBS | BBB RMBS |

	Tranche	Rating	P&I Paid	% of Deal	Cumulative Loss to Default	Yield	CDS	
Senior	A1	AAA	1st	37.1%	62.9%	5.17%	0.17%	
	A2	AAA	2nd	23.2%	39.7%	5.35%	0.35%	
	A3	AAA	3rd	9.3%	30.4%	5.45%	0.45%	<----Sell CDS
	A4	AAA	4th	7.6%	22.8%	5.30%	0.30%	
	B	AA	5th	10.3%	12.5%	5.55%	0.55%	
	C	A	6th	3.3%	9.2%	6.55%	1.55%	
Mezzanine	D	BBB	7th	5.7%	3.5%	8.25%	3.25%	<----Buy CDS
	E	BB	8th	1.5%	2.0%	10.00%	5.00%	
Equity		Unrated	Last	2.0%				
			Total	100%				

Exhibit 11.4   Typical CDO Structure Issued in 2006, BBB-Rated RMBS as Collateral

would begin to suffer a loss. If losses hit 9.2 percent, investors would lose all their original investment.

Anyone who has ever bought insurance knows that one has to pay an insurance premium for the contract. To buy those CDS contracts on BBB-rated CDOs, Mr. Hubler would have to pay around 3.25 percent of the notional amount of protection each year to pay for that insurance. In other words, to buy insurance on $2 billion of BBB-rated CDOs, he would have to pay $65 million a year. Now, Mr. Hubler might have the right idea, but the timing was a bit tricky. Defaults in the subprime market might increase right away, or the market might hold on for another year or two. This is where Mr. Hubler got "too clever by half." To generate cash to make the premium payments, Mr. Hubler sold insurance on AAA-rated CDOs backed by BBB-rated RMBS. On the surface, this seemed like a low-risk trade. After all, defaults rarely occur on AAA-rated securities and the collateral supporting the CDO would have to suffer a 30.4 percent loss, before the cash flows on an AAA-rated tranche become encumbered. Said another way, 60.8 percent of the collateral supporting the CDO in conjunction with a 50 percent recovery rate would have to occur before the cash flows on this AAA-rated tranche would suffer a loss. Up until this point in time, such an event was historically unprecedented.

The problem with this idea is that the AAA-rated CDOs provide a very skinny yield premium. In early 2007, senior AAA-rated CDOs paid a credit-risk yield premium of approximately 0.17 percent of the notional amount of the swap. In other words, selling insurance on $2 billion of AAA-rated CDOs generated only $3.4 million. Junior AAA-rated CDOs, which have a longer average life, yielded more at about 0.45 percent. At this higher spread, selling insurance on $2 billion of junior AAA-rated CDOs would generate $9 million. Needless to say, selling $1 of CDS on any AAA CDOs hardly made a dent in the cost of carrying $1 of CDS on

BBB-rated CDOs, which cost 3.25 percent each year. Not to be deterred, all one has to do is sell more CDSs on AAA tranches to generate more cash flow. We estimate Hubler sold CDSs on $16 billion of various trancjes of junior AAA-rated CDOs backed by BBB-rated collateral. In so doing, he was able to generate $65 million (and possible more) in cash flow needed to offset the premiums required to maintain the CDS on the BBB-rated CDOs.

At the end of the day, this structure made the bet that there would be a rise in defaults but not an enormous rise. Diversification would ensure that the AAA tranches would not suffer when the BBB tranches did. After all, each RMBS was backed by thousands of mortgages. The CDO was backed by 20 to 30 BBB tranches drawn from different RMBS. Thought of in this way, this is a complex trade. One has to make a judgment on mortgage default and recovery rates, and when those default rates would occur. The wild card is the consideration of correlation of defaults. Is the default of one mortgage associated with defaults of other mortgages? If some homeowners default, will it encourage other homeowners to default? Furthermore, one has to consider how the rating and price of an AAA-rated tranche might change if one or more of the support tranches goes away. At the end of the day, if defaults rose above historical averages but did not skyrocket, Howie would collect on the BBB-rated CDS purchased and the AAA-rated CDSs sold would expire worthless. If the spike in defaults never occurred, Howie would neither make nor lose money. If defaults spiked far higher than historical experience, most of the BBB-rated RMBS could become worthless or nearly so. This would cause all tranches, including the AAA rated ones, of CDOs backed by BBB collateral to become worthless. It would not matter what the rating of the CDO happened to be, or how much credit support existed.

An option trader knows that buyers of credit-risky debt are synthetically writing put options. The lower the credit rating, the higher the strike price on the synthetic put. With this perspective in hand, an option trader would set aside the complexities of the trade, and quickly identify Hubler's trade as a *short ratio put spread*. Recall, that in a short ratio put spread, one buys a put with a strike price at or near the money, while selling a greater number of further out-of-the-money puts. High ratio put spreads are dangerous in that they are highly levered transactions. Under normal circumstances, both options expire worthless, and the investor breaks even. Alternatively, the price of the underlying falls somewhat and the investor earns a profit as the high-strike put goes in the money and the downside put expires worthless. The probability that the price of the underlying falls below the lower strike is relatively small. But if is does, the losses mount very fast, and it is possible for the investor to lose most or all of his or her capital. When a short ratio put spread goes bad, it does so big time. Take the following as an example of an idealized short ratio put spread.

In this idealized example of the 8:1, short ratio put spread done 2 billion times, the value of the spread reaches its apex of just under $2 billion. This profit will be

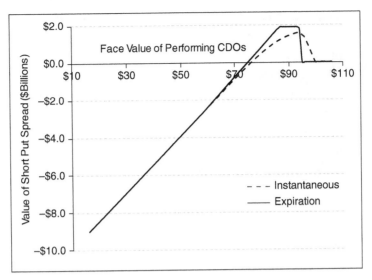

Exhibit 11.5 Short Ratio Put Spread (Analog and with Special Features)

achieved if the BBB-rated CDO tranche completely defaults while the AAA-rated CDO tranche remains untouched at the time the CDS expires. The value of the position at expiration remains steady as the value of the underlying assets that are still performing falls, until the quantity of performing loans can no longer support the AAA tranche. If defaults rise beyond this point, the losses mount up fast. From this point forward, the trade loses $8 for every $1 lost in the value of the performing underlying collateral. With defaults on home mortgages skyrocketing, most of the collateral supporting this and other CDOs like it disappeared and even the highest-rated tranches became junk. Just as one must post collateral to support a short option position to ensure that they will perform on their financial obligation, so must those who write CDSs. As the value of this short ratio put spread lost value, Morgan Stanley had to post collateral to cover the losses reflected in the market value of the CDS contracts. In the end, Howie was finally forced to cover his position and crystalize the loss, which was said to exceed $9 billion. The moral of this story is simple. Analyze trades and investment strategies, and find the hidden options. Then take the perspective of an option trader to get a very quick sense of the risks that exists in a transaction. Once you have a good idea of the downside risk, ask yourself, "Is it worth it?"

The Latrell Sprewell Trade (Exercise In-the-Money Options)

Latrell Sprewell is a former NBA basketball star. During his professional career, he played for the Golden State Warriors, the New York Knicks, and the Minnesota

Timberwolves and was named to the NBA All-Star team four times. As a professional, he put up some impressive statistics. Including the playoffs, he played in 975 games, producing over 18 points a game with an average field goal percentage of over 42 percent. He also converted over 80 percent of his free-throw attempts.

Even as he put up great numbers, his career was overshadowed by an incident in 1997 while playing for the Golden State Worriers. During practice on December 1, he attacked the head coach P. J. Carlesimo. Seems that Sprewell was not in the mood for criticism and warned the coach to keep his distance. Ignoring the warning, Carlesimo approached Sprewell, who quickly threatened to kill him. Seconds later, Sprewell dragged the head coach backward by the throat, choking him for at least 7 seconds. Sprewell's teammates and assistant coach freed Carlesimo and Sprewell left the floor for about 20 minutes. After taking a shower, Sprewell returned to the practice floor, where he attacked Carlesimo once again, this time landing a glancing blow to Carlesimo's cheek. This time, he was dragged away by the assistant coaches, never to return again. Initially, Sprewell was suspended for 10 games without pay, but that did not go down well with the fans, at which point the Warriors voided his contract and the NBA suspended him for one year. This could have been a serious financial blow, as his contract would have earned him $23.7 million over the following three years. In an act of defiance, Sprewell took the case to arbitration, where the contract voiding was overturned and the suspension was reduced to the 68 games remaining in the season. Sprewell had a history of violence. In 1995, Sprewell fought with teammate Jerome Kersey, and after practice, he returned with a two by four and may have threatened to return with a gun. In 1993, Sprewell fought with Byron Houston, a 250-pound power forward.

Sprewell was traded to the New York Knicks after the choking incident, where he had five very productive years. To be sure, this was a risk for the Knicks, but Sprewell assured the franchise he was a changed man. Sprewell became part of the starting lineup for the 1999/2000 season, and captured a five-year/$62 million contract. In 2003, Sprewell made NBA history by sinking a record nine shots in a row from the three-point arc against the Los Angeles Clippers. At the end of the season, Sprewell was traded to the Minnesota Timberwolves in a complex trade between four different teams. During that year, Sprewell finished the season second in team scoring with an average of 20 points a game.

In October 2004, the Timberwolves offered Sprewell a three-year/$21 million contract extension. This was far less than his current expiring contract. Insulted by the offer, he went public with his outrage, stating "I told you I needed to feed my family," at a press conference. "They offered me 3 years at $21 million. That's not going to cut it. And I'm not going to sit here and continue to give my children food while this front office takes money out of my pocket. If [owner Glen] Taylor wants to see my family fed, he better cough up some money. Otherwise, you're going to see these kids in one of those Sally Struthers commercials soon."* Needless to say, he declined the contract extension. This is where the experienced option trader would say he made his big mistake. He chose not to exercise an option that was $21 million in the money. He instead chose to play out his existing contract and hope for something better. The 2004/2005 season was a bad one for Latrell and better offers were not forthcoming. While he might have taken the $7 million per year contract, that was now off the table and all he could get from the Timberwolves was the league minimum of $1 million a year. He went so far as to reject the possibility of a $5 million "mid-level exception." (An MLE allows a team to sign a player for a maximum of a four-year/$5 million contract once a year for teams that are over their salary cap. This amount can be paid if the team did not pay a "luxury tax" in the previous season for exceeding its salary cap. Teams that paid the tax are limited to paying just $3 million. The rules get even more complicated from there.) In the final analysis, Sprewell refused to play for $1+ million a year and his career came to an abrupt end. The moral of this story is, if you have an option that is $21 million in the money and about to expire, exercise it, and don't look back.

Final Thought

Most individual investments and many investment strategies have some kind of hidden option in them. This option is usually a put option, which is sold short. The values of these put options skyrocket during bear markets and this is often the reason why banks, hedge funds, and other levered investors suffer significant losses. If investors, individual and institutional alike, look to uncover these hidden options, price them accordingly, and understand their characteristics, big losses are avoidable. This is a task anyone can master. All one has to do is expand the way they think about investments, uncovering the asymmetries in investment payoffs, and identifying the true source of returns. When properly done, you will have a better, and if for no other reason simpler, way of understanding risk.

---

*TheBrushback.Com, November 9th, 2004, Volume 1 Issue 74.

Chapter 2

1. The appropriate model one should use to value an option is dependent, at least in part, by the underlying asset. The binomial option-pricing model is a generalized numerical method professionals use to value options on instruments whose behavior changes over time. A good example of this is options on fixed income instruments. Long-term bonds are more volatile than short-term bonds. As a result, the volatility of returns on a bond falls as it ages. Furthermore, the price of a bond drifts to par as it ages. As a result, Brownian motion is not a good descriptor of a bond's price behavior. A Brownian bridge process is a better description as it captures the "pull to par" of the underlying instrument. A binomial option-pricing model is superior to the B–S–M model in cases where the price of the stock is expected to be noncontinuous and binomial in nature. A good example is a short-term option on a biotech stock that is about to get approval or rejection of a blockbuster drug. If approval is granted, the price is expected to jump enormously. If it is rejected, the stock is expected to crater. Whereas the B–S–M is a volatility-based model, binomial models allow the user to model specific outcomes.

2. If one is pricing options on futures, one should use a models that takes into account of the forward price of a futures contract. Modifying the inputs to the B–S–M option-pricing model does this. Specifically, one should substitute the futures price for the current market price of the underlying asset. Since the futures price already incorporates drift attributable to the risk-free rate, this should be entered as zero. The formulas for pricing options on other asset classes and special situations can be found in books listed in the reference section of this book.

## Chapter 4

1. Monthly Return Characteristics (in percent) for One-Month Puts

	90	92	94	96	98	100	102	104	106	108	110
Median	−100	−100	−100	−100	−100	−100	−67.1	−30.6	−18.9	−13.8	−10.7
Average	−93.9	−86.7	−74.2	−62.6	−52.2	−34.3	−24.1	−15.1	−9.3	−6.4	−4.7
St. Dev.	54.1	67.0	103	117	117	112	94.0	76.5	62.0	51.4	43.4
Alpha	−91.3	−82.3	−67.0	−53.3	−41.9	−23.3	−14.1	−6.6	−2.2	−0.4	0.4
Beta	−5.0	−8.3	−13.6	−17.3	−19.3	−20.5	−18.6	−16.0	−13.4	−11.2	−9.5
R-Sqrd	0.17	0.32	0.36	0.45	0.56	0.68	0.81	0.90	0.96	0.98	0.99
Correlation	0.42	0.56	0.60	0.67	0.75	0.83	0.90	0.95	0.98	0.99	1.00

2. Monthly Return Characteristics (in percent) for Three-Month Puts

	90	92	94	96	98	100	102	104	106	108	110
Median	−52.7	−51.0	−47.9	−43.3	−38.4	−34.1	−28.8	−23.0	−17.9	−13.8	−10.9
Average	−25.8	−24.1	−22.1	−19.8	−17.3	−14.4	−12.4	−9.9	−7.6	−5.8	−4.5
St. Dev.	68.8	66.3	63.9	61.5	59.0	56.2	52.2	47.8	43.3	39.0	35.1
Alpha	−18.9	−17.4	−15.6	−13.4	−11.1	−8.4	−6.7	−4.6	−2.8	−1.3	−0.4
Beta	−12.7	−12.5	−12.2	−11.9	−11.6	−11.2	−10.6	−9.9	−9.1	−8.3	−7.5
R-Sqrd	0.7	0.7	0.8	0.8	0.8	0.8	0.8	0.9	0.9	0.9	0.9
Correlation	0.8	0.9	0.9	0.9	0.9	0.9	0.9	0.9	1.0	1.0	1.0

3. Monthly Return Characteristics (in percent) for 12-Month Puts

	90	92	94	96	98	100	102	104	106	108	110
Median	−13.5	−12.8	−12.2	−11.7	−11.0	−10.4	−9.8	−8.7	−8.2	−8.0	−7.7
Average	−4.2	−4.2	−4.2	−4.1	−4.0	−3.7	−3.8	−3.6	−3.4	−3.2	−3.0
St. Dev.	33.2	31.8	30.6	29.4	28.3	27.2	26.2	25.1	24.0	23.0	21.9
Alpha	−0.8	−0.9	−1.0	−1.0	−0.9	−0.8	−0.9	−0.9	−0.8	−0.6	−0.5
Beta	−6.4	−6.2	−6.0	−5.8	−5.6	−5.5	−5.3	−5.1	−4.9	−4.8	−4.6
R-Sqrd	0.8	0.8	0.8	0.8	0.8	0.8	0.8	0.9	0.9	0.9	0.9
Correlation	0.9	0.9	0.9	0.9	0.9	0.9	0.9	0.9	0.9	0.9	0.9

4. Monthly Return Characteristics (in percent) for One-Month Calls

	90	92	94	96	98	100	102	104	106	108	110
Median	7.1	7.8	7.7	3.2	−10.6	−48.5	−100	−100	−100	−100	−100
Average	1.0	0.4	−0.1	−1.1	−5.2	−12.8	−36.3	−69.5	−82.1	−92.2	−98.5
St. Dev.	40.6	47.2	54.7	64.2	79.2	98.5	105.9	92.1	73.7	45.4	14.5
Alpha	−3.7	−5.0	−6.3	−8.1	−13.2	−21.6	−44.4	−75.2	−86.0	−94.1	−98.9
Beta	8.7	10.0	11.4	12.9	14.8	16.3	15.2	10.6	7.2	3.6	0.8
R-Sqrd	1.0	0.9	0.9	0.8	0.7	0.6	0.4	0.3	0.2	0.1	0.1
Correlation	97	97	97	97	97	97	97	97	97	97	97

5. Monthly Return Characteristics (in percent) for Three-Month Calls

	90	92	94	96	98	100	102	104	106	108	110
Median	4.7	4.6	4.2	3.5	0.2	−4.7	−9.9	−15.5	−23.9	−39.2	−54.5
Average	0.9	0.7	0.2	−0.5	−1.6	−3.0	−6.7	−11.0	−15.4	−19.2	−20.8
St. Dev.	29.2	32.0	35.3	39.2	43.7	48.9	53.6	58.6	64.8	74.7	94.3
Alpha	−2.4	−3.0	−3.8	−4.9	−6.4	−8.3	−12.3	−17.0	−21.7	−25.9	−28.2
Beta	6.3	6.8	7.5	8.2	8.9	9.770	10.5	11.1	11.8	12.538	13.631
R-Sqrd	0.95	0.94	0.92	0.89	0.86	0.821	0.78	0.74	0.68	0.579	0.430
Correlation	97	97	97	97	97	97	97	97	97	97	97

6. Monthly Return Characteristics (in percent) for 12-Month Calls

	90	92	94	96	98	100	102	104	106	108	110
Median	3.7	3.5	3.2	2.8	2.3	2.7	2.0	1.2	1.0	0.7	−1.0
Average	1.1	1.0	0.9	0.8	0.7	0.4	0.4	0.3	0.1	−0.1	−0.5
St. Dev.	18.6	19.6	20.6	21.7	22.9	24.2	25.9	27.7	29.7	32.0	34.7
Alpha	−1.0	−1.2	−1.4	−1.6	−1.9	−2.3	−2.4	−2.7	−3.0	−3.5	−4.0
Beta	4.0	4.1	4.3	4.5	4.8	5.0	5.3	5.6	5.9	6.2	6.6
R-Sqrd	0.93	0.92	0.91	0.90	0.89	0.87	0.85	0.83	0.81	0.78	0.74
Correlation	97	97	97	97	97	97	97	97	97	97	97

7. Constructing a binomial tree

Binomial trees are used to price more complex options that do not fit the assumptions of the B–S–M model. They are most commonly used to price options on bonds and options on stocks, commodities or currencies that have unique features. Generically, it takes the following form.

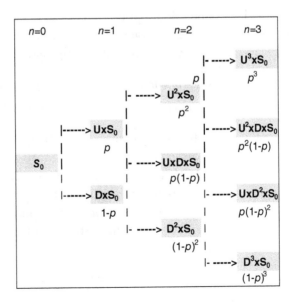

Starting at the evaluation date where the current price is known, the tree of prices is constructed by working forward to expiration. At each step, price can either move up or down. The amount that the value of the underlying security increases (U) or falls (D) is approximately equal to one standard deviation adjusted for the time duration considered at each step along the tree.

$$U = e^{\sigma\sqrt{t/n}} \quad\text{where}\quad U \geq 1$$

$$D = e^{-\sigma\sqrt{t/n}} = {}^1/_u \quad\text{where}\quad 0 < D \leq 1$$

The new up price (S_{up}) is equal to $U \times S$, while the new down price (S_{down}) is equal to $D \times S$. Cox, Ross, and Rubinstein originally developed this method for estimating the up and down factors. These factors are very convenient as they allow for internal consistency. The probabilities of landing at a particular point are not path dependent. It does not matter if price changes up first then down, or down first then up. This allows for each node along the tree to recombine without regard to the path price followed to get there. This property also allows the value of the underlying asset to be calculated directly without requiring the tree to be constructed first by applying the following formula (where N_U is the number of up ticks and N_D is the number of down ticks).

$$S_n = S_0 x U^{(N_U - N_D)}$$

The probability that price rises (p) is computed with the following equation, and the probability that price falls is $(1 - p)$.

$$p = \frac{e^{rt/n} - D}{U - D}$$

To find the value of an option, one starts at expiration and works backwards. Valuation at this point is straightforward. The value of each of the final nodes at expiration is simply the intrinsic value of the option.

Value of Call at Nodes at Expiration $= Max(S_n - K, 0)$

Value of Put at Nodes at Expiration $= Max(K - S_n, 0)$

Recall that **K** is the strike price and $\mathbf{S}_n$ is the spot price of the underlying asset at the node in the nth period.

To arrive at the option's price at the evaluation date, one works backwards from the expiration date computing the value of the option at each node along the way. In the case of a call option the value of the option at any particular node is the probability weighted average of the potential outcomes discounted at the risk-free rate. It is computed with the following formula.

$$C_{t-\Delta t, i} = e^{-r\Delta t}(pC_{t, i+1} + (1 - p)C_{t, i-1})$$

where $C_{t,i}$ is the opiton value for the ith node and time t, and

$$p = \frac{e^{(r-q)\Delta t} - D}{U - D}$$

The end result is a binomial tree that simulates the results of geometric Brownian motion of the underlying instrument with parameters r (risk-free rate), q (dividend yield), and σ (volatility).

NOTES

American option   An American option gives the owner the freedom to exercise at anytime during its life. Most options listed on U.S. exchanges are of this type.

assignment   Assignment represents the transfer of ownership of the underlying asset that takes place when an option is exercised.

at the money   An option is said to be at the money if the current asset price is equal to the strike price. Numerically, it has a moneyness of 100.

Bermudan option   A Bermudan option is a hybrid between a European and American option. A Bermudan option is exercisable only on predetermined dates stated in the contract, typically monthly.

borrowing costs   The fee paid to a security lender by the person who borrows the asset.

buy to close   A term used by the futures and options industry to indicate an existing contract has been terminated. A contract is terminated when someone purchases a position held short in his or her account. Buying to close decreases the open interest in the number of contracts outstanding.

buy to open   A term used by the futures and options industry to indicate a new contract has been created. A new contract is created when someone purchases a contract and is not closing a position held short in his or her account. Buying to open increases the open interest in the number of contracts outstanding.

calendar spread   A calendar spread trade involves the simultaneous purchase and sale of futures or options contracts that mature or expire on differing dates. Calendar spreads are often referred to as time or horizontal spreads.

call option   A call option represents the right but not the obligation to buy an asset at a predetermined price within a predetermined time frame.

call spread   An option strategy constructed by simultaneously purchasing a call with a specific strike price and selling another call option with the same expiration date but at a higher strike price. It is often referred to as a "bullish call spread."

cash-covered put   An option strategy constructed by selling a put option and simultaneously setting aside enough cash to buy the asset in the event the asset is put to the option writer.

collar   An option strategy that entails owning an asset while simultaneously holding a short risk reversal. More specifically, a strategy that is simultaneously long an asset, short a call, and long a put on the same asset. This is a less-than-perfect hedging strategy that allows the investor to sell the underlying asset if its price falls to or below the strike of the put. The investor will enjoy limited gains if the price of the asset exceeds the price of the call option sold.

contract multiplier   The contract multiplier defines the amount of the underlying security a single contract references. A typical equity option (call or put) gives the owner the right to buy or sell 100 shares of the underlying security. The contract multiplier in this case is 100.

covered call   An option strategy constructed by selling a call option while holding the underlying asset for delivery to the call buyer if the buyer chooses to call the stock away.

credit   The amount of cash received by an option writer when selling an option.

debit   The amount of cash paid to the option writer when buying an option.

deliverable   The asset that satisfied the obligation of a futures or options contract. For options on stocks, it is the stock itself. For indexes, it is cash in the amount equal to the difference between the market price and exercise price of the index referenced.

delta   A measure of an option's price sensitivity for a small change in the price of the underlying asset. Mathematically, delta is the first derivative of an option's price with respect to the price of the underlying asset.

dividend yield   The amount of dividend paid or expected to be paid by a corporation to shareholders over a one-year time period divided by the market price of the company's stock.

European option   A European option gives the owner the right to exercise only on its expiration date.

exercise   The process by which an owner of an option demands performance by the seller. When exercising a call, the owner of the option demands delivery of the underlying asset in exchange for cash in the amount of the strike price of the contract. When exercising a put, the owner of the option sells the underlying asset to the option writer. The put writer must pay the strike price defined by the contract upon delivery of the underlying asset.

expiration date   The date an option expires or ceases to exist.

forward price   The specified price in a forward contract. An arbitrage condition defines the fair value of the forward price. It is determined based on the current price plus the cost of carry less any dividends that might have to be paid before the expiration date of the contract.

gamma   A measure of the sensitivity of an option's delta given a change in the price of the underlying asset. Mathematically, gamma is the second derivative of an option's price with respect to the price of the underlying asset.

gamma scalping   A method of trading volatility. It entails buying an asset and selling calls, or selling an asset and buying puts, on a delta-neutral basis. Gamma causes the delta of an option to drift in a beneficial direction, ensuring the price of the option moves more than the price of the underlying asset. A gain is locked in when the delta of the arbitrage trade is reset to zero.

hedge ratio   A measure of the price movement of one asset relative to another. It is used to weight trades to produce the desired risk/return characteristics. For example, if one buys 1 dollar of asset X and hedges it with A dollars of asset Y, A is the hedge ratio.

implied volatility   The volatility used in an option-pricing model that causes the model to generate a theoretical valuation that is equal to the market price of the option. As a result, it is another measure of an option's price.

in the money   A call option is said to be in the money if the current asset price is greater than the strike price of the contract. Numerically, it has a moneyness greater than 100. A put option is said to be in the money if the current asset price is less than the strike price of the contract. Numerically, it has moneyness less than 100.

intrinsic value   The value the owner of an option would capture if they exercised an option. For a call option, it is measured by subtracting the strike price of the option from the market price of the underlying security. For a put option, it is measured by subtracting the market price of the underlying instrument from the strike price of the option. Only options that are in the money have intrinsic value.

lambda   A measure of the percentage change in the price of an option for a percentage change in the price of the underlying security. It is a measure of an option's leverage to the price of the underlying asset. Mathematically, lambda is delta multiplied by the price of the underlying asset divided by the price of the option.

moneyness (absolute)   A measure of the position of an option's strike price, relative to the market price of the underlying asset. The measure is standardized to the price of the underlying asset. As a result, 100 percent moneyness represents an option that has a strike price equal to the market price of the underlying asset. 90 percent moneyness indicates the strike price of the option is 10 percent below the market price of the underlying asset and 105 percent moneyness indicates the strike price of the option is 5 percent higher than the market price of the underlying asset.

moneyness (standardized)   A measure of moneyness relative to the implied volatility of an at-the-money option. It indicates how much an option is in or out of the money in terms of the riskiness of an option.

naked options   An option position that is not collateralized by the underlying instrument or cash (e.g., selling a call on a stock without owning the stock, or selling a put without enough cash to pay for the stock if it is put to the seller).

notice of delivery   The process by which the option writer is informed that the owner of a call option has exercised the right under an option agreement to take ownership of the underlying asset.

open interest   A measure of the number of options or futures contracts outstanding at any point in time.

Option Clearing Corporation (OCC)   The OCC was founded in 1973 and operates under the jurisdiction of the Securities and Exchange Commission (SEC) and the Commodities Futures Trading Commission (CFTC). It is a clearing organization for listed options in the United States. It provides central counterparty clearing and settlement service to all the listed option-trading platforms. By acting as a central counterparty, the OCC is on the opposite side of all positions held by investors. In taking this position, it ensures that the obligations will always be honored.

out of the money   A call option is said to be out of the money if the current asset price is less than the strike price of the contract. Numerically, it has moneyness more than 100. A put option is said to be out of the money if the current asset price is more than the strike price of the contract. Numerically, it has moneyness less than 100.

parity   An option is trading at parity when its price is equal to its intrinsic value.

phi   A measure of the sensitivity of an option's price for a change in the dividend yield on the underlying instrument. Mathematically, phi is the first derivative of an option's price with respect to the dividend yield.

put option   The right but not the obligation to sell an asset at a predetermined price within a predetermined time frame.

put–call parity   The relationship between European puts and calls with the same expiration date and strike price, the underlying instrument, and cash equivalents. It states that the value of cash plus a call is equal to the value of the underlying asset and a put.

put spread   An option strategy constructed by simultaneously purchasing a put with a specific strike price and selling another put option with the same expiration date but a lower strike price. It is often referred to as a "bearish put spread."

ratio spread   An option strategy that involves buying a certain number of options and selling a different number of options. Both options reference the same underlying instrument but have different strike prices. Ratio spreads usually have the same expiration date, but this is not required. For example, in a 1 × 2 ratio call spread, one option is purchased for every two that are sold.

realized volatility   A measure of uncertainty that actually took place in the past. It is often referred to as historical volatility.

real option   The right but not the obligation to acquire the present value of a stream of cash flows by making an investment on or before the opportunity ceases to exist in an uncertain environment. An example would be a power plant that can deliver electricity to two different grids. It has the option to sell its power to the grid paying the highest price.

rho (r)   A measure of the sensitivity of an option's price for a change in interest rates. Mathematically, rho is the first derivative of an option's price with respect to the risk-free rate.

risk-free-rate   The rate of interest associated on a debt instrument that is free of credit risk. Investors are guaranteed to earn this yield over an investment horizon that matches the tenor of the instrument.

risk reversal   Option strategy that produces a return profile that is similar to owning the underlying security. It entails being short an out-of-the-money put and long an out-of-the-money call. Both options must have the same time to maturity.

strike price   The price at which an owner of an option can transact. A call buyer has the option of purchasing a stock at the strike price and the put buyers have the option to sell at the strike price. It is also commonly referred to as the *exercise price*.

sell to close   A term used by the futures and options industry to indicate an investor is closing out an existing position. Selling to close decreases open interest in the number of contracts outstanding.

sell to open   A term used by the futures and options industry to indicate an investor is initiating a new position. Selling to open increases the open interest in the number of contracts outstanding, as a new position has been created.

short interest   The quantity of stock or other financial interest that investors have sold short and not yet covered. It is measured in the absolute number of shares sold short or as a percentage of the number of shares outstanding.

short interest ratio   The amount of stock sold short divided by the average daily trading volume. Think of it as the number of days trading it would take to cover all short sales outstanding if no other transactions took place. Many look at the SIR as a sentiment indicator. A high SIR would suggest the stock is heavily shorted because there is a great deal of investor pessimism. A contrarian would suggest this is a positive for the stock.

short squeeze   A situation where a heavily shorted stock or commodity moves sharply higher causing short sellers to buy and pushing the price higher still. Short squeezes typically result in violent price movements.

theta (Q)   A measure of the sensitivity of an option's price for the passing of time. It tells us the rate at which an option price decays as time passes. Mathematically, theta is the first derivative of an option's price with respect to time to expiration.

time decay   Options have a predetermined life. As it ages, an option loses value. Time decay is a description of how an option loses value as it ages.

time premium   The portion of an option's price that exceeds its intrinsic value. Volatility and time to expiration are the primary drivers of time premium.

time to expiration   The length of time over which an option will remain outstanding.

underlying instrument   The asset an option or futures contract references to derive its value.

vega (n)   A measure of the sensitivity of an option's price for a change in the volatility of the underlying asset. Mathematically, vega is the first derivative of an option's price with respect to implied volatility.

vertical spread   An option strategy involving the simultaneous purchase and sale of option's contracts with differing strike prices but identical expiration dates. In a typical *bullish vertical spread (aka call spread)*, one buys a call and simultaneously sells one with a higher strike price. In a typical *bearish vertical spread (aka put spread)*, one buys a put and simultaneously sells one with a lower strike price.

volatility   A measure of the risk associated with the return on investment. It is computed by taking the standard deviation of historical returns.

volatility arbitrage   A trading strategy that attempts to capitalize on the differences between forecasted future volatility of an asset and the implied volatility imbedded in option prices on that asset.

volatility skew   A description of the typical relationship between implied volatility and moneyness. Under most circumstances, options with moneyness less than 100 are priced with an implied volatility greater than options with moneyness of 100. In this situation, the option string is said to have a positive skew.

volatility smile Another description of the typical relationship between implied volatility and moneyness. Under some circumstance, options with moneyness less than 100 are priced with an implied volatility greater than options with moneyness of 100. At the same time, options with moneyness greater than 100 possess an implied volatility higher than at-the-money options. A graph of this relationship takes on the shape of a smile.

volatility surface A three-dimensional chart showing the relationship between implied volatility on the z-axis, to moneyness found on the x-axis and time to maturity plotted on the y-axis.

volatility term structure The relationship between implied volatility and the time to expiration on a series of options. Terms structures are typically upward sloping, but often take an inverted shape when discounting a near-term event or financial distress.

zeta A measure of the probability that an option will expire in the money.

zeta$_{Ever}$ A measure of the probability that an option will trade in the money at some point over its life.

REFERENCES

1. Abramowitz, Milton, and Irene A. Stegun. *Handbook of Mathematical Functions with Formulas, Graphs, and Mathematical Tables.* New York: Dover Publications, Ninth printing, 1970.

2. Adams, Henry. *History of the United States of America (1801–1817). Vol.2: During the First Administration of Thomas Jefferson.* Cambridge University Press, 2011 [1889].

3. Antonopoulos, Andreas M. *Mastering Bitcoin. Unlocking Digital Crypto-Currencies.* O'Reilly Media, April 2014.

4. Baseball-Reference.com Lenny Dykstra Player Page, November 27, 2013.

5. Bennett, Colin, and Miguel A. Gil. "Volatility Trading: Trading Volatility, Correlation, Term Structure and Skew." *Grupo Santander* (April 2012).

6. Berkshire Hathaway Form 10-K, 2012.

7. BitCoin.Org. "Bitcoin: A Peer-to-Peer Electronic Cash System"(PDF). October 2008.

8. Black, Fischer, and Myron Scholes. "The Pricing of Options and Corporate Liabilities." *Journal of Political Economy* (1973).

9. Bondarenko, Oleg. "Why Are Put Options Expensive?" White Paper, Department of Finance, University of Illinois at Chicago, November 2003.

10. Cerami, Charles A. *Jefferson's Great Gamble.* Sourcebooks, 2003.

11. Chriss, Neil A. *Black-Scholes and Beyond: Option Pricing Models.* New York: McGraw-Hill, 1997.

12. Cox, John C., and Mark Rubinstein. *Options Markets.* Upper Saddle River, NJ: Prentice Hall, 1985.

13. Davis, Joshua. "The Crypto-Currency: Bitcoin and Its Mysterious Inventor." *The New Yorker*. October 10, 2011.

14. Demeterfi, Kresimir, Emanuel Derman, Michael Kamal, and Joseph Zou. "More than You Ever Want to Know about Volatility Swaps." Goldman Sachs Quantitative Strategies Research Notes (March 1999).

15. ESPN Classic - Sprewell's Image Remains in a Chokehold.

16. ESPN: New York Magazine on Latrell Sprewell in 1999 January 25, 2006.

17. "The Fall of Lenny Dykstra." *MAXIM*, October 17, 2011 www.maxim.com/sports/the-fall-of-lenny-dykstra-part-2.

18. Fama, Eugene F., and Kenneth R. French "Common Risk Factors in the Returns on Stocks and Bonds." *Journal of Financial Economics* 33, no. 1 (1993): 3–56.

19. Fama, Eugene F., and Kenneth R, French. "The Capital Asset Pricing Model: Theory and Evidence." *Journal of Economic Perspectives* 18, no. 3 (Summer 2004): 25–46.

20. Fleming, Thomas J. *The Louisiana Purchase*. Hoboken, NJ: John Wiley & Sons, 2003.

21. "Former Baseball Star Lenny Dykstra Pleads Not Guilty to Federal Charges." *Contra Costa Times*, June 13, 2011.

22. "Former MLB Star Lenny Dykstra Admits to Financial Fraud." CBS Sports. Retrieved July 13, 2012.

23. Frankie, Christopher (2013). Nailed! The Improbable Rise and Spectacular Fall of Lenny Dykstra, Running Press

24. Gatheral, Jim. "Modeling the Implied Volatility Surface." Stanford Financial Mathematics Seminar (February 2003).

25. GoldenStateOfMind.Com, #1 Hoops Feud of All Time May 21, 2006

26. Guthner, Mark W. CFA. *Quantitative Analytics in Debt Valuation & Management*. New York: McGraw-Hill, 2012.

27. Hosmer, James Kendall. *Louisiana Purchase*. New York: D. Appleton & Co, 1902.

28. "How Lenny Dykstra Got Nailed." *Sports Illustrated* (February 11, 2011), http://sportsillustrated.cnn.com/vault/article/magazine/MAG1195702/.

29. http://www.investopedia.com (2013).

30. "Historical Mortgage Rates," Freddie Mac, www.freddiemac.com/pmms/pmms30.htm.

31. Huag, Espen Gaarder. *The Complete Guide to Option Pricing Formulas, 2nd ed*. New York: McGraw-Hill, 2008.

32. "Introduction into the New Bloomberg Implied Volatility Calculations." Bloomberg LLC, March 2008.

33. Jane Wells. "Lenny Dykstra's Former Mansion Is Sold." CNBC.com, January 29, 2011.

34. Latrell Sprewell BasketballReference.Com

35. Lawson, Gary, and Guy Seidman. *The Constitution of Empire: Territorial Expansion and American Legal History*. New Haven, CT: Yale University Press, 2008.

36. "Lenny Dykstra Files for Chapter 11." ESPN. Reuters, July 8, 2009.

37. Lenny Dykstra's Investment website, www.nailsinvestments.com.

38. "Lenny Dykstra Sentenced for Fraud." ESPN. Retrieved December 3, 2012.

39. Lewis, Michael. *Moneyball: The Art of Winning an Unfair Game*, 45–47. New York: W. W. Norton & Company.

40. Lintner, John. "The Valuation of Risk Assets and the Selection of Risky Investments in Stock Portfolios and Capital Budgets." *Review of Economics and Statistics*, 47, no. 1 (1965), 13–37.

41. Mandelbrot, B., and R. L. Hudson. *The (Mis)Behaviour of Markets: A Fractal View of Risk, Ruin, and Reward*. London: Profile Books, 2004.

42. Markowitz, H.M. *Portfolio Selection: Efficient Diversification of Investments*. New York: John Wiley & Sons, 1959.

43. Marshall, Thomas Maitland. *A History of the Western Boundary of the Louisiana Purchase, 1819–1841*. Whitefish, MT: Kessinger Publishing, 1914.

44. Merton, Robert. "An Analytic Derivation of the Efficient Portfolio Frontier." *Journal of Financial and Quantitative Analysis* 7 (September 1972): 1851–1872.

45. Miller, Merton C. "Theory of Rational Option Pricing." *Bell Journal of Economics and Management Sciences,* 4, no. 1 (Spring 1973): 141–183.

46. Modigliani, Franco, and Merton Miller. "The Cost of Capital, Corporate Finance and the Theory of Investment." *American Economic Review* 48, no. 3 (1958): 261–297.

47. Nakamoto, Satoshi. "Bitcoin: A Peer-to-Peer Electronic Cash System." www.Bitcoin.Org, December 2008.

48. Natenberg, Sheldon, and Jeffery M. Cohen. *Option Volatility & Pricing*. New York: McGraw-Hill, 1994.

49. NBA.Com/Stats Latrell Sprewell

50. Nielson, Lars Tyge. "Understanding $N(d_1)$ and $N(d_2)$: Risk-Adjusted Probabilities in the Black-Scholes Model." INSEAD White Paper, October 1992.

51. Nugent, Walter. *Habits of Empire: A History of American Expansionism*. New York: Random House, 2009.

52. "Once-Celebrated Reckless Leads to Dykstra's Financial Fall," *New York Times*. July 19, 2011, www.nytimes.com/2011/07/20/sports/baseball/the-financial-fall-of-lenny-dykstra.html?&uscore;r=0.

53. Options Clearing Corporation, Infomemo #30059, January 3, 2012.

54. "Regulation of Bitcoin in Selected Jurisdictions." The Law Library of Congress, Global Legal Research Center, January 2014.

55. Ross, Stephen A. "The Capital Asset Pricing Model (CAPM), Short-sale Restrictions and Related Issues." *Journal of Finance* 32, no. 177 (1977).

56. Sharpe, William F. "Capital Asset Prices: A Theory of Market Equilibrium under Conditions of Risk. *Journal of Finance* 19, no. 3 (1964): 425–442.

57. "Want to Live Like Wayne Gretzky? 13,000 sq.-ft. Mansion Built for Hockey Great Hits the Market for $15M." *National Post*. Retrieved August 24, 2013.

Reading this book is a great first step in becoming a skilled option trader and investor, but the development of your skills should not stop here. To continue your development and to help put newly developed skills into practice, we have built an educational website called **TheOptionsEdge.Com**. TheOptionsEdge.Com is designed to take the skills of the novice or even the skilled practitioner to the next level. We take the next steps in educating our followers by delivering educational videos and articles designed to discuss some of the basic concepts in a different way, and delving deeper into some of the more nuanced issues of successful option trading. As part of the educational process, we will employ the techniques discussed in this book and in our educational videos, to discuss investment opportunities in real time. Some readers might want to follow these ideas to see how they develop over time. Others might want to go further and put money at risk. To be sure, TheOptionsEdge.Com is not intended be just another investment website. It is designed to take advantage of all the new techniques in social media to build a community of educated and skilled members.

Here at TheOptionsEdge.Com we realize that investors are continuously, bombarded with information. Some of it is useful to the investment process, while much of it is not. Bringing cutting edge technology to aid in the analytics process is the future of investing. Every trader knows that news and information flows fast and furious and market prices are constantly changing. As the economic environment, competitive landscape, and consumer preferences change, so does the intrinsic value of companies across the globe. This creates opportunities for investors who do their homework and act accordingly. Savvy investors look for opportunities with asymmetric return possibilities. There is nothing more enticing than risking a dollar with the potential of earning 5 or 10 times that amount.

To that end, we want to help the investor understand the market environment in real time and give people the analytic tools and market data to build upon their skills.

There are a number of investor services that attempt to support the individual and professional investor. We have worked with many of these tools and are constantly on the lookout for next new tool in financial technology. In evaluating these tools, we look for a number of important attributes. Firstly, we are looking for tools that go beyond the same old analytical methods. We search for analytic tools that help investors develop a repeatable, systematic process that suits the investor's style. Second, we are looking for systems that will help investors consistently earn high-risk adjusted returns. "Consistent" and "repeatable" are key words here. It is not enough to deliver high returns on a sporadic basis. An ideal investment tool and process will help investors succeed in all investment environments. Thirdly, we want the tools to be intuitive and easy to use. We have worked with difficult tools in the past. Over time, those tools become tedious as investors end up spending more time managing their tools than their portfolios.

To help you take the next step in your trading success, we have joined forces with the folks at OptionsPlay.Com.

OptionsPlay has combined market data and artificial intelligence based on fundamental and technical analysis, to develop an easy to use analytics tool. This online tool is designed to help investors find opportunities and structure trades accordingly. Most of the information you need is presented in one screen view. That screen view is arranged in three sections.

On the left-hand side, you have the trade ideas panel. Here you will find trade ideas generated by the system each night. At times there are just a few promising ideas. At other times, there will be more than you can handle. To find the ideas that fit your industry expertise or preferences, investors can sort through these ideas based on a number of factors. One can parse trades based by bullish or bearish tilts. This is particularly useful for investors that want to be both long and short as a means of managing market risk. If one needs a few short positions, OptionsPlay can help with that. Some investors like to focus on stocks with certain market caps, as they go in and out of favor. OptionsPlay can help with that. Some investors have expertise in particular sectors because on hobbies or work experience. OptionsPlay can focus on the names in those sectors that are most relevant to you. These ideas are ranked on a scale of 1 to 10. Those rated 7–10 are expected to rise in price, those rated 4–6 are expected to be range bound and those rated 1–3 are expected to fall in price. The system will also assign a trend indicator and rank index so that the user can quickly see when it might be time to act.

Every investor has a list of favorite stocks to watch. OptionsPlay enables investors to build a watch list and the system will provide the OptionsPlay score and trend indicators to each of the positions on that list.

The middle panel shows a chart of the recent price action of a stock. Layered on that chart in that standard view are potential points of price support and resistance to help identify entry and exit points. OptionsPlay satisfies the needs of more sophisticated market technicians. The system comes with a host of technical tools that traders can incorporate into their analysis and on their price charts. Fundamentals are part of the picture as well. Accompanying each price chart are some valuation measures like the price-to-earnings ratio and the dividend yield. Understanding the news flow is critical as well. By clicking on the News Feed button, investors can quickly see published news that describes what is happening to a particular company and the industry in which it competes. Earnings announcements are an important catalyst, one that often drives big price movements. The next earnings data, if announced by the company, is shown below the price chart to keep investors aware of a potential price-moving event.

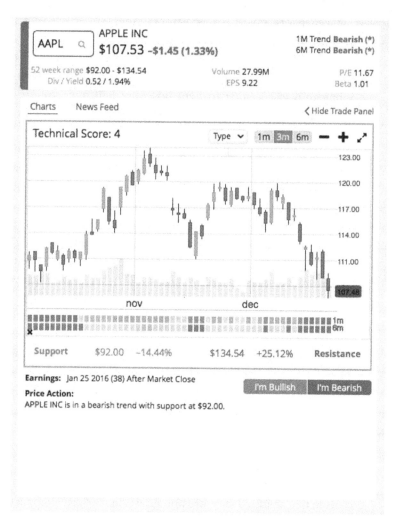

At the bottom of that panel, investors do their analysis and indicate whether they are bullish or bearish on a stock. Given the investor's bias, the system allows the investor to change hats from analyst to trader and portfolio manager.

The panel on the right-hand side helps the investor structure their trade based on their directional bias, conviction, and risk tolerance. The first chart will show a total return analysis assuming one buys or sells the shares of the company under review. The middle chart shows the total return payoff pattern using a single-leg option. If one is bullish it shows the payoff pattern of a call. If the investor is bearish, it shows the payoff pattern of a put. The third window will show the payoff pattern of a two-legged structure. If one is bullish it shows the payoff pattern of a vertical call spread. If the investor is bearish, it shows the payoff pattern of a vertical put spread.

Inside each of these windows is the proprietary OptionsPlay score. This score is driven by the probability of success and the price target generated by the technical analysis. A value in excess of 100 suggests the risk–reward ratio is acceptable. A score less than 100 suggest the risk–reward ratio is suboptimal. The user can modify each of these structures from the recommended strikes and expirations as they see fit to create the payoff pattern and OptionsPlay score that is best for the situation at hand.

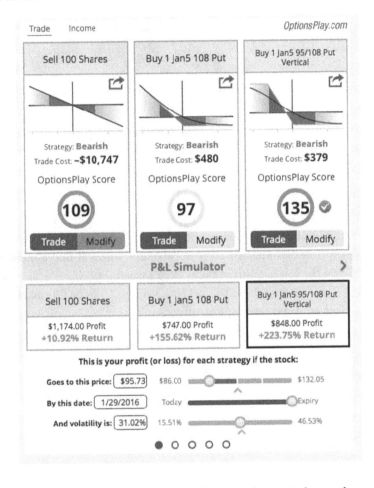

If you click on any one of the three total return chart windows, the system will reveal some important information such as the cost of the trade, the probability of earning a profit, and highlight breakeven levels. Below the three trade structures, there is additional information as well. Here you can find a more robust description of each trade. More importantly, you will find a distribution of potential outcomes driven by the implied volatility priced into option prices. This way you can quickly see the probabilities of the share price going to a specific level or trading within some range. In addition, one can place boundaries on potential outcomes and the system will re-rank the potential structures.

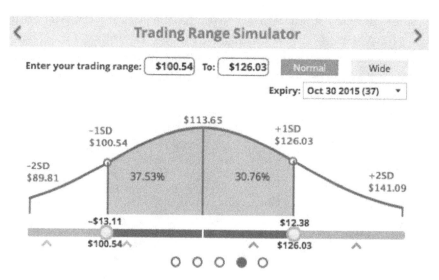

This discussion is just a primer of the capabilities of this unique and powerful system. To be sure, more tools are in the works. We encourage everyone who has read this book to learn more about OptionsPlay. This is easy to do. Simply go to the OptionsPlay channel on YouTube and you will find a number of videos that show you the full breadth of the system's capability.

To learn more go to TheOptionsEdge.Com or OptionsPlay.Com websites to see free trial and subscription offers.

ABOUT THE FREE TRIAL

OptionsPlay.Com is pleased to offer purchasers of this book a free trial and subscription discounts to their options analytics services delivered over the web. To learn more about these valuable offers, go to OptionsPlay.Com/Book.

See the card at the back of the book for instructions and your unique pin code. Only one discount per promo code is allowed.

Absolute skew, 73
Alpha:
    creating, 189
    in put option performance, 109–112
American-style options, 15, 208, 211
Anticipatory hedging, 159–161
Asian debt crisis, 295–296, 298
Assigning options, 15–16
Autocorrelation, 67, 120–123

Back testing indicators, 236
Bankers Trust, 283
Barrier option, 276
Bear Stearns High Grade Credit Fund,
    293
Berkshire Hathaway, 266–268
Bermudean-style options, 15
Beta, 102–103, 112–113
Bid/offer spread, 32
Binomial events, 31
Binomial trees, 121
Bitcoin, 272–278
Black, Fisher, 29
Black–Scholes–Merton option-pricing
    model, 21, 29–64
    assumptions of, 30–35, 70
    for a company of index paying a
        continuous dividend, 36

and discrete dividends, 208–210
European-style options assumption,
    36
example, 37–39
intuition behind, 36–39
and put options, 105–108
BNP Paribas ABS Eonia, 294
Bonaparte, Napoleon, 271–272
Bonds. *See also* IBOXX high-yield
        index
    convertible, 244
    PIK (pay in kind), 244
Borrowing and lending line, 101
Borrowing costs, 33–34. *See also* Phi
    company takeovers, 232
    forward borrowing rates, 231–232
    implied, on underlying instruments,
        227–232
    term borrowing/lending, 229
Brent North Sea oil, 259
Brownian motion, 30–32
Buffett, Warren, 266–267
Buy to open, 13
Buy-write tactic. *See* Covered calls

Calendar spreads, 91–94, 180, 187, 188,
    190, 224–227
Caliber Global Investment, 293

Call options:
    call butterfly spread, 220
    call spread risk reversals, 143–146,
        202–205
    covered calls, 146–149
    defined, 12
    embedded, 244
    historical returns analysis on, 114–117
    long calendar spread, 224–227
    long calls, 126–128
    synthetically replicating, 241
Call spread risk reversals, 143–146,
    202–205
Cantarell, Rudesindo, 258
Capital asset pricing model (CAPM),
    101–105, 108–110
Capital commitment, reducing, 182
Capital market investors, 244
Capital market line, 103
Capital structure, 244
Carlesimo, P.J., 304
Carry trades, 280–281. *See also*
        Convergence trades
Cash, synthetically replicating, 242–243
Cash-covered puts, 149–152
CDS (credit default swaps), 299–303
Collateralized debt obligations (CDOs),
    300–303
Commissions. *See* Transaction costs
Common currencies, 294–295
Continuous dividend payments, 35–36
Contract multiplier, 12
Contract terms and conditions, 12
Convergence trades, 294–298
Convertible bonds, 244
Corporate debt, creating synthetically,
    243–253
Corzine, Jon, 296–297
Cost of carry, 23–24
Covered calls, 60, 146–149
Credit default swaps (CDSs), 299–303
Credit risk:
    credit risk-free rate, 297
    credit-risk free assets, 168, 245, 247

debt and, 164–165, 247
    in mortgages, 290–291
    in residential mortgage-backed
        securities (RMBSs), 288–292,
        297–302
Cryptocurrencies. *See* Bitcoin
Currency options, 30
Cypress banking system crisis, 277

Debt securities. *See* Corporate debt,
        creating synthetically
Deliverables, 16
Delta, 40–43, 85
    in 1 x 2 ratio put spreads, 184–185
    in diagonal put spreads, 174–175
    intuition behind, 40–41
    in iron condor trades, 153
    vs. price of underlying security, 41
    relationship to theta, 181
    in straddles, 88
Derivatives, overview of, 27
Diagonal put spreads, 172–182
    aging of, in high-volatility environment,
        181
    alternatives to reduce capital
        commitment, 182
    ratio diagonal put spreads, 188–192
Dillon Read Capital Management, 293
Discrete dividends, 208–210
Distribution analysis, 218–227
Diversification, 99
Dividend capture, 207–213
Dividend escrow method, 208–210
Dividend yield, 55–58
Dividends, 35–36, 210–211
Dooley, Evan Brent, 296
Dotcom bubble, 285–287
Drivers of options prices, 39–58. *See also*
        Greeks
Dykstra, Lenny, 6–10
Dynamic replication, 238

Early excercise, 15, 208, 211–212, 227
Earnings reports, 72

Efficient frontier, 100–101, 167–168, 189–190
Efficient market hypothesis, 69, 103, 215–216, 219
Embedded call options, 244
European debt crisis, 276–277, 297–298
European Union, 294–296
European-style options, 15, 208
Exchange-traded options, 15–16
Exercising an option, 12, 14–15, 16
Expected volatility, 66
Expiration dates, 12. *See also* Time decay
    and call options, 114–117
    and put options, 107–108
    time decay vs. time to expiration, 52, 170–171

Fear, 73, 202
FIFO (first-in, first-out), 16
Financial Crimes Enforcement Network (FinCEN), 277
Financial crisis of 2008, 161–162, 180
Forward price, 23–24
Francis Baring and Company, 272
Frictionless markets, 32
Fundamental investing, 157–158
Fundamental strategies, 125–155
    income-generating (*see* Income-generating strategies)
    ratio spreads, 135–139
    risk reversals, 139–146
    single-leg puts and calls, 126–129
    vertical spreads, 129–135
Futures contracts, 282

Galena Street Fund, 294
Gamma, 43–46
    in diagonal put spreads, 174–175
    equation for, 45
    intuition behind, 44
    relationship to theta, 118
Gamma scalping, 82–87, 119, 238
Geometric Brownian motion, 30–31
Global Proprietary Credit Group (GPCG), 300

Gold:
    call spread risk reversals on, 201–207
    put/call ratio example, 234–235
Golden State Warriors, 303–305
Greek banking system crisis, 276–277, 297
Greeks, 40–58
    benefits of using, 58–60
    delta (*see* Delta)
    gamma, 43–46, 118, 174–178 (*see also* Gamma scalping)
    phi, 55–58
    return attribution and, 59–60
    rho, 53–55
    theta (*see* Theta)
    vega, 46–50, 85, 188
    zeta, 60–63, 218–221

Hedging, 33–34. *See also* Gamma scalping; Portfolio hedging
High-yield bonds, historical performance, 176–182. *See also* IBOXX high-yield index
High-yield debt, hedging with equity, 164–169
Historical volatility, 67–68
Hope and Company, 272
Horizontal spreads. *See* Calendar spreads
Howie Hubler trade, 298–303
Hubbard, M. Kin, 257
Hubler, Howie, 298–303

IBOXX high-yield index, 165–169, 176–182, 187–188
Implied volatility, 46, 66, 68–70, 94–95
    in diagonal put spreads, 180
    relationship to realized volatility, 80–82
    relationship to strike price, 71–73
    skew chart, 70–71
    volatility smile, 70–71
Income-generating strategies, 146–155
    cash-covered puts, 149–152
    covered calls, 146–149
    iron condor, 152–155

Information extraction, 215–236
    implied borrowing costs on underlying
        instruments, 227–232
    option-implied distribution of future
        prices, 218–227
    put/call ratio, 232–235
Institutional investors, 244
Insurance companies, as investors, 244
Interest rates, effect on options, 53–55
Interest-rate risk, 280, 291–292
Internet bubble, 285–287
Intrinsic value, 17–18, 20, 52, 275
Intuition in options pricing, 36–39
Investing disasters, 279–305
    carry trades, 280–281
    convergence trades, 294–298
    dotcom bubble, 285–287
    Howie Hubler trade, 298–303
    Latrell Sprewell trade, 303–305
    portfolio insurance, 281–285
    subprime mortgage-backed securities,
        287–294
Investment choices, 3–4
Investor fear, 73, 202
Investor optimism/pessimism, 217
Iron condor, 152–155
IWM, 176, 190

Jefferson, Thomas, 271–272
Jump risk, 72

LEAPS (Long-Term Equity Anticipation
    Securities), 107, 252–253
Leland, Hayne, 281
Leverage, 27
Liquidity, 14
Long calls, 126–128
Long volatility, 80, 83
Long-Term Capital Management (LTCM),
    295–296, 298
Lottery tickets, 6
Louisiana Purchase, 269–272

Market corrections/crashes, 161–162
Market panic behavior, 71–72

Market portfolio, 101
Mean reversion, 81–82
Mean variance analysis, 189
Mechanics of options. *See* Option
    mechanics
Merton, Thomas, 29, 296
MF Global, 296–298
Minnesota Timberwolves, 303–305
Modern portfolio theory (MPT), 99–101
Momentum investing, 158
Moneyness, 23–25, 51, 73, 181–182
    and put options, 106
    and skew charts, 69–70
    vs. time decay, 58, 171
    in volume terms, 181
Monte Carlo simulation, 282
Morgan Guarantee, 283
Morgan Stanley, 300
Mortgage hedge funds, 292–293

Nakamoto, Satoshi, 274
Naked options, 62–63, 119
NBA (National Basketball Association),
    303–304
Net credit, 19
Net debt, 19
New York Knicks, 303–304
News announcements, 72
News information flow, 215–216
No-borrowing cost assumption, 33–34

O'Brian, Leland, 283
Oil investments, 255–265
    crude oil consumption, historical, 257
    crude oil prices, historical, 256
    crude oil volatility term structure,
        262–263
    exploration and production (E&P)
        companies, 259–262
    free straddle on, 264
    oil fields as options, 259–262
    oil-field production cycle, 258
    peak oil theory, 257–258
    volatility skew, 263
One-time dividends, 210–211

Open interest, 14
Open-source software, 274–275
Optimal hedge ratio, 189
Optimism/pessimism, 217
Option mechanics:
  assignment, 15–16
  basic concepts, 11–12
  contract terms and conditions, 12
  creating, extinguishing, settling, 13–14
  deliverables, 16
  exercising, 14–15, 16
  leverage and risk, 27–28
  moneyness, 23–25
  option premium, 20–23
  price behavior, 17–20
  underlying assets and volatility, 25–27
  valuation, 21–23 (*see also* Pricing
    models)
Option performance curve, 50
Option premium, 18–19, 20–23
Option price, vs. underlying security
    price, 39–40, 43
Option prices, information from,
    215–236. *See also* Information
    extraction
Option pricing theory, 246, 291–294
Option-implied distribution of future
    prices, 218–227
Options:
  fundamental strategies (*see* Fundamental
    strategies)
  overpriced behavior of, 118–123
  overview of, 1–10
  as part of all investment choices, 4–5
  pricing and performance, 97–99
    capital asset pricing model (CAPM),
      101–104
    conclusions about, 117–118
    historical returns analysis on calls,
      114–117
    historical returns analysis on puts,
      105–114
    modern portfolio theory (MPT),
      99–101

real options, 273–274
real-world examples, 1–3, 6
Options Clearing Corporation (OCC),
    14, 15
Over-the-counter (OTC) options, 16
Overwrite tactic. *See* Covered calls

Parvest Dynamic ABS, 294
Path dependence, 62, 86, 121
Pay in kind (PIK) bonds, 244
Peak oil theory, 257–258
PEMEX (oil company), 258
Performance drag, 50, 88, 175,
    176
Permanent hedging, 161–162
Phi, 55–58
  equation for, 57–58
  intuition behind, 56–57
PIK (pay in kind) bonds, 244
Portfolio hedging, 157–193
  1 x 1.1 ratio diagonal put spreads,
    188–192
  1 x 2 ratio put spreads, 183–188
  alternatives to reduce capital
    commitment, 182
  anticipatory hedging, 159–161
  building a proper hedge, 170–172
  diagonal put spreads, 172–182
  equity for hedging high-yield debt,
    164–169
  finding optimal hedge ratio, 189
  optimal strategies for, 162–164
  performance simulation, 176–182
  permanent hedging, 161–162
  put options as insurance, 160–161
Portfolio insurance, 281–285
Price decay, measuring. *See* Phi; Theta
Pricing, and probability, 218–222
Pricing models, 21, 29–30. *See also*
    Black–Scholes–Merton
    option-pricing model
''The Pricing of Options and Corporate
    Liabilities,'' 29
Probability and pricing, 218–222

Property and casualty (P&C) insurance, 266–268
Put options, 104–105
  1 x 2 ratio put spreads, 183–188
  30-delta puts, 160–161, 168–169, 171, 172–174
  calendar put spreads, 180, 187
  cash-covered puts, 149–152
  defined, 12
  diagonal put spreads, 172–182
  historical returns analysis on, 105–114
  as insurance, 160–161, 299
  put/call ratio, 232–235
  ratio calendar put spreads, 180, 187, 188, 190
  ratio diagonal put spreads, 188–192
  short, ratio put spread, 298–303
  short puts, 128, 129
  synthetically replicating, 242
Put writing, 280
Put-call parity, 26–27, 229, 237–239, 268

Quasi-equity securities, 244

Ratio put spreads, 183–192
  calendar, 180, 187, 188, 190
  capital outlay, 183
  characteristics of, 183
  diagonal, 188–192
  Howie Hubler trade, 298–303
  profit and loss pattern, 186
Ratio spreads, 135–139
Real estate. *See* Subprime mortgage-backed securities
Real options, 273–274, 275
Realized volatility, 46, 66–69, 80–82, 94–95
Real-world option examples, 1–3
Relative skew, 73–74
Repo financing, 280
Residential Mortgage Backed Securities (RMBS), 288–294, 300–301
Return attribution, 59–60

Rho, 53–55
  equation for, 54–55
  intuition behind, 53–54
Risk management, 27
Risk reversals, 139–146, 182
Risk-free-rate lending/borrowing, 33
Rubinstein, Mark, 281, 283
Russell 2000 index, 165–166, 168, 176
Russian debt crisis, 295, 298

S&P 500 index, 105, 166
Scholes, Myron, 29, 296
Security market line, 102–103
Sell to close, 13
Sell to open, 13
Short interest, 196
Short interest ratio, 196
Short put risk reversal, 145
Short puts, 128, 129
Short ratio call spreads, 197–200
Short ratio put spreads, 299–303
Short selling, 55–56
Short squeezes, 196–201
Short volatility, 80, 83
Simple moneyness, 23–25
Single-leg puts and calls, 126–129
Skew, 70–75, 133, 195
  absolute, 73
  measuring, 73–75
  predictive benefits of, 201–207
  price of gold vs., 202
  reasons for, 72–73
  relative, 73–74
  in short squeezes, 200
Skew charts, 69–70, 222–223, 263
SPDR S&P 500 ETF (SPY), 105
Special dividends, 210–211
Special situations. *See* Strategies for special situations
Spot price, 23–24
Spreads:
  1 x 2 ratio put spreads, 183–188
  calendar spreads (*see* Calendar spreads)
  call butterfly, 220

diagonal put spreads, 172–182
ratio spreads (*see* Ratio put spreads;
    Ratio spreads)
vertical spreads, 129–135
Sprewell, Latrell, 303–305
Static replication, 238
Statistical volatility. *See* Realized volatility
Stick diagrams, 17
Stock market crash of 1987, 283–284
Straddles, 87–89, 264
Strangles, 89–91
Strategies for special situations, 195–213
    dividend capture, 207–213
    opportunities in skew, 201–207
    stocks under heavy short interest,
       196–201
Strike price, 12
Subprime borrowers, 288
Subprime mortgage crisis, 287–294,
    300–303
Subprime mortgage-backed securities,
    287–294
Success stories:
    Berkshire Hathaway, 266–268
    Bitcoin, 272–278
    Louisiana Purchase, 269–272
    oil trade, 255–265
Synthetic options, 7, 229
Synthetics, 237–253
    corporate bonds, 248–253
    corporate debt, 243–253
    put-call parity, 237–239
    synthetically replicating a call, 241
    synthetically replicating a put, 242
    synthetically replicating cash,
      242–243
    synthetically replicating stock,
      239–241

Tail risk, 155
Tech bubble, 285–287
Technical investing, 158
Term borrowing/lending, 229
Term structure of volatility, 70

"Theory of Rational Option Pricing," 29
Theta, 50–53, 170
    and cost vs. price, 50
    in diagonal put spreads, 174–175
    equation for, 52–53
    intuition behind, 51–52
    relationship to delta, 181
    relationship to gamma, 118
"thread the needle" trades, 137
Time decay, 27, 50–52. *See also*
    Expiration dates
    management, 123
    vs. moneyness, 58, 171
    in risk reversals, 145
    in straddles, 87
    in strangles, 90–91
    vs. time to expiration, 52
    vs. time to expiration, 170–171
    and vertical spreads, 133
Time premium, 18–19
Time to expiration:
    theta and, 51
    vega and, 49
Time value, 18–19, 275
Total differential, 58–59
Tranches, 288–289
Transaction costs, 32, 86–87, 176, 177,
    190, 240
Trend, and measure of risk, 67
Trend-following investing, 158

Underlying instruments, 11
    delta and, 41
    fractional amounts of, 32–33
    implied borrowing costs on,
      227–232
    price of, vs. delta, 41–42
    price of, vs. option price, 39–40, 43
    price of, vs. phi, 56–57
    price of, vs. rho, 54
    and put-call parity, 26–27
    volatility of, 46 (*see also* Vega)
United Capital Markets Holdings Inc.:
    Horizon Funds, 294

Value investing, 157–159
Vega, 46–50, 85, 155
   equation for, 49
   intuition behind, 47–48
   vs. price of underlying security, 48
   vs. time to expiration, 49
Vertical spreads, 129–135
Volatility:
   defined, 65
   effect on option performance curve, 50
   expected, 66
   implied, 46, 66, 68–70, 94–95
   long and short, 80, 83
   managing, 233
   realized, 46, 66–69, 94–95
   relationship between implied and
      realized, 80–82
   statistical (*see* Realized volatility)
   term structures of, 75–78
   trading
      calendar spreads, 91–94
      gamma scalping, 82–87
      straddles, 87–89
      strangles, 89–91
Volatility arbitrage, 46
Volatility expectations, 20–22
   and underlying assets, 25–27
Volatility instruments, 19, 64
Volatility premium, 18–19
Volatility skew, 70–71
Volatility surface, 70, 78–80,
   105

Wells Fargo, 283

Zeta, 60–63
   calculating, 218–221
   equation for, 62

CPSIA information can be obtained
at www.ICGtesting.com
Printed in the USA
FSHW020317230920
73970FS